THE BLACK AGED
IN THE UNITED STATES

Recent Titles in
Bibliographies and Indexes in Afro-American and African Studies

Martin Luther King, Jr.: An Annotated Bibliography
Sherman E. Pyatt, compiler

Blacks in the Humanities, 1750-1984: A Selected Annotated Bibliography
Donald Franklin Joyce, compiler

The Black Family in the United States: A Revised, Updated, Selectively
Annotated Bibliography
Lenwood G. Davis, compiler

Black American Families, 1965-1984: A Classified, Selectively Annotated
Bibliography
Walter R. Allen, editor

Index to Poetry by Black American Women
Dorothy Hilton Chapman, compiler

Black American Health: An Annotated Bibliography
Mitchell F. Rice and Woodrow Jones, Jr., compilers

Ann Allen Shockley: An Annotated Primary and Secondary Bibliography
Rita B. Dandridge, compiler

Index to Afro-American Reference Resources
Rosemary M. Stevenson, compiler

A Richard Wright Bibliography: Fifty Years of Criticism and Commentary,
1933-1982
*Keneth Kinnamon, compiler, with the help of Joseph Benson, Michel Fabre,
and Craig Werner*

Index of Subjects, Proverbs, and Themes in the Writings of Wole Soyinka
Greta M. K. Coger, compiler

Southern Black Creative Writers, 1829-1953: Bio-bibliographies
M. Marie Booth Foster, compiler

THE BLACK AGED
IN THE UNITED STATES
A Selectively
Annotated Bibliography

Revised and Updated Second Edition

Compiled by
LENWOOD G. DAVIS

Bibliographies and Indexes in Afro-American and African Studies, Number 23

GREENWOOD PRESS
NEW YORK • WESTPORT, CONNECTICUT • LONDON

Library of Congress Cataloging-in-Publication Data

Davis, Lenwood G.
    The Black aged in the United States : a selectively annotated
bibliography / compiled by Lenwood G. Davis.—Rev. and updated,
2nd ed.
        p.   cm. — (Bibliographies and indexes in Afro-American and
African studies, ISSN 0742-6925 ; no. 23)
    Includes index.
    ISBN 0-313-25931-3 (lib. bdg. : alk. paper)
    1. Afro-American aged—Bibliography.   2. Old age assistance—
United States—Bibliography.   I. Title.   II. Series.
Z1361.N39D354   1989
[E185.86]
016.3052 '6 '08996073—dc19   88-32359

British Library Cataloguing in Publication Data is available.

Library of Congress Catalog Card Number: 88-32359
ISBN: 0-313-25931-3
ISSN: 0742-6925

First published in 1989

Greenwood Press, Inc.
88 Post Road West, Westport, Connecticut 06881

Printed in the United States of America

(∞)™

The paper used in this book complies with the
Permanent Paper Standard issued by the National
Information Standards Organization (Z39.48-1984).

10 9 8 7 6 5 4 3 2 1

FOR
Jacquelyne Johnson Jackson
"The foremost authority on the Black Aged"
and
Eunice Jacks Wright

Contents

Introduction

This annotated bibliography is a revision of the one that I published in 1980. Within the last eight years however, a number of studies, articles, pamphlets, and books on that subject have been published. This updated work, like the earlier one, is primarily designed as a reference for those who want to know more about the Black aged in the United States.

This book differs from the earlier one in many respects. More than forty references have been added to the section on the Black Aged and Slavery. Fifty-seven new sources were added to the section on Major Works. Twenty-three additional references were added to the General Works section. Further, special attention was devoted to the section dealing with dissertations and theses. The previous bibliography listed thirty-six dissertations and theses; this work discusses eighty-one. The previous book listed one hundred and sixty-five articles; this work discusses over three hundred and ten. This book includes several topics that were either not fully developed or not mentioned earlier: Black aged abuse, alcoholism, Black organizations, crime, depression, hypertension, life satisfaction, legal services, planning, professional training, Black centenarians, and Black octogenarians. Some attention has been given to autobiographies and autobiographical works. Many of these works give us keen insight into how aged Blacks felt about their pains, dreams, disappointments, hopes, and sufferings, and of racism in this country. This book includes works published as recently as 1987. Because of the current proliferation of materials on the Black aged however, the user must consult various indexes to see what is presently available.

The Black aged have been neglected as a group, since most gerontologists do not acknowledge their problems as any different from those of the White aged. That contention has been challenged by such writers as Jacquelyne J. Jackson, James H. Carter, Hobart C. Jackson, Wilbur H. Watson, Rose C. Gibson, Roosevelt H. Wright, Jr., and others. They believe that the Black aged have special and different problems because they are for the most part poorer than their white counterparts. It is even worse for the elderly Black female. She is not in "triple jeopardy": she is in "quadruple jeopardy" -- Black, old, poor, and female.

Blacks have always taken care of their senior citizens, since long before they came to the United States. In African society elders were the leaders and most respected members of the community. Even during slavery in America during the 1800s, the Black elderly were looked upon with respect by both slaves and free Blacks. Moreover, free Blacks during the slave era founded organizations that had as their primary objective the care for the elderly, widows, and orphans. Blacks have traditionally made special efforts to care for their old, sick, and homeless.

Another little-known fact is that Blacks with the assistance of Whites established homes for the Black aged even during the slave era. One of the earliest homes was the Home for Aged Colored Women that was founded in Boston about 1860. Another was the Stephen Smith Home for the Aged that was organized in 1864 in Philadelphia. Although there were between two and three hundred homes established for the Black aged between 1860 and the present, the Stephen Smith Home is one of the few that is presently still in existence and functioning.

Although presently there is an increased awareness of the plight of the Black elderly, some attention should be focused on the historical role of the Black aged because their role has not changed drastically in some ways since slavery. They still are, in many instances, the stabilizing force in the Black family structure.

Some writers such as Herbert G. Gutman, Leslie Howard Owen, Kenneth M. Stampp, Eugene D. Genovese, Robert W. Fogel, Stanley L. Engerman, J. C. Furmas, Bishop Meade, Joseph H. Ingraham, Nehemiah Adams, Stanley Feldstein, Bertram W. Doyle, James Redpath, and others give their impressions of the status of the aged slave. However, it is the narratives of former slaves such as Frederick Douglass, Solomon Northup, Louis Hughes, Austin Steward, Williams Wells Brown, Charles Ball, John Brown, John Mercer Langston, and others that give us a clearer picture of the position of the elderly slaves and the way they were treated.

There are two arguments concerning the status of aged slaves presented in these selections. One position is that old slaves were not cared for by their masters but left to beg in the streets for a scanty and precarious subsistence. Old slaves were "doctored up" and sold for less than a good dog, in one case for a mere dollar. Another instance involved a slave who was sold for a meager ten dollars. Still another case shows that two aged slaves were sold together for only thirteen dollars. Some aged slaves were not cared for when they were ill but were left to die. Other accounts state that old slaves were mistreated and even whipped by their mistresses and masters. One writer reports that masters emancipated some aged slaves as a reward for a lifetime of faithful service, "but other planters intended many of these seeming generosities simply as part of a larger scheme to set themselves and their relatives free of responsibility for care of the old persons." Although some of the slaves were in their 80s and 90s, they still waited on their mistresses and masters. They had to continue to work to "pay" for their support.

The other argument is that old slaves were properly cared for by their masters after years of services. Some writers note that some planters built cottages for old slaves and provided them with "pensions." Other authors add that aged slaves had the "light" duties of babysitters, nurses, seamstresses, cooks, weavers, and coach drivers. Another author contends that "the aged slaves had a high degree of security, emotional as well as physical." "Their master's error," this writer continues, "lay in the supposition that the modest protection of the Big House accounted for their widespread cheerfulness and contentment, for the old folks' ability to live decently and with self-respect depended primarily on the support of their younger fellow slaves."

Some of the slave narratives and slave testimonies state that some old slaves had "light" duties and that some were mistreated. What is most significant, however, is that the narratives and testimonies tell us how the slaves themselves viewed their aged mothers. Frederick Douglass, for example, recalls the influence that his grandmother had on him during the period that he was a slave. Douglass surmises that his grandmother's kindness and love stood in the place of his mother, whom he did not know. His grandmother, according to Douglass, was a woman of power and spirit. The abolitionist also argues that the mechanics were called "uncles" by all of the younger slaves, not because they really sustained that relationship to any, but according to plantation etiquette, as a mark of respect due from the younger to older slaves. He concludes that "strange, and even ridiculous as it may seem, among a people so uncultivated, and with so many stern trials to look in the face, there is not to be found, among any people, a more rigid enforcement of the law of respect to elders, than they maintain...."

Solomon Northup, another ex-slave, wrote that aged slaves were patriarchs among other slaves. He recalls "Old Abram was a kindhearted being, a sort of patriarch among us, fond of entertaining his younger brethren with grave and serious discourse. He was deeply versed in such philosophy as is taught in the cabin of the slave." Louis Hughes declares that when a slave woman was too old to do much of anything, she was assigned to be in charge of young babies in the absence of their mothers, usually with no one to help her. Austin Steward, a slave for twenty-two years and a freeman for forty years, recalls how the old slaves were treated on his former plantation in Virginia. According to him, his mistress had old slaves "punished by having them severely whipped by a man, which she never failed to do for every trifling fault."

William Wells Brown states that one of his jobs was to prepare the old slaves for the slave market. He remembers shaving the old men's beards and plucking out their gray hairs. If there were too many gray hairs, he colored them black. The owner passed these slaves off as being middle-aged, thereby cheating the buyers. Brown also mentions an old slave called "Uncle Frank," who was a fortune-teller. He told both slaves' and planters' fortunes. Charles Ball relates that as a child he passed many long nights with his grandfather "listening to his narratives of the scenes through which he had passed in Africa," and hearing of his grandpa's religion with its strong injunction of "tenderness to wives and children."

John Brown, an ex-slave from Georgia, recollects that on his plantation there was an old slave by the name of "Minney," the mother of thirteen children, who was stoned by her master because she would not run fast enough for him. Her master laughed after the stone broke her arm. The author also describes how old "Aunties" and "Uncles" generally took care of the sick, using methods learned from other slaves over the years. John Mercer Langston, a former slave and the first Black elected from Virginia to the United States House of Representatives, recalls that his master freed his aged slaves in his will. One, Billy Quarles, was also given two hundred and twenty dollars.

Later testimonies of ex-slaves support the positions of the slave narratives that are told in George P. Rawick's The American Slave: A Composite Autobiography. Three ex-slaves from Georgia: Georgia Baker, Martha Colquitt, and Callier Elder, recall the influence that their grandparents had on them. Georgia Baker declares she spent much of her early childhood in the company of her grandfather, who slept "on a trundle bed in the kitchen" and who tended Georgia and her siblings while their parents were in the fields. Martha Colquitt states her grandmother helped provide material comfort for her: "Grandma helped to cook, wash, and make clothes." Callier Elder recalls that her "Grandpa helped supply wild nuts, garden produce, and meat for the family table." Perry Jemison, a former slave from Ohio, remembers that "My grandmother wuz named Snooky and my grandfather Anthony. I thought der wuzn't a better friend in all de world den my grandmother. She would do all she could for her grandchildren. Der wuz no food allowance for chillun that could not work and my grandmother fed us out of her and my mother's allowance." Austin Grant, of Texas, says that his grandfather used to "tell us things, to keep the whip off our backs."

One of the most interesting stories about aged slaves is discussed in William Still's The Underground Railroad. The author writes about Jane Davis, a slave woman of about seventy, from the Eastern Shore section of Maryland. She was a mother of twelve children and "married." Because she was often mistreated and about to be sold to a new master, she decided to leave her children and husband and escape to Buffalo, New York, where her brother was living. She escaped by the Underground Railroad. Although she was nearly seventy years old, she slept in the woods for nearly three weeks with little or no food. The author concludes that Miss Davis doubtless represents thousands of aged slave mothers, who, after having been worn out under the yoke, were frequently either offered for sale for a trifle, turned out to die, or compelled to eke out their existence on the most stingy allowance.

Other slaves' testimonies presented here point out that aged slaves were "highly esteemed by both the slaves and the masters." One writer argues that often the aged female slave was the "confidential adviser" of the older members of the slave household. Moreover, the aged slave added "dignity" to her position and "her regime." According to some, the "grannies" were genuine matriarchs--powerful, stabilizing figures who performed a profoundly important service. The slave testimonies reveal that younger slaves learned trades from older slaves. In many instances the "granny" or aged slave was a kind of "glorified nurse and was the authority in nursery matters." The younger slave who attended to the children as guardian and companion, and who was called "nurse," was subordinate to her. Another writer notes that an old slave woman might act as plantation physician, midwife, and more or less secretly, "witch doctor." One writer gives his idea of the aged slave's role in the "courtship" of slaves on plantations. The author states that almost every large plantation had an experienced old slave who instructed young male slaves in the delicate matter of winning the girls of their choice.

A Northerner who traveled in the South gives an interesting account of his conversation with an old slave. According to the writer, the aged female slave's maternal affection for her children was very strong. The aged slave emphasized that she and other slaves "were not" content to be in slavery contrary to reports of White plantation owners.

Although the foregoing accounts give various roles of and attitudes toward aged slaves, it is noted by Kenneth M. Stampp, Theodore Weld, Robert Fogel, Stanley L. Engermann and others that in 1860 only 1.2 percent of slaves were over seventy; thus the owner of as many as a hundred slaves seldom had more than one or two elderly slaves to support. In many cases a slave was considered "old" at about thirty or thirty-five, and few lived beyond fifty-five. Fogel and Engermann add that "40 percent of the slaves died before age nineteen."

The aged slave played a vital part on the plantation and was treated with respect by the younger slaves. Perhaps the younger slaves were aware that most of them would not reach old age. What is most important is that aged slaves knew that they had to share their knowledge and experience with younger slaves in the hopes that they would beat the "slave system." Some aged slaves could no longer tolerate the system and escaped to freedom. While other aged slaves were content with their own status, since most knew that they were too old to escape to freedom, they assisted and sometimes encouraged younger slaves to escape, in hopes that they would live their lives in "free" territory and not under the yoke of slavery.

One of the greatest contributions that the aged slaves made to the Black race was that of transmitting the Black culture. The aged slave was usually the closest one to Africa and had more knowledge about it than the younger generation. It was she or he who transmitted the history and songs of Africa. One writer points out that one of the Black childrens' chief diversions was to listen to the songs and tales of Africa from their grandparents. Thus the Black aged played a significant role then, as well as now, because they were and are the transmitters of the Black heritage.

There are a number of organizations, institutions, centers, and individuals who have done extensive research on the Black aged since the mid 1970s. The National Center on Black Aged in Washington, D.C. is the leading organization that does research on the Black aged. It puts out a number of studies and reports and also holds various conferences on the Black elderly. The Center for the Study of Aging and Human Development at Duke University Medical School is another leading institution engaged in research on the Black aged. Other institutions such as the Ethel Percy Andrus Gerontology Center at the University of Southern California, the Institute of Gerontology at the University of Michigan-Wayne State University, and the Center on Aging at San Diego State University have done extensive research on the Black Aged. The National Council on the Aging as well as the federal government publish a number of studies and reports on the Black aged.

This work could not have been completed without the assistance of several people to whom I am grateful. I am indebted to Ursula Bost for helping with the original typing and indexing. I would also like to thank Martha Rokahr for typing the final draft of the manuscript and giving some valuable suggestions. Several librarians also assisted me: The Schomburg Center for Research in Black Culture; the Moorland-Spingarn Research Center; Winston-Salem State University Library; University of North Carolina at Chapel Hill Library; Wake Forest University Library; Duke University Library; and the Library of Congress.

Although this is the most comprehensive annotated bibliography on the Black aged ever compiled, a limited number of books, articles, reports, and other works are excluded because for various reasons they were not available to the compiler. I take full responsibility for any errors or omissions and for all of its shortcomings.

A few words must be said about the dedication of this book. This work is dedicated to Dr. Jacquelyne Johnson Jackson, the foremost authority on the Black aged. She has been in the forefront of research, writing, and espousing the rights of Black senior citizens. Professor Jackson has done more than anyone in the United States to draw attention to the uniqueness and special needs of the Black elderly. Moreover, she, along with the late Hobart C. Jackson, were the founders of the National Caucus on the Black Aged. Dr. Jackson was one of the founders of Black Aging, as well as its first editor. This journal later expanded its coverage and became Minority Aging and Professor Jackson serves as its editor. The sociologist continues to lecture all over the world on the uniqueness and special needs of the Black aged.

This book is also dedicated to Mrs. Eunice Jacks Wright, an ageless Black woman who paid her dues. She was in her 70s when she passed away a few months ago. She and her late husband, Fred Wright, educated all of their five children (Betty, Carolyn, Fred, Jr., Gloria, and Dean). Although the family was relatively poor and from the South, they managed to have two and sometimes three children in college at the same time. Three of the five children have master's degrees. Mrs. Wright had the respect and admiration of her children and grandchildren and was a source of inspiration for her family. Very, very few aged Black women, anywhere, can boast of having three children with advanced degrees. Although the Wrights were not college-educated, they wanted their children to have the best education possible. Mrs. Wright Paid Her Dues and deserved All of the love, admiration and respect that she received.

THE BLACK AGED
IN THE UNITED STATES

1.

BLACK AGED AND SLAVERY

Books

1. SLAVE NARRATIVES
INDIVIDUAL

1. Asher, Rev. Jeremiah. <u>Incidents in the Life of The Rev. J. Asher.</u>
London: Charles Gilpin, 1850, pp. 15-21.

   The author states that most of the information he acquired about
   Africa came from Gad, his grandfather, who was stolen from the
   coast of Guinea when he (Gad) was four years old. Gad fought in
   the American Revolution and was promised his freedom by his owner
   after the war was over. After the war was over Gad was put back
   into slavery. He eventually purchased his freedom from his master
   and moved out of town. When he died he was almost one hundred
   years old.

2. Ball, Charles. <u>Slavery in the United States: A Narrative of the
   Life and Adventures of Charles Ball, A Black Man, Who Lived Forty
   Years in Maryland, South Carolina and Georgia, As A Slave Under
   Various Masters, and Was One Year in The Navy With Commodore Barney
   During the Late War.</u> Lewiston, PA: J. W. Shugert, 1836, pp. 9, 12,
   15, 78.

   As a child the author recalls that he passed many long nights with
   his grandfather "listening to his narrative of the scenes through
   which he had passed in Africa," and hearing of his grandpa's religion with its strong injunctions of "tenderness to wives and
   children." It was suggested that younger slaves respected old
   slaves.

3. Brown, John. <u>Slave Life in Georgia: A Narrative of the Life,
   Sufferings, and Escape of John Brown, A Fugitive Slave, Now in
   England.</u> Edited by Louis Alexis Chamerovzow. London: Anti-Slavery
   Society, 1855, pp. 26-27, 56-57.

Brown, John (continued)

The author points out that old slaves were mistreated. Brown recalls that an old slave by the name of Mirney, the mother of thirteen children, was stoned by her master because she would not run fast enough for him. Her master even laughed at her after the stone broke her arm. The writer argues that slaves, young and old, were "doctored" up to look younger when they were being sold. He also states that old "Aunties" and "Uncles" generally took care of the sick. They learned this "trade" from other slaves over the years. He asserts that younger slaves respected elder slaves.

4. Brown, William Wells. <u>Narrative of William W. Brown, A Fugitive Slave</u>. Boston: The Anti-Slavery Office, 1847, pp. 42-45, 92-93.

The author states that one of his jobs was to prepare the old slaves for the slave market. Mr. Brown was ordered to shave the old men's beards and pluck out their gray hairs. If there were too many gray hairs, he colored them black. After "doctoring" the slaves, they looked ten or fifteen years younger. The owner passed those old slaves off as being middle aged; thereby cheating the buyers, especially in ages of the slaves which they bought. Mr. Brown also mentions a slave called "Uncle Frank," who was a fortune teller. He told slaves' and Whites' fortunes and was well respected.

5. Craft, William and Ellen Craft. <u>Running A Thousand Miles For Freedom, Or, The Escape of William and Ellen Craft From Slavery</u>. London: William Tweedie, 1860, pp. 9-10, 12, 22.

One of the writers, William Craft, points out that although his old master had the reputation of being a very humane and Christian man, he thought nothing of selling his aged father and mother, at separate times, to different slave owners. He also argues that his aged parents were very religious and devoted to the service of God. The reason his master sold his parents, and other aged slaves, was that "they were getting old, and would soon become valueless in the market, and therefore he intended to sell off all the old stock, and buy in a young lot." This action was typical of many slave owners.

6. Douglass, Frederick. <u>My Bondage and My Freedom</u>. New York: Miller, Orton and Mulligan, 1855, pp. 35-40, 45-49, 69-70, 114.

The writer states that the mechanics were called "uncles" by all the younger slaves, not because they really sustained that relationship to any, but according to plantation <u>etiquette</u>, as a mark of respect, due from the younger to the older slaves. The orator declares, "strange, and even ridiculous as it may seem, among a people so uncultivated, and with so many stern trials to look in the face, there is not to be found, among any people, a more rigid enforcement of the law of respect to elders, than they maintain." He continues to say that "a young slave must approach the company

Douglass, Frederick (continued)

of the older with hat in hand, and woe betide him, if he fails to
acknowledge a favor, of any sort, with the accustomed 'tank'ee,"
etc. So uniformly are good manners enforced among slaves, that I
can easily detect a 'bogus' fugitive by his manners," contends
Douglass. The orator concludes that " . . . it is considered bad
luck to . . . 'sass' the old folks."

7. _____. Life and Times of Frederick Douglass Written by Himself: His Early Life As A Slave, His Escape From Bondage and His
Complete History to Present Time. Boston: DeWolfe & Fiske Co.,
1892, pp. 26-33, 56-58.

The author recalls the influence that his grandmother had on him
during the period that he was a slave. He states that his grandmother's job was that of babysitter. Douglass surmises that his
grandmother's kindness and love stood in place of his mother, whom
he did not know. His aged grandmother, according to the writer,
was a woman of power and spirit.

8. _____. Narrative of the Life of Frederick Douglass, An
American Slave. Boston: Published at the Anti-Slavery Office,
1845, pp. 48-51.

The leader discusses his old grandmother. He suggests that if any
one thing in his experience, more than another, served to deepen
his conviction of the infernal character of slavery, and to fill
him with unutterable loathing of slaveholders, it was their base
ingratitude to his poor, old grandmother. Douglass surmises that
his grandmother had served his old master faithfully from youth
to old age. He argues: "She had been the source of all his
wealth; she had peopled his plantation with slaves; she had become
a great grandmother in his service. She had rocked him in infancy,
attended him in childhood, served him through life, and at his
death, wiped from his icy brow the cold death-sweat, and closed
his eyes forever...."

9. Grandy, Moses. Narrative of the Life of Moses Grandy, Late a
Slave in the United States of America. Boston: Oliver Johnson,
1844, pp. 10, 41.

The writer asserts that his mother was blind and very old and was
living in a little hut in the woods, "after the usual manner of
old, worn-out slaves." Mr. Grandy recalls that some slaves, including old slaves, were treated so badly that they asked God to
take them away from that life.

10. Griffiths, Martha. Autobiography of a Female Slave. New York:
Bedfield, 1857, pp. 12, 14, 320, 333-336, 372.

Griffiths, Martha (continued)

The author was a mulatto slave and fair enough to pass for white. She mentions her grandfather and other aged slaves. Miss Griffiths states that her old grandfather was called the patriarch slave because he was the oldest slave in the whole neighborhood.

11. Grimes, William. Life of William Grimes, The Runaway Slave, Brought Down to the Present Time. New Haven, CT: The Author, 1855, pp. 9-10, 20-21.

The ex-slave mentions that once when he attempted to escape, he told Planter George, an old slave, of his plans. George told his master of his escape plans and Grimes was caught and severely beaten. He also writes about another old slave called Frankee, whom he believed to be a witch.

12. Hughes, Louis. Thirty Years A Slave: From Bondage to Freedom. The Institution of Slavery as Seen on the Plantation and in the Home of the Planter: Autobiography of Louis Hughes. Milwaukee: South Side Printing Co., 1897, pp. 43-45.

The author states that when a slave woman was too old to do much of anything, she was assigned to be in charge of young babies in the absence of their mothers. He concludes that it was rare that she had anyone to help her. Mr. Hughes suggests that his mistress was very cruel.

13. Jackson, John Andres. The Experience of a Slave in South Carolina. London: Passmore and Alabaster, 1862, pp. 7-23.

The writer asserts that his grandfather was stolen from Africa and his father learned the African method of curing snakebites and was called Dr. Clavern. He also mentions that his owner was very cruel even to old Black slaves. He would whip them unmercifully. The author observed that all the slaves, and especially aged slaves, were happy when their owner died. He discusses several aged slaves: "Old George," "Old Prince," "Old Bob," "Old Peter."

14. Langston, John Mercer. From the Virginia Plantation to the National Capitol: An Autobiography. Hartford, CT: American Publishing Co., 1894, pp. 25, 28-30.

The author pointed out that his master freed in his will, his aged slaves, including Billy Quarles, to whom he also gave two hundred and twenty dollars. Billy was the oldest and most experienced of the slaves and was a deeply religious man. The writer also re-calls that Billy was a staunch believer in ghosts. And not in-frequently, declared Langston, sounds and movements which excited his attention and attracted his interest, were ascribed to such agency, at work for man's good, as he would claim, by appointment of divine Providence. Had Uncle Billy, as he called him, not been superstitious, afraid of ghosts, and easily disturbed by strange

Langston, John Mercer (continued)

noises and curious sights, so commonly found figuring in the imagination of the too credulous Virginia slave of the older time, he would have been by reason of his natural endowments and general qualities of character, with his experience and observation, eminently successful in any efforts which he might have been called to make in such capacity, concludes Mr. Langston.

15. Northup, Solomon. Twelve Years A Slave: Narrative of Solomon Northup. A Citizen of New York, Kidnapped in Washington City in 1841, and Rescued in 1853, From a Cotton Plantation Near the Red River, in Louisiana. Auburn, NY: Derby and Miller, 1853, pp. 141-143, 169, 172-173.

The writer points out that aged slaves were patriarchs among other slaves. He recalled "Old Abram" was a kind-hearted being, a sort of patriarch among us, fond of entertaining his younger brethren with grave and serious discourse. He was deeply versed in such philosophy as is taught in the cabin of the slave. Mr. Northup recalled that younger slaves respected older slaves.

16. Roper, Moses. A Narrative of the Adventures and Escape of Moses Roper with a Preface by the Rev. T. Price. London: Darton, Harvey and Darton, 1838, pp. 1-3.

The author was born in Caswell County, North Carolina. He states that his mistress was going to kill him when he was born because he was the son of her husband. His grandmother stopped the owner's wife from killing Roper. He suffered all during slavery because he was half white.

17. Smith, Mrs. Amanda. The Story of The Lord's Dealings with Mrs. Amanda Smith: An Autobiography. Chicago: Meyer & Brother, Publishers, 1893, pp. 19-24, 27.

Mrs. Smith states that her grandmother was a woman of deep piety and great faith. She heard her mother often say that it was to the prayers and mighty faith of her grandmother that they owed their freedom. The author also praised the Lord for a Godly grandmother. She states that her grandmother often prayed that God would open a way so that her grandchildren might be free. The writer concludes that the families into which these young ladies were to marry, were not considered by the Black folks as good masters and mistresses as they had, and that was one of the grandmother's anxieties. And so she prayed and believed that somehow God would open a way for their deliverance. Mrs. Smith was an evangelist and missionary. She traveled in America, England, Ireland, Scotland, India and Africa.

18. Smith, James L. Autobiography of James L. Smith. Norwich, CT:
     Press of the Bulletin Co., 1881, pp. 4-5.

     The author, an ex-slave, told how his grandmother cared for him
     during slavery. He mentions that an old Black "root" doctor, told
     his master that Cella, a slave, poisoned his mother and father.
     This "root" doctor gave his parents some medicine and they re-
     covered from their illness. The author suggests that his mistress
     was cruel to old house slaves, including Jinny, the cook. Mr.
     Smith also discusses another Black doctor who was also a fortune
     teller. The fortune teller told Smith that he would escape to
     freedom, which he did.

19. Steward, Austin. Twenty-Two Years A Slave, and Forty Years A
     Freeman. Rochester, NY: William Allring, Publisher, 1857, pp. 16-
     17, 24-25, 27.

     The author states that on his master's plantation in Virginia, it
     was the usual practice to have one of the old slaves set apart to
     do the cooking. All field slaves were required to give into the
     hands of the cook a certain portion of their weekly allowance
     either in dough or meal, which the cook prepared. He pointed out
     that his mistress had older servants punished by having them se-
     verely whipped by a man, which she never failed to do for every
     trifling fault.

                         2.   SLAVE NARRATIVES
                              COLLECTIONS

20. Armstrong, Orland Kay. Old Massa's People: The Old Slaves Tell
     Their Story. Indianapolis: Bobbs-Merrill Co., 1931, pp. 86-120,
     196-208.

     The ex-slaves recall that some former aged female slaves were
     cooks, seamstresses, weavers and nurses. They relate that younger
     slaves learned these and other "trades" from older slaves. It was
     also suggested that younger slaves respected older slaves.

21. Egypt, Ophelia Settle, J. Masuoka and Charles S. Johnson, Editors.
     Unwritten History of Slavery: Autobiographical Accounts of Negro
     Ex-Slaves. Nashville, TN: Fisk University, Social Science Insti-
     tute, 1945, pp. 104-109, 181-188, 201-225, 276-282.

     These interviews with ex-slaves were conducted during 1929 and
     1930. The subjects resided, for the most part, in Tennessee and
     Kentucky. Some ex-slaves recall that they worked some aged slaves
     almost to death. Others relate that the aged slave would serve as
     "doctor" and use homemade remedies and administer them to the other
     slaves. Some aged ex-slaves declare that they went through a lot
     for young Blacks and that this later generation should be more ap-
     preciative than they are. Many ex-slaves recollect that their for-
     mer masters were good to them. Others relate that they were
     treated very badly by their former masters. One ex-slave claimed
     to be about 120 years old.

22. Escott, Paul D. Slavery Remembered: A Record of Twentieth-Century
     Slave Narratives. Chapel Hill: University of North Carolina Press,
     1979, pp. 28-30, 32-34, 50.

     Several ex-slaves discuss how old slaves were treated during the
     ante-bellum era. Several state that aged slaves were treated
     badly by their owners.

23. Hurmence, Belinda, Editor. My Folks Don't Want Me To Talk About
     Slavery. Winston-Salem, NC: John F. Blair, Publisher, 1984.
     103 pp.

     This work includes twenty-one oral histories of former North
     Carolina slaves that were collected by the Federal Writers Project
     in the 1930s. These former slaves were from North Carolina and
     were about ten years of age or older at the end of the Civil War
     (1865). Their ages ranged from 80 years to 103. Many state that
     slaves in general were treated well by their former owners. Others
     suggested that slaves, including older slaves, were mistreated by
     their former owners. The majority of these were females and were
     interviewed in Raleigh, North Carolina.

24. Killion, Ronald and Charles Waller, Editors. Slavery Time: When I
     Was Chillun Down on Marster's Plantation. Savannah, GA: Beehive
     Press, 1973, pp. 3-123.

     This work discusses interviews in Georgia with former slaves.
     These interviews were made in the 1930s. Most of the former
     slaves were in their eighties and nineties. Some were over one
     hundred years old. Many ex-slaves were treated well by their
     masters, according to the interviewees.

25. Nichols, Charles H. Many Thousand Gone: The Ex-Slaves' Account of
     Their Bondage and Freedom. Bloomington: Indiana University Press,
     1963, pp. 15-17, 24, 94-95, 179.

     Various references are made to old slaves throughout this book.
     It was pointed out that younger slaves had a deep respect for
     aged slaves.

26. Perdue, Charles L., Jr., Thomas E. Barden and Robert K. Phillips,
     Editors. Weevils in the Wheat: Interviews with Virginia Ex-
     Slaves. Charlottesville, VA: University Press of Virginia, 1976,
     pp. 2-348.

     These interviews were conducted during the 1930s as part of the
     Virginia Writers' Project. Many of these former slaves were in
     their eighties and nineties. A few were over one hundred. Many
     state that they were treated kindly by their former masters.
     Others declare they were treated very cruelly by their former
     owners.

27.   Rawick, George P. The American Slave: A Composite Autobiography.
       Westport, CT: Greenwood Press, 1977. 19 Volumes.

       These autobiographies were based on the 1930s Federal Writers'
       Project interviews. In the 1930s most of these ex-slaves were in
       their 80s and 90s. A number were over 100 years old. They state
       how they were treated during slavery. Many recollect that they
       were treated kindly by their masters. Others recall that their
       masters treated them very cruelly. The ex-slaves also comment on
       how aged slaves were treated. Some were cared for in their old
       age and others were not.

28.   Tyler, Ronnie C. and Lawrence R. Murphy, Editors. The Slave
       Narratives of Texas. Austin, TX: Encino Press, 1974, pp. 15-32,
       48-62, 64-79, 113-127.

       The writers' interviews were based mainly on the Federal Writers'
       Project collection of the 1930s. Other interviews include works
       found in family papers, and archives in libraries in Texas. Most
       of the ex-slaves were in their 80s and 90s in the 1930s. Nearly
       25 of the 120 interviewed were over 100 years old. Many of the
       ex-slaves stated that they and their families were treated well by
       their former masters. As to be expected, most of the aged ex-
       slaves believed in Jesus Christ and were deeply religious. Several
       had interesting stories to tell about their childhood experiences
       under slavery.

29.   Workers of the Federal Writers' Program. The Negro in Virginia.
       New York: Hastings House Publishers, 1940, pp. 38-46, 60-63, 72-
       78, 93, 102.

       A number of ex-slaves in their eighties and nineties recall how
       old slaves were treated. It was pointed out that a number of aged
       slaves were: butlers, cooks, housemaids, nurses and coachmen.

30.   Yetman, Norman R. Life Under the "Peculiar Institution": Selection
       From the Slave Narrative Collection. Huntington, NY: Robert E.
       Krieger Publishing Co., 1976, pp. 7-338.

       These narratives were done in the 1930s by ex-slaves. Most of the
       interviewers were white. The ex-slaves were mainly in their 80s
       and 90s. Several were over one hundred years old. Some state
       they were treated well by their masters. Others declare they were
       treated very badly.

3.   AGED SLAVES AND AFRICA

31.   Edwards, William J. Twenty-Five Years in the Black Belt. Boston:
       The Cornhill Co., 1918, pp. 1-6.

       The author was born in Alabama four years after the War Between
       the States. He states that most of the history he knew about
       Africa and his family came from his old grandfather. His

Edwards, William J.   (Continued)

grandfather had ten children and was a local preacher. Mr. Edwards
suggests that old ex-slaves tell of their bitter experience during
slavery. The author mentions that both his mother and grandmother
were very religious. He, like many Black children in the South,
was raised by his grandmother. His grandmother died when he was
only eleven years old.

32. Herskovits, Melville J. The Myth of the Negro Past. New York:
     Harper and Brothers, 1941, pp. 150-151, 176-177, 197.

     The writer points out that one of the things that slaves brought
     to America from Africa was their respect for their elders. Prof.
     Herskovits states that the early slaves in America referred to
     their elders as "almost ghosts." The validity of this explanation
     is best indicated by referring the assertion that "old folks" are
     "almost ghosts" to the tenets of the ancestral cult which, as one
     of the most tenacious Africanisms, has left many traces in the New
     World Negro customs, states the author. He continues to state the
     belief in the power of the ancestors to help or harm their descend-
     ants is a fundamental sanction of African relationship groupings,
     and this has influenced the retention of Africanisms in many as-
     pects of Negro life in the New World.

33. Huggins, Nathan Irvin. Black Odyssey: The Afro-American Ordeal
     in Slavery. New York: Pantheon Books, 1977, pp. 138-139, 169.

     The author asserts that there was in most established households
     an oral tradition, often sustained by Black folk who remembered
     and never tired of telling of the earlier folk, of remembered
     Africans with strange ways and words, the generations gone. When
     such aged slaves died, the Afro-American past was just that much
     more obscured in darkness. Prof. Huggins states that the nursery
     on the plantation was under the care of an old slave woman or man
     who was too feeble for other work.

34. Ingraham, Joseph Holt. The Sunny South; or, The Southern at Home,
     Embracing Five Years' Experience of a Northern Governess in the
     Land of Sugar and the Cotton. Philadelphia: G. G. Evans, 1860,
     pp. 86-87, 104-106, 114-116.

     The writer mentions a ninety-two year-old slave named Juba, who
     was sort of a patriarch over the other slaves. Although he had
     been in the United States for seventy-eight years, he had not for-
     gotten his African language, which he spoke when he was vexed . . . .
     Prof. Ingraham also discusses Old George, a slave fiddler. The
     author observed Aunt Phillisy, a slave over a hundred years old,
     who still retained much of her African language. She had a hus-
     band named Daddy Cusha, who was also over one hundred years old
     and blind. It was stated that their master cared for them in
     their old age.

4. SLAVE LETTERS

35.   Blassingame, John W., Editor. Slave Testimony: Two Centuries of
      Letters, Speeches, Interviews, and Autobiographies. Baton Rouge,
      LA: Louisiana State University Press, 1977, pp. 9-10, 163, 401,
      554, 629.

      Various references are made to aged slaves throughout this book by
      former slaves. Many point out that when aged slaves could not be
      of any service to planters, they were turned loose upon the mercy
      of the world. Others surmise that the old slaves were generally
      left to sit around in rags and dirt and to take care of the child-
      ren; and when they cannot do this, they just lay around and suffer,
      until they die, and there was no great account taken of them any-
      way. Others contend that some old slaves were mistreated and
      abused by their masters. There are a few letters from old slaves
      written to their former masters for financial assistance. Most
      former masters did not send any money. Several newspaper and
      magazine interviews are also included in this collection. Some of
      the slaves and ex-slaves interviewed were eight and ninety years
      old; several were over one hundred years old.

36.   Miller, Randall M., Editor. "Dear Master": Letters of A Slave
      Family. Ithaca, NY: Cornell University Press, 1978, pp. 69, 187-
      207, 227, 236-237, 258.

      Various references are made to aged slaves throughout the book.
      Some aged slaves were cooks, coachmen, shoemakers, preachers,
      carters, stonemasons, and gardeners. Some aged slaves mentioned
      were: "Old" Ben, Judy, Kessiah Morse, Washington, "Uncle Charles,"
      Etta, etc.

37.   Starobin, Robert S., Editor. Black in Bondage: Letters of
      American Slaves. New York: New Viewpoints, 1974, pp. 3, 24, 105.

      The letters were written by house servants, drivers and artisans
      who made up an elite group of perhaps 5 to 10 percent of the total
      slave population. A few letters were written by ordinary slaves.
      Many of these letters were written by aged slaves and refer to
      aged slaves. The letters were written in the 1800s. Many of
      these letters were written to their masters and former masters by
      young and aged slaves. Most of the letters were of a complimentary
      nature. One letter written by an aged female slave stated that she
      would be freed by her master if anyone would support her.

5. WHITES' VIEWS OF THE AGED SLAVE

38.   Adams, Nehemiah. South-Side View of Slavery: or Three Months At
      The South. Boston: T. R. Marvin, 1854, pp. 47-48, 79-80.

      Mr. Adams argues that every slave had an inalienable claim in law
      upon his owner for support for his whole life. He states that he

Adams, Nehemiah (Continued)

observed that on one plantation was a white-headed Black who had done no work for ten years. The aged slave enjoyed all the privileges of the plantation, garden, and orchard; he was clothed and fed as carefully as though he were useful, contends Adams. The author also gives examples of other aged slaves. One aged slave had been confined to his bed with rheumatism for thirty years and was cared for by his master, states the writer.

39. Berlin, Ira. Slaves Without Masters: The Free Negro in the Antebellum South. New York: Oxford University Press, 1974, pp. 152-153.

Prof. Berlin surmises that although manumission codes carefully prescribed the maximum age at which slaves might be freed in order to prevent worn-out bondsmen from becoming community charges, masters found it profitable to unload elderly, enfeebled slaves. Slaveholders often deposited these unwanted thralls in nearby cities, and almost every southern municipality sprouted a complement of "retired" bondsmen, concludes the author.

40. Blassingame, John W., et al., Editors. The Frederick Douglass Papers. 1847-1854. Vol. 2. New Haven: Yale University Press, 1982, pp. 37-39.

Douglass points out that slaveholders kept slaves in bondage from infancy to old age and soon as they became old and decrepit - the moment they were unable to toil - their masters, from benevolence and humanity, of course, gave them their freedom. The inhabitants of the states, to prevent this burden upon their community, made the master liable for their support under such circumstances, concludes the Black abolitionist.

41. _____. The Slave Community: Plantation Life in the Antebellum South. Revised and Enlarged Edition. New York: Oxford University Press, 1979, pp. 266-270.

It was suggested that one of the key figures in the white child's socialization was the ubiquitous aged Black mammy to whom he frequently turned for love and security. It was the Black mammy who often ran the household, interceded with his parents to protect him, punished him for misbehavior, nursed him, rocked him to sleep, told him fascinating stories, and, in general, served as his second, more attentive, more loving mother. The historian concluded: "Often the child formed a deep and abiding love for his mammy and, as an adult, deferred to her demands and wishes."

42. Breeden, James D., Editor. Advice Among Masters: The Ideal in Slave Management in the Old South, Westport, CT: Greenwood Press, 1980, pp. 6-7, 9, 28, 40, 47, 55, 80, 91, 106, 108, 118, 133, 151, 184, 200, 205-207, 247, 289-290, 297, 301-302, 310, 314.

Breeden, James D. (Continued)

According to Dr. Breeden, the protection of the slave in old age
was one of the aspects of slavery frequently pointed to by the
institution's defenders. He concludes, in part: "But this . . .
shockingly small contents make clear the old age benefits did not
command more than the incidental attention of the writers on
slave management. . . ."

43.   Child, L. Maria, Editor. "The Child's Anti-Slavery Book: Con-
       taining a Few Words About American Slave Children and Stories of
       Slave-Life. New York: Carlton & Porter, Publisher, 1859, pp.
       109-153.

       One chapter, "Aunt Judy's Story: A Story From Real Life," by
       Matilda G. Thompson, discusses an aged slave. The ex-slave told
       how she was a slave, freed, put back into slavery and freed again
       in her old age. She relates how she was "tricked" into slavery
       by several planters. Aunt Judy had several children and attempted
       to find them in her old age, but could not. Unlike some aged
       slaves, she had no one to depend on in her old age.

44.   Ingraham, Joseph Holt. The South-West, By a Yankee. New York:
       Harper & Brothers, 1835, Vol. 2, pp. 236-239, 241-242, 249, 254.

       There is one section entitled "Indulgence to Aged Negroes." The
       author, a Northerner, traveled in the Southwest and made the fol-
       lowing observations. He states that aged slaves were sometimes
       allowed to go with their children when they were sold, providing
       their children would care for them. The author declares, "Negroes
       have a peculiarly strong affection for the old people of their own
       colour. Veneration for the aged is one of their strongest charac-
       teristics." Ingraham also points out that planters address the
       aged slaves in a "mild" and "pleasant manner" as "Uncle" or
       "Aunty" -- titles as peculiar to the old Blacks as "boy" and
       "girl", to all under forty years of age. Some aged slaves were
       allowed to spend their last years on the master's plantation,
       without doing any kind of work. Some, however, did raise a few
       vegetables in order to purchase a few extra comforts. Some
       planters were kind to their slaves and indulged them, concludes
       the writer.

45.   Lowery, Irving E. Life on The Old Plantation in Antebellum Days
       or a Story Based on Facts. Columbia, SC: The State Company,
       Printers, 1911, pp. 45-58, 62, 65, 73-87.

       Chapter III is entitled "Granny, The Cook, On the Old Plantation."
       The author argues that one of the most important slaves on this
       plantation in South Carolina was Granny, the cook. He points out
       that she fed, clothed and raised her master's son and the master's
       son "slept in Granny's own bed with his lily white arms around her
       black neck." Rev. Lowery concluded that Granny, though she was
       Black, considered herself the mistress of the plantation because

Lowery, Irving E. (Continued)

her owner made her head of the household. The author, eighty years old, was born on this plantation in 1850, and concludes that "when Granny gave orders, those orders had to be obeyed. White and Colored respected and obeyed her."

46. Mason, Isaac. Life of Isaac Mason As a Slave. Worcester, MA: The Author, 1893, pp. 9-12.

The author discusses his grandfather, Richard Graham Grimes, who was an old slave in Maryland. When Grimes' master died, in consideration of Grimes' old age and the time he spent serving his master, he was "handsomely" rewarded with his freedom, an old horse called "the old bay horse" - which was also past the stage of usefulness - and an old cart. He was not, however, given a home to live in or a place to shelter his head from the storm.

47. McManus, Edgar J. A History of Negro Slavery in New York. Syracuse: Syracuse University Press, 1966, pp. 144-150.

A number of slaves were manumitted in their masters' wills. The author observes an interesting situation whereby James Thorne, a Flushing, New York farmer, required all of his slaves to contribute 3 shillings annually into a fund to provide for their old age. Some owners cared for their aged slaves and others did not.

48. _____. Black Bondage in the North. Syracuse: Syracuse University Press, 1973, pp. 144-148.

It was pointed out that certain northern states had laws that imposed certain obligations on slaveholders to care for their slaves, particularly aged slaves. New York slaveholders were punished by a fine if their Negroes had to beg for sustenance, and the bondsmen were invited to report cases of maltreatment or neglect to the authorities. The masters were expressly forbidden to abandon slaves who had become too old or sick to be of further service. Massachusetts and Connecticut had laws making the owner responsible for indigent Blacks who had been cast adrift under the pretense of freeing them. In Rhode Island, the masters had to reimburse the overseers of the poor for any public assistance given to abandoned slaves, concludes Prof. McManus.

49. Meade, Bishop. Sketches of Old Virginia Family Servants. Philadelphia: Isaac Ashmead, Printer, 1847, pp. 135-200.

Various references are made to aged slaves. The writer points out that they were nurses and deeply religious people. Some could read and write. He surmises that although some of the aged slaves were in their 80s and 90s, they still waited on their mistresses and masters. The author discusses certain individual aged Blacks: "Old Milly," "Blind Lucy," "Aunt Betty," "Springfield Bob," "Mammy Chris," Uncle Sam," "Uncle Jim," "Aunt Diana," "Aunt Margaret," "Rachel Parker," "Nelly Jackson," "Aunt Beck."

50.   Page, Thomas Nelson. The Negro, The Southerner's Problem. New York: Charles Scribner's Sons, 1904, pp. 167, 171, 174-181, 193-202.

The author states that as a young lieutenant in a volunteer company he kissed his old "Black Mammy" on the parade ground in sight of the whole company. He points out that in one instance, at a wedding in the executive mansion at Richmond, Virginia, the aged slave was left outside and when it was discovered that the bride's aged "Mammy" had not come in, the Governor, himself, went out and brought her in on his arm to take the place beside the mother of the bride.

51.   _____. Social Life in Old Virginia Before the War. New York: Charles Scribner's Sons, 1897, pp. 57-62.

The aged slave was the White children's nurse in the sense that they were placed in her charge with general supervision from the mistress. She also assisted the mistress in everything pertaining to the training of the children.

52.   Pollard, Edward A. Black Diamonds: Gathered in the Darkey Homes of the South. New York: Pudney & Russell, Publishers, 1859, pp. 22-25, 30-36, 74-77, 79, 88, 94-98.

The author argues that aged slaves were cared for by their masters in their old age and treated well . . . . The work was first published in 1850 under the title The Southern Spy: Or Curiosities of Negro Slavery in the South.

53.   Rose, Willie Lee. Slavery and Freedom. Expanded Edition. Edited by William W. Freehling. New York: Oxford University Press, 1982, pp. 44-45, 66-67, 69-70.

It was pointed out that an old slave, on St. Helena Island, South Carolina, never worked in his life because his master was convinced he was a cripple. The author stated that being a nurse was a favorite assignment for an old slave, who had far too many children in charge to allow much time for individual needs. Prof. Rose also discussed duties assigned to old slaves.

54.   Syrgley, F. D. Seventy Years in Dixie. Nashville, TN: Gospel Advocate Publishing Co., 1893, pp. 41-51.

Chapter III is called "Black Mammies." The author was raised by a "Black Mammy" on his father's plantation in Tennessee. He states that the "Black Mammy" was the highest authority in the nursery in all matters pertaining to the management of the children. According to Mr. Srygley, the aged slave was a necessity as his own mother died not long after his birth. The aged slave cared for him as a mother would and did not give up her tender care until he was eighteen years old, at which time she died.

Srygley, F. D. (Continued)

The author states that he was proud of the fact that this slave taught him how to count up to ten in an African dialect.

55. Strother, David Hunter. Virginia Illustrated: Containing a Visit to the Virginia Cannan and The Adventures of Porte Crayon. New York: Harper and Brothers, 1857, pp. 64-65, 70, 226, 236-238, 253-258.

General references are made to elderly slaves. The author recalls that when the slave became too old for active service, visitors to the plantation came to see the old nurse who had been so active in the life of the family group. The author argues that it would have been an insult both to the aged slave and to the family if they did not pay their respects to her. She was a personage not to be over-looked, however old she might become.

6. SLAVERY IN THE STATES

56. Brown, Letitia Woods. Free Negroes in The District of Columbia: 1790-1846. New York: Oxford University Press, 1972, pp. 75-120.

The author states that many elderly slaves in the District of Columbia were manumitted by wills and deeds of their master. Some aged slaves were left with a bequest in the will of their owners and other aged slaves were not given anything except their freedom. The Court in the District decided that manumission was valid if provision was made by the testator to prevent the slave from becoming a burden on the public.

57. Coleman, J. Winston, Jr. Slavery Times In Kentucky. Chapel Hill: University of North Carolina Press, 1940, pp. 32-40, 66, 121.

The author points out that many aged slaves were cared for by their masters. In some instances the owners provided for the up-keep and care of the old slave in his will. In some cases, old slaves did continue to work on the plantations as butlers, cooks and coachmen. Some aged slaves sold for as little as $175.00.

58. Fields, Barbara Jeanne. Slavery and Freedom on the Middle Ground: Maryland During the Nineteenth Century. New Haven: Yale University Press, 1985, pp. 32-34.

Dr. Fields suggests that though the Maryland state law discouraged the manumission of slaves too old or infirm to take care of them-selves - between 1796 and 1832 owners were forbidden to emancipate slaves over 45 - manumission provided a tempting means of casting aside slaves who had become a burden to their owners. It was also surmised that the higher rate of manumission among slaveowners of modest means may owe something to this fact. The author declared that the free Black population of northern Maryland had a smaller proportion of children and older people because so many of its free Blacks were migrants who tended to be adults in the prime of life.

59. Greene, Lorenzo Johnston. The Negro in Colonial New England: 1620-
     1776. New York: Columbia University Press, 1942, pp. 138-139.

     It was stated that many masters, after their slaves had become old
     and useless in their service, set them free, as they would a worn-
     out horse, with the results that they became public charges and a
     burden to the towns. In order to save the towns this expense, all
     masters were required to support their former slaves should they
     come to want. The following states passed laws requiring masters
     to care for their old slaves: Connecticut (1702), Massachusetts
     (1703), Pennsylvania (1726), and Rhode Island (1729).

60. Sellers, James Benson. Slavery in Alabama. University, AL:
     University of Alabama Press, 1950, pp. 129-132, 347, 359-360.

     This work discusses various aspects of aged slaves in Alabama. The
     author repeatedly argues that when slaves became old most of them
     could count on being pensioned and allowed to live out their lives
     without working as part of the plantation family. He concludes
     that "social pressure was brought to bear on planters who failed
     to discharge this part of a slaveowner's responsibility." The
     writer cites several excerpts from planters' will books whereby
     they stated that old slaves should be provided for after their
     death. Some were and others were not.

61. Smith, Julia Floyd. Slavery and Plantation Growth in Antebellum
     Florida, 1821-1860. Gainesville, FL: University of Florida Press,
     1973, pp. 91-99, 205-212.

     The author points out that the slaves who were too old to work in
     the field were assigned regular duties which took less physical
     effort. Old men worked as gardeners, wagoners, carters, and stock-
     tenders. Aged women were employed as hospital nurses, assistant
     cooks, workers in the dairy or poultry yard, caretakers of Black
     children in the plantation nursery, or in sewing and repairing
     garments and in spinning and weaving. Aged slave women were used
     as midwives.

62. Sterky, H. E. The Free Negro in Antebellum Louisiana. Rutherford,
     NJ: Fairleigh Dickinson University Press, 1972, pp. 130-133.

     A number of aged slaves were freed by their masters' wills for
     their "faithful service." In a number of instances, they were
     also given money and sometimes land.

63. Sydnor, Charles Sackett. Slavery in Mississippi. New York: D.
     Appleton-Century Co., 1933, pp. 65-66.

     The writer declares that as slaves grew old, their tasks were
     lightened in proportion to their failing strength. He continues
     to state that on most of the larger plantations there were (old)
     Negroes who either did no work or not enough to compensate for

Sydnor, Charles Sackett (Continued)

their food, clothing and shelter. Dr. Sydnor surmises that he
found no instance of a master's failing to care for such slaves
and they generally seem to have been treated well as able-bodied
field hands. The writer also points out that some planters' wills
provided for the care or freedom of their aged slaves "who had been
faithful for a number of years," or "who have been good, dutiful,
and obedient."

64. Zilversmit, Arthur. The First Emancipation: The Abolition of
     Slavery in the North. Chicago: University of Chicago Press,
     1957, pp. 17-19.

It was observed that as early as 1702, Connecticut passed a law
regulating manumissions, but its object was merely to prevent masters from escaping the responsibility of maintaining old or sick
slaves by freeing them "after they have spent the principal part
of their time and strength in their master's service." A number of
other states, such as Massachusetts, Rhode Island, Pennsylvania,
New York and New Jersey, passed similar laws.

7. FEMALE AGED SLAVES

65. Child, L. Maria. The Freedmen's Book. Boston: Ticknor and
     Fields, 1865, pp. 206-218.

There is one essay written in this collection by Harriet Jacobs,
a Black woman called "The Good Grandmother." Miss Jacobs discusses
her grandmother, who was a slave for fifty years. Her grandmother
was purchased by the sister of her former mistress, who was
seventy years old at the time. Her new owner immediately gave her
her freedom. Her grandmother helped her (Jacobs) escape to freedom, and gave her a small bag of money.

66. Coffin, Levi. Reminiscences of Levi Coffin, The Reported President
     of The Underground Railroad. Cincinnati: Robert Clarke Co., 1898,
     pp. 160-170, 312-318.

The author, a White abolitionist, discusses several aged slaves.
He mentioned one Aunt Betsey, who escaped with her family to freedom. She was a trusty old slave of her master and he reposed considerable confidence in her. She had a husband and eight children.
They lived in Kentucky. When Betsey found out that her master intended to sell her children, she decided to escape to Ohio, a free
state, and this she did. She loaded her family in a wagon, covered
them up and pretended to be going to the market in Cincinnati to
sell some vegetables. She and her family left and never returned.
They later moved to Canada to escape the slave catchers that her
former master sent to bring them back. She did not return to her
master.

67. Doyle, Bertram Wilbur. The Etiquette of Race Relations In the
     South: A Study in Social Control. Chicago: University of Chicago
     Press, 1937, pp. 13-17, 71, 74, 78.

     The author points out that during slavery the aged female slave's
     position and relation to the mistress and children was perhaps
     closer than that of any of the other slaves. According to Doyle,
     she was a kind of "glorified" nurse and was the authority in nurs-
     ery matters. The younger slave who attended the children as guar-
     dian and companion, and who was called "nurse" was subordinate to
     her, states the writer. Moreover, it is said, the mistress
     "humoured her claims of authority," hence the intimacy doubtless
     begot its own etiquette, concludes the author. Doyle also makes
     references to various aged slaves.

68. Frazier, E. Franklin. The Negro Family in the United States.
     Chicago: University of Chicago Press, 1939, pp. 146-159.

     Chapter 8 is entitled "Granny: The Guardian of the Generations."
     Dr. Frazier points out that during slavery the Black grandmother
     occupied, in many instances, an important place in the plantation
     economy and was highly esteemed by both the slaves and the masters.
     She was the repository of the accumulated lore and superstition of
     the slaves and was on hand at the birth of Black children as well
     as of White children. The granny took under her care the orphaned
     and the abandoned children. The writer argues that when emanicpa-
     tion came, it was often the old grandmother who kept the genera-
     tions together. The Black grandmother's importance is due to the
     fact not only that she had been the "oldest head" in a maternal
     family organization, but also to her position as "granny" or mid-
     wife among a simple peasant folk, according to the author. Prof.
     Frazier concludes that the Black grandmother has not ceased to
     watch over the destiny of the Black families as they moved in ever
     increasing numbers to the cities during the 1930s.

69. Furmas, J. C. Goodbye To Uncle Tom. New York: William Sloane
     Associates, 1956, pp. 17, 110, 126, 145, 262.

     Various references are made to the aged slave throughout the book.
     The author points out that some old slave women might choose to act
     as plantation physician, midwife and -- more or less secretly --
     witch doctor. It was observed that younger slaves looked to older
     slaves for advice.

70. Murray, Lindley. Narratives of Colored Americans. New York:
     William Wood & Co., 1875, pp. 16-18, 46-48, 103-111.

     Various references are made to aged Blacks throughout the book.
     Most were former slaves. Two particular slaves, "Old Dinah" and
     "Old Susan" stand out. Dinah was a slave who was baptized by a
     Roman Catholic priest. She learned to read and was deeply religious.
     Susan also was deeply religious and believed in the power of God.
     Susan was over seventy and she cared for her aged mother who was
     101 years old.

71. Myers, Minnie W. <u>Romance and Realism of the South Gulf Coast</u>.
     Cincinnati: Robert Clarke Co., 1898, pp. 56-57, 86-87.

     The writer points out that the aged slave was the first person to
     whom children visiting the plantation ran to see, for she was
     amiable in her greeting, and it was she who saw to all their wants.
     She showered the children with attention and could be kind and in-
     dulgent or stern and exacting as the occasion demanded. The writer
     declares: "Such a thing as rebellion against her was almost un-
     dreamt of, for she was high in authority."

72. Pickens, William. <u>The Heir of Slaves: An Autobiography</u>. New York:
     Pilgrim Press, 1911. pp. 5-7.

     The author points out that his grandmother lived with his mother
     and father and raised all of the grandchildren. He recalled that
     she could thread her own needles when she was eighty years old.
     She lived for forty years with a broken back, the upper part of her
     body being carried in a horizontal position, at right angles to her
     lower limbs, so that she had to support her steps with a walking
     cane, if she walked far. This was one of the results of slavery,
     states the writer. She had been beaten and struck across the back
     with a stick. He concludes that even in her old age her temper
     rose quickly, but was volatile and she was a very dear and helpful
     grandmother.

73. Redpath, James. <u>The Roving Editor: Or, Talks with Slaves in the
     Southern States</u>. New York: A. B. Burdick, Publisher, 1859.
     pp. 116-117, 129-132.

     The author discusses his talk with an old slave mother who was
     sixty-two. He was shocked because according to him, she did not
     look that old. Redpath points out that her maternal affections
     for her children were very strong. The aged slave emphasizes that
     she and other slaves were not contented to be in slavery as was
     reported by White slave owners, asserts Redpath.

74. Scarborough, Dorothy. <u>On Trail of Negro Folk-Songs</u>. Cambridge,
     MA: Harvard University Press, 1925, pp. 144-145, 151-152, 164,
     173, 287.

     The author tells of an overseer who complained to his uncle that
     the insolence of one of the old women slaves was becoming so un-
     bearable that he needed advice about punishing her. When told that
     the old woman's name was "Mammy," the uncle replied: "What! What!
     Why, I would as soon think of punishing my own mother! Why man,
     you'd have four of the biggest men in Mississippi down on you if
     you even dare suggest such a thing, and she knows it! All you can
     do is knuckle down to Mammy." There are also other aged slaves
     mentioned in this book. This book has racist overtones.

75. Still, William. <u>The Underground Railroad</u>. Philadelphia: Porter &
     Coates, 1872, pp. 118, 394-395.

     The writer alludes to various aged slaves throughout this book.
     One specific case involves Jane Davis, a slave woman about seventy,
     from the Eastern Shore section of Maryland. She was the mother of
     twelve children and "married." Because she was to be sold and of-
     ten mistreated, she decided to leave her children and husband and
     escape to Buffalo, New York, where her brother was living. She
     escaped by the Underground Railroad. Although she was nearly
     seventy, she suffered hunger, and slept in the woods for nearly
     three weeks with little or no food. The author concludes that
     Jane, doubtless, represented thousands of aged slave mothers, who
     after having been worn out under the yoke, were frequently either
     offered for sale for a trifle, turned off to die, or compelled to
     eke out their existence on the most stinted allowance.

76. Stroyer, Jacob. <u>My Life in the South</u>. Salem, MA: Newcome &
     Gause, Printers, 1898, pp. 8-9, 10-12.

     The author points out that when Black female slaves were too old
     to work in the fields on the plantation, they were used as nurses
     to look after slave children. Some of these aged female slaves
     were also cooks. He states how his old Uncle Benjamin saved him
     from getting a whipping from a slave boy.

                    8.   MALE AGED SLAVES

77. Carleton, George Washington. <u>The Suppressed Book About Slavery!</u>
     New York: Carleton Publisher, 1864, pp. 190, 228-229, 277-278, 281,
     325-326.

     A number of references are made to aged slaves throughout this
     book. There is the case of a ninety year old slave named Johnson,
     from Louisiana, who was whipped, stamped and kicked to death by
     his master.

78. Poole, William F. <u>Anti-Slavery Opinions: Before the Year 1800</u>.
     Cincinnati: Robert Clark and Co., 1873, pp. 21-23, 28.

     The author discussed "Negro Tom," an Alexandria, Virginia slave
     who died December 19, 1790 at age 80. Tom was described as a
     calculator, prodigy, untaught arithmetician and untutored scholar.
     Poole concluded: ". . . . Had his opportunities of improvement
     been equal to those of thousands of his fellow men, neither the
     Royal Society of London, the Academy of Science at Paris, nor even
     a Newton himself need have been ashamed to acknowledge him a
     brother in science."

79. Rogers, George C., Jr., et al., Editors. <u>The Papers of Henry
     Laurens</u>. Columbia: University of South Carolina, 1968, Vol. 4,
     p. 148N.

Rogers, George C., Jr. (Continued)

It was pointed out that an old Black slave named Cudgo (Cudjoe)
continued to work, even at his age. The editors declare that the
young slaves respected and loved him. The elderly slave was living
and working in South Carolina in 1770. His owner states that if
Cudgo was too old to work, he would provide for him . . . .

80. Starobin, Robert S. Industrial Slavery in the Old South. New
     York: Oxford University Press, 1970, pp. 167-168.

It was pointed out that old slaves, especially men, were used in
the factories. Prof. Starobin suggests that 4 percent in the
factories were slaves over sixty years old.

9. TREATMENT OF AGED SLAVES

81. Drew, Benjamin. A North-Side View of Slavery: The Refugee, or the
     Narrative of Fugitive Slaves in Canada, Related by Themselves.
     Boston: John P. Jewett and Co., 1856, pp. 19, 48, 88, 138, 155,
     175, 182-183, 212, 248-254, 280-282, 338, 350.

Various former slaves recall how old slaves were treated in the
South. Some said old slave men were treated worse than a horse or
a hog. . . . A large number of the narratives in this collection
were written by both male and female mulatto ex-slaves.

82. Feldstein, Stanley. Once A Slave: The Slaves' View of Slavery.
     New York: William Morrow and Co., 1970, pp. 125-128.

There is one section in this work entitled "The Aged Slave." The
author surmises that "one of the shabbier characteristics of
slavery described in the slave narratives, and one which tended to
deepen the slave's conviction of the infernal character of the institution and to fill him with utter loathing of slaveholders, was
the master's alleged lack of gratitude to the aged slave." Prof.
Feldstein declares that if no work of any value could be found for
them, or if they outlived their original masters and fell into the
hands of strangers, they would either be sold for any price they
could bring, or simply turned out to fend for themselves. It was
pointed out that in some cases of aged slaves being sold for one
dollar "to men not worth one cent." In some instances after they
had to fend for themselves, some were found starved to death, and
half eaten up by animals. Some aged slaves became so embittered
at being replaced by younger men that their contempt was directed
toward their fellow slaves. The elderly slaves were, in the most
real sense, the end result of the dehumanization process, concludes
the writer.

83. Genovese, Eugene D. Roll, Jordan, Roll: The World the Slaves
     Made. New York: Pantheon Books, 1974, pp. 519-521.

There is one section entitled "The Old Folks." The author argues
that the reliance of the quarters on folk medicine gave the old

Genovese, Eugene D. (Continued)

folks a special role--one that made them feel especially useful and
respected and that brought them a consideration born of religious
sanction as well as physical service. The aged slaves attended the
sick, comforted those in pain, and taught the younger slaves the
mysteries of medical magic. Dr. Genovese contends that suicide
appeared rarely among old slaves. He concludes that the aged
slave had a high degree of security, emotional as well as physical.
Their masters' error, continues the historian, lay in the supposition that the modest protection of the Big House accounted for
their widespread cheerfulness and contentment, for the old folks'
ability to live decently and with self-respect depended primarily
on the support of their younger fellow slaves.

84. Liston, Robert. Slavery in America: The History of Slavery.
     New York: McGraw-Hill Book Co., 1970, pp. 72, 79-80, 83, 89.

     The writer points out that old slaves had their gray hair dyed
     black and their silver whiskers plucked out to make them appear
     younger. Liston contends that planters were ridiculing old slaves
     when they called them "auntie" and "uncle." Another form of ridi-
     cule, declares Liston, is when old slave domestics were consulted
     for their advice on family and plantation affairs. It was also
     mentioned by the author that some old slaves were babysitters and
     had other "light" duties to perform.

85. Owens, Leslie Howard. The Species of Property: Slave Life and
     Culture in the Old South. New York: Oxford University Press,
     1976, pp. 47, 109, 113-120, 203.

     Prof. Owen asserts that many of the masters assigned some of the
     aged light duties such as taking care of children. Many slave-
     holders also saw the presence of some of the old ones as a tax on
     plantation resources. Masters emancipated some as a reward for a
     lifetime of faithful service, but other planters intended many of
     these seeming generosities simply as part of a larger scheme to
     set themselves and their relatives free of responsibility for care
     of the old persons, according to the author. The aged slaves some-
     times drifted aimlessly, winding up in cities where urbanites
     thought them burdensome additions to the population. Cunning
     slaveholders doctored the appearance of the old to make them appear
     a few years younger, rested them, and then sold them to anyone who
     paid a respectable price, asserts Dr. Owens. The author concludes
     in all, the aged slave could not look forward to leisurely final
     years with certainty. On the larger estates, a planter might be
     unfamiliar with the care and food rations actually given to the
     old ones by an overseer. If they moved about, he assumed it was
     because of age and little else.

86. Parks, Willis B., Editor. The Possibilities of the Negro in
     Symposium. Atlanta, GA: Franklin Publishing Co., 1904, pp. 69-
     73.

Parks, Willis B. (Continued)

There is one article, "Aged Ex-Slaves Gather At Home of Old Master,"
by Robert Timmons included in this work. Fifteen ex-slaves
joined in this reunion in 1899. The oldest member of the party,
"Uncle" Edmund Menefee, who was 80 years old, came from near
Hiram, Georgia, and walked the entire distance, about fifty miles.
They came to see the old homestead and the other slaves with whom
they associated during slavery. The author states that the ex-
slaves told of how well they had been treated as slaves and how,
though they wanted freedom, yet when freedom came, they wanted to
remain on the same plantation and continue to work for their mistress, after the death of their master. The ex-slaves also told
how their master had taught them to be religious, to be neat and
clean, to be always honest and give the proper respect to the
Whites. These lessons, they said, had remained with them and they
were teaching them to their children.

87. Stampp, Kenneth M. The Peculiar Institution: Slavery in the Ante-
     Bellum South. New York: Alfred A. Knopf, 1972, pp. 58, 318-319,
     323-325, 328-329, 336.

     Prof. Stampp argues that a substantial number of aged "aunties"
     and "uncles" did not spend their declining years as pensioners
     living leisurely and comfortably on their masters' bounty. A few
     did, but not enough reached retirement age to be more than a negli-
     gible expense to the average owner. Dr. Stampp surmises that
     doubtless most Blacks in their sixties were not very productive,
     but they usually did enough work at least to pay for their support.
     Even slaves over seventy were not always an absolute burden,
     though it may be assumed that most were. In 1860 only 1.2 percent
     were over seventy; thus the owner of as many as a hundred seldom
     had more than one or two senile slaves to support, concludes the
     historian.

88. Weld, Theodore Dwight, Editor. American Slavery As It Is:
     Testimony of a Thousand Witnesses. New York: American Anti-
     Slavery Society, 1839, pp. 54, 101, 114, 135, 136, 161, 167.

     Various mention of the treatment of old slaves was seen throughout
     this book. A number of cases state that old slaves were severely
     whipped by their owners. In a few instances, the owner's wife
     flogged the aged slaves, including female slaves . . . .

              10. THE BLACK AGED AND THE SLAVE FAMILY

89. Gutman, Herbert G. The Black Family In Slavery and Freedom:
     1750-1925. New York: Panthron Books, 1976, pp. 185-229, 252, 307.

     The writer argues that slaves' social beliefs caused slaves to
     transfer quickly the names of grandparents to grandchildren. The
     evidence means that children often knew their grandparents. This
     also suggests that elderly slaves played prominent roles in fami-
     lies formed by their children, and especially in socializing and

Gutman, Herbert G.   (Continued)

enculturating the young. Gutman concludes that naming practices
among plantation slaves reveal concern for symbolic ties to older
Black kin. There is also one section dealing with elderly slaves
called "Aunts and Uncles and Swap-Dog Kin."

90.   Webber, Thomas L. Deep Like the River: Education in the Slave
      Quarter Community, 1831-1865. New York: W. W. Norton & Co.,
      1978, pp. 157-179.

Chapter 13 is entitled "The Family." The author declares that although aged slaves maintained their own cabins until death, the
general rule in most quarter communities was for single and aged
slaves to move in with one of their married children after they became too old to work in the fields. Respected for their age and
for their position as head of the family, grandparents often enjoyed a venerated authority in the family, states Prof. Webber.
In most quarter families, states the author, children learned that
when their family gathered together, it was the commands of grandparents that were to be obeyed first. Often one or more grandparents assumed the role of the arbiter in family disputes and
quarrels. The author concludes that grandparents also played an
important educational role in transmitting the songs and stories
of Africa and of plantation history. One of childhood's chief diversions, according to the writer, was to listen to the songs and
tales of grandparents.

11.   ECONOMIC VALUE OF AGED SLAVES

91.   Armistead, Wilson, Editor. Five Hundred Thousand Strokes for
      Freedom: A Series of Anti-Slavery Tracts, Of Which Half a Million
      Are Now First Issued By Friends of The Negro. London: W. & E.
      Cash, Publishers, 1853, p. 17.

Anti-slavery series number 17 is entitled "Sale of Aged Negroes."
This sale took place in Winnsboro, South Carolina at an auction.
An aged male about 70 years old and his wife about the same age
were sold for a meager $13.00. They were almost worn out with
stripes and hard work and both their hair was nearly white because
of old age. This ad was taken from "Report of an English Travel-
ler."

92.   Catterall, Helen Tunncliff, Editor. Judicial Cases Concerning
      American Slavery and the Negro. Washington, DC: Carnegie Insti-
      tution of Washington, 1926. Vol. 1, pp. 204-205, 458, 463-464.

A number of aged slaves were freed in their owners' wills. One
case was in Virginia as seen in the John Randolph case and the
other case involved Kentucky; and concerns aged slaves named
Milly, Nancy and Harry:

Coalter v. Bryan, 1 Grattan 18, May 1844. (19) "In May 1833,
John Randolph of Roanoke died, unmarried and childless; leaving

Catterall, Helen Tunncliff (Continued)

a very large estate, both real and personal. His slaves numbered
nearly or quite four hundred . . . After the death of John Randolph, it was ascertained that he had left several wills . . (20)
The will of 1821, and the codicil of the 5th December of that year,
'In the name of God. Amen! I John Randolph of Roanoke, do ordain
this my last will and testament, hereby revoking all other wills
whatsoever. 1. I give and bequeathe all my slaves their freedom,
heartily regretting that I have ever been the owner of one. 2. I
give to my ex'or a sum not exceeding eight thousand dollars, or so
much thereof as may be necessary to transport and settle said
slaves to and in some other state or territory of the U.S. giving
to all above the age of forty, not less than ten acres of land each.
3. To my old and faithful servants Essex and his wife Hetty who I
trust may be suffered to remain in the (21) state, I give and bequeath three and a half barrels of corn, two hundred weight of
pork, a pair of strong shoes, a suit of clothes and a blanket each,
to be paid to them annually, also an annual hat to Essex, and ten
pounds of coffee and twenty of brown sugar. 4. To my woman servant
Nancy the like allowance as to her mother. 5. To Juba (alias Jupiter)
the same; to Queen the same; to Johnny my body servant, the same,
during their respective lives. . . Monohon v. Caroline (of color),
2 Bush 410, November 1867. (411) "Mrs. Lucy Fine, by her last
will gave freedom to her slaves, and directed that her brother,
Nathan Mardis, should take them to Cincinnati, Ohio, or other
suitable place, and execute deeds of manumission. She also made
some specific bequest to each of them, and directed her residence
to be sold, and its proceeds to be divided among them or their
descendents. The Slaves John and Matt had belonged to her de-
ceased husband, and fell to her for life only. Caroline was not
to enjoy freedom until the death of an aged Negro named Milly,
who had been a faithful slave to the testatrix . . . . Farmers'
Bank v. Johnson, 4 Bush 411, January 1869. "The original judgment,
ordering a sale of Johnson's lands, slaves, etc., to pay his cre-
ditors, and directing that the aged and infirm slaves, Nancy and
Harry, should be sold to the lowest bidder--that is, to the one
who would provide for them, and bury them plainly and decently, for
the least sum--to be paid out of the assets of the insolvent deb-
tor, was only providing out of his estate for both the legal and
moral obligation resting on him to take care of his aged and infirm
slaves. Had these slaves not been sold, Johnson would have been
released from this obligation when the United States Government
abolished the relation of master and slave; .. (412) The bank got
Johnson's legal rights to these aged and infirm slaves, and was
entitled to their services, whatever may have been the value thereof, and became legally responsible for their maintenance whilst
remaining slaves, and for decent burial if they should die in slavery; but when the right to control the service of these slaves
ceased by the political action of the Government, the bank's legal
liability to maintain and bury them was also abolished . . . dis-
miss all proceedings against the bank to compel it to maintain said
infirm negroes since the adoption of the Thirteenth Amendment to
the United States Constitution." (Williams, C. J.)

93. _____. Judicial Cases Concerning American Slavery and the Negro. Washington, DC: Carnegie Institution of Washington, 1932, Vol. 3, pp. 182, 628.

A number of elderly slaves were set free by their masters' wills as seen in an Alabama and Louisiana case: Roberson v. Roberson, 21 Ala. 273, June 1852. Will of John Roberson, 1844: (274) "for good services and regard that I have for my four slaves, .. Old Peter and . . his wife, and Little Peter and . . his wife, I hereby set them free at my death." They were sold by the executors. Held: the bequest was void. They go to the residuary legatees. State v. Executors of McDonough, 8 La. An. 171, April 1853. Will, executed in 1838: (174) "I, John McDonough, a native . . of Baltimore, . . now an inhabitant of the Town of McDonough in . . Louisiana, . . do make this, my Olographic Will, . . I have never been married, . . I . . bequeath, their freedom, (as a reward for their long and faithful services,) to my (ten) old servants, Gabriel (et al.) . . I direct my executors, . . immediately after my death, to correspond with the American Colonization Society, at . . Washington, . . for the purpose of ascertaining, when said Society, intends sending a vessel to Liberia . . with emigrants, from New Orleans, and by the first vessel . . to send all the rest . . of my black people, . . (with the exception of the black man, Philip (et al.) . . all of whom I have lately purchased, as it is my will, that they . . (175) with any other black, or colored people, whom I may acquire . . subsequent to the date of this . . Will, . . shall serve those, (by being hired out . . or kept employed on my plantations, . .) to whom I have . . willed the . . residue . . of my Estate . . fifteen years from . . my death; when . . my Executors . . will deliver (them) . . up to the American Colonization Society . . to be also sent to Liberia, . .)

94. _____. Judicial Cases Concerning American Slavery and the Negro. Washington, DC: Carnegie Institution of Washington, 1929. Vol. 2, pp. 101-102, 186-187.

The editor lists two cases relating to aged Blacks in North Carolina. They are: Lane v. Wingate, 3 Iredell 326, June 1843 (327) "the plaintiff declined selling him, alleging that he wanted Daniel to wait upon an old negro woman . . . named Rhoda, who was upwards of one hundred years of age, . . . defendant replied, that if the plaintiff would let him have Daniel, he would support old Rhoda during her life; the parties valued Daniel at two hundred dollars, and the defendant executed the agreement." Rhoda remained with the defendant (327) for about four weeks, after which time she returned to the house of the plaintiff, where she has remained ever since . . . it was worth twenty-five dollars a year to support Rhoda . . . (328) verdict for the plaintiff, assessing his damages at seventy-five dollars." The other case includes Joiner v. Joiner, 2 Jones Eq. 68, December 1854. Will: (69) "to my son Noah . . . the cooper Joseph, . . . and James." Codicil, three years later: "that Robert Hines have . . . the boy James: "one . . . was a valuable young man. The other . . . was very old, supposed to be near one hundred, and not only without value, but an expense." Held: "we cannot . . . believe that a father would

Catterall, Helen Tunncliff (Continued)

mock his son by giving him, as an apparent bounty, an old Negro, who was . . . a burden."

95. Davis, Edwin Adams, Editor. Plantation Life in Florida Parishes of Louisiana, 1836-1846 As Reflected in the Diary of Bennet H. Barrow. New York: Columbia University Press, 1943, pp. 392-410.

Under the "Rules of Highland Plantation," the planter stated that if a slave would work for him until he got old and could no longer maintain himself, that he would care for him. In the 1855 "Inventory of the Estate of Bennet H. Barrow," it listed several aged slaves and their value: Betsy age 59, $100.00; Old Sukey age 56, $100.00; Lucy, age 71, only $10.00; Dennis, age 44, $150.00; Josh age 69, $100.00; Phil, age 75, $100.00; Old Hannah, age 70, only $5.00, Old Cato, age 60, $400.00; Judis, age 56, $100.00; Ceely, age 54, $100.00. This book also gives "Slave Deaths: 1831-1845." Two slaves, Old Pat, age 80 and Old Jack age 85 died in 1831, and 1834 respectively. Two other slaves, Old Rheuben, age 60 and Old Betty, age 65, both died in 1836.

96. Fogel, Robert William and Stanley L. Engerman. Time on the Cross: The Economics of American Negro Slavery. Boston: Little, Brown and Co., 1974, pp. 74-77, 153-155.

Various references are made to the economic status of aged slaves. The authors argue that earnings of sixty-five year olds were still positive and, on an average, brought the owners as much net income as a slave in the mid-teens. They declare that the above statement does not mean that every slave aged sixty-five produced a positive net income for his owner. Some of the elderly, according to Fogel and Engerman, were a net loss. However, the income earned by the able-bodied among the elderly was more than enough to compensate for the burden imposed by the incapacitated, conclude the authors. Fully 40 percent of the slaves died before age nineteen, conclude the authors.

12.   BLACK AGED AND RELIGION

97. Henderson, Donald H. The Negro-Freedman: Life Conditions of the American Negro in the Early Years After Emancipation. New York: Henry Schuman, 1952, pp. 98-109.

The writer discusses aged Blacks and their views on education, superstitions and religion. It was pointed out that aged Blacks went to public schools to acquire an education. The old people wanted to learn to read the Bible before they died, and wished their children to be educated. Dr. Henderson states than an investigator reported having seen three generations--a grandmother, a daughter, and a granddaughter--sitting on the same bench, spelling the same lesson, and having seen classes that included pupils from six years of age up to sixty. The aged also were deeply superstitious and religious.

98. Miller, Harriet Parks. Pioneer Colored Christians. Clarksville, TN: W. P. Titus, Printer, 1911. 103 pp.

This book includes the Christian views of ex-slaves. They were born between 1810 and 1850. Most of these aged Blacks state that they never would have reached old age except for the grace and will of God. He was the one that carried them through, they argued.

99. Woofter, Thomas J., Jr. Black Yeomanry: Life on St. Helena Island. New York: Henry Holt and Co., 1930, pp. 103-109, 208-211.

The writer states that there are many ex-slaves who are near ninety. He argues this longevity is, in itself, a striking commentary on the health of the Island. Prof. Woofter concludes that theirs is not a bedridden old age and seldom are they entirely dependent. Many are straight as a string and do occasional field work or odd jobs up to the time of their last illness. The ex-slaves were also deeply religious people.

13.   THE BLACK AGED SLAVE AS A STORYTELLER

100. Dundes, Alan, Editor. Mother Wit From the Laughing Barrel. Englewood Cliffs, NJ: Prentice Hall, Inc., 1973, pp. 199-205, 251-257.

Various references are made to the Black aged throughout this book on Black Folklore. One section of particular interest is "Dialogues of The Old and The New Porter." This is a conversation between a young Black Pullman porter and an elderly Black porter. The young Black convinced the aged Black porter to join the Pullman Sleeping Car Porters' Union. Another section, "Old-Time Courtship Conversation," discusses the Black aged. This essay discusses "courtship" of slaves on plantations. The author states that almost every large plantation had an experienced old slave who instructed young slaves in the way in which they should go in the delicate matter of winning the girls of their choice. It was also suggested that younger slaves respected aged slaves.

101. Levine, Lawrence W. Black Culture and Black Conscience: Afro-American Folk Thought From Slavery to Freedom. New York: Oxford University Press, 1977, pp. 45-46, 57-58, 64-66, 71, 223, 403.

The writer makes various references to the Black aged. He points out that on some plantations, the aged Black slaves were "doctors" or "root doctors" who used herbs and "roots" as medicine. A number of slave practitioners won considerable renown for their skill. In 1729 the governor of Virginia traded an elderly slave "who had performed many wonderful cures of diseases" his freedom in return for the secret of his medicine, "a concoction of roots and barks." The writer also related that old slaves had signs for everything. These were signs indicating what the weather would be; signs telling of the coming of strangers or loved ones; signs prophesying bad luck or good fortune; signs warning of an impending whipping or the approach of white patrols; signs foretelling imminent illness

Levine, Lawrence W. (Continued)

or death. Dreams were taken seriously as an important source of
such signs, concludes the writer.

14. THE AGED SLAVE AND THE UNDERGROUND RAILROAD

102. Annual Report of the American Anti-Slavery Society for the Year
      Ending May 1, 1860. New York: American Anti-Slavery Society,
      1861, pp. 47, 52-55.

      Various references are made to aged slaves throughout this report.
      Several old slaves, along with their families, attempted to escape
      to freedom.

103. Gara, Larry. The Liberty Line: The Legend of the Underground
      Railroad. Lexington: University of Kentucky Press, 1961, pp. 20-
      21.

      Several aged ex-slaves state what slavery was like. One former
      slave declares: "We all had freedom in our bones." Another ex-
      slave told his interviewer not to believe anyone who said he
      would rather be a slave than a free man.

104. Siebert, Wilbur H. Vermont's Anti-Slavery and Underground Rail-
      road Record. Columbus, OH: The Spahr and Glenn Co., 1937, pp. 2-
      5, 67.

      It was pointed out that in some instances when slaves were infirm,
      old, sick and blind, some owners discarded them and towns had to
      take care of them. Some towns forced the former owners to take
      care of them in their old age.

105. Smedley, R. C. History of the Underground Railroad in Chester
      and the Neighboring Counties of Pennsylvania. Lancaster, PA:
      Office of the Journal, 1883, pp. 108-111.

      William Parker, a former slave in Anne Arundel, Maryland, tells
      how his grandmother, a cook in the "great house" took care of him
      on the plantation when his mother died.

15. LIFE EXPECTANCY OF SLAVES

106. Betts, Edwin M., Jr., Editor. Thomas Jefferson Farm Book.
      Princeton, NJ: Princeton University Press, 1953, pp. 5-9, 15-18,
      24, 30, 57, 128-129.

      This book gives a list of the names of slaves on Thomas Jeffer-
      son's plantation. Many slaves were in their 70s and 80s. A few
      were in their 90s. These slaves were unusually old for slaves
      during the 1770s - 1790s.

107. Goldin, Claudia Dale. Urban Slavery in the American South 1820-
      1860: A Quantitative History. Chicago: University of Chicago
      Press, 1976, pp. 16, 62-64, 127, 134, 138.

      The writer argues that the 1830 and 1840 urban percentage for
      older slaves is not much different from the total United States
      figures. Some cities, for example, Norfolk and Richmond, had a
      slightly older female slave labor force than the other cities,
      but this older age bracket does not, according to Dr. Goldin,
      show an abnormal bulge before 1840. The author concludes that
      this had changed somewhat by 1850 and differences had become
      striking by 1860. At that time all cities except New Orleans had
      become older in population. At that time, argues Goldin, all
      cities except New Orleans had a greater percentage of females
      older than 54, than did the United States in general. In some
      cities, for example, Norfolk and Washington, the percentage was
      double that of the United States.

108. Oakes, James. The Ruling Race: A History of American Slave-
      holders. New York: Alfred A. Knopf, 1982, pp. 195-196, 247-250.

      It was pointed out that with an average life expectancy of less
      than forty years, most slaves were dead before they reached the
      age of forty-four. The majority of slaves were children eighteen
      years of age or under. Demographically, therefore, the most
      common master-slave relationship was between a middle-aged White
      man and a Black child, concludes Prof. Oakes. Only about 4.0%
      slaves were over forty-nine years old.

                      16. HOMES FOR THE AGED

109. Home For Aged Colored Women. Forty-Seventh Annual Report of the
      Directors of the Home for Aged Colored Women. Boston: J. Wilson
      and Son, 1860. 7 pp.

      It was pointed out that outside relief is given to aged and infirm
      colored women, in sums from two dollars to six dollars per month.
      Applicants for admission must be sixty years old or over, except
      in special cases of illness or infirmity. The report goes on to
      state that the number of outside beneficiaries has steadily in-
      creased. It is the intention of the directors to make this work
      as comprehensive as possible, and the Committee on Admissions has
      taken it diligently in hand, conferring with other agencies and
      individuals, and personally investigating all applications. They
      also visit those who already receive an allowance, to make sure
      that it is proving sufficient and being wisely spent, and to re-
      commend an increase when advancing age and infirmity render it
      necessary. There are many pathetic cases where relatives or
      friends are making a hard struggle to support these aged and fee-
      ble women, or a neighbor, on whom there is no claim, has taken one
      in for charity's sake, and a small addition to the family income
      eases the strain and makes better care possible. There are also
      women who have supported themselves all their lives, and cannot
      bear to sit down quietly in a Home as long as they can do a little
      work outside, and this monthly allowance helps them to maintain

Home For Aged Colored Women (Continued)

their independence. The Home stands ready as a refuge for all
when outside resources fail. In it they find rest and warmth,
good food and care, a little work for those who are able, and an
atmosphere of cheerfulness and good-will which is rarely equalled
elsewhere. Matron and help, inmates and directors, feel the
mutual helpfulness and dependence on each other of a real family,
while everyone is free to follow her own way provided they do not
interfere with the safety or comfort of others.

110. Home for Aged and Infirm Colored Persons. Proceedings of the
      Second Annual Report. Philadelphia: Merrihew and Son, 1866.
      28 pp.

      This work contains the Constitution, By-Laws and Rules of the Home
      for Aged and Infirm Colored Persons. The proceedings of the
      second Annual Report were taken from a meeting held January 12,
      1866 in Philadelphia. The report points out much is being done in
      the city to help the Black aged and infirm, but much, much more
      needs to be done.

Articles

1. FEMALE AGED SLAVES

111. Brown, Clarence. "Reflections on 119 Years of Living," Jet,
     July 4, 1974, pp. 22-25.

     This article concerns Mrs. Mary Mood, born a slave on an Augusta,
     Arkansas plantation almost 10 years before the signing of the
     Emancipation Proclamation. She has been called the "oldest Black
     woman in the United States." Mrs. Mood has lived under the rule
     of 23 presidents. She gives her views on sex, President Nixon,
     her longevity, the moon landing, today's fashions, airplanes,
     and food prices.

112. Flander, Ralph B. "Two Plantations in a County of Antebellum
     Georgia." Georgia Historical Quarterly, Vol. 7, March, 1928,
     pp. 1-24.

     The writer points out that aged, infirm or crippled slaves wove
     baskets, mended or made clothes, or were assigned light tasks
     about the place. The old women often canned fruit and cared for
     the children.

113. Jacobs, Harriet. "The Good Grandmother" in The Freedmen's Book,
     L. Maria Child, Editor. Boston: Ticknor and Fields, 1865,
     pp. 206-218.

     The writer, a slave, states that her grandmother was a remarkable
     woman in many respects. Her grandmother, also a slave, made
     enough money baking crackers at night to purchase the freedom of
     her children. The grandmother was purchased for fifty dollars by
     an old White lady who gave her her freedom. The author, who also
     gained her freedom, along with her grandmother, moved to the
     North.

114. Parkhurst, Jessie W. "The Role of the Black Mammy in the Planta-
      tion Household," Journal of Negro History, Vol. 23, No. 3, July,
      1938, pp. 349-369.

      Various references are made to the aged "Black Mammy." The author
      points out that she was considered self-respecting, independent,
      loyal, forward, gentle, captious, affectionate, true, strong, just,
      warmhearted, compassionate-hearted, fearless, popular, brave, good,
      pious, quick-witted, capable, thrifty, proud, regal, courageous,
      superior, skillful, tender, queenly, dignified, neat, quick,
      competent, possessed with a temper, trustworthy, faithful, patient,
      tyrannical, sensible, discreet, efficient, careful, harsh, devoted,
      truthful, neither apish nor servile. The aged mammy, according to
      the author, was a diplomat and knew how to handle delicate situa-
      tions with such a fine sense of appropriateness that her purpose
      was usually accomplished. From being a confidential servant she
      grew into being a kind of prime minister, states the writer. The
      writer states that it was well known that if she espoused a cause
      and took it to the master, it was sure to be attended to at once,
      and according to her advice. The aged Black Mammy was at the top
      of the social hierarchy of slaves and occupied a position to be
      envied as well as to be strived for. The old Black Mammy was
      skillful in making old home remedies and upon them the White
      plantation had to depend when medicine gave out and no more was to
      be had, concludes the writer.

                    2. TREATMENT OF THE AGED SLAVE

115. Corlew, Robert E. "Some Aspects of Slavery in Dickson County
      (Tennessee)," Tennessee Historical Quarterly, Vol. 10, 1951,
      pp. 224-248, 344-365.

      The author argues that occasionally, if a slave was old, the
      owner would provide for both emancipation and support in old age.
      Such was the case with John Humphries and many others. Humphries
      in 1826 provided in his will that "my old negro woman Amy . . . is
      to be permitted to live with which of my children she pleases,
      but not as a slave, and which ever she chooses to live with shall
      be bound to maintain her as long as she lives . . . ."

116. "In the South the Slaves Are Taken Care Of for Past Services."
      New York Herald Tribune, March 8, 1860, p. 4.

      This article discusses four old Black slave pensioners in Alabama;
      one eighty years old. Another one was seventy-five years old.
      The other two were fifty years old. The writer states that all
      four were well taken care of by their masters.

117. "Old Slaves (Homeless)." Richmond (VA) Daily Dispatch, May 29,
      1858, p. 3.

      The writer suggests that old slaves were abandoned by their owners
      so they would not have to care for them since they could not work.
      "Old Negroes, like old horses, are often turned loose to go where
      they wish. . . ," declares the writer.

This article discusses four old Black slave pensioners in
Alabama; one eighty years old. Another one was seventy-five
years old. The other two were fifty years old. The writer states
that all four were well taken care of by their masters.

118.   "Old Slaves (Wards of the City)". Louisville Daily Courier,
        June 12, 1855, p. 4.

        It was pointed out that old slaves were set free by their masters
        and since they were penniless, they had to be taken care of by
        the cities.

3.   ECONOMIC VALUE OF THE AGED SLAVE

119.   "A Great Slave Auction." Douglass' Monthly, Vol. 1, No. 11, April,
        1859, pp. 56, 59.

        At a slave auction in Savannah, Georgia, the highest price paid
        for a slave man was $1,750 and the highest price paid for a female
        slave was $1,250. The lowest price paid was for a grey-haired
        couple who were purchased for only $250.00 each. It was stated
        that since they were over fifty years old and worn out, they were
        not worth much . . . .

120.   Pollard, Leslie J. "Aging and Slavery: A Gerontological Perspec-
        tive." Journal of Negro History, Vol. 66, No. 3, Fall, 1981,
        pp. 228-234.

        According to the writer, reverence for the aged survived the en-
        slavement process and was maintained by their performance of a
        valuable function that allowed them to enjoy dignity, self-respect
        and the veneration of the young. Prof. Pollard argues that in a
        production-based system, the slave community learned to care for
        those who, because of infirmity or old age, became incapable of
        productive labor, emphasizing their inclusion and belonging to a
        Black community that did not define its existence solely in terms
        of the Big House. This community, then, learned to cope with the
        senescent slave the same way as industrial societies must learn
        to provide for the obsolescent corporate worker. He concludes:
        "No doubt the benefit was reciprocal as older slaves taught
        younger ones how to cope with life, the meaning of survival over
        destruction, indeed, life over death . . . ."

4.   LIFE EXPECTANCY OF SLAVES

121.   Sydnor, Charles S. "Life Span of Slaves," American Historical
        Review. Vol. 35, No. 3, April, 1930, pp. 566-574.

        Prof. Sydnor discusses the life span of slaves in the state of
        Mississippi. He also compares the life span of whites with slaves.
        Much of his data is based on the United States Census for 1850.
        He points out that a slave twenty years old seems to have had a
        smaller chance than a white person of the same age to reach the
        age of thirty, forty, fifty, or sixty. Beyond sixty, slaves'
        chances of living to one of the higher ages were greater than
        that of the whites.

5. HISTORICAL PERSPECTIVES OF THE BLACK AGED

122. Blassingame, John W. "Status and Social Structure in The Slave Community: Evidence From New Sources." Perspectives and Irony in American Slavery. Harry P. Owens, Editor. Jackson, Mississippi: University Press of Mississippi, 1976, pp. 137-151.

The author makes various references to aged slaves. He points out that aged slaves were deeply religious and they stressed the importance of it on young slaves. Old slaves also taught young male slaves the "proper" formula of "courtship." Aged slaves, according to the historian, often demonstrated their verbal skills at church. One of the primary marks of a slave's piety was his or her ability to bear public witness to God in the form of prayer. Religious testimony was so important, states Dr. Blassingame, that slaves reduced prayers to formulas and taught them to young converts. Aged slaves also carved exquisite walking canes or whistles for youngsters and slave women were skillful seamstresses and made beautiful quilts. Prof. Blassingame surmises that old men and women with great stores of riddles, proverbs, and folktales played a crucial role in teaching morality and training the young to solve problems and to develop their social structure with elders being viewed as the possessors of wisdom, the closest link to the African homeland, and persons to be treated with respect, concludes the author.

123. Wylie, Floyd M. "Attitude Toward Aging Among Black Americans: Some Historical Perspectives." Aging and Human Development, Vol. 2, 1971, pp. 66-70.

The writer surmises that fortunately many of the cultural values and attitudes regarding the elderly have apparently changed little over the several centuries since Africans were snatched from their home continent. Wylie contends that the period of the slave trade and slavery did not divest Africans and their descendants of many basically African cultural values. The author concludes that it is clear that among the more important of these values that continue to the present time are a certain respect and even veneration of age, and frequently strikingly different attitudes about the aging process and the role and place of older persons within the culture. He also states this historical perspective will hopefully provide a different understanding, appreciation, and recognition of the essentially humanitarian view that Black Americans take of their older folk.

2.

MAJOR BOOKS AND PAMPHLETS

124. American Association of Retired Persons. A Portrait of Older Minorities. Washington, DC: American Association of Retired Persons, 1986. 16 pp.

There is one section on the "Black Elderly" in this short pamphlet. Black aged are discussed as they relate to: "Living Arrangements," "Education," "Employment," "Income," "Poverty Status," and "Health." According to this report about 2.1 million (8%) of the Black population in the United States are are 65 or over. Of that group, about 155,000 (7.5%) are age 85 or over. Nearly 60% of the Black aged are concentrated in the Southeastern states. The Black elderly are also compared to other minority elderly groups: Hispanic, Asian/Pacific Islander, and Native American.

125. Bell, Bill D., Editor. Contemporary Social Gerontology. Springfield, IL: Charles C. Thomas, 1976, pp. 321-362.

Section VIII of this book is devoted to "The Minority Elderly." The essays include: "Situational Factors Affecting Minority Aging," by Joan W. Moore; "Aged Negroes: Their Cultural Departures from Statistical Stereotypes and Rural-Urban Differences," by Jacquelyne J. Jackson; Ben M. Crouch wrote "Age and Institutional Support: Perceptions of Older Mexican-Americans;" "Patterns of Aging Among the Elderly Poor of the Inner City" was contributed by Margaret Clark; the final essay, "Widows and Minority Group," was penned by Helena Z. Lopara. References followed each essay.

126. Bell, Duran, et al. Delivering Services to Elderly Members of Minority Groups: A Critical Review of the Literature. Santa Monica, CA: The Rand Corp., April 1976, 103 pp.

One of the authors' avowed objectives was "to improve future research in such a way that it will be more useful to public policy."

Bell, Duran, et al. (Continued)

The authors in their review of the literature conclude that race
may be important in the design and implementation of a service
delivery system for elderly and nonelderly Blacks; the relevance
of race arises however not from the higher incidence of Blacks
among lower socioeconomic categories, but because of the cultural,
historical and educational factors that affect the extent to
which race neutral programs can be effective in actually providing
services to similarly situated persons from different racial
groups. The authors criticize Black researchers when they argue:
"The promotion of research on problems of the Black elderly has
tended to rest on the claim that Black elderly have qualitatively
different problems than other groups. The contention is that
Black elderly have unique problems and needs that should be
studied separately perhaps in the context of special institutes
or training programs. But if it turns out that apparent race
differences are simply a function of the differences in the distribution of racial groups across SES categories, the special
significance of research on Black elderly would be less compel-
ling." The authors went on to state that the literature fails to
define any problems that would indicate a need for methods of
service delivery unique to Blacks and that although it may be useful to know that the average Black is poorer than the average non-
Black, such information has little or no bearing on a service delivery process except to imply that Blacks need more of such
services, conclude the authors.

127. Birdsall, Stephen, Shannon P. Hallman and Richard J. Kopec.
      North Carolina Atlas of the Elderly. Chapel Hill: University of
      North Carolina, Department of Geography, 1979, pp. 3-68.

      Various references are made to the Black elderly throughout this
      book: number of the elderly, residential location, race and sex
      balance, growth and change, migration, marital status and isola-
      tion, work and the aged, income and poverty, mortality and health.

128. Browne, William P. and Laura Katz Olson, Editors. Aging and
      Public Policy: The Politics of Growing Old in America. West-
      port, CT: Greenwood Press, 1983, pp. 67-102.

      There is a thirty-five page essay in this collection by Jacque-
      lyne Johnson Jackson entitled, "The Politicization of Aged Blacks,"
      which explores the three major issues of the political implica-
      tions of racial differences between aged Blacks and whites, the
      adequacy of the Older Americans Act Amendments (OAA) of 1981 and
      the Summary Reports of the Committee Chairmen, the 1981 White
      House Conference on Aging (WHCOA) in recognizing aged Blacks as a
      distinct group, and the diversity of political "pushes and pulls"
      to which aged Blacks are being increasingly subjected, states the
      author. The major conclusions reached were that demographic dif-
      ferences between aged Blacks and whites are politically important,
      that OAA and WHCOA did not recognize aged Blacks as a distinct
      group, and that the political attitudes and behaviors of aged

Browne, William P. and Laura Katz Olson (Continued)

Blacks are not homogeneous. However, it is probable that aged
Blacks are more concerned about racism than about ageism, argues
Dr. Jackson.

129. Butler, Frieda R. A Resource Guide on Black Aging. Washington,
      DC: Howard University, Institute for Urban Affairs and Research,
      1981. 167 pp.

      This Resource Guide is a compilation and codification of sources
      of existing publications concerning the Black elderly. In addi-
      tion to literary references, the Guide provides a listing of (1)
      major organizations serving the elderly, (2) the major journals
      and periodicals on aging, and (3) selected statistical tables.
      As a guide to reference sources, the book provides a comprehensive
      coverage of materials available, but cannot be considered complete
      and exhaustive. Although a thorough search of the literature was
      conducted, and numerous contacts with agencies and individuals
      were made, it is quite possible that there are some gaps and
      omissions, states the writer. This source was compiled from
      primary and secondary sources . . . .

130. Chan, Peter, Editor. Reading in Black Aged. New York: MSS
      Information Corp., 1977. 212 pp.

      This is a collection of twenty-two previously published articles.
      Of this number, seven are by Jacquelyne Johnson Jackson, the lead-
      ing authority on the Black Aged. These essays deal with four
      areas: overview, research, services and social policy. Most of
      the articles have appeared in Aging and Human Development, Pro-
      ceedings of Research Conference on Minority Groups Aged in the
      South, Gerontologist, Phylon, and Family Coordinator.

131. Dancy, Joseph, Jr. The Black Elderly: A Guide for Practitioners.
      Ann Arbor, MI: The Institute of Gerontology, University of
      Michigan-Wayne State University, 1977. 56 pp.

      This book discusses the following major points: (1) raise the
      consciousness of practitioners and their employing institutions
      and agencies in regard to the particular needs, problems, and
      strengths of the Black elderly; (2) suggest how the Black elderly
      can be served more appropriately and supportively; (3) provide the
      practitioner with a better understanding of the cultural heritage
      and traditions of the Black elderly; and (4) encourage the practi-
      tioner to reexamine his or her own attitudes about aging and min-
      orities. The author also gives some of the strengths of the Black
      elderly: (1) an accumulation of wisdom, knowledge, and common sense
      about life that comes not only from age, but from their particular
      experience of hardship and suffering; (2) they have a creative
      genius in doing much with little; (3) their ability to accept
      their own aging and regarding old age as a reward in itself; (4)
      they hold a sense of hope and optimism for a better day, in spite

Dancy, Joseph, Jr. (Continued)

of a past full of hardships. Dancy concludes that in these
strengths of good sense and resourcefulness, acceptance and hope,
elderly Blacks offer an inspiration for us all. This work has a
comprehensive bibliography and appendices that include some institutions with special concerns for the Black elderly and selected films and videotapes. The author included a 14-page bibliography at the end of this work.

132.   Davis, Frank G. The Black Community's Social Security.
        Washington, DC: University Press of America, 1978. 189 pp.

        This book is designed to test and evaluate the validity and the
        social security implications of the author's basic hypothesis of
        declining personal income of the lower income masses of the Black
        community relative to the income of the White community, and to
        demonstrate the resultant permanent high incidence of poverty and
        personal income security in the Black community, notwithstanding
        the insurance provisions of the present Social Security Act. The
        author concludes: (1) Old-age insurance tax costs in the Black
        community substantially exceed old-age insurance benefits; (2)
        Old-age insurance benefits payable to the Black community are far
        below the poverty level when at the same time, almost two-fifths
        of Blacks age 65 and over are below the poverty level as compared
        to only 14 percent of Whites; (3) Over-all rises in Social Secu-
        rity benefits, accruing to the Black community are more than
        washed out by ultimate rises in Social Security taxes.

133.   Davis, Richard H., Editor. Community Services and the Black
        Elderly. Los Angeles: The Ethel Percy Andrus Gerontology Center,
        University of Southern California, 1972. 46 pp.

        This work is a collection of papers presented at a training pro-
        gram for persons providing services to the Black elderly. The
        contents include: "Introduction," by Victor E. Coppin; Barbara
        Solomon penned "Social and Protective Services;" Differential Use
        of Time" was written by Marion Marshall and Azelia Upshaw; Bernice
        Harper essayed "Physical and Mental Health Services;" Hobart C. Jack-
        son essayed "Social Policy Which Facilitates These Services." An
        Appendix and Bibliography on the Black Aged rounded out this work.

134.   Faulkner, Audrey Olsen, et al, Editors. When I Was Comin' Up:
        An Oral History of Aged Blacks. New York: Archon Books, 1982.
        223 pp.

        The aged Blacks in this study lived in the Central Ward, the Black
        heartland of Newark, New Jersey. Most of the aged Blacks were
        women and were born between 1880 and 1910; and had migrated to the
        North from the South. These biographies do much to demolish the
        negative images of old Southern Blacks that are current in our
        society. Political apathy, the absence of anger, docility, lack
        of initiative, family disorganization--these and many more

Faulkner, Audrey Olsen (Continued)

stereotypes are refuted in histories that have been recorded by
real people from the Central Ward of Newark, not cardboard cari-
catures of bygone times, state the editors. Their biographies
form the first, and major, portion of this book, followed by a
brief chapter examining some historical data relevant to the
personal histories.

135.   Gelfand, Donald E. and Alfred J. Kutzik, Editors. Ethnicity and
Aging: Theory, Research, and Policy. New York: Springer Publishing Co., 1979, pp. 11, 15-23, 38-44, 51-61, 141-158, 161-166, 168-
173, 277-307.

There are two essays in this collection that deal specifically
with the Black elderly: John Lewis McAdoo, "Well-Being and Fear
of Crime Among the Black Elderly," and Donald C. Snyder, "Future
Pension Status of the Black Elderly." There are several references to the Black elderly throughout the book: church activity,
health, income, life satisfaction, mutual age societies, parent-
child patterns of assistance, pension coverage of males, pension
income, pension status, perception of aging, poverty, social
interaction, Social Security system, social support systems, and
spouses.

136.   Jackson, Jacquelyne Johnson, Editor. Proceedings of The Research
Conference on Minority Group Aged in the South. Durham, NC:
Center for the Study of Aging and Human Development, Duke Univer-
sity Medical Center, 1972. 233 pp.

Twenty-two papers are discussed in this collection. There are
also four major Appendices: (1) Selected Statistical Data on Aging and Aged Blacks; (2) Profile of Aged Blacks in Nonmetropolitan
Areas: Statistical Tabulations; (3) Aged Blacks: A Selected Bibliography; (4) Selected Bibliography on the Aged in Ethnic Minorities. This conference focused upon completed, on-going, and
needed research on Black aged. Its major purposes--examining the
current status of research on Black aged, with special emphasis
upon identifying critical research gaps, and encouraging more re-
search--to investigate carefully Black aged--can best be realized
through significant increases in such researches and researchers
as direct or indirect outgrowths of this Conference, concludes
the editor of these papers. There is a bibliography for each
section.

137.   _____, Editor. Proceedings of Conference on Black Aged in
the Future. Durham, NC: Center for the Study of Aging and Human
Development, Duke University, 1973. 140 pp.

The title tells what this book is about. The topics include:
"Black Aged in the Future in a Predominantly Black Southern Town,"
by Johnny Ford; "Death and Dying: A Cross-Cultural View," by
Richard A. Kalish; "Housing and Geriatric Centers for Aging and

Jackson, Jacquelyne Johnson (Continued)

Aged Blacks," by Hobart C. Jackson; "Housing for the Aged Blacks,"
by Abraham Isserman; "Medical Aspects of the Aged American Black,"
by Nathaniel O. Calloway; "Dental Health of Aged Blacks," by
Reginald Hawkins; "Nursing Care of the Aged," by Jeanne J.
Penn; "The Future of the Black Aged in America," by Charles H.
Palm; "A Psychiatric Strategy for Aged Blacks in the Future," by
James H. Carter; "Curriculum Development on Aged Blacks in Predominantly White Environments," by Walter Beattie and Harry Morgan;
and "Social Stratification of Aged Blacks and Implications for
Training Professionals," by Jacquelyne J. Jackson, the editor of
these proceedings.

138.   _____, Editor. Action for Aged Blacks: When? Washington, DC:
National Caucus on the Black Aged, Inc., 1975. 87 pp.

This book is a collection of the proceedings of a Conference of
the National Caucus on the Black Aged, Inc., held May 16-17,
1973 in Washington, DC. More than twenty people participated in
this conference. One of the main purposes of this gathering was
to call attention to and give as much visibility to the plight of
the Black elderly as possible in every area of their concern such
as Income, Health, Housing Programs, Services and Facilities, Research and Training, etc. This conference also declared that it
would take whatever action seems indicated within the resources of
the Caucus to change this situation for the better and to improve
the quality of life for older Black Americans--including in this
process urging others at national, state, and local levels to join
with them . . . .

139.   _____. Minorities and Aging. Belmont, CA: Wadsworth Co.,
1980. 256 pp.

This is one of the latest and most complete works on minorities
and aging by the leading authority on Black Aging. Much of this
book deals with the Black aged. The basic theme of Black aged is
that they have special and unique needs that must be met by aggressive programs by the federal, state and local governments.
Some attention is also devoted to the role of the National Center
On The Black Aged. The writer includes an extensive bibliography.

140.   Jackson, Maurice and James L. Wood. Aging in America: Implications for the Black Aged. Washington, DC: National Council on
the Aging, 1976. 42 pp.

This monograph was based on the study The Myth and Reality of
Aging in America conducted by Louis Harris and Associates, Inc.,
that was commissioned by the National Council on the Aging. The
writers argue that in American society there are few real advantages in being old and compared to other groups such as younger
whites, older whites and younger Blacks, the Black aged rarely
emerge superior in terms of their income, occupation, housing or

Jackson, Maurice and James L. Wood (Continued)

family relations, which would be predicted by the double jeopardy hypothesis. What the double jeopardy hypothesis fails to comprehend is that the Black aged are not always disadvantaged relative to these other comparison groups, and at times they are better off than at least some of the other groups. In terms of their self-image and patterns of helping relationships, for example, the Black aged have shown surprising strength. The double jeopardy hypothesis would not predict that, according to the authors. The researchers conclude: ". . . we must revise our understanding of the Black aged; double jeopardy is not uniform in all major areas of their lives. The Black aged have problems--moreso than many other groups in American society. Yet it is also a group that exhibits a variety of strengths, strengths surely needed as its members continue to face barriers of race and age.

141. Kraft, John and Carter C. Osterbind, Editors. Older People in
      Florida: 1980-1981, A Statistical Abstract. Gainesville, FL:
      University Press of Florida, 1981, pp. 17, 19, 21-22, 66, 68-69,
      79, 84, 90, 95, 99, 113, 116, 119-124, 131-134, 163, 195.

The Black elderly are discussed in this work as it relates to their deaths, diseases, employment status, energy expenditure, family income, heads of households, housing unit, HUD programs, money income, population, poverty levels, rent paid, Social Security beneficiaries, supplemental security income, unemployment and value of housing.

142. Manuel, Ron , Editor. "Minority Aging: Sociological and Social
      Psychological Issues. Westport, CT: Greenwood Press, 1982, pp.
      36-39, 41-51, 77-82, 95-114, 171-178, 231-247.

A number of essays in this collection deal specifically with the Black aged: "To Be Old and Black: The Case for Double Jeopardy on Income and Health," by Maurice Jackson, Bohdan Kolody, and James L. Wood; "Mental Health and Successful Coping Among Aged Black Women," by Sue Perkin Taylor; "Religion and the Black Elderly: The Historical Basis of Social and Psychological Concerns," by Allen C. Carter; "The Black 'Granny' and the Soviet 'Babushka': Commonalities and Contrasts," by Gari Lesnoff-Caravaglia; "Service Delivery and the Black Aged: Identifying Barriers to Utilization of Mental Health Services," by Oliver W. Slaughter and Mignon O. Batey; "The Dimensions of Ethnic Minority Identification: An Exploratory Analysis Among Elderly Black Americans," by Ron C. Manuel. This book also includes a 23-page bibliography.

143. McNeely, R.L. and John L. Colen, Editors. Aging in Minority
      Groups. Beverly Hills, CA: Sage Publications, 1983, pp. 15-27,
      42-49, 123-136, 153-160, 185-193, 195-225.

The central premise of this book is that minority aging warrants particular attention. This work discusses four topics: "The

McNeely, R.L. and John L. Colen (Continued)

Demography of Minority Aging"; "Exemplars of Aging in a Cultural
Context: Three Minority Groups"; "Selected Social Problems and
the Minority Aged"; and "Guidelines for Service Delivery." The
following articles deal with the Black elderly: Wilbur H. Watson,
"Selected Demographic and Social Aspects of Older Blacks: An
Analysis with Policy Implications"; Nellie Tate, "The Aged Experience"; Adam W. Herbert, "Enhancing Housing Opportunities for the
Black Elderly"; John Lewis McAdoo, "Fear of Crime and Victimization: Black Residents in a High-Risk Urban Environment"; Gaylene
Perrault and Gilbert L. Raiford, "Employment Problems and Prospects of Older Blacks and Puerto Ricans". A number of the other
essays discuss the Black elderly in conjunction with other ethnic
groups. There are references at the end of each essay.

144. Minority Aged in America. Detroit, MI: The Institute of Geron-
      tology, University of Michigan-Wayne State University, 1971.
      63 pp.

      This book is a collection of papers from a symposium entitled
      "Triple Jeopardy: The Plight of Aged Minorities." It was held
      April 17, 1971 in Detroit, Michigan. The essays included are:
      "Welfare Policies for the Aged Poor: A Contradiction," by Elias S.
      Cohen; Jacquelyne J. Jackson contributed "Compensatory Care for
      the Black Aged"; "Changing Welfare to Serve Minority Aged" was
      written by Donald P. Kent; Robert B. Hill essayed "A Profile of
      Black Aged"; "A Profile of Indian Aged" was penned by Robert
      Benedict; Joyce Stephens wrote the final article, called "The
      Aged Minority." There are brief references at the end of most
      of the essays.

145. National Council on the Aging. Triple Jeopardy--Myth or Reality?
      Washington, DC: National Council on the Aging, April, 1972.
      40 pp.

      This work is a collection of four papers that deal with the theme,
      Triple Jeopardy, being old, and poor, and a member of a minority
      group. Daniel Saenz discusses "Triple Jeopardy--Myth or Reality?"
      Dr. Saenz presents his views of how aging and poverty affect this
      minority group. Willie R. Jeffries wrote on "Our Aged Indians".
      The author lets us know the aged Indian is an individual with
      feelings and pride, who often will not accept our help. E. Grant
      Youmans contributed "Age Group, Values, and the Future". Dr.
      Youmans reports on a study comparing age group differences between
      people 20 to 29 years and those over 60 years living in two geo-
      graphical areas--one a rural county in the Southern Appalachian
      region and the other a metropolitan center adjacent to that region.
      Dr. Jacquelyne Johnson Jackson penned the fourth essay entitled
      "Black Aged: In Quest of the Phoenix". Dr. Jackson focuses on the
      Black aged in "quadruple jeopardy," i.e., those who are Black, old,
      poor--and female. She also gives the reader many needed facts,
      judgments and suggestions for dealing with the aged Black popula-
      tion.

146. National Urban League. Double Jeopardy: The Older Negro in
      America Today. New York: National Urban League, 1964. 28 pp.

      The League states that aged Blacks are in "double jeopardy" be-
      cause they are (in 1964) the most desperate of any American group.
      Moreover, it argues that "Today's (1964) aged Negro is different
      from today's White because he is a Negro." This organization went
      on to point out that since 10.5% of White old-age-assistance reci-
      pients in a national study were found to be institutionalized,
      then 10.5% of the Negro recipients, rather than 2.4% as was the
      case, should also have been institutionalized. Some writers dis-
      agree with this theory.

147. Newsome, Barbara L. Insights on the Minority Elderly. Washington,
      DC: National Center on Black Aged, 1977. 35 pp.

      Part One of this short work was called "A Conversation Among
      Noted Black Gerontologists." The participants included: Nathaniel
      O. Calloway, Dolores A. Davis, Calvin Fields, Robert B. Hill,
      Hobart C. Jackson, Inable Lindsay, Barbara L. Newsome and E.
      Percil Stanford. Part Two of this work was entitled "Issues
      Related to Working with the Minority Elderly." One essay dealing
      specifically with Blacks was penned by Calvin Fields and was en-
      titled, "The Black Elderly: A Collection of Concepts and Ideas."

148. Palmore, Erdman B., Editor. Handbook on the Aged in the United
      States, Westport, CT: Greenwood Press, 1984, pp. 7-8, 54, 65, 68,
      83, 115, 128-129, 188-191, 204, 219-233, 344-345, 403.

      There is one essay in this work on the Black aged by Ruth L.
      Greene and Ilene C. Sogler. The essayists suggest that as
      socioeconomic trends and race relations change in America, they
      will have a great impact upon the social, economic, and psycho-
      logical characteristics of the future Black elderly . . . . They
      conclude: "Our own work in coping and adaptation shows that the
      differences that the Black elderly display may be differences in
      style and expression - more a reflection of the process of adapta-
      tion than differences in outcome measures." There are also other
      references made to aged Blacks: avoidance of doctors, centenarians,
      church attendance, deficient housing, disabled, fear of crime,
      institutionalized, religion of, retirement, social contact, sui-
      cide rates, widows, and women.

149. _____. Minority Aging and the Legislative Process. San
      Diego, CA: Center on Aging, San Diego State University, 1977.
      96 pp.

      More than seventeen people participated in this third institute
      on minority aging that is presented in this book. The essays and
      comments in this monograph represent a look at some of the many
      directions in which legislators, policy makers, and administrators
      have gone in developing programs and policy that may have an im-
      pact on the minority older person. The materials included in this

Palmore, Erdman B., Editor (Continued)

work provide insights into the considerations and actions of
some planners and legislators. Attention is also given to determining strategies for the future. The editor concludes that the
body of available knowledge suggests that significant changes can
be made without causing major negative reactions. A 26-page
bibliography is also included.

150.   . Institute Proceedings on Minority Aging and the
Legislative Process. San Diego, CA: Center on Aging, San Diego
State University, 1977. 180 pp.

The title tells what this book is about. The following topics are
discussed: "Strategies for Effective Input By The Elderly,"
"Historical and Current Perspectives on Legislation," "Role of the
Regional Office," "Policy Issues and Their Impact on the Ethnic
Elderly," "Policy and the Minority Aged," "Policy and the Minority
Aged at the State Level," "The Minority Aging--An Action," "Re-
tirement Legislation and The Minority Aged," "Strategies for Af-
fecting Legislative Priorities," "Social Security and Supplemental
Income," "The State Office on Aging and Legislative Implications,"
and "Political Consideration For Change." There is also a good
Bibliography and Appendices.

151.   . The Elder Black: A Cross-Cultural Study of Minority
Elders in San Diego. San Diego, CA: Center on Aging. San Diego
State University, 1978. 63 pp.

This work deals with three specific objectives. First, it analy-
zes characteristic lifestyles and customs, as well as primary
interactional networks of ethnic minority groups and in this case,
especially those of Black elders. Second, it explores and deline-
ates the perceptions and viewpoints of the Black elders toward
formal programmatic assistance and human services networks with
the overall intent of tracing, where possible, the interactions
between the formal programs and the primary networks. Third, it
tested out a methodology appropriate to obtaining information
about ethnic minority populations and specifically the elders of
these populations. The writer concludes that generally, the findings in this study indicate that the services available and the
services actually used by the elderly Blacks in the sample are two
divergent issues. Services are often available and may even be
accessible. The reality is that too many of the elderly in the
sample were not aware of the specifics of the services and had
they been aware, many would have, in fact, used some of the services. This work has an annotated bibliography on Black Aging and
also other works on Black Aging.

152.   , Editor. Minority Aging: Policy Issues for the '80s.
San Diego, CA: University Center on Aging, San Diego State
University, 1981, pp. 3-8, 25-28, 125-144, 210-212.

Palmore, Erdman B., Editor (Continued)

This work lists the Proceedings of the Seventh National Institute on Minority Aging held at San Diego State University, February 6-8, 1980. The following essays deal specifically with the Black elderly: Malvin Goode, "A Case for the So-Called 'Aged'"; "Retirement Income for the Black Elderly" was penned by Edward C. Wallace; Esther Jones Langston contributed "Kith and Kin: Natural Support Systems: Their Implications for Policies and Programs for the Black Aged." There is also an Appendix that gives Recommendations for Black Caucus.

153. Pollard, Lu Lu. Retirement--Black and White. New York: Exposition Press, Inc., 1973. 75 pp.

The author discusses the retirement of the Black aged with the White aged. She compares certain facets of retirement such as "Fears of Retirement," "Retirement Income," "Retirement Housing," "The Counselor's Role," and "The Role of the Community." The concluding chapter is entitled "White vs. Black Retirement." The writer asserts that too frequently the Black retiree must seek aid from welfare, not because he does not want to work, but because for so many years he was denied an opportunity to earn a decent livelihood, which would be reflected in his retirement pension. She concludes that the Black worker has been denied knowledge that could help him in retirement because no one in management thought it important to prepare him for retirement in the same way the White worker was prepared.

154. Sherman, George A., Editor. Curriculum Guidelines in Minority Aging. Washington, DC: National Center on Black Aged, 1980, pp. 1-49.

Ron Manuel contributed "An Expanded Outline and Resourse for Teaching A Course in the Sociology of the Black Aged." Parts of the outline deal with the following topics: "Demography and the Elderly Black," "Research Methodology and the Study of the Black Aged," "Theoretical Orientations and the Study of the Black Aged," "Social Intervention Among the Black Aged," "The Socio-Living Circumstances Surrounding the Black Aged." There are selected readings at the end of each section. There is also A Selected List of Films on Black Aging. The films are "A Man Named Charlie Smith," "Old, Black and Alive," and "The Invisible Minority."

155. Stanford, E. Percil, Editor. Comprehensive Service Delivery Systems for Minority Aged. San Diego, CA: Center on Aging, San Diego State University, 1977. 180 pp.

The 24 papers in this collection are the proceedings of the Fourth National Institute on Minority Aging, held April 28-30, 1977. The institute dealt with four major topics: "Research and Service Perspectives," "Health," "Federal Council on the Aging," and "Innovative Community Programs and Resources for the Ethnic Minority Elderly."

156. _____. Editor. <u>Aging Black Women: Selected Reading for the</u>
<u>Caucus on the Black Aged (NCBA)</u>. Washington, DC: The National
Caucus on the Black Aged, 1975. 449 pp.

Many of the following essays in this collection are reprinted
from previous journals. They include: Robert W. Genther and
Stuart P. Taylor, "Physical Aggression as a Function of Racial
Prejudice and the Race of the Target"; J. Richard Udry, Karl E.
Bauman and Charles Chase, "Skin Color, Status, and Mate Selec-
tion"; Warren D. TenHouten, "The Black Family: Myth and Reality";
Jessie Bernard, "Marital Stability and Patterns of Status Varia-
bles"; Andrew E. Slaky and Joan R. Sealy, "Black Liberation,
Women's Liberation"; Jacquelyne J. Jackson, "But Where Are the
Men?"; Benjamin Quarles, "Frederick Douglass and the Woman's
Rights Movement"; Alex Gitterman and Alice Schaeffer, "The White
Professional and the Black Client"; Wayne A. Burroughs and Cabot
L. Jaffee, "Attitudinal Reaction of White Females Toward Two Black
Female Collaborators"; Thomas J. Pugh and Emily H. Mudd, "Atti-
tudes of Black Women and Men Toward Using Community Services";
H. B. Kaplan, "Self-Derogation and Social Position: Interaction
Effects of Sex, Race"; Patricia Gurin, "Social Class Constraints
on the Occupational Aspirations of Students Attending Predomi-
nantly Negro Colleges"; Warren S. Blumenfeld, "College Preferences
of Able Negro Students: A Comparison of Those Naming Predominantly
White Institutions"; Fred H. Borgen, "Differential Expectations?
Predicting Grades for Black Students in Five Types of Colleges";
Bernice J. Miller, "Inner City Women in White Schools"; Kent G.
Mommsen, "Differentials in Fertility Among Black Doctorates";
Toni Cade Bambara, "How Black Women Educate Each Other"; Sonia
Pressman, "Job Discrimination and the Black Woman"; E. Wilbur
Bock, "Farmer's Daughter Effect: The Case of the Negro Female
Professionals"; Peter J. Weston and Martha T. Mednick, "Race,
Social Class and the Motive to Avoid Success in Women"; Alan L.
Sorkin, "Occupational Status and Unemployment of Nonwhite Women";
James Ledvinka, "Race of Employment Interviewer and Reasons Given
By Black Job Seekers for Leaving Their Jobs"; Gerald E. Hills,
Donald H. Granbois and James M. Patterson, "Black Consumer Per-
ceptions of Food Store Attributes"; Gordon F. Sutton, "Assessing
Mortality and Morbidity Disadvantages of the Black Population";
Clayton T. Shaw, "A Detailed Examination of Treatment Procedures
of Whites and Blacks in Hospitals"; Joel Fisher, "Negroes and
Whites and Rates of Mental Illness: Reconsideration of a Myth";
Earl L. Biassey, "Paranoia and Racism in The United States";
John J. Schwab, Nancy H. McGinnis and George J. Warheit, "Social
Psychiatric Impairment: Racial Comparisons"; George J. Warheit,
Charles E. Holzer, III, and John J. Schwab, "An Analysis of Social
Class and Racial Differences in Depressive Symptomology: A Commu-
nity Study"; Andreas M. Pederson, George A. Awad and Alan R.
Kindler, "Epidemiological Differences Between White and Non-White
Students at a Predominantly White University"; Ed B. Chung, Jack
E. White, and LaSalle D. Leffall, "Neoplastic Lesions of the Colon
and Ano-Rectum in Blacks"; J. Kovi and M. Y. Heshmat, "Incidence
of Cancer in Negroes in Washington, DC and Selected African
Cities"; Jacquelyne J. Jackson, "Aged Negroes and Their Cultural
Departure from Stereotype and Rural-Urban Differences"; Jacque-
lyne J. Jackson, "Aged Blacks: A Potpourri in the Direction of

Stanford, E. Percil, Editor (Continued)

the Reduction of Inequities"; Jacquelyne J. Jackson, "Comparative Life Styles and Family and Friend Relationships Among Older Black Women"; Jacquelyne J. Jackson, "Sex and Social Class Variations in Black Aged Parent-Adult Child Relationships"; Rose M. Somerville, "The Future of Family Relationships in the Middle and Older Years: Clues in Fiction"; Jacquelyne J. Jackson, "Marital Life Among Aging Blacks"; Helena Zaniecki Lopata, "Social Relations of Black and White Widowed Women in a Northern Metropolis"; H. L. Hearn, "Career and Leisure Patterns of Middle-Aged Urban Blacks"; Mary L. Lambing, "Social Class Living Patterns of Middle-Aged Urban Blacks"; Jacquelyne J. Jackson, "Social Impacts of Housing Relocation Upon Urban, Low-Income Black Aged." Most of these articles are discussed throughout this bibliography.

157.   Sterne, Richard S., et al. The Urban Elderly Poor: Racial and Bureaucratic. Lexington, MA: Lexington Books, 1974. 145 pp.

This book deals with the elderly in Rochester, New York. Blacks in (1974) made up more than 18 percent of the population in that city. Much of this book is about the poor, mostly Black elderly, in the inner city of Rochester. According to the writers, elderly Blacks transmit a different message. In general, they admire white people, are genuinely enthusiastic about joining with whites in common programs, but express a greater measure of material want. They argue that it is now clear that a large portion of the elderly population are poor because they lack money, not because they lack social services. The answer is to supply them with money, not with social services. This approach, cash supplements or a negative tax, constitutes an important alternative to the notion that coordination of and an increase in the supply of services are the answers to satisfying the needs of the elderly poor, conclude the authors. This book has four Appendices and a Bibliography as well as an Index.

158.   Watson, Wilbur, et al., Editors. Health and the Black Aged. Washington, DC: National Center on Black Aged, 1978. 151 pp.

The title tells what this work is about. The following topics were discussed: "The Study of Hypertension Compliance in a Group of Elderly Third World Patients," "Carcinoma of the Prostate Gland in California: A Candid Look at Survival Trends in Regards to Stage, Race, and Social Class," "Health Indicators and Life Expectancy of the Black Aged: Policy Implications," "Mobility Among the Physically Impaired Black Aged," "Doctor Can't Do Me No Good: Social Concomitants of Health Care Attitudes and Practices Among Elderly Blacks in Isolated Rural Populations," "Poverty, Folk Remedies and Drug Misuse Among the Black Elderly," "Perceived Health Status of the Black Elderly in an Urban Area: Findings of a Survey Research Project," "Ethnicity and Aging in Elderly Black Women: Some Mental Health Characteristics," "The Social Psychology of Black Aging: The Effects of Self-Esteem and Perceived Control on The Adjustment of Older Black Adults," "Health

Watson, Wilbur, et al., Editors (Continued)

Status of a Successful Black Aged Population Related to Life
Satisfaction and Self-Concept," "The Aged and Aging Black Prison
Inmate: An Inquiry into Some Mental Health Consequences of Im-
prisonment," "A Community-Based, Consumer Controlled, Comprehensive Approach to Health Care for the Black Elderly," and "Medical
Screening Project: One Answer to a City's Problem." There are
also Research Notes: "Planning Scientific Research." Dr. Robert
Butler wrote an "Afterword". Selected references followed each
of the essays.

159.   Watson, Wilbur H.   Stress and Old Age: A Case Study of Black
        Aging and Transplantation Shock.   New Brunswick, NJ: Transaction
        Books, 1980.   127 pp.

This is a study of the stressful effects of forced migration on
elderly Black people, and their coping behavior following relocation from a long-term care institution. The general setting was
the metropolitan area of a major city in the northeastern United
States. At the inception of the study, the ages of these elderly
Blacks ranged from fifty-eight to 102 years. All had lived from
three to fifteen years in the home that was called the Griot House
--a ninety-eight percent Black residential facility. Because
state officials had ruled that Griot House was in violation of
federal and state life safety codes, two buildings housing a total
of 126 people were closed in 1976 for renovation and/or demolition
and reconstruction, states Dr. Watson. About fifty percent of
these elderly persons were moved to predominantly white long-term
care facilities. Some were moved to other predominantly Black
settings, and approximately eight percent moved to private homes
with family members of friends. Whatever the place and nature of
their new homes, all experienced varying degrees of disturbance in
the ways of life that they had become accustomed to. There were
signs of distress associated with the changes in place of residence and the demands or requirements for personal adjustments to
their new sociocultural environments, states Prof. Watson. In
some instances, the requirements for adjustment to social change
were complicated by physical and mental impairments. In combination with social change, the infirmities of body and mind made the
process of residential relocation a harrowing experience for some
of these seniors. The dynamics and observable effects of their
experiences are the central objects of attention in this study,
concludes the researcher.

160.   Weeks, Herbert A. and Benjamin J. Darsky.   The Urban Aged: Race
        and Medical Care.   Ann Arbor, MI: University of Michigan, School
        of Public Health, 1968.   136 pp.

The writers point out that the urban Black aged receive less medical care than other ethnic groups. The medical facilities are not
always easily accessible to the Black elderly. Therefore, they
are at a great disadvantage when it comes to proper health care.

161. Wilson, Emily Herring, Narrator. Hope and Dignity: Older Black
     Women of the South. Philadelphia: Temple University Press, 1983.
     200 pp.

     The title of this book is misleading because all of the twenty-
     seven Black women interviewed in this book were from one state -
     North Carolina. The ages of these women range from 76 to 104
     years old. This book presented the Black women in a variety of
     roles - as mothers, and midwives, church workers, gospel singers,
     artists, editors, teachers, business leaders, and community
     activists. It was stated that these women provide witty, humorous,
     dramatic, and revealing testimonies of hope and dignity . . . .

3.

GENERAL WORKS

1. BLACK AGED AND CHILDREN

162. Harrison-Ross, Phyliss and Barbara Wyden. The Black Child: A Parent's Guide. New York: Berkley Medallion Book, 1973, pp. 223-225.

Chapter 33 is entitled "What Grandma Doesn't Know." The authors surmise that what the older generation of Blacks doesn't know about cuddling--If you don't respond to a young child's needs, he won't respond to you and others later. The authors state, "Don't expect the older generation to accept all new ideas." The writers argue that in many cases Black mothers depend on grandmothers to discipline and help raise their children.

163. Hill, Robert B. The Strengths of Black Families. New York: Emerson Hall Publisher, 1971, pp. 5-6, 42.

In Part 1 of this work there is one section entitled "Absorption of Individuals: Minors and the Elderly." The writer contends that the families headed by elderly Black women take in the highest proportion (48 percent) of children. He declares that about the same proportion of Black and White families have elderly persons living with them, except in families headed by a woman where a higher proportion of White (10 percent) than Black (4 percent) families had elderly members. These elderly persons play important roles in many of these families such as baby-sitting with grandchildren. These services often provide additional income to elderly persons. Dr. Hill concludes that elderly Black women are more likely to take children into their own households than be taken into the household of younger kin.

164. Lewis, Hylan. Blackways of Kent. Chapel Hill, NC: University of North Carolina Press, 1950, pp. 100-120, 239, 244-246.

Lewis, Hylan (Continued)

The writer argues that in general, the attitude of Black young
people toward the Black aged is one of respect and kindness;
there tends to be marked filial respect and obedience among all
groups. The author concludes that a significant amount of the
respect for the older persons is related to the following facts:
they control a significant part of the wealth or means of support
as propertied heads of families or widows, and; pension payments
give many a measure of support and release them from dependence
upon relatives and friends. The older Blacks play another important role in Kent society; they are not only significant links with
the ways of previous generations of Kent Blacks, but they are also
significant links with present and past generations of Kent Whites.

165. Martin, Elmer P. and Joanne Michell Martin. The Black Extended
Family. Chicago: University of Chicago Press, 1978, pp. 49-57,
112-114.

Chapter Five is entitled "Relations Between Old and Young Child
Rearing" and discusses the Black elderly. The authors point out
that the Black aged extended family member, believing that the
"old fashioned" ways of preparing young members for living in
America have made for the maintenance of the family and the welfare of its members, seek to impart those ways to the young. The
writers see the Black aged, though still among the most respected
individuals in the extended family, experiencing a sense of un-
easiness as, day after day, they see their roles as child raisers
diminish. The educators conclude that the Black aged are finding
it more difficult to have an impact on the lives of their extended
families as the mass media, peer-group influence, the educational
system, and a mechanistic conformity to fads and fashions push
their influence further into the background. To the Black aged,
those old-fashioned ways of reacting to oppression by patience,
by indirection, and by perseverance, are the cornerstone of Black
extended family stability. When members of their extended family reject the time-proven ways of confronting life, the aged re-
proach them for rejecting their truest heritage, conclude the
authors.

166. Powdermaker, Hortense. After Freedom: A Cultural Study in the
Deep South. New York: Atheneum, 1969, pp. 143-174.

The author points out that grandmothers are present in many households, and are likely to loom larger than mothers on the child's
horizon, even when the real mother retains the chief authority.
She also states that, frequently, they are at home when the mother
goes out to work, although, because of the early marriages, the
grandmother too is often young enough for strenuous labor. Where
an elderly woman is head of a household, including married daughters, she carries authority with the children, and even where her
position is less dominant, she is likely to take over a share of
responsibility for their welfare and behavior, concludes the
writer.

167. Stack, Carol B. All Our Kin: Strategies for Survival in a Black
      Community. New York: Harper and Row, Publishers, 1974, pp. 13-
      16, 63-65, 113-116.

      Various references are made to Black grandmothers and Black grand-
      fathers. It is pointed out that many Black children are raised by
      their grandmothers. Many of these grandparents live with their
      children and grandchildren.

168. Staples, Robert. Introduction to Black Sociology. New York:
      McGraw Hill Book Co., 1976, pp. 135-136.

      There is one section on "The Aged." The author states that in
      most cases, the grandmothers are more likely to take children
      into their own households than to be taken into the household of
      their kinfolk. Dr. Staples argues that about half (48 percent) of
      elderly Black women have other related children living with them--
      in contrast to only 10 percent of similar White families. He con-
      cludes that this is but one more indication of the strong cohesive-
      ness and prevalent concern for one another within Black families.
      Most aged Black parents desire to live independently of, but in
      close contact with, their children.

169. Wright, Richard. Black Boy: A Record of Childhood and Youth.
      New York: Harper & Brothers, 1945, pp. 24-25, 32, 43, 52, 73-78,
      84-90, 92-97, 102-110.

      The author discusses the many conflicts that he had with his
      grandmother during his childhood. She was a deeply religious
      woman and attempted to convert him to her faith. This he refused
      to do. Although he was raised partly by his grandmother, Wright
      had many disagreements with her. He did, however, love her very
      much. He did what was almost unheard of in the Black community
      and that was to speak up and disobey his grandmother's wishes.

                    2. BLACK AGED AND THE BLACK FAMILY

170. Bernard, Jessie. Marriage and Family Among Negroes. Englewood
      Cliffs, NJ: Prentice-Hall, Inc., 1966, pp. 92-96.

      The author asserts that the position of the oldest woman in a
      family was, traditionally, an extremely important one: it was
      she, not the male head of the family, who had the role of the
      matriarch. Dr. Bernard argues that the grandmother played an
      important part even during slavery, "highly esteemed by both the
      slaves and the masters." Often she was the confidential adviser
      of the older members of the slave household. Moreover, age added
      "dignity" to her position and "her regime." The writer concludes
      that these "grannies" were genuine matriarchs--powerful stabiliz-
      ing figures who performed a profoundly important service--but
      they have all but disappeared from the scene.

171. Kingsley, Andrew. <u>Black Families in White America</u>. Englewood
      Cliffs, NJ: Prentice-Hall, Inc., 1968, pp. 106-117.

      Various references are made throughout the book about the Black
      aged in Africa, during the slavery era, and in present day Ameri-
      can society. The author points out the influence that various
      Black aged middle class families had on the children and grandchildren.
      Some of the aged familied discussed include the Hildrus Poindexter
      family, the Langston Hughes family and the Martin Luther King, Sr.
      family.

172. Birmingham, Stephen. <u>Certain People: America's Black Elite</u>.
      Boston: Little, Brown, and Co., 1977, pp. 55-78.

      Part Three, "The Old Guard," is a discussion of aged Blacks. They
      prefer "Negro." Most of the aged Black elite are proud of their
      family backgrounds, according to the author.

173. Haley, Alex. <u>Roots: The Saga of An American Family</u>. New York:
      Doubleday & Co., 1974, pp. 24-137.

      Aged Blacks and the role they played in Africa, slave family and
      freed family are discussed throughout this classic. Some of the
      aged include Grandmother Yaisa, Juffure's Council of Elders, Omoro,
      Binta Nyo Boto, Old Fiddler, Kizzy, Will Palmer, etc. He discusses
      the influence that aged Blacks had on him and other Blacks through-
      out history.

174. Kennedy, Carroll E. <u>Human Development: The Adult Years and
      Aging</u>. New York: Macmillan Publishing Co., 1978, pp. 57-62.

      There is one section in this work that deals with the Black fami-
      lies. The author points out that the fact that there are few
      Blacks in nursing homes suggests something of the nature of the
      extended-family concept in the Black community. Moreover, many
      Black relatives, however, are more likely to be children than
      older relatives. Older women tend to take in children and
      younger persons rather than being taken in themselves.

175. Ladner, Joyce A. <u>Tomorrow's Tomorrow: The Black Woman</u>. Garden
      City, NY: Doubleday & Co., 1971, pp. 50, 60-66.

      The author discussed the extended family and the role of the
      grandparents in the family. It was stated that grandmothers
      often live in the homes of their children and grandchildren.
      Here they probably exercise more influence over the behavior of
      the child than do the parents because of the continuous involve-
      ment with them. Occasionally, the child becomes confused about
      whom he should relate to and be supervised by as the authority
      figure, concludes Dr. Ladner.

176. Lichtman, Allan J. and Joan R. Challinor, Editors. Kin and Communities: Families in America. Washington, DC: Smithsonian Institution, 1979, pp. 145-154.

There is a short article in this collection by Jacquelyne Johnson Jackson and Bertram Emmanuel Walls. They discuss "Aging Patterns in Black Families." In an effort to counteract the trend of spurious generalizations about aging patterns of the later years in Black kinship networks, as well as their inappropriate comparisons with white kinship networks, this paper provides an overview of available data about aged patterns in Black kinship networks in the South, and, to the extent possible, comparisons of those patterns with non-Southern Black kinship networks and with white kinship networks. Finally, the authors suggest several types of studies which may be crucial in furthering our sociological and anthropological knowledge and understanding of kinship patterns for aged Blacks, the results of which could be applied readily to continuing social programs for the aged involving, but not restricted to, Blacks, conclude the scholars.

177. Mindel, Charles H. and Robert W. Habenstein, Editors. Ethnic Families in America: Patterns and Variations. New York: Elsevier Scientific Publishing Co., Inc., 1976, pp. 221-247.

There is one article in this work on the Black family by Robert Staples. In this essay Dr. Staples points out that the Black aged is not as likely to live with one of his children as are the white aged. In most cases, the grandmothers are more likely to take children into their own households than to be taken into the household of their kinfolk. According to this sociologist, about half (48 percent) of elderly Black women have other related children living with them - in contrast to only 10 percent of similar white families. He concludes that the extended kin structure in the Black community manages to buttress the psychological isolation and poverty of the Black aged. Most aged Black parents desire to live independently of, but in close contact with, their children. Where their socioeconomic conditions permit, the adult children assist their elderly parents, according to Prof. Staples.

178. Obudho, Constance E., Editor. Black Marriage and Family Therapy. Westport, CT: Greenwood Press, 1983, pp. 191, 209-213.

Several references are made to the Black elderly throughout this work. It was mentioned that it is not uncommon for Black youngsters to assume the moral and ethical characteristics of their elders. The concept of child-rearing had its linkage on the African soil and was transcended and ingrained on the American soil. Therefore, the Black elderly have been traditionally an integral part of the total family structure, concludes Dr. Obudho.

179. Quinn, William H., and George A. Hughston, Editors. Independent
      Aging: Family and Social Systems Perspectives. Rockville, MD:
      Aspen Systems Corporation, 1984, pp. 164-181.

      Chapter 11 was written by E. Percil Stanford and Shirley A. Lock-
      ery and is called "Aging and Social Relations in the Black Commu-
      nity." The essayists argue that the interaction patterns of Black
      families in the community have been such that the older person has
      been supported, in most instances, through the volunteer efforts
      of immediate family members or of extended formal and informal
      kinships in the community. They declare: "The Black community
      has been, and continues to be, supported by Black families. This
      support often manifests itself in a variety of ways. One way is
      community interaction through voluntarism . . . ."

180. Sager, Clifford J., Thomas L Brayboy, and Barbara R. Waxenberg.
      Black Ghetto Family in Therapy: A Laboratory Experience. New York:
      Grove Press, 1970, pp. 45-46, 102-127, 204-207.

      One Black grandmother was discussed in this book. It was pointed
      out that the Black grandmother was not the domineering force in
      the Black family. The authors surmise that in many cases the
      Black grandmother does not want to dominate the family; she only
      wants to be included in it, to feel as though she's important. . . .

181. Staples, Robert. The Black Woman in America: Sex, Marriage, and
      the Family. Chicago: Nelson Hall publishers, 1978, pp. 153-154.

      The author states that the grandmother is frequently an important
      figure in the Black child's life, even in West Africa. In the
      United States, it was suggested that a Black child is much more
      likely to have a grandmother in the same household with her. In
      many cases the grandmother is more likely to take children into
      her own household than to be taken into the household of younger
      kinfolk, according to Prof. Staples.

3. BLACK AGED FEMALES

182. Carson, Josephine. Silent Voices: The Southern Negro Woman Today.
      New York: Dell Publishing Co., pp. 25, 27, 85, 96, 103, 123, 125,
      137, 161, 165, 178, 207, 231.

      This book, edited by a white woman, is based on interviews with
      several Black women throughout the South; some were Black aged.
      The women tell what they think and feel--about themselves, their
      futures, their religions, their friends, their employers, their
      leaders, about their politics or lack of them, about segregation
      and integration, about White people and White culture, about love
      and old age and death, above all, about human dignity. The author
      points out that in 1968 seventy-five percent of aged Black women
      lived alone. Ninety-six percent had less than $2,000 a year to
      live on. Sixty-eight percent had less than $1,000 a year. Sever-
      al aged Black women that Miss Carson interviewed fall into the
      above category.

183. DuBois, W. E. Burghardt. Dusk of Dawn: An Essay Toward An Auto-
      biography of Race Concept. New York: Harcourt, Brace & World,
      Inc., 1940, pp. 12, 114-117.

      The author discusses his grandmother and grandfather. He states
      they raised him and influenced him greatly. Dr. DuBois surmises
      that with Africa he had only one direct cultural connection and
      that was the African melody which his great-grandmother violently
      used to sing.

4. BLACK AGED POPULATION

184. Achenbaum, W. Andrew. Old Age in the New Land: The American Ex-
      perience Since 1790. Baltimore: Johns Hopkins University Press,
      1978, pp. 8, 29, 61-62, 92-96, 147, 150-151, 158-160, 190n. 32.

      Various topics discuss the Black aged: "Slavery and the Black
      Aged," "Black Aged Farmers," "Population Statistics of the Black
      Aged," "Current Situation of the Black aged," "Need for Further
      Study on the Black Aged," and "Differences Among Aged By Race."

185. Berghorn, Forrest J., et al., Editors. The Dynamics of Aging.
      Boulder, CL: Westview Press, 1981, pp. 155, 158-159, 182-183,
      203-210, 228, 234, 237.

      The Black aged are discussed in a variety of ways: "Black Aged
      and Double Jeopardy," "The Black Elderly," "Poor Black Aged,"
      "Black Aged and Social Security," "Widowed Aged Blacks," "Black
      Aged and Population," "Black Aged and the Black Church." It was
      stated that perhaps a lifetime of struggle has indeed enabled the
      Black person to meet old age with toughness and strength of
      character.

186. Binstock, Robert H. and Ethel Shanas, Editors. Handbook of Aging
      and The Social Sciences. New York: Van Nostrand Reinhold Co.,
      1985, pp. 264-303.

      Various references are made to the Black aged throughout this book.
      One Chapter, "Race, National Origin, Ethnicity and Aging," by
      Jacquelyne Johnson Jackson, deals mainly with the Black aged.

187. Breslau, Lawrence D. and Marie R. Haug, Editors. Depression and
      Aging: Causes, Care, and Consequences. New York: Springer
      Publishing Co., 1983, pp. 55-58, 195.

      Chapter 4 was written by John F. Santos, Richard W. Hubbard, and
      John L. McIntosh and was entitled "Mental Health and the Minority
      Elderly." One part of this essay discussed "The Black Elderly."
      It was pointed out that marital problems, deaths in the family,
      and other "exit events" occur more often and, therefore, may be
      expected to stimulate depression more frequently in Blacks than
      whites. It was suggested that aged Blacks have less suicides
      than aged whites. . . .

188. Brotman, Herman B. Facts and Figures on Older Americans. Wash-
      ington, DC: Administration on Aging, No. 2, 1971, p. 3.

      The writer points out that shorter life expectancy for Negroes
      produces a smaller proportion of older persons. The 22.7 million
      Negroes of all ages represent 11.2% of the total resident popula-
      tion. The older Negro population increased from 1.2 million in
      1960 to 1.6 million in 1970 and, since this was a higher rate of
      growth than that of the total Negro population, they made up 6.9%
      of all Negroes as compared with 6.2% in 1960. Like the White
      population, moreover, the older women outnumber the older men and
      the discrepancy is increasing. The ratio of women per 100 men
      among 65+ Negroes rose from 115.0 in 1960 to 131.0 in 1970. While
      this ratio is not quite as large as it is for the White population,
      the ratio for Negroes of all ages is over 110 as compared with
      only 105 for Whites, states Mr. Brotman.

188a. _____. Facts and Figures on Older Americans. Washington, DC:
      Administration on Aging, No. 5, 1972, p. 3.

      The writer surmises that the first counts from the 1970 census
      enumeration show a total of 22.7 million Blacks of all ages or
      11.27% of the total population, an increase of about 3.8 million
      since 1960 when the figure was 18.9 million or 10.5% of the total
      population. As a result of lower life expectancy than is true for
      Whites, however, the Black aged in 1970 came to 1.6 million or
      only 7.8% of all the aged. This was still an improvement over
      1960 when the 1.2 million Black aged represented only 7.1% of all
      of the older persons in the United States. Stated another way,
      only 6.9% of the total Black population is aged 65+ as compared
      with over 10% for the Whites, concludes the author.

189. _____. Facts and Figures on Older Americans: State Trends,
      1960-1970. Washington, DC: Administration on Aging, No. 6, 1974,
      pp. 4-5.

      The author states that between 1960 and 1970 the number of Negroes
      65 years of age and older grew faster than the total Negro popula-
      tion. This age group increased from 1.2 million in 1960 to 1.6
      million in 1970. Since that was a higher rate of growth than
      that of the total Negro population, the 65+ Negroes accounted for
      6.9% of the total Negro population as compared to 6.2% in 1960.
      Although 6.9% is the national average for the aged Negro popula-
      tion, the trend in numbers and in proportion of this population
      varied considerably among the States, states the writer. He also
      points out that in terms of rates of change between 1960 and 1970,
      six states had substantial growth of 100 percent (doubling) or
      over in their aged Negro population--North Dakota 175.0%, Alaska
      142.2%, Nevada 122.7%, Hawaii 108.8%, Maine 107.3%, and Wisconsin
      104.5%. These increases, however, were over very low numbers in
      1960, ranging from a low of 8 to a high of 2,051. In 1970, no
      state had exactly the same percentage of aged Negroes as the
      national average, 6.9%. There were 16 states with larger propor-
      tions than the national average. The author concludes that at

Brotman, Herman B. (Continued)

the lower end of the distribution, 35 states had a smaller percentage of aged Negroes than the national average. Eight of these
states were within one percentage point lower than the national
average (5.9-6.8). Thirteen states were within two percentage
points (4.9-5.8), and seven within three points (3.9-4.8). Seven
more states were between four and six percentage points below the
national average.

190. Brown, Mollie, Editor. Readings in Gerontology. St. Louis, MO:
C. V. Mosby Co., 1978, pp. 95-113.

Chapter 10 was called "Myths and Realities About Aged Blacks" and
was penned by Jacquelyne J. Jackson and Bertram E. Walls. This
study, which was primarily concerned with the resolution of prevalent myths about aged Blacks and Whites, was based on an analysis
of the 1974 Harris data about aging attitudes and behaviors in the
United States. The finding of a general absence of any significant
racial differences between paired groups of low- and high-income
aged and young Blacks and Whites in the Harris survey suggested
strongly the vast similarity of aging processes and patterns among
American Blacks and Whites, declare the authors. They suggest that
the most important implication of their study for aging programs
involving Blacks is the need to structure such programs on adequate
knowledge about the conditions under which race is and is not a
factor. Furthermore, advocates for racially separated programs
should avoid hiding behind aged Blacks when they are clearly more
concerned about building Black power bases for themselves. The
writers conclude: "Finally, aging training programs should place
greater emphasis on training individuals of various races to provide services to individuals of various races. They should also
aid their students in distinguishing clearly between significant
differences between populations, such as aged Blacks and Whites,
and significant differences between individuals who happen to be
aged Blacks or Whites."

191. Hall, Gertrude and Geneva Mathiasen, Editors. Guide to Development of Protective Services for Older People. Springfield, IL:
Charles C. Thomas Publishers, 1973, pp. 62-63.

The editors point out that in Houston and Philadelphia a higher
proportion of Negroes received protective services than their
ratio in the communities. In Houston, 25.6 percent of the protective service clients were Negroes as compared with 16 percent
Negro population in the community. In Philadelphia, the respective figures were 25 percent and 17 percent; in San Diego, 11
percent and 3 percent, argued the writers.

192. Harwood, Alan, Editor. Ethnicity and Medical Care. Cambridge,
      MA: Harvard University Press, 1981, pp. 37-129.

      Jacquelyne Johnson Jackson wrote "Urban Black Americans" for this
      work. Various references are made to aged Blacks throughout this
      essay as it related to their "Population," "Death," "Suicide,"
      and "Health." There is also a nine and one-half page bibliography
      at the end of this essay.

193. Hendricks, Jon, and C. Davis Hendricks. Aging in Mass Society:
      Myths and Realities. Cambridge, MA: Winthrop Publishers, Inc.,
      1977, pp. 349-382.

      Chapter 13 is called "Minority Groups in the Later Years" and
      deals mainly with aged Black Americans. The authors point out
      that "Triple Jeopardy" means old, poor, and a member of a racial
      or ethnic group. It was suggested that Blacks who reach the age
      of 70 years might prove to be in better health than similarly
      aged white elderly. The writers conclude that family ties are a
      particularly strong source of support for Blacks . . . and fami-
      lies may accord their older relatives more esteem than in the
      case of the general population.

194. _____, Editors. Dimensions of Aging: Readings. Cambridge,
      MA: Winthrop Publishers, Inc., 1979, pp. 115-119, 189, 248-263,
      278-285, 348-359.

      Various references are made to the Black aged throughout this
      book as they relate to: their attitudes toward death, their
      health, living in the inner city, nutrition, and their population.

195. Kerschner, Paul A., Editor. Advocacy and Age: Issues, Experiences
      and Strategies. Los Angeles: Ethel Percy Andrus Gerontology
      Center, University of Southern California, 1976, pp. 97-112.

      Hobart C. Jackson penned "Black Advocacy, Techniques and Trials"
      for this collection. The writer surmises that the Black elderly
      had few persons to represent them in their fight for higher social
      security benefits, better housing and overall protection.

196. Lesnoff-Caravaglia, Gari, Editor. Aging and the Human Condition.
      New York: Human Sciences Press, Inc., 1982, pp. 15-29.

      E. Percil Stanford and Clifford Alexander contributed "Elderly in
      Transition" for this collection. They argue that the Black elder-
      ly will continue to be in transition for several years. Continu-
      ous involvement in the mainstream and a sense of self-worth and
      pride will aid them in being more recognized as a meaningful force
      in the larger society. More are accepting the challenge willingly
      and with a fine sense of purpose. With some of the merging social
      policies and reinforcements, there is a much greater chance that
      the Black elderly will continue to emerge as a vital force in our

Lesnoff-Caravaglia, Gari, Editor (Continued)

society. The older Black person has been quietly serving as a pillar of strength in the American society through the years, and it appears that this will be true for years to come, conclude the authors.

197.   Levitan, Sar A., William B. Johnston and Robert Taggart. Still a Dream: The Changing Status of Blacks Since 1960. Cambridge, MA: Harvard University Press, 1975, pp. 134, 216-227.

The authors point out that overall, Blacks represented nearly one in ten Old Age Survivors and Disability Insurance (OASDI) recipients in 1971. Because Blacks have shorter life expectancy, they accounted for only 7.5 percent of all retired workers receiving benefits, which was nearly equivalent to their 7.9 percent share of the elderly population (age sixty-two and over). Under the survivors' segments, 7.7 percent of widows receiving benefits were Black. The writers state that Black life expectancies are considerably shorter than Whites, meaning that Blacks are paying into a system which is less likely to benefit them in later years. They concluded that one approach which would correct some of these problems would be to supplement payroll taxes which contributed from general revenue. Prof. Levitan also suggests that elderly Blacks are less likely to be in homes for the aged; but rather than better health in old age, this reflects higher incomes for whites (since most nursing homes are private and costly) and the extended family structures among Blacks, who are more likely to care for grandparents in the home, conclude the authors.

198.   McCann, Charles W. Long Beach Senior Citizens Survey. Long Beach, CA: Community Welfare Council, 1955, p. 18.

The author points out that in 1955 less than 1% of Blacks lived in Long Beach that were 65 years old or older. This was in contrast to the State of California as a whole where Blacks constituted 6% of the population. Since the beginning of World War II, Blacks have been coming to Long Beach in increasing numbers. Drawn by work opportunities, they represented a relatively younger age group. Sadly, only one-half page of fifty pages mentions the Black aged.

199.   Riessman, Frank, Editor. Older Persons: Unused Resources for Unmet Needs. Beverly Hills, CA: Sage Publications, 1977, pp. 62-67.

Herbert Golden penned "Black Ageism" for this work. According to Prof. Golden what is clear is that attempts to apply research findings based on undifferentiated comparisons between Black and white elderly toward the solution of problems faced by Black elderly are doomed to ineffectiveness. Social scientists by and large agree that race is an American social reality and, as such, must be regarded as an independent variable in any study attempting

Riessman, Frank, Editor (Continued)

to offer policy and/or planning objectives. "It is then only when Blacks are studied as a group without necessarily making compari- sons to the larger white elderly population that we will have a good base for attacking the unique problems that this minority group membership imposes on people's adaptation to aging," con- cludes the author.

200. Riley, Matilda White, Beth B. Hess and Kathleen Bond, Editors. Aging in Society: Selected Reviews of Recent Research. Hillsdale, NJ: Lawrence Erlbaum Associates, Publishers. 1983, pp. 115-137.

There is one essay on "Minority Aging," written by Kyriakos S. Markides. Much of the discussion is centered around the Black aged. Moreover, much of this article comes from previous essays listed throughout this bibliography. There is a five-page, 112 citation bibliography at the end of this essay.

201. Rowan, Carl T. Just Between Us Blacks. New York: Random House, 1974, pp. 131-134.

Section 65 discusses the Black Aged. The writer declares that about 1.6 million Black Americans are sixty-five years and over. More than half of them still live in the South, although the largest single concentration is in New York City. Rowan argues that we should find ways to give property-tax relief to the elder- ly. He concludes that another way to aid older men and women is to find some kind of work for them. This would provide extra in- come, and it would furnish a big psychological boost, letting them know they still belong and are useful.

202. Seltzer, Mildred M., et al. Editors. Social Problems of the Aging: Readings. Belmont, CA: Wadsworth Publishing Co., 1978, pp. 273-283.

The following articles were excerpted from the U. S. Senate Spe- cial Committee on the Aging, The Multiple Hazards of Age and Race: The Situation of Aged Blacks in the United States: Robert B. Hill, "The Black Elderly"; Donald L. Davis, "Growing Old"; and Hobart C. Jackson, "Information About the National Caucus on the Black Aged." Cary Lacklen also contributed "Aged, Black and Poor: Three Case Studies". This essay also appears elsewhere in this bibliography.

203. Troll, Lillian E., Joan Israel and Kenneth Israel, Editors. Looking Ahead: A Woman's Guide to the Problems and Joys of Growing Older. Englewood Cliffs, NJ: Prentice Hall, Inc., 1977, pp. 149- 156.

In this collection Prof. Jacquelyne Johnson Jackson discusses the physical environment, income and work, family and health of older Black women. The underlying thesis of this essay about older

Troll, Lillian E., et al. (Continued)

Black women is the paucity of gerontological knowledge about them.
The problem is also complicated by inadequate methodologies for
determining the precise impacts of race upon aging. Yet it is
highly likely that significant improvements will occur within the
gerontological literature about older Black women in the future
for several different reasons. One important reason is the sheer
increase in the presence of older Black women within the American
society, argues the sociologist. Some of the trends in the physical and income work environments of older Black women are pro-
gressive, others are regressive. By the end of the century, vir-
tually all older Black women will have at least minimal access to
physical comforts currently regarded as necessary for minimal
living. But their income levels are likely to remain relatively
low in comparison with other major race-sex groups within the
United States. Important, however, is the fact that more of their
concerns will be shifting toward the quality, and not the quantity
of life, concludes Dr. Jackson.

204. Watson, Wilbur H. Aging and Social Behavior: An Introduction to
Social Gerontology. Monterey, CA: Wadsworth Health Sciences
Division, 1982, pp. 138-155.

Chapter 10 is devoted to "Black Aging." It was stated that in
addition to being the largest minority elderly group, many Black
elderly (about 36% in 1975) are poverty-stricken and in a large
measure deprived of life-sustaining health services. Dr. Watson
suggested that the increasing numbers and longevity of Blacks
since 1970 is attributed in part to the support of family and
kinship groups, along with community reverence for elders . . . .

205. White, Joseph L. The Psychology of Blacks: An Afro-American
Perspective. Englewood Cliffs, NJ: Prentice-Hall, Inc., 1984,
pp. 4, 6-7, 13, 44-46, 67, 71-72.

Dr. White declares that the elderly in the Black community are
valued because they are the storehouse of the oral tradition, the
basic teaching of life. He concludes, in part: ". . . Older
(Black) people have stood the test of time and adversity, paid
their dues, transcended tragedy, and learned how to keep on
keepin' on . . . ."

5. BLACK AGED AND MENTAL HEALTH

206. Butler, Robert N. and Myrna I. Lewis. Aging and Mental Health:
Positive Psychological Approaches. St. Louis, MO: C. V. Mosby
Co., 1982, pp. 8-10, 114-117.

There is one section that discusses the Black Elderly. The authors point out that since Black older people die at a younger
age, they may never become eligible for retirement benefits even
if they have them. It was also pointed out that old people of all
races make up only 4% to 5% of community mental health clientele,

Butler, Robert N. and Myrna I. Lewis (Continued)

so one can see that only a small fraction of the total are Black. Also less than 3% of nursing homes and homes for the aged residents are Black, according to the authors. The authors argue that the Black church has proved to be a stabilizing force, providing the elderly with social participation, prestige, and power in the internal life created by parishioners.

6.   BLACK AGED AND OLD FOLKS' HOMES

207. DuBois, W. E. Burghardt and Augustus Granville Dill. Morals and Manners Among Negro Americans. Atlanta, GA: Atlanta University Press, 1914, pp. 97-103.

Section Eleven discusses "Caring for Old People." The authors declare that from early times Blacks in the United States have established old folks' homes and have now (1914) perhaps a hundred such homes throughout the land. They sent out questionnaires to twenty-five states concerning the care of the Black aged. The writers found that the Black elderly were being provided for by relatives, friends or some charitable institutions. In most cases they were receiving adequate care.

208. _____. Efforts for Social Betterment Among Negro Americans. Atlanta, GA: Atlanta University Press, 1909, pp. 65-77.

Section 11 in this book is devoted to "Old Folks' Homes." The writer discusses the various homes for the Black aged all over the United States from the first one established in 1864 in Philadelphia to the latest one established in 1907 in Detroit. He mentioned 61 Black Old Folks' Homes. Dr. DuBois points out the breaking up of families in slavery by sale and during the war and Reconstruction times, greatly aggravated the suffering of the old, while the loosened family ties, due to the slave system, left in post-bellum times numbers of neglected old folk. The author concludes, however, that even loose family ties were not able to overcome the native African reverence for parents, and before the war began Old Folks' Homes for Negroes had begun to be established, some by Negroes themselves, others by their friends.

209. National Council on the Aging. The Golden Years . . . A Tarnished Myth. Washington, DC: National Council of the Aging, 1970, pp. 9, 11, 14-15, 25, 27, 29, 31, 37, 40, 58-59, 68, 84, 91-95, 113-114.

This was a report prepared for the Office of Economic Opportunity. About 13% of the Black elderly was included in this report. Blacks were poorer, less educated and were receiving less funds from Medicare than aged whites.

7. BLACKS AND MINORITY AGED

210.   Butler, Robert N. Why Survive? Being Old in America. New York:
        Harper & Row, 1975, pp. 6, 29-32, 148, 163-164, 257, 262, 267,
        288, 339, 358, 368.

        The author looks to more sensitive treatment of minority aged at
        the point of service provision as a factor that could be effec-
        tive in increasing their utilization of social services. Noting
        that minority groups are extremely poorly represented in the
        service professions as doctors, nurses, and social workers, But-
        ler suggests that those providing services to minority aged
        "should have the assistance of interpreters and training with
        respect to language and culture when this is appropriate. The
        service provider must understand the differing patterns of beha-
        vior that affect the giving and receiving of service."

8. BLACK URBAN AGED

211.   Drake, St. Clair and Horace R. Cayton. Black Metropolis: A
        Study of Negro Life in a Northern City (Chicago). New York:
        Harcourt, Brace and Co., 1945, pp. 58-64.

        Various aged Black residents of Chicago recall the "good" old
        days in that city. They were referring to the 1900-1940s. Many
        state that things were relatively "good" for Blacks before a
        large number of Blacks migrated from the South to that Northern
        city.

212.   Frazier, E. Franklin. The Negro Family in Chicago. Chicago:
        University of Chicago Press, 1932, pp. 235-240.

        Several "old" Black residents of Chicago viewed with alarm the
        influx of the ignorant masses from the South migrating to Chicago.
        They saw their neighborhoods deteriorating and met racial barriers
        where none had existed before. To them, the migrants constituted
        a threat to the standards of behavior which they had safeguarded
        as a heritage. The aged Blacks even formed such clubs as "The
        Old Settlers Club" in order to separate themselves from those
        "hordes of barbarians," concludes Dr. Frazier.

9. BLACK RURAL AGED

213.   Dougherty, Molly Crocker. Becoming a Woman in Rural Black Cul-
        ture. New York: Holt, Rinehart and Winston, 1978, pp. 45-53,
        101-104.

        This is a case study of Black womanhood in a north central
        Florida community. The role and influence of the Black grand-
        mother is also discussed. In many instances mothers, fathers,
        and their children live with their grandmother and she is head
        of the household.

214. Youmans, E. Grant, Editor. Older Rural Americans: A Sociological
      Perspective. Lexington: University of Kentucky Press, 1967,
      pp. 262-280.

      There is one essay in this collection entitled "The Older Rural
      Negro" written by Stanley H. Smith. The essay discusses:
      selected demographic characteristics of aged rural Negroes; data
      on educational level, employment and income; some data on the in-
      volvement of aged rural Negroes in American life; and a small
      amount of data which are designed to allow an assessment of some
      of the subjective reactions to aged Negroes to their social and
      economic conditions.

                    10. BLACK AGED IN STATES

215. Beck, Amanda A., et al. Michigan Aging Citizens: Characteristics,
      Opinions, and Service Utilization Patterns. Ann Arbor, MI: In-
      stitute of Gerontology, University of Michigan-Wayne State Uni-
      versity, 1975, pp. 1-2, 24-25, 28, 31, 33, 36-37, 40, 42-43, 45,
      47, 50, 54, 56, 62-66, 114, 137, 163, 181, 207, 349.

      About 10% of the aged in this study were Black. The following
      areas were discussed: "Demographic Characteristics," "Problems
      for Older Americans," "Income and Expenditures," "Employment and
      Retirement," "Neighborhood and Housing," "Transportation," "Phy-
      sical Health and Nutrition," "Social and Psychological Well-
      Being," and "Leisure and Civic Activities."

216. Berghorn, Forrest J., et al. The Urban Elderly: A Study of Life
      Satisfaction. New York: Allanheld, Osmun and Co., Publishers,
      1978, pp. 1, 44, 46, 48, 50, 94-95, 112, 119-120, 127-129.

      This study dealt mainly with Kansas City, Kansas. It was pointed
      out that aged Blacks more than whites tend to be dependent soci-
      ally and/or psychologically on their friends and neighbors. It
      appeared that Blacks have fewer relatives in the Kansas City
      metropolitan area to whom they could turn for assistance. . . .

217. New Jersey Conference of Social Work. The Negro in New Jersey.
      Trenton, NJ: The New Jersey Conference of Social Work, 1933,
      pp. 54-55, 72, 79, 87, 97.

      It was pointed out that in the 1930s fourteen county welfare
      homes and nine municipal almshouses provided public institu-
      tional care for aged Blacks. This report declared that approxi-
      mately 11 percent of Blacks seventy years and over in New Jersey
      benefited from the old age relief law. There were about 3,000
      Blacks in New Jersey eligible for this relief . . . . There were
      also three private nursing homes for the Black elderly.

11.   COMPARATIVE BLACK AND WHITE AGED

218.   Butler, Robert N.   Why Survive? Being Old in America.   New York:
       Harper & Row, 1975, pp. 6, 30-32, 69-70, 107-108, 124-126, 262,
       267, 288, 303, 331, 398.

       Various references are made to the Black aged throughout the
       book. The author declares in absolute numbers more Whites than
       Blacks are elderly poor (85 percent of the total elderly poor are
       White, 15 percent Black). Black poverty, however, is more pro-
       found than White poverty. The percentage of aged Blacks living
       in poverty is twice that of aged Whites. Forty-seven percent of
       all aged Black females have incomes under $1,000. In rural areas
       two out of three aged Blacks fall below the poverty line. Fur-
       thermore, elderly Blacks tend to have more people dependent on
       them than do the White elderly. More elderly Black people live
       with younger people than do White elderly; 28 percent of them
       live in families with a young head of household compared to 8.9
       percent for all elderly, regardless of race. There are many
       reasons why a larger percentage of Black elderly live with their
       children: the importance of the role of grandmother because the
       mother works or is away; the need for the sharing of income with-
       in a family, including the older person's Social Security and
       public assistance payments; and the respect and sense of respon-
       sibility, said to exist more strongly in Black households, in
       caring for and protecting one's parents, particularly the aged
       mother. The author continues to surmise that those older Blacks
       who do not live with relatives are in a much more disadvantaged
       economic situation: 75 percent of all elderly Blacks living
       alone fall below the poverty line, and Project FIND reported
       that of Black widows an amazing 85 percent were living in poverty,
       with another 5 percent on the borderline.

219.   Gelfand, Donald E. Aging: The Ethnic Factor. Boston: Little,
       Brown and Co., 1982, pp. 1, 9-10, 20, 35-37, 46-54, 61-67, 70,
       74-81, 87-88, 97, 104-105.

       It was pointed out that Blacks comprise the fastest growing group
       of ethnic older persons. The Black aged over sixty-five in-
       creased 28 percent between 1970-1978 in comparison to an increase
       of 19 percent among Whites over 65. Among both Blacks and Whites
       the number of women over sixty-five far exceeds the number of
       men. Approximately one-third of both Black and White elderly are
       living alone, but 29 percent of elderly Black families are headed
       by women as compared to only 11 percent of elderly White families.

220.   Grier, William H. and Price M. Cobbs. Black Rage. New York:
       Basic Books, 1968, pp. 26-30, 45.

       Various references are made throughout the book to aged Blacks.
       The writers point out how young and old Blacks resent White peo-
       ple. Some Blacks express their resentfulness openly and others
       suppress it. One example in this work, an eighty-seven year old
       Black woman still recalls how her mother spoke up for her to her
       White employer in the South during slavery.

221. Harris, Louis and Associates. The Myth and Reality of Aging in
      America. Washington, DC: National Council on the Aging, 1975,
      pp. 4, 7, 15, 18, 51, 66-69, 76, 95, 115, 121-122, 124, 133-136,
      185, 234-235, 241-242.

      Four hundred and seventy-nine Blacks were interviewed for this
      study as compared to two thousand and forty-four Whites. The
      Black aged were compared to the White aged in such areas as
      "Income," "Education," "Health," "Religion," "Public Policy."
      The Black aged were not seen favorably in this study . . . .

222. Haug, Marie R., et al., Editors. The Physical and Mental Health
      of Aged Women. New York: Springer Publishing Co., 1985, pp. 19,
      136, 153, 166-181, 255.

      There is one essay in this work by Jacquelyne Johnson Jackson
      called "Poverty and Minority Status." Most of the illustrations
      given are about old, Black women, primarily because quadruple
      jeopardy was coined specifically to refer to poor, old, Black
      women, argues Dr. Jackson. Old women classified as a racial
      minority are Black. In 1981, of all old women in the United
      States, 90.7 percent were white and 8.2 percent were Black.
      Further, most of the few empirical data available about quadruply
      jeopardized people pertain only to Blacks, declares Prof. Jack-
      son. She concludes: "The vulnerabilities and strengths of old
      women who live for a very long time, despite their poverty and
      minority status, are probably quite vast, but research to date
      prevents us from knowing definitively what those vulnerabilities
      and strengths might be, aside from their rather obvious biologi-
      cal elitism. We also do not know whether they differ greatly
      by their vulnerabilities and strengths from old white women who
      are poor and live for a very long time."

223. Hoffman, Adeline M. The Daily Needs and Interests of Older
      People. Springfield, IL: Charles C. Thomas, Publisher, 1970,
      pp. 315-316.

      The writer asserts that one might hypothesize that the Black
      aged have fewer problems than Whites in accommodating the
      normative demands of the kin group because of previous experience
      and identification within it. The author concludes that the ser-
      vice orientation is more pronounced among the Black subculture,
      especially the lower classes and undoubtedly there are heightened
      reciprocal activities among its members and a useful service role
      for the aged Black.

224. Kalish, Richard A. Late Adulthood: Perspectives on Human Deve-
      lopment. Monterey, CA: Brooks/Cole Publishing Co., 1975, pp. 5,
      13-20, 88-90.

      Various references are made to the Black aged throughout the
      book. In most of the references the author compares them with
      other minority ethnic groups as well as with the White aged. He

Kalish, Richard A. (Continued)

contends that the Black aged have led a doubly difficult life.
First, they are victimized by overt or covert prejudice and discrimination or by their lack of language skills, vocational training, and opportunity. Second, they now find themselves under
attack for not having been aggressive enough at an earlier age
against these injustices or for not being able to alter their
values sufficiently in their later years. Kalish concludes,
however, that there is an increasing appreciation of the plight
of the general community.

225.   Kent, Donald P. and Carl Hirsch, et al. Needs and Use of Ser-
        vices Among Negro and White Aged. Vol. I. University Park, PA:
        Pennsylvania State University, July, 1971. 241 pp.

The writers state differentials in income level, with the oldest
Black respondents suffering greatest financial deprivation, occurred at levels below those determined to be minimal for adequate maintenance among the sample as a whole. Disparities that
do occur on a racial basis were found to exist only between
Blacks and Whites residing with family members who may be seen
to serve as a buffer between the Black aged and the most severe
consequences of such limited financial resources. The author
found that a greater proportion of Black respondents than White
were working, even if retired, in order to maintain their present
income levels. While more Blacks than Whites were dependent on
welfare allotments for income maintenance, this pattern seems to
result from lesser degrees of eligibility among Blacks for both
private and government pension programs based on employment in
earlier years, according to the authors. Through the authors'
general knowledge of rampant discrimination against Blacks compared to Whites even in a group selected from areas of low
socio-economic status in a city. Differences between the racial
groups were also found in the area of informal social interaction.
However, while Black respondents were found to have fewer living
children than Whites, the total ability for dependence within
the social networks of the respondents was not uniformly weighted
in favor of the White aged in this sample. The authors conclude
that the answer may call for greater attention to poor aged
community residents, both Black and White, by government and
voluntary agencies whose defined goals include supports for an
improved quality of life among urban residents. This study was
done in the Philadelphia Model Cities area.

225a.   _____. Health Conditions, Social Adjustments, and Utiliza-
        tion of Community Resources Among Negro and White Aged. Vol. II.
        University Park, PA: Pennsylvania State University, 1972. 255 pp.

The title tells what this work is about. The authors state that
in all areas, health conditions, utilization of community resources, housing, financial aid counseling, employment services,
transportation, one finds that the Black aged is at the bottom
of the ladder. This work is a follow-up of Vol. I by the same

Kent, Donald P., et al (Continued)

authors. They conclude that it would be self deluding to imagine
that the earlier reporting (Vol. I) of these findings would have
significantly contributed to be a change of conditions in the
lives of the sampled population or in the activities of the
agencies delegated by society to work with the aged. On the
other hand, continue the authors, it is also disappointing to
appreciate that little change has occurred within these two
spheres in the time that has passed since fieldwork began. This
study was done in the Philadelphia Model Cities area.

226. Manard, Barbara Bolling, et al. Old-Age Institutions. Lexing-
      ton, MA: Lexington Books, 1975, pp. 44, 51, 77, 80, 96, 122,
      136.

The author points out that the states with the largest non-White
elderly populations are Southern. The seventeen states in which
fewer than 3 percent of the elderly are non-White--Colorado,
Connecticut, Florida, Massachusetts, Minnesota, Montana, Nebras-
ka, New Hampshire, North Dakota, Oregon, Rhode Island, South
Dakota, Utah, Vermont, Washington, Wisconsin, and Wyoming--are
predominantly north central and eastern. Two urban northeastern
states, Massachusetts and Rhode Island, have elderly populations
that are less than 2 percent Black; in New York and New Jersey,
the proportion is about 6 percent. Thus, the distribution of
the states with respect to the proportion of the elderly population that is non-White closely mirrors the distribution along
other dimensions we have found to be associated with low rates
of institutionalization, state the authors. This fact probably
contributes to the underrepresentation of Blacks in the total
Old-Age Institutions (OAI) population: Blacks are less likely
than Whites, nationally, to be in OAI because Blacks, by and
large, live in states where old people in general are less likely
to be in OAI. Looking at Virginia, Blacks comprise 18 percent of
the elderly population and 12 percent of the elderly population
in OAI. In Virginia, elderly Blacks are about as likely as elderly Whites to live in extra-familial situations, declare the
writers. The proportions are 24 and 26 percent respectively.
Since Blacks in Virginia are proportionately more likely than
Whites to be in institutions other than OAI, when we group together the elderly populations in all types of institutions, we
find little difference between Blacks and Whites, conclude the
authors. In Virginia, 4.5 percent of the elderly Whites and 4.4
percent of the elderly Blacks are in institutions and group
quarters. A similar situation occurs in Massachusetts, which
has both a high proportion of its elderly in OAI and a low proportion of non-Whites generally. Almost 2 percent (1.9) of the
Massachusetts elderly population is Black, and 1.7 percent of
the elderly OAI population is Black, according to the authors.

227. Smith, Bert Kruger. Aging in America. Boston: Beacon, 1973, pp. 52-55.

Part of Chapter Three is devoted to "Problems of Race and Poverty." The author asserts that almost one half of all the older Blacks are living below the poverty level. He also argues that with poverty came the ragged companions of poor housing and poor health. Life expectancy is much lower for Blacks than for Whites. The author concludes that although the Black aged do not use the medical services as frequently as Whites do, they have more intense illnesses, resulting in significantly more bed-disability days than Whites of similar ages. The compound problems of age and poverty and minority status, argues Smith, make older years a constant hardship for many Americans.

228. Ward, Russell A. The Aging Experience: An Introduction to Social Gerontology. New York: J. B. Lippincott Co., 1979, pp. 57-60, 210-213, 302-308.

The Black elderly is compared to the White and Spanish aged in terms of: "Median years of education," "Percent married and living with spouse," "Percent in labor force," "Median individual income," "Percent in poverty." In most of these areas, Blacks are behind aged Whites and ahead of aged Spanish . . . .

12. BLACK AGED AND THE BLACK CHURCH

229. Walls, William J. The African Methodist Episcopal Zion Church: Reality of the Black Church. Charlotte, NC: A.M.E. Zion Publishing House, 1974, pp. 113, 118-119, 428-429.

Chapter 27 is entitled "Concern for Aged Ministers, Widows and Children." As early as 1848, the A.M.E. Zion Church provided for worn out (Aged) ministers. In 1896 the General Conference organized a "Committee on Worn-Out Preachers." The church felt a responsibility to its aged ministers. The by-laws of the church said that "if a minister is permanently incapacitated by reason of sickness or accident he is eligible for retirement and pension."

230. Barrow, Georgia M. and Patricia A. Smith. Aging, Ageism and Society. With Cartoons by Bulbul. St. Paul, MN: West Publishing Co., 1979, pp. 259-276.

Chapter 13 is devoted to "The Minority Aged." The authors rely on data from previous printed works by other writers for their material on the "Black Aged." The writers conclude that Blacks are the largest group of the aged minorities followed by Hispanics, American Indians, and Asian Americans. According to the authors, the numbers of persons do not reflect, however, the variety in these groups in terms of races, cultures, languages, socioeconomic status, and historical or traditional attitudes and beliefs. They also point out that upgrading the status of the minority elderly requires recognition of the various factors that prevent them from utilizing services followed by the establishment of outreach programs designed to overcome them.

231. Hess, Beth B. and Elizabeth W. Markson, Editors. Growing Old in
      America. New Brunswick, NJ: Transaction Books, 1985, pp. 377-383.

      Several articles on the Black Aged in this collection are reprinted
      from previously published works. There are, however, several re-
      ferences to the Black aged that present a different viewpoint.
      The editors in their "Introduction" declare "While it may be a
      facile truism to say to be Black and to be old in America is a
      double yoke of oppression, the precise ways in which race and age
      interact to influence one's treatment at the hands of functionaries
      (and well-meaning sociologists), the allocation of scarce resources,
      or access to opportunities for self-fulfillment are very subtle
      indeed." Other articles in this book also allude to the Black
      aged.

                    13. BLACK AGED AND HOUSING

232. Lawton, M. Powell and Sally L. Hoover, Editors. Community Housing
      Choices for Older Americans. New York: Springer Publishing Co.,
      1981, pp. 59-89.

      Two essays in this collection are devoted to the Black elderly:
      "Housing for the Black Elderly--The Need Remains," by Edward C.
      Wallace; and "Black and Spanish Elderly: Their Housing Charac-
      teristics and Housing Quality," by Sally L. Hoover. Mr. Wallace
      argues that except for public housing, elderly Blacks have been
      virtually excluded from federally financed elderly housing. The
      irony of the situation, concludes Wallace, is that they are the
      ones who need that help most, now and in the future. Ms. Hoover
      points out that although there are fewer older Blacks than White
      homeowners, it appears that the Blacks are more likely to remain
      in a home once it is purchased; therefore, as a group they may be
      slightly more likely to experience the tangential problems of
      overhousing and structural deterioration, concludes the researcher.

233. Rebeck, Ann H. A Study of the Developments in Programs for the
      Care of the Aged: With Emphasis on New York State and New York
      City. New York: New York State Department of Social Welfare,
      May 1, 1943. 141 pp.

      In 1941 there were 73 private homes for the aged in and around
      the metropolitan area serving residents from New York City. Of
      that number, there were only three (3) for the Blacks, two for
      Black women and one for men and women. About six homes cared for
      both Blacks and Whites. The writer concludes that although there
      were long waiting lists for all homes, the need for facilities
      for Blacks was the most acute. The author also gives an example
      of a small home for Black women.

4.

DISSERTATIONS AND THESES

1. BLACK AGED AND THE FAMILY

234. Brown, Gwendolyn S. "When Do Black Elderly Persons Live With Younger Relatives: An Analysis of Factors Affecting Multigenerational Living in the United States." Unpublished Master's Thesis, Howard University, 1982. 179 pp.

The author answers the question, "when do Black elderly relatives live with younger relatives?" in this way: "The best chance of finding an elderly Black person living with a younger relative exists when the elder's income is less than $3,000 and the younger relative is between 45 and 64 years of age, lives in an urban center, lives in the South, and has an income above $3,000 per year. This relative may be male or female, but may increasingly be found to be female." The writer also states that the increasing number of elders sharing housing with another person of the opposite sex must be noted as one way elders are choosing to manage their resources better <u>and</u> maintain independence. . . .

235. Burton, Linda M. "Early and On-Time Grandmotherhood in Multigeneration Black Families." Unpublished Doctoral Dissertation, University of Southern California, 1985. 269 pp.

This study explores the consequences of "early" versus "on-time" entry to the grandmother role by examining the relationship among three variables--timing of role entry, intergenerational cohesion, and grandparental satisfaction--in a sample of multi-generation Black female lineages. Two key issues are addressed. First, with a focus on the grandmother as the unit of analysis, the effect of timing of entry to the grandmother role on role satisfaction is evaluated. The second issue focuses on the grandmother, but as part of the lineage family system. This issue concerns the effect of timing of role entry for the concurrent transitions of the other lineage members (daughter to mother, grandmother to great-grandmother) on intergenerational cohesion and, subsequently, grandparental role satisfaction, states the writer. Results indicate that early grandmothers are significantly less satisfied with their role than on-time grandmothers. Differential

Burton, Linda M. (Continued)

satisfaction was mirrored in satisfaction scores, as well as grandmothers' assessments of the appropriate age for role entry. Early
grandmothers reported the appropriate age for grandparental role
entry 12-30 years higher than their own chronological ages while
on-time grandmothers reported a minimal or non-existent difference
(0-2 years), concludes Dr. Burton.

236.   Graves, Conrad. "Family and Community Support Networks and Their
        Utilization by the Black Elderly." Unpublished Doctoral Disserta-
        tion, New York University, 1981. 237 pp.

        This dissertation was based on the study of 208 Black men and
        women who lived in a high-crime, low-income, predominantly Black
        community of a large northeastern city. The following issues
        were dealt with in this study: (1) more information about the
        characteristics of the client population, the Black aged, with a
        differentiation between the Black elderly living in urban areas
        and those who still live in the rural sections of this country;
        (2) more information about the methods and techniques of service
        delivery that lead to the most effective utilization of service by
        the poor, Black elderly; (3) more information as to whether social
        services that are offered and utilized have a positive effect on
        the social health of the client population.

237.   Hirsch, Carl. "Primary Group Supports Among a Sample of Elderly
        Black and White Ethnic Residents of Urban, Working-Class Neighbor-
        hoods." Unpublished Doctoral Dissertation, Pennsylvania State
        University, 1979. 225 pp.

        This study explored the instrumental support received by elderly
        working class and ethnic group residents of urban neighborhoods
        from their families, friends and neighbors. Dr. Hirsch concludes
        that non-kin helpers of the ethnic and working-class elderly do
        play an important role in the provision of instrumental support
        for those not living with family members, or who reach out of the
        family household for support on issues requiring either long-term
        or short-term support. The role played by non-kin helpers was
        found to be especially significant for the childless elderly. . . .

238.   Langston, Esther R. L. "Kith and Kin: Natural Support Systems:
        Their Implications for Policies and Programs for the Black Aged."
        Unpublished Doctoral Dissertation, University of Texas at Arling-
        ton, 1982. 102 pp.

        This dissertation examined the accessibility and utilization of
        informal support systems by the Black aged and whom the Black can
        call on in a crisis such as illness; the effects of residential
        environment on the use of and accessibility of informal support
        systems by the Black aged in the United States. The author argues
        that the residential environment (urban, semi-urban) was found to
        be a major factor in examining the use of informal support systems.

Langston, Esther R. L. (Continued)

The kith system had the highest frequencies of visits and lived
closer to the respondent in all geographic areas. The kin system
was found to be the first choice for support in time of a crisis
such as illness except in the semi-urban area where the formal
system was the first choice. According to Dr. Langston, the data
in this study indicated that geographic location was a major factor for understanding the effects of and sources of support for
the Black aged in the United States.

239. Nkweti, David A. "The Aged in Black Middle Class Families: A
      Study in Intergenerational Relations." Unpublished Doctoral
      Dissertation, American University, 1982. 184 pp.

      In terms of living arrangements, it was found that the ideal and
      general preference for both the elderly individuals and their
      adult children was an independent household for each generation.
      However, the majority of the elderly sample (sixty-eight percent)
      were living in households containing kin other than spouses. For
      instance, the aged brought adult children, grandchildren, and
      sometimes other elderly siblings to live with them. The same
      thing was true for the middle generation who adopted various stra-
      tegies to keep in touch with their parents. For example, many de-
      vised a technique of information gathering and sharing among sib-
      lings. Another finding revealed that there was general good will
      and readiness among both generations regarding medical assistance,
      although the older the individual the more aid was needed. The
      study found a discrepancy between the attitudes of the elderly and
      the young. The elderly were experiencing a feeling of social dis-
      tance while the young did not, states Dr. Nkweti. To conclude,
      the study reveals that general perceptions about the aged and
      their relations to kin do not correspond perfectly with social
      realities of the elderly. Middle class families maintained a
      dynamic relationship with their elderly members despite numerous
      factors and demands that tend to impede ongoing social interaction.
      Finally, attitudinal discrepancies between the elderly and the
      young and a feeling of social distance by the elderly did not rup-
      ture relations between the two generations.

240. Peoples, Beverly, Y. C. "An Exploration Study of Noninstitution-
      alized Black Urban Elderly Living in Age-Homogenous Apartments in
      Detroit, Michigan and Their Informal Social Support Systems."
      Unpublished Doctoral Dissertation, Iowa State University, 1984.
      219 pp.

      The purpose of this research study was to identify the primary
      groups that noninstitutionalized, Black elderly living in federal-
      ly subsidized age-homogenous residential apartments located in
      Detroit, Michigan, perceived as being instrumental components in
      their informal social support system. Elderly persons go from
      being a totally independent person to being partially independent
      and mutually interdependent based upon the support given to them
      by family, friends and neighbors. Therefore, a functional

Peoples, Beverly Y. C. (Continued)

informal social support system must be available if the independent elderly persons are to maintain a feasible level of independence and a satisfactory social adjustment, according to the researcher. It was found that relatives provided the majority of
support for the respondents in matters that required long-term
support (help in financial matters, help during long-term and
short-term illness and help during socioeconomic upsets, etc.) and
in short-term commitments (borrowing monetary and nonmonetary
items, help in storing and fixing small household items). They
had definite high expectations concerning the provisions of filial
support or financial matters and assistance with activities of
daily living, when needed. Leisure-time activities were spent
with friends and neighbors. Frequent interaction with family and
friends was noted. The results of this study showed that noninstitutionalized Black urban elderly are not isolated and abandoned by family, friends and neighbors. They are an integral unit
within an active, nurturing and interacting informal social support system that provides a heterogenous array of support, when
needed, concludes Dr. Peoples.

241.   Rosebud-Harris, Marcy C. "A Description of the Interactional and
       Subjective Characteristics of the Relationships between Black
       Grandmothers and Their Grandchildren Enrolled in the University
       of Louisville." Unpublished Doctoral Dissertation, University of
       Iowa, 1982, 449 pp.

       The purpose of this study was to obtain descriptive data about the
       interactional and subjective characteristics of the relationships
       between Black grandmothers and their adult, college-educated
       grandchildren, as perceived by both grandmothers and grandchildren.
       The data generally supported the hypothesis. Interactional and
       subjective relationships between Black grandmothers and grand-
       children were extremely strong. While maternal grandmothers,
       granddaughters, younger grandmothers, and younger grandchildren--
       with fewer variations--interacted with greater frequency than
       paternal grandmothers, grandsons, older grandmothers, and older
       grandchildren, the differences were insignificant, according to
       Prof. Rosebud-Harris. Irrespective of the maternal or paternal
       blood ties of the grandmother to the grandchild, age of grand-
       mothers, and age and sex of grandchildren, interactional and sub-
       jective relationships between these Black grandmothers and their
       adult, college-educated grandchildren were extremely strong,
       concludes the author.

242.   Yelder,   Josephine. "Generational Relationships in Black
       Families: Some Perceptions of Grandparents' Role." Unpublished
       Doctoral Dissertation, University of Southern California, 1975,
       220 pp.

       This study investigated themes and variations in the role of
       grandparents in Black families. The research involved a descrip-
       tive analysis of grandparenting and its relationship to other

Yelder, Josephine   (continued)

variables. A purposive sample of forty-one Black grandparents
with a grandchild between the ages of four and five years was
selected. The primary method of data collection was through interviews with these participants in their homes. Data were gathered during a three month period regarding demographic factors,
perceptions of family relationships, grandparent role, child
rearing opinions, and relationships outside the family. Three
major working hypotheses guided this study: (1) the style of
grandparenting will vary with the changing circumstances of grandparents, parents, and/or grandchildren; (2) generational relationships in Black families are a network of roles in which the grandparent role is an acquired role that is in part influenced by the
significance of the role to the occupant; and (3) the degree of
comfort in being a grandparent will be related to factors which
influence what is perceived as normative in the performance of the
grandparent role. The author concludes that the respondents
ranged in age from 43-75 and had 107 children, 246 grandchildren
and 52 great-grandchildren. Close family ties were indicated by
most of the group. Most of the respondents felt that child-rearing practices should be flexible to fit the needs of the child....

2. BLACK AGED WOMEN

243. Carter, Carla A. "An Investigation of the Attitudes of Elderly
      Clients Toward Social Workers." Unpublished Master's Thesis,
      Howard University, 1981, 56 pp.

      This study expressed the following trends: (1) as the elderly
      women viewing the young social worker perceived that worker as
      being at least 30 years of age, they tended to assign a more
      favorable rating of her, than if the perceived age assigned was
      under 30; and (2) as the elderly women viewing the older social
      worker, perceived that worker as being 50 years of age or older,
      they assigned less favorable ratings of that worker. According
      to the writer, this suggests that though the age of the helping
      person may not significantly influence the attitudes of the elder-
      ly Black females used in this research, in the monotonic fashion
      hypothesized, age does influence ratings to some extent. During
      post hoc interviews with the subjects conducted by the investiga-
      tor at the conclusion of the study, subjects expressed their
      favorability toward the younger helper person if the younger per-
      son demonstrated enough "life" experience to understand their
      special needs and concerns as elderly people, concludes Ms. Carter.

244. Chapman, Sabrina Coffey. "A Social-Psychological Analysis of
      Morale In a Selected Population: Low-Income Elderly Black Females."
      Unpublished Doctoral Dissertation, Pennsylvania State University,
      1979. 184 pp.

      This study concerned itself with the relationships existing be-
      tween certain social-psychological variables and morale in a
      select minority population, low-income elderly Black females, and
      also analyzes the differences in morale existing between the

Chapman, Sabrina Coffey (Continued)

study population and low-income elderly White females. It was
reasoned that, although the low-income elderly Black female is in
a precarious position of multiple jeopardy in the larger sociocultural milieu, her position within the Black Community itself
is a highly esteemed one. Historically, and of necessity, aged
Black females have often, over their life-spans, typically assumed
both the instrumental role, that of providing the family's economic support, and the integrative, expressive role, that of providing intergenerational family support, declares Prof. Chapman. Ac-
cordingly, the theoretical constructs of the role continuity--role
dicontinuity and activity theory, as well as those of relative
deprivation--relative gain and disengagement theory, were utilized
as pertained to the research problem. It was found that no significant relationship could be established between race and morale.
The fact that the difference in morale levels was not verifiable
as statistically significant between low-income elderly Black
females and low-income elderly White females seems to suggest that
the life experiences of these two populations are more parallel
than anticipated; and, that the similarities attendant to the experience of being old, poor and female are greater than the dis-
similarities of that experience, regardless of race, argues the
writer.

245.   Hamlett, Margaret Lucylle. "An Exploratory Study of the Socio-
        Economic and Psychological Problems of Adjustment of 100 Aged
        and Retired Negro Women in Durham, North Carolina During 1959."
        Unpublished Master's Thesis, North Carolina College at Durham,
        1959. 69 pp.

        The author states that three-quarters of the women were reasonably
        well adjusted. According to Ms. Hamlett, an analysis of the data
        indicated that a greater proportion of the women had problems in
        the economic than in either the psychological or social areas.
        Most of the social activities they performed prior to old age
        were continued. It was also found that the factor of race was not
        a basis for the maladjustment of these women. She concludes that
        the generally accepted beliefs with reference to the problems of
        the aged are inadequate in many respects when applied to a selec-
        ted sample of aged and retired women residing in Durham, North
        Carolina during 1959.

246.   Irvin, Yvonne F. "The Relationship of Age and Adjustment to the
        Subjective Well-Being of Older Black Women." Unpublished Docto-
        ral Dissertation, University of Pittsburgh, 1982. 92 pp.

        This study investigated the relationship between age, observed
        adjustment and subjective well-being in a "young-old" group (60-
        75 years of age) and an "old-old" group (76 years and older) of
        Black women who were participants in multi-service daycare pro-
        grams. Subjective well-being was measured by the Revised Phila-
        delphia Geriatric Morale Scale (PGC) and the Life Satisfaction
        Index A (LSIA), while the New Adjustment Check List was used to

Irvin, Yvonne F. (Continued)

obtain estimates of adjustment. The results indicated that the
"young-old" group had higher subjective well-being scores on both
measures of subjective well-being, although a significant difference was only obtained with the PCG scores, states the writer. No
differences in observed adjustment were obtained nor were any of
the interactions between age, adjustment and subjective well-being
significant. However, a significant positive correlation was obtained between observed adjustment and subjective well-being as
measured by the PGC for the "old-old" group while the same measures correlated around zero for the "young-old" group. The results
were interpreted as indicating for these subjects that the PGC was
a more discriminating measure of subjective well-being than the
LSIA. Furthermore, the facts that age differences were found on
the measures of subjective well-being and that the relationship
between adjustment and subjective well-being tended to differ for
the two age groups, were taken as evidence supporting Neugarten's
contention that old age should be viewed as consisting of at least
two different stages: the "young-old" and the "old-old", concludes Dr. Irvin.

3. BLACK AGED MEN

247.   Adam, Antenor Joseph. "An Exploratory Study of the Relation of
       the Adjustment of 100 Aged Negro Men in Durham, North Carolina
       with Their Education, Health, and Work Status." Unpublished
       Master's Thesis, North Carolina College at Durham, 1961. 88 pp.

The writer found that the over-all adjustment levels of the subjects studied were, on the average, high. There was no difference
between economic status and adjustment, and social status and adjustment. Adam found that there was no difference between psychological status and adjustment and economic status and adjustment.
The highness of the mean scores of the social, economic, and psychological adjustment areas is accounted for in part by the selectivity of the group studied. Non-welfare status, which indicates
a relative absence of poverty, was used as a reference point in
the choice of subjects.

4. RELIGION AND THE BLACK AGED

248.   Gray, Cleo J. "Attitudes of Black Church Members Towards the
       Black Elderly as a Function of Denomination, Age, Sex, and Level
       of Education." Unpublished Doctoral Dissertation, Howard Univer-
       sity, 1977. 185 pp.

As an initial empirical venture in the study of attitudes held--
and thus communicated--by Blacks, this study focuses only on the
response of this population to the aged Black. The study is further limited with respect to age, sex, level of education and membership in a Black church, the major interacting institution in
the life of the aged. Using a study sample drawn from the total
population of male and female members of three different denomina-
tions and churches (N=210), and employing Kogan's Attitude Toward

Gray, Cleo J. (Continued)

Old People Scale (a Likert-type scale of 17 matched positive-
negative pairs), the following null hypotheses were tested: (1)
There is no significant difference in the attitude of Black church
members toward the elderly as a function of denomination. (2)
There is no significant difference in the attitude of Black church
members toward the elderly as a function of age. (3) There is no
significant difference in the attitude of Black church members toward the elderly as a function of sex. (4) There is no significant difference in the attitude of Black church members toward the
elderly as a function of level of education. The writer concludes that as the data suggest that a positive attitudinal climate exists in the Black church and is thus communicated. Recommendations were made to structure and implement programming and
activities which serve to enlarge the positive climate and to
mitigate against the propagation of negative attitudes toward the
elderly.

5. BLACK AGED AND HOUSING

249. Anderson, Peggye D. "The Black Aged: Dispositions Toward Seeking
Age Concentrated Housing in a Small Town." Unpublished Doctoral
Dissertation, Northwestern University, 1975. 189 pp.

This work is an exploratory study in which the author searched for
elderly Blacks' attitudes toward seeking aged concentrated housing
as well as factors that influence their desire to seek this style
of living. The study includes 208 Black elderly people sixty-five
years and older. The setting in which the study was conducted is
Tuskegee, Alabama. The lives and lifestyles of the Black elderly
people in the study do not vary much from the general aged population. Their level of education, marital and health status reflect
the typical aged person. Thus, the people in this study have an
average of eight years of schooling. The majority of the females
are widowed and the majority of the males are married. Most of
the people are in good to fair health. The author also found that
even though some variables do not help explain why aged Blacks may
seek age concentrated housing; nevertheless, they provide interesting insight into the lives and lifestyles of Black elderly people.
Such variables that help us understand more about elderly Black
people's lives, but not help explain why the elderly would seek
age concentrated housing, include: family relations, sex, age and
age identification, concludes Prof. Anderson.

250. Hawkins, Brin D. "A Comparative Study of the Social Participation
of the Black Elderly Residing in Public Housing in Two Communities:
The Inner City and the Suburbs." Unpublished Doctoral Dissertation, Brandeis University, 1976. 181 pp.

This study was based on a sample of 145 elderly Black men and
women residing in two public housing projects in the Washington
D.C. area. The Claridge Project is located in an inner city, high
crime, high density, predominantly Black census tract. The Re-
gency is located in a low crime, low density, predominantly White

Hawkins, Brin D.   (Continued)

suburban fringe census tract. The basic premise of this study is
that social participation can serve as a mediating function between the role loss experienced in the later years and morale, because it provides supports to the individual's role identities
which are prerequisites for a positive self-concept. A major factor influencing social participation is the residential environment, which may inhibit or facilitate social interaction. Personal characteristics were also considered as they influence social
participation in old age; i.e., sex, age, marital status, education, income, and relocation experience. The findings of this
study support the adaptability of older persons, particularly the
ability of the Black elderly to adjust to new and unfamiliar residential environment. The findings further indicate a higher level
of interaction in clubs or organized activity in a pleasant and
safe community where opportunities for social interaction are
available.

251.   Stretch, John J.   "The Development and Testing of a Theoretical
Formulation That Aged Negroes with Differences in Community Secu-
rity are Different in Coping Reactions." Unpublished Doctoral
Dissertation, Tulane University, 1967. 155 pp.

This study conceptualized and tested a beginning theory developed
by the author from social-psychological and neo-psychoanalytic
sources, that there are differences in coping reactions between
two populations of aged Blacks who have differences in community
security. The sample used was seventy-two Blacks, predominantly
sixty years old and above, not living with spouse, and meeting
eligibility requirements for residence in the William Guste public
housing apartment. The findings in general, confirmed the beginning theoretical formulation as conceptualized. No significant
differences were found between the Guste-Community group on nineteen extraneous variables thought to influence coping, states the
author. Significant differences in the predicted direction for
the Low Security sample on six of these variables were found
between the High-Low Security group. Differences in the six community security scores were in the predicted direction of higher
scores for the Guste Homes sample than for the Community sample,
with two scores, total community security and self-fulfillment,
significant beyond the five percent level. Of the two empirical
indicators of community security, larger sample differences in
coping reaction scores were found between the High-Low Security
group than between the Guste-Community group. Most differences
in coping reaction scores, nineteen out of twenty-four, were in
the predicted direction, and in the High-Low Security group eight
were significant, concludes the writer.

252.   Sugg, Michael L.   "A Comparative Study of Morale and Activity
Levels Among Lower Socio-Economic Elderly Residents Living in
Age-Segregated vs. Age-Integrated Housing Arrangements." Unpublished Doctoral Dissertation, University of Pittsburgh, 1975.
132 pp.

Sugg, Michael L. (Continued)

The central concern of this study is the theoretical and policy implications related to what type of living arrangements are most suitable for elderly poor persons. A comparative design was implemented utilizing the theoretical orientation of the so-called Activity theory and Disengagement theory while assessing the activity and morale levels of age-segregated versus age-integrated living arrangements among a total research population of 402 elderly poor obtained from two social service agencies in Allegheny County, Pennsylvania. Three separate residential groups were compared: (1) Public housing, age-segregated elderly; (2) Public housing, age-integrated elderly; (3) Private housing, age-integrated elderly. The findings indicated that both theories were rejected in relation to age-segregated elderly, but not entirely in the case of private dwelling, age-integrated elderly, observed Dr. Sugg. Activity and morale scores regardless of health, age, or other variables, were consistently higher for both age-segregated and age-integrated elderly living in public housing arrangements. Private housing, age-integrated elderly with satisfactory morale levels and low activity scores reflected a disengaged style of life. The overall findings, then strongly support a policy of expanded development in public housing for the elderly in our society, concludes Dr. Sugg.

253.   Wyckoff, Shelley A. R. "The Effects of Housing and Race Upon Depression and Life Satisfaction of Elderly Females." Unpublished Doctoral Dissertation, George Peabody College for Teachers of Vanderbilt University, 1983. 143 pp.

The population used in the study were Black and white females, 65 years of age and older, from Huntsville, Alabama. From this population, four samples were randomly selected from planned and unplanned housing, states the author. The study failed to report a significant difference between subjects in planned and unplanned housing relative to depression and life satisfaction. Among the reasons that were noted for this were the failure of some studies to include control variables and the possible differences in well-being for the unplanned housing groups used in previous studies and the current study. Those in the current study may have been too close to asymtote (relative to well-being) to permit a significant change. Another reason for the discrepancy in findings is that planned housing, when considered in isolation, may not be a very potent variable for enhancing the well-being of senior citizens, argues Dr. Wyckoff. Relative to race, white females in planned housing displayed a higher level of life satisfaction than Black females residing in planned housing, while Black females in unplanned housing reported a lower level of depression than white females residing in unplanned housing, concludes Dr. Wyckoff.

6. BLACK AGED AND HEALTH

254. Brown, Norman B. J. "Societal Determinants of Cultural Factors Related to the Dental Health of Older Black Americans." Unpublished Doctoral Dissertation, University of Michigan, 1982. 167 pp.

The purpose of this study was to explore the efficacy of the Health Belief Model in explaining the dental health of older Black Americans by examining the relationship between the dental health status of older Black Americans and the following societal determinants: (1) ethnicity; (2) environment; (3) education; and (4) economics. Dental health beliefs and practices of this population were examined to determine the effect on their dental health (i.e., the number of decayed, missing, and filled teeth). In addition, the participants' perceived susceptibility to, and perceived severity of, dental caries were analyzed to ascertain decision-making behavior for taking action to prevent or minimize dental problems. The sample employed in this study consisted of 122 Black American males and females between the ages of 55-97. They were either retired, employed, or unemployed members of the United Auto Workers (UAW) Retired and Older Workers Department. The proposed relationships between the indicated societal determinants and the dental health of older Black Americans were generally supported, states Dr. Brown. The degree of the differential in personal oral health habits and use of dental services was significantly related to environmental factors (i.e., social conditions and geographic locations), education, and income. Dental health beliefs and practices were generally positively correlated to dental health, concludes the researcher.

255. Butler, Frieda R. "Factors Related to Compliance with a Treatment Regimen in Black Elderly Diabetic Women," Unpublished Doctoral Dissertation, University of Maryland, 1980. 137 pp.

This study consisted of 68 Black diabetic women aged 60-79 who attended an ambulatory care facility in an urban, inner-city area. The dependent variables indicating compliance were three direct indicator items on the interview schedules, measuring self-reported medication omissions and one indirect indicator item, measuring daily checking of urine for glucose. A weight gain of six or more pounds within a two month period was also used as an indicator for non-compliance. The criterion, non-compliance, was measured in this study sample by the identification of the respondents according to weight gain or by the identification of the respondents who provided negative responses to two or more of the indicator questions on the initial interviews. The results indicated that of the six variables studied, knowledge of diabetes was statistically significant beyond the .05 level and was hence the sole significant predicator of compliance with the diabetic treatment regimen, declares Dr. Butler. The data indicated that compliers tended to be knowledgeable of diabetes, had a self-perceived level of high understanding of the condition and followed their diets. Non-compliers tended to display low knowledge of the disease, had a self-perceived low level of understanding of the

Butler, Frieda R. (Continued)

condition and did not adhere to their diets. The additional factor of high knowledge of the disease by the compliers indicates a
greater belief in their susceptibility to the disease and the
severity of the disease, concludes Prof. Butler.

256.   Edmonds, Mary M. "Social Class and the Functional Health Status
        of the Aged Black Female." Unpublished Doctoral Dissertation,
        Case Western Reserve University, 1982. 201 pp.

        This investigation centers around the question of whether a rela-
        tionship exists between social class and the noninstitutionalized
        aged Black female's ability to accurately assess her functional
        health status. One hundred women, residing in Cleveland, Ohio,
        and meeting the above criteria, were asked to self assess specific
        activities of daily living and were then asked to demonstrate
        their ability to perform the activities. Those whose scores were
        congruent with the rater's scores were conceptualized as being
        realistic; those who rated themselves as performing better than
        the interviewer's ratings of their performance were considered
        optimistic; and those who rated their ability to perform as less
        adequate than the interviewer's ratings were considered pessimis-
        tic. It is hypothesized that the higher social class, the more
        realistic the rating. It is further hypothesized that the rela-
        tionship between social class and the score will hold when the
        intervening variables, cognitive health knowledge, experimental
        health knowledge, geographic location where reared, current self
        assessed physical health, chronicity, self assessed physical limi-
        tations, current utilization of health services, and willingness
        to assume the sick role are introduced. The hypotheses are not
        supported. Fifty-eight women were realistic, 21 were mildly pes-
        simistic, and 21 were mildly optimistic, asserts Prof. Edwards.

257.   Harper, Doreen C. "The Effects of a Medication Self-Care Program
        on Knowledge of Medication, Health Locus of Control and Self-Care
        Behavior Among Black Elderly Hypertensive Women." Unpublished
        Doctoral Dissertation, University of Maryland, 1980. 220 pp.

        The purpose of this study was to determine the effect of a medica-
        tion self-care program on knowledge of medication, health locus of
        control, self-care behaviors, medication error and self-care beha-
        viors among Black elderly women. The study was conducted from May
        to November, 1979, with women who attended a primary care clinic.
        The sample consisted of 60 volunteer Black hypertensive women who
        had provider-reported or self-reported problems with medication
        administration. In the first criterion measure the medication
        self-care program significantly increased knowledge of medication,
        health locus of control, and self-care behaviors. Medication
        errors were significantly reduced. These treatment effects were
        greatly diminished in the second criterion measure. Although
        blood pressures were lower for women in the experimental group
        than the control group, there were no significant differences in
        blood pressures between the groups. It was also found that blood

Harper, Doreen C. (Continued)

pressure levels were normotensive throughout the study for women
in both groups. Dr. Harper concluded that the medication self-
care program did improve knowledge of medication, perceived control over health, self-care behaviors and medication errors among
Black elderly hypertensive women. The diminution effect which
occurred, however, led to the conclusion that programs for the
Black elderly aimed at changing health behaviors require follow-
up supervision and support from providers to reinforce new health
behaviors.

258.   Monroe, Lillie M. "An Assessment of Nutrition Education Needs of
        Elderly Blacks and a Comparison of Four Methods of Instruction."
        Unpublished Doctoral Dissertation, Howard University, 1978.
        322 pp.

The purpose of the present investigation was to undertake as assessment of the nutrition education needs of the elderly, and then
to compare the effectiveness of four methods of instruction on the
elderly's awareness of nutrition; rentention of nutrition knowledge; and attitudes and opinions about food, nutrition, and health.
Two hundred participants in a Title VII-Nutrition Program for the
Elderly, sixty years of age or older, were the subjects of this
investigation. The study group consisted of one-hundred-two females and ninety-eight males. The subjects were divided into four
groups of fifty, and one method of instruction was conducted on
each of the four different groups. Percentage change was used to
compare effectiveness of instruction among methods. There were
statistically significant differences in the frequencies and means
of the pretest and immediate post test, pretest and follow-up post
test, and to a degree immediate post test and follow-up post test
for each method of instruction. The greatest percentage change
between the frequencies of pretest and immediate post test; and
pretest and follow-up post test occurred in the dietetic interview. The greatest percentage change between the immediate post
test and follow-up post test occurred in the self-instructional
materials, concludes Dr. Monroe.

259.   Morrison, Barbara J. "Black Aged in Nursing Homes: An Applica-
        tion of the Shared Function Thesis." Unpublished Doctoral Disser-
        tation, Columbia University, 1979. 318 pp.

The data for this dissertation was drawn from five selected nursing homes in New York City. A combination of random and purposive
sampling resulted in the selection of 93 residents who were interviewed as part of the study between January and September 1978.
Sixty-four of the 93 residents in the study sample had family
available. Twenty-seven of these family members were interviewed.
Data on the demographic characteristics of this population were
compared to existing norms for Black aged in the community. The
institutionalized persons in the study sample were significantly
older and there were many more widowed and never married persons.
These findings would seem to indicate that lack of spouse or

Morrison, Barbara J. (Continued)

other familial supports in the face of advancing age and impairment is a major reason for admission to the nursing home. It was
also found that availability of family was significantly related
to sex of the older person. Black aged males in the study sample
were less likely than aged females to have family available, according to Prof. Morrison. The nursing homes which serve a
majority of Black residents and were therefore defined as "ethnic"
were more likely than the non-ethnic nursing homes to include cultural components in routine activities. These components included
the celebration of holidays important to Black aged, the regular
provision of ethnic foods and the inclusion of Black music and art
in social activities. The second finding was that consumer attitudes were related to the ethnic orientation of the host facility.
This was especially true for issues of matching provider and consumer on the basis of ethnicity than for the inclusion of cultural
components in routine activities for which there was ample support
from most residents and family members, states Dr. Morrison.

260. Richardson, Julee J. "The Motivating Factor Influencing Compli-
      ance in Older Black Diabetics." Unpublished Doctoral Dissertation,
      University of California at San Francisco, 1984. 212 pp.

According to Dr. Richardson, maturity-onset diabetes is a serious
problem for older Black Americans. Noncompliance with the prescribed diabetic regimen affects the health professional's treatment of diabetes, the control of hyperglycemia and diabetic com-
plications. Using a modified version of the Health Belief Model,
this study examines the influence of health beliefs, costs and
barriers in carrying out the treatment regimen, and food attachments upon the diabetic compliance of thirty-seven older Black
subjects diagnosed as having maturity-onset diabetes melitus. The
data indicate that the majority of subjects were noncompliant.
Although 89 percent of the noncompliers adhered to the medication
regimen, 85 percent of these subjects did not adhere to diet. Non-
compliers were grouped according to specific types based upon the
qualitative influence of: (1) health beliefs; (2) behavior and
attitudes; and (3) food attachments. Compliance was influenced by
perceptions of the treatment efficacy, fear of illness consquence,
response to food, and sociocultural barriers, observed the researcher. It was also pointed out that 81 percent (N=27) of the
subjects were overweight. Eating patterns of the obese diabetic
involved an emotional response to food, which resulted in overeat-
ing and persistent hyperglycemia, aggressively treated with hypo-
glycemic therapy treatment, concluded the author.

261. Ross, Ruth E. "Comparative Health Measures: The Relationship
      Between Self-Perceptions of Health and Medical Health in a Popula-
      tion of Poor Urban Elderly Blacks." Unpublished Doctoral Disser-
      tation, Rutgers University, 1986. 255 pp.

Relationships among Self Perceived Health, Activities of Daily
Living, Use of Health Care Services, Physician Assessed Health

Ross, Ruth E. (Continued)

and Clinical Health Status were explored in a sample of 155 low income, urban, elderly Blacks. It was hypothesized that Self . Perceived Health would be congruent with Physician Assessed Health and useful to predict clinical/medical health status. Self perceived Health and Use of Health Care Services had low, but significant correlations with Physician Assessed Health. Forty-seven percent of the Self Perceived Health and Physician Assessed Health ratings were congruent. Activities of Daily Living had an r of .40 with Physician Assessed Health, Activities of Daily Living and clinical/medical health problems worsen with age, while the other measures do not. Analysis reveals that Self Perceived Health rather than Physician Assessed Health plays a pivotal role in determining Use of Health Care Services, while Activities of Daily Living predicts clinical/medical health status, declares Dr. Ross.

7. BLACK AGED AND MENTAL HEALTH

262. Cato, Susie M. "A Study of the Alterations in the Mental Status of Older Clients During Acute Hospitalization." Unpublished Master's Thesis, Howard University, 1984. 83 pp.

This study's findings found changes in mental status of older clients after four days of hospitalization. However, this study expanded the exploration of the cognitive domain as identified by other writers with the use of the Mini-Mental State Examination. An analysis of each client's nursing care plan provided data not revealed in Roslaniec's investigation. It is recommended that this study be replicated and that further investigation proceed to include nursing care plan recordings, control of client environmental conditions and Mini-Mental State evaluation during a specified home follow-up visit, concludes the researcher.

8. BLACK AGED AND LIFE SATISFACTION

263. Bailey, Shirley Barrett. "A Study of Selected Factors Related to the Social Satisfaction of the Residents of a Facility for Senior Citizens--The Roosevelt For Senior Citizens." Unpublished Master's Thesis, Howard University, 1975. 118 pp.

The author looks at the factors related to the social satisfaction of residents of the Roosevelt for Senior Citizens. The study was done to find out if residents were satisfied with living conditions with friends and relatives, and if lower income residents were as pleased as higher income residents.

264. Brooks, James, Jr. "Social Indicators and the Life Satisfaction of a Group of Black Elderly Americans." Unpublished Doctoral Dissertation, Catholic University of America, 1985. 146 pp.

This study examines the relationship between social activity, social relations and demographic factors and life satisfaction, using the Life Satisfaction Index A Scale (LSIA) as a measure of the dependent variable. 159 Black elderly Americans living

Brooks, James, Jr. (Continued)

primarily in age-heterogeneous environmental settings in both rural and urban areas were the subjects of the study. The data was
collected in ten senior citizen centers in and surrounding Jackson,
Mississippi. According to Dr. Brooks, bivariate analyses revealed
significant relationships between social activity and social relations and life satisfaction, therefore, supporting the proposi-
tions of the activity theory of aging. Regression analyses revealed that subjective health and social relations accounted for
13.1 percent of the variance in life satisfaction for the total
sample. For the rural respondents, subjective health and social
relations and distance from the nearest child accounted for 33.7
percent of the variance in life satisfaction. For the urban respondents, subjective health, perceptions of social problems, and
objective social relations accounted for 16.5 percent of the variance in life satisfaction, states the author. Partial correla-
tional analyses revealed no difference in rural-urban life satisfaction contrary to the Donnenwerth et al. (1978) study in which
rural Black elderly had higher life satisfaction than their urban
counterparts, concludes the writer.

265.   Hailstorks, Robin J. "Life Satisfaction Among Black Elderly
Women: A Retrospective Analysis." Unpublished Doctoral Dissertation, Ohio State University, 1983. 83 pp.

Sixty noninstitutionalized Black elderly women from two urban
areas served as subjects for this study. They were between the
ages of fifty-nine and eighty years of age. Subjects were selected based on two criteria: (1) thay they would be willing to be
interviewed for several hours; and (2) that they were not institutionalized (i.e., they did not reside in a nursing home). Several subjects were members of senior centers and served as hostesses
for these centers. The three periods of time were: young adulthood, middle adulthood and old age. Health, income, religiosity,
social affiliations, and attitude toward work, family, and life in
general were the aspects of life under study. The objective of
this study was to determine which of these variables were more
important in explaining the dependent measure life satisfaction,
and at what point in time were these variables more important in
explaining the dependent measure. Dr. Hailstorks concludes that
health, social affiliations, and religiosity were the variables
which accounted for more variance in the dependent measure than
any other variable at all periods of time under study. Results
also supported the recent findings regarding correlates of life
satisfaction for the general population . . . .

266.   Peterson, John L. "Personality Effects of Self-Esteem, Need
Motivation, and Locus of Control on the Life Satisfaction of Older
Black Adults." Unpublished Doctoral Dissertation, University of
Michigan, 1974. 106 pp.

The author points out that although the psychological effects of
aging have begun to receive considerable attention among white

Peterson, John L. (Continued)

adults, few studies have been concerned with these effects among
other ethnic groups. If similar results could be found for different ethnic groups as that available for White samples, there
would be greater support for theories concerned with personality
effects of aging. This assumption prompted the investigation of
the influence of personality factors on life satisfaction among
older Black adults. Specifically, the personality factors which
were assumed to affect life satisfaction were: (1) self-esteem;
(2) need motivation: need achievement (n Ach), need affiliation
(n Aff), and need power (n P); and (3) internal-external locus of
control: individual-system blame and individual-collective action.
The results indicated support for the effects of self-esteem and
internal-external control on life satisfaction among elderly Black
adults. However, with the exception of the findings for need
power, the effects associated with need motivation were negligible,
concludes Dr. Peterson.

267.   Sears, June L. "Selected Environmental Factors Related to Life
        Satisfaction of Black Senior Citizens." Unpublished Doctoral
        Dissertation. Michigan State University, 1975. 99 pp.

        This study was designed to answer questions relative to the degree
        of life satisfaction of low-income Black elderly people and their
        relationship to the following selected environmental factors:
        nutrition, activities, interpersonal relationships, income and
        health. The purposive, urban population sample selected consisted
        of 100 low-income Black men and women 60 years of age or older.
        Each was living independently (not receiving convalescent or home
        care) in either general or public housing or in a Senior Citizens'
        Center within the city of Inkster, Michigan. The feeling of life
        satisfaction among respondents was notably high in terms of scores
        reported on the life satisfaction index employed. Sixty percent
        scored three-fourths (15 or more) of the items positively. These
        findings may be interpreted to mean they were well satisfied with
        their lives, argues Dr. Sears. The study provided some guidelines
        for identifying needs and concerns of the elderly sample selected.
        It also gave some insights as to their attitudes, perceptions, and
        interests.

268.   Harper, Dee Wood, Jr. "Socialization for the Aged Status Among
        the Negro." Unpublished Master's Thesis, Louisiana State Univer-
        sity at Baton Rouge, 1967. 212 pp.

        The author points out that the larger Black community should take
        more interest in the Black aged and should be more responsive to
        their needs. According to the writer, the aged Black should have
        more contact with their own age group than with the larger Black
        community.

269. Tate, Nellie . "Social Interactional Patterns and Life Satisfac-
      tion of a Group of Elderly Black Widows." Unpublished Doctoral
      Dissertation, Brandeis University, 1981. 207 pp.

      This study examined the relationship between the social interac-
      tion patterns and life satisfaction of a group of elderly widowed
      Blacks. It was anticipated that those widows with high levels of
      interaction and those who obtained support from informal systems
      would be more satisfied with their lives. Survey data were exa-
      mined from 65 vulnerable widowed Blacks in Philadelphia. They
      ranged in age from 64-92 (mean age 78.04). Almost two-thirds
      (42 or 64.6 percent) were 75 years of age and older. The mean
      educational level was 6.9 years. In terms of previous occupation,
      30 or 46.2 percent were employed in professional, skilled and
      semi-skilled positions. The overwhelming majority, 55 or 85 per-
      cent indicated they had adequate incomes. Only 36 of these women
      had living children. They had been widowed a mean of 21.4 years
      and had lived a mean of 48.4 years in the Philadelphia area.
      While it was found that these widows were embedded in a network
      of family and friends, communication appeared to flow from the
      widow to other members of the network. Communication between the
      various members of the network was almost nonexistent, stated
      Dr. Tate. Although these women had numerous physical complaints,
      the majority (54 or 83.5 percent) were satisfied with life, in-
      come, attitude toward present living situation, perceived health
      status, and the presence of a confidante were found to be the best
      variables in predicting life satisfaction for these widows,
      asserts the writer.

                    9.   BLACK AGED AND EDUCATION

270. Christian, Judy A. "An Investigation of the Educational Preferen-
      ces of Older Aged Black Adults." Unpublished Doctoral Disserta-
      tion, Catholic University, 1982. 194 pp.

      This study identified the educational preferences of aged Blacks
      (i.e., persons 60 and over) participating in the Continuing Edu-
      cation for Older Adults (CEOA) Program, Institute of Gerontology
      (IOG), University of the District of Columbia (UDC), Washington,
      DC. The educational preferences were identified with respect to
      content areas, instructional strategies, and logistical techniques
      as perceived by the primary sample of aged Blacks, CEOA/IOG/UDC
      (n=560) and the secondary sample of Institute (IOG/UDC) staff
      (n=20). This was done to develop an educational program state-
      ment for aged Blacks, states Prof. Christian. Three hypotheses
      were tested: (a) the educational preferences of aged Blacks
      (CEOA/IOG/UDC) with respect to content areas, instructional stra-
      tegies, and logistical techniques vary according to sex, age, edu-
      cational level, and income level; (b) there is difference in the
      perceptions of the educational preferences between aged Blacks
      (CEOA/IOG/UDC) and Institute (IOG/UDC) staff; and (c) if there is
      a difference in the perceptions of the educational preferences,
      agreement can be achieved through a consensus development tech-
      nique. The findings of the study indicate that: generally, aged
      Blacks agree on their educational preferences; consumers and

Christian, Judy A. (Continued)

gerontology practioners disagree on the educational preferences; and agreement can be achieved through a consensus development technique, concludes the writer.

10. BLACK AGED AND CRIME

271. McMurray, Harvey L. "The Criminal Victimization of the Elderly in Washington, DC." Unpublished Master's Thesis, Howard University, 1982. 108 pp.

As a result of this study, the following recommendations were made as possible means by which community action can be initiated to minimize the criminal victimization of the elderly residents of Washington, DC:
1. Black men, women, low-income and unmarried persons should be the primary focus of public or community action programs relative to crime and the elderly.
2. The elderly should be encouraged to participate in community crime watch programs.
3. The elderly should avoid travelling alone whenever possible.
4. A committed effort should be made in providing employment for the youth of the District of Columbia, especially Black males.
5. Programs to educate youth about the elderly should be implemented in the school system, especially on the subject of the impact of crime on the elderly.
6. The police should give special attention to residential areas known to be occupied by elderly persons.
7. The police should make victim information a part of their crime statistics and analysis.
8. The police should be utilized more as a referral and information network in providing the types and ways to contact support systems to those persons victimized.
9. The elderly should avoid carrying cash on their person when possible.
10. Fact sheets and other forms of information dissemination should be distributed among elderly persons to educate them on crime related issues, crime prevention, and support services.

11. URBAN BLACK AGED

272. Beard, Virginia Harrison. "A Study of Aging Among a Successful, Urban Black Population." Unpublished Doctoral Dissertation, St. Louis University, 1976. 138 pp.

In this investigation an effort was made to identify some distinguishing characteristics more or less common to successful Black aged persons. The areas of investigation were life satisfaction, adjustment, the person's self perception of being Black in a predominantly White society. The group was identified by the criteria: 1. Education, at least a high school graduate, 2. Income, more than $3999 annually of a single aged person. 3. Health, reported to be in fair to excellent health, with no more than one chronic illness. Data was gathered by an extensive questionnaire

Beard, Virginia Harrison   (Continued)

including the Life Satisfaction Scale Index Z (LISZ), the Stages
of Black Awareness Scale, and several questions constructed for
use in this study to measure adjustment and change with age. Subjects were selected at random from rosters of Black organizations
in St. Louis City and County and on recommendation of community
people. The sample was 100 men and women ranging in age from 34
to 91 years, however, only six were below age 50. Conclusions indicated that successful Black aged, very much alike in certain
socioeconomic ways, still appeared quite heterogeneous in terms
of life satisfaction, Black self perception and by other variables. The researcher recommended that more studies of a descriptive and exploratory nature be done using larger numbers of subjects of successful Black aged and for other sub-groups in order
to provide more information and to identify predictor variables.
It was also recommended that the exclusion of Blacks from important aging studies should only be done when it can be determined
and validated that race is an extraneous variable for the researching of a particular construct.

273.   Benton, Beverly C. "Quality-Of-Life Measurements Among Inner-
City Black Older People." Unpublished Doctoral Dissertation,
Tulane University, 1983. 150 pp.

Dr. Benton argues that little research has been undertaken with
inner-city elderly minorities; consequently, no scale has been
constructed or adapted that shows sensitivity to unique historical experiences or cultural differences among these population
groups. The primary aims of this research are to: (1) examine
the appropriateness of the Life Satisfaction Index A(LSI-A) for
measuring successful aging among Black inner-city older people,
and to (2) construct a morale index, drawing from Kutner Moral
Scale, the Life Satisfaction Index-A (LSI-A), and others to
measure successful aging among Black inner-city older people.
Also, an instrument to measure religiosity, and a second one to
measure specific value orientations will be constructed. These
instruments will be suitable for social science research among
this population group, states Prof. Benton.

274.   Dancy, Joseph, Jr. "Religiosity and Social-Psychological Adjustment Among the Black Urban Elderly." Unpublished Doctoral Dissertation, University of Michigan, 1978. 297 pp.

This study addresses itself to two universal phenomena, aging and
religion in an examination of the relationship of religion to the
socio-psychological adjustment of the urban Black elderly. The
data for this study is taken from an earlier study conducted by
Gary T. Marx of the University of California which originally
focused on anti-semitism in the United States. The total sample
of that study included 1,119 Black metropolitan residents of
which 182 persons were age 60 and over. The latter group constitutes the respondents in this present study. These data include
six questions which could serve as measures of religiosity. These

Dancy, Joseph J.   (Continued)

questions related to (1) belief in God, (2) Jesus as Savior, (3) importance of religiosity, (4) life beyond death, (5) existence of the devil, and (6) attendance at worship services. The primary mode of examining the relationship between religiosity and socio-psychological adjustment was through use of cross-tabulations and correlations. In an effort to determine the extent to which this relationship could be explained by the demographic variables, multi-variate tables, partial correlations, and multiple regres-sion were utilized. According to the author, the results indi-cated that those factors which most decidedly separated those Black elderly who measured high in religiosity from those who measured low in religiosity were: income, being raised on a farm, sex, educational level, and number of years at present residence. The Black elderly, overall, showed a high level of religiosity by responding quite strongly to the extreme favorable position of the six religiosity items, concludes Dr. Dancy.

275.   Dhaliwal, Sher Singh. "A Sociological Description and Analysis of A Non-Random Sample of Low-Income, Washington, DC, Aged Negroes." Unpublished Master's Thesis, Howard University, 1967. 152 pp.

The author describes selected social characteristics of an elderly group living in a low-income area of Washington, DC. The charac-teristics studied were living arrangements and conditions, eco-nomic status, social and leisure time activities, religious and civic activities, and attitudes toward themselves, death, living arrangement and programs for the aged.

276.   Harris, Roland A. "A Study of Black Aged Persons." Unpublished Doctoral Dissertation, University of Tennessee, 1981. 245 pp.

According to Dr. Harris the consequences of age segregation and peoplehood segregation were examined for three subgroups of Black aged persons. The term "peoplehood" rather than race was pre-ferred for use in this study to reduce the extent of racial over-tones, states the writer. Contextual settings for the subgroups were (A) age and peoplehood segregated; (B) age segregated and peoplehood integrated; and (C) age integrated and peoplehood se-gregated. Demographic characteristics were very similar for the subgroups. Depth interviews were conducted with the 235 subjects who were ages fifty-five or older. They were low-income and not highly educated. Most had migrated to the small urban area of Knoxville and had been residents over ten years. Variables for each subgroup were compared. Chi-square was used as a test of significance and phi-square used to measure the strength of asso-ciation. When compared with peoplehood integrated subjects, peoplehood segregated subjects were more satisfied with their housing. Also, peoplehood segregated subjects compared with peo-plehood integrated subjects walked more and used other transpor-tation less on weekdays. Age segregated subjects were less fami-liar than age integrated subjects with public and private agencies,

Harris, Roland A. (Continued)

according to the author. The senior citizens center in the peoplehood segregated site promoted activities, interaction, and
communications to a greater extent than those at the other two
sites. The greater use of agencies by persons dwelling at site
A was a possible consequence, concludes the writer.

277.   Heisel, Marsel A. "Learning and Information Seeking Activities
          of Urban, Aged, Black Adults." Unpublished Doctoral Disserta-
          tion, Rutgers University, 1983. 156 pp.

This study explored the extent and ways in which a group of 132
older educationally disadvantaged, urban Black men and women engaged in formal and non-formal learning activities. A Learning
Activity Label (LAL) scale was developed from the data, and
factors associated with high LAL scores were identified using
multiple regression analysis. Learning was broadly defined to
include all purposeful attempts to acquire knowledge and information. There was great variability in both educational history
and current learning activity levels among respondents. Much of
what they learned was self-taught and they preferred educational
activities in informal places. The majority were regular readers,
mostly reading newspapers and the Bible, states the researcher.
Few reported difficulty in meeting daily reading demands, but 68
percent said they would like to learn to read better and 44 percent said they would attend instruction if it were made available. Results also showed women, and those who consider their
reading ability to be good, tend to be more active learners ($p <$
.001). Age and educational attainment had no independent effect
on learning, asserts Prof. Heisel.

278.   Holden, Cedric M. "An Analysis of Need Among the Black Elderly:
          Implications for Administering Human Services Delivery Systems."
          Unpublished Doctoral Dissertation, University of Michigan, 1984.
          219 pp.

This study was designed to uncover the needs of 100 low income
Black elderly residing in public housing in the inner-city of
Detroit, Michigan. Findings disclosed an average ten percent
greater level of impairment than was found in several other comparable studies or reported in governmental statistics. Moreover, 96% of the subjects reported full impairment in the area
of income/economics, according to Dr. Holden. Persons providing
assistance to the elderly were among the members of the informal
social network (i.e., friends and family). Friends and their
families were often given fictive-kin relationships. Evidence
of the existence of an extended family was found. Offspring
were often absent in the day-to-day lives of their elderly
parent(s), concludes the author.

279.   Lambing, Mary L. "A Study of Retired Older Negroes in an Urban
        Setting." Unpublished Doctoral Dissertation, University of
        Florida, 1969.   224 pp.

        The purpose of this study was to investigate the lifestyle of
        American Blacks retiring from the professions, from stable blue-
        collar work, and from the service occupations, domestic work, and
        common labor. Data were obtained from interviews of 101 retired
        Blacks in Alachus County, Florida. About one-third of the inter-
        views were carried out by non-Whites. Because social class mem-
        bership has repeatedly been found to be an important determinant
        of behavior, this factor was emphasized throughout the study.
        The A. B. Hollingshead Two-Factor Index of Social Position was
        used to ascertain social status of respondents. Thirteen pro-
        fessionals were interviewed, which constituted a local availabi-
        lity sample made up primarily of school teachers. There were
        only 15 retirees from blue-collar occupations who could be in-
        cluded in the study. A representative sample of 73 people drawn
        from the rolls of the Department of Public Welfare had been in
        service occupations, domestic work, and common labor. Some of
        the latter group were also recipients of social security bene-
        fits. Retired Blacks had an average of 3.02 living children.
        Of those with living children, 25% lived in the same household
        with a child and 52% had at least one child living in the same
        town. Fifty-six percent saw their children weekly or more often.
        Indications were that these Blacks had much closer relationships
        with siblings than retired people in studies made with White
        subjects. Mutual assistance patterns were similar to those
        found in earlier gerontological research. When a study of active
        roles was made, these Blacks did not show evidence of disengage-
        ment after the age of 65, concludes Dr. Lambing.

280.   Mason, Elaine F. "Fear of Death in Elderly Black Women."
        Unpublished Doctoral Dissertation, Boston University, 1979.
        170 pp.

        For this research, forty Black women between the ages of sixty-
        five and eighty-nine were interviewed and tested in individual
        sessions of 2-4 hours each. All lived independently in the Bos-
        ton area and were free from medical problems that would limit
        physical activity. Experiences with the death of others explains
        the most variance in measured fear of death. This finding was
        the most consistent throughout the study in that those women who
        had experienced the deaths of many relatives had few negative
        thoughts about death, little fear of their own impending death
        and few inconsistent thoughts about death, declares Dr. Mason.
        She states that a high percentage of deaths among friends, on
        the other hand, was associated with many negative thoughts about
        death, suggesting that the deaths of friends are more emotionally
        significant to older women and therefore increase negative death
        conceptions. Violent deaths among friends and relatives were
        associated with fear of one's impending death while witnessing
        those deaths was associated with many death fantasies. Prof.
        Mason concludes: "The study suggests that greater individualized
        assessment and programming is indicated for elderly Black women.

Mason, Elaine F. (Continued)

Although the small sample size limits generalizability, longitudinal research efforts should consider the impact of death events, religious affiliation and locus of control on the fear of death."

281.   McCumming, Betty L. H. "The Incrementalist Nature of Public Policy: Service Utilization Implications for the Black Elderly Under the Older Americans Act." Unpublished Doctoral Dissertation, Syracuse University, 1977. 148 pp.

The purpose of this study was to critically examine and assess the incrementalist nature of public policy development, and to discern through the analysis of selected performance measures how incrementalism affects the manner in which the Black elderly determines to utilize services legislated under the Older Americans Act of 1965. Data were gathered from three different populations of persons: (a) Black elderly users of the Nutrition Program, (b) Black elderly non-users, and (c) administrators, planners and implementors associated with the Nutrition Program in Syracuse, New York. The findings of this study, supported by data from all three groups of respondents confirmed that the incrementalist nature of public policy carries serious implications for the Black elderly citizens of Syracuse, New York. This is especially true in their use of the Nutrition Program, Title VII of the Older Americans Act, asserts Dr. McCumming. These groups-users, non-users and administrators, planners and implementors, all agreed that were it not for serious breaches in the program's accessibility, accountability, comprehensiveness, coordination, ability to disseminate knowledge about the service and willingness to allow participation, this program would be much more greatly used and appreciated by the Black elderly, concludes the author.

282.   Nall, Hiram A. "Just Like Brothers: An Ethnographic Approach to the Friendship Ties of an Urban Group of Elderly Black Men." Unpublished Doctoral Dissertation, University of California at Los Angeles, 1982. 243 pp.

The study helps to fill the gap in knowledge about the lifeways of elderly Black men, and reveals the importance of one type of life-enriching resource (friendship ties) and one type of life-sustaining resource (a coffee shop) in the process of growing old. A delineation and examination of the group's significance is carried out in conjunction with analysis of its various unique structural aspects which promote its viability. These include: (1) a sense of belonging which involves the sharing of resources and services and the mutual support of group members, (2) the presence of status and leadership roles which promote positive self-images among group members, (3) flexibility of social structure which accommodates the needs of individual group members, (4) and a structuring of social relations that allows the group to function as an adaptive mechanism promoting successful adaptation to the aging process. . . .

283.   Sauer, William J.   "Morale of the Urban Aged: A Regression Analysis By Race." Unpublished Doctoral Dissertation, University of
Minnesota, 1975.   208 pp.

Past research in the field of social gerontology has paid little
concern to morale of aged Blacks. The purpose of this research
was to develop a model, based primarily on previous research on
aged White samples, and examine the degree to which the predictors of morale were isomorphic for aged Whites and aged Blacks.
A search of the literature revealed that such a model would consist of the following variables: Age, sex, race, education, occupation, income, marital status, health, participation in voluntary associations, interaction with relatives, friends and neighbors. The data consisted of a random sample of low income aged
Blacks and Whites in Philadelphia and were collected by the late
Donald P. Kent as part of the Aged Services Project he was directing. The sample consisted of 936 elderly, 722 of which were
Black and 214 of which were White. All respondents were 65 years
of age or older, states the author. The author argues that the
results of the analyses indicated for Blacks the only two significant predictors of morale were health and participation in solitary activities, with the former being the most important. For
Whites, in addition to health and solitary activities, interaction with family and sex were also found to be significant. Unlike Blacks, however, solitary activities were the most important
followed by health, with sex and family interaction being of
lesser importance, suggests Prof. Sauer. It was concluded that
for these data the predictors are not isomorphic between races;
further work is needed using more heterogeneous samples to demonstrate the differences the proposed model suggests exist
between races.

284.   Smith, Alicia D.   "Life Satisfaction and Activity Preference
Among Black Inner City Center Participants: An Exploratory
Study." Unpublished Doctoral Dissertation, University of
Massachusetts.   Massachusetts, 1978.   109 pp.

The purpose of this investigation was to identify Black senior
center participants who reside in a northeastern urban community,
and to determine if there is a relationship between individual
preferences for particular learning activities and those living
conditions which account for life satisfaction. In addition, the
study was intended to investigate the elderly's perception of
"survival" or coping needs. The results indicate that (1) the
population of Black senior center participants tend to be as diverse as the general population, (2) health, length of residency
and age are significant correlates of life satisfaction, (3)
length of residence is the single best predictor of life satisfaction, and (4) participants prefer activities which are personal
and health related. The importance of the leisure and social atmosphere at the centers in attracting participants and the possi-
bility that survival skills perceptions may be a result of the interaction between reality and attitudes as defined by life and
cultural experiences, are emerging issues. It is concluded that,
for this population, aging adjustment means engaging in and enlarging upon social interactions and experiences rather than disengaging.

285.   Taylor, Sue P.   "Aging in Black Women: Coping Strategies and
        Lifeways Within an Urban Population."   Unpublished Doctoral Dis-
        sertation, University of Massachusetts, 1978,   250 pp.

        The study is based on data collected during a 1976-77 ethnogra-
        phic study of the lifeways and coping strategies of Black women
        between the ages of 59 and 97 in a metropolitan New England com-
        munity.   The bicultural experiences of Black women are revealed
        through life histories.   Today, the women, like the general aging
        population, represent a heterogenous group.   Yet, similarities in
        behavior, attitudes, and coping strategies exist and are attri-
        buted to cultural patterns which have persisted throughout the
        women's lifespan.   Their personal/cultural coping mechanisms
        serve as a sustaining force in face of the adversities of being
        old, Black, female and sometimes poor in urban America, Dr.
        Taylor concludes: "Values orientations which emphasize faith,
        family and a strong adherence to the American work ethic shape
        adaptive mechanisms and enable individuals to use kinship con-
        nections as problem-solving devices."

286.   Williams, Kamalee H.   "Perceptions of Retirement Activities in
        Retirement of Some Urban Low-Income Black Elderly."   Unpublished
        Doctoral Dissertation, United States International University,
        1980.   178 pp.

        This descriptive analytic study investigated perceptions of re-
        tirement and activity participation among a selected group of
        noninstitutionalized urban low-income Black elderly men and wo-
        men aged 60 and older.   The purpose of the study was to determine
        and describe (1) perceptions of the retirement experience, (2)
        social activities participation, (3) selected demographic cha-
        racteristics associated with those opinions of retirement and
        activity participation among selected urban low-income Black el-
        derly individuals.   On the basis of the data presented in the
        study, the following conclusions were evident: (1) Retirement
        was perceived as occurring primarily because an individual was
        unable to continue employment.   Very few were of the opinion that
        people retired specifically to devote more time to leisure acti-
        vities.   While low-income urban Black elderly may retire volun-
        tarily, negative situations that provide feelings of uselessness
        seemed to be determinants for initiating retirement.   (2) Early
        retirement was not favored.   Employment preferences included job
        maintenance as long as permitted by health or employer.   (3)
        During retirement, job maintenance should not be a requisite for
        survival, but an available option.   (4) There was significant
        involvement of respondents with family, church related activities,
        and current political issues.   Low-income urban Black elderly
        seemed proud of their ability to "make do" with the little they
        possessed, suggests Dr. Williams.

287.   Williams, Lois L.   "Analysis of Social and Community Needs of
        Black Senior Citizens in Inner City Detroit."   Unpublished Docto-
        ral Dissertation, University of Michigan, 1977.   157 pp.

Williams, Lois L. (Continued)

The purpose of this study was to make available some of the information concerning the complex needs of the Black senior citizen and to identify supportive services designed to enhance the
capacity of this elderly population to improve its quality of
life. The results indicated that the majority of the Black
senior citizens were found to be satisfied with their living conditions despite a multitude of seemingly negative characteristics
such as: (1) substandard housing facilities located in the midst
of an urban area, (2) Presence of an unusually high crime rate,
(3) A relatively low socio-economic status, (4) Apparent psychological conditions of resignation, (5) A sense of complacency
with respect to those areas over which they felt they had no control, states Prof. Williams. The results and implications of the
study suggest future research in the following areas: (1) A
study to delineate the peculiar problems attendant to the aging
Black urban poor in America as contrasted to those common to
other urban populations, (2) A study to determine the needs of
Black senior citizens living in their own home sites as opposed
to those living in public facilities, (3) a comparative study of
the success of social service agencies in delivering identical
basic social services to (a) senior citizens in public high-rise
housing as contrasted to (b) senior citizens in their own home
sites.

12. RURAL BLACK AGED

288.   Ball, Mercedes Elizabeth. "Comparison of Characteristics of
       Aged Negroes in Two Counties." Unpublished Master's Thesis,
       Howard University, 1967. 223 pp.

       This study was done to find selected characteristics of an elder-
       ly group of rural and urban Blacks to compare patterns of aging
       in Dodge and Chatham counties in Georgia. The characteristics
       included housing, family and friendship relationships, leisure
       and recreation, religious and social activities, use of local
       programs and facilities, health, education, and economic status.

289   Davis, Abraham, Jr. "Selected Characteristic Patterns of a
       Southern Aged Rural Negro Population." Unpublished Master's
       Thesis, Howard University, 1966. 149pp.

       This is a descriptive survey of selected social characteristics
       of the aged, rural Blacks in Macon County, Alabama. The author
       discusses such characteristics as living conditions, family and
       friendship relationships, leisure time and religious activities,
       attitudes toward desired residential patterns, problems and
       death, awareness and use of facilities for the aged and health
       problems.

290.   Nicken, Lois C. "Functional Assessment and Coping Behavior
       Among the Rural Black Elderly." Unpublished Doctoral Disserta-
       tion, University of Florida, 1984. 185 pp.

Nicken, Lois C. (Continued)

Research for this dissertation was conducted from 1981 to 1984 among rural elderly residents living independently in their communities in Alachus County, Florida. Fifty-four elderly persons, Black and white, were recruited through the snowball sampling procedure to participate in the Functional Assessment phase of the study. Subsequently, the Black elderly persons participated in an in depth examination of coping behaviors, according to the researcher. The Black elderly scored higher on the FAI than their white counterparts. Scores of 17 or more on the FAI are believed to indicate possible need of institutionalization and many of the sample were in this category. However, these Black elderly, their FAI scores notwithstanding, were not in need of institutionalization. The high scores of the Black elderly are attributable to the language of the instrument often not being understood and standardization procedures of the language to their education, surmises Dr. Nicken. The author concludes that the results showed that the Black elderly have made adaptive adjustments to their cultural milieu which included rural living, poverty and lack of transportation.

291.   Page, Helan E. "Praxis in the Life-World: Intentional Structures Binding the Rural Black Elderly and Their Help." Unpublished Doctoral Dissertation, Northwestern University, 1984. 195 pp.

The author spent 18 months of resident field-work in a Afro-American community. The researcher learned of the residents' taken-for-granted knowledge about (1) their "place" in the white world; (2) how at-risk the "place" of the elderly is in light of changes in local, national and world existential conditions; and (3) how data produced by the research activity is unavoidably co-constituted through the communicative relationship between the researcher and the community who makes a "place" for her. The conclusions: that the community's life-world is not divorced from, but rather is dialectically related to the Euro-American life-world; that unequal access to upward mobility and exploitive treatment by whites is accepted by most residents as being "just the way life is," and, that most Afro-American residents assume that Euro-America will maintain the advantage of affirming its own thematic significations (cultural meanings) and so will continue imposing them on relatively powerless minorities until an awareness of their own innate potential motivates these minorities to co-constitute a life-world they prefer.

292.   Randall-David, Elizabeth W. "Mama Always Said: The Transmission of Health Care Beliefs Among Three Generations of Rural Black Women." Unpublished Doctoral Dissertation, University of Florida, 1985. 237 pp.

This research examines the transmission of health care information, attitudes and practices among three generations of women in a representative rural Black community in the American South. Rather than looking at the community as a single entity, this

Randall-David, Elizabeth W. (Continued)

study examines the continuities and discontinuities in health care beliefs and practices among three generations of family members in four age cohorts. Hypertension, a prevalent health problem in the Black community, was chosen as the focus of inquiry. Research findings indicate that older women in the community are still perceived as important sources of general health care information. However, their influence has been attenuated through contact with the health care system and through health information provided by the mass media and school based health education. The four age cohorts reported differential degrees of reliance on the various sources of health information, younger women relied more heavily on the mass media and health care professionals for health information than did older women, argues the writer. However, data regarding health care practices related specifically to hypertension indicate that in actuality there are few differences among the age groups. Although in general the responses across generations were similar, there was a trend towards more biomedically congruent beliefs and practices among younger respondents, concludes the researcher.

293.   Spencer, Mary L. S. "The General Well-Being of Rural Black Elderly: A Descriptive Study." Unpublished Doctoral Dissertation, University of Maryland, 1979. 158 pp.

This study was based on 60 Black males and females who were residing in the rural areas of southern Prince George's County, Maryland. The general well-being assessment showed that 62% of the population was functioning without any or with slight impairment, while 38% had impairments of greater severity or in more than one area of functioning. When each of the functional areas was examined, it was found that 82% of the sample scored excellent or good in social functioning, and 70% scored good or excellent in mental health functioning. In the area of physical health, 40% of the subjects were functioning at a good or excellent level, and 56% were functioning at a good or excellent level in the activities of daily living. However, in the area of economic resources, 47% of the population was moderately impaired or worse. Dr. Spencer concludes: "The findings also revealed that there were no significant differences between males and females in the general well-being status or in any of the five areas of functioning. Likewise, there were no significant differences in general well-being among those subjects who were married, widowed, or single, separated or divorced."

294.   Wilson, Vanessa. "The Impact of Social-Psychological Factors on the Life Satisfaction of the Rural Black Elderly." Unpublished Doctoral Dissertation, Ohio State University, 1985. 136 pp.

The sample chosen for this study consisted of 140 randomly selected Black elderly people who reside in the rural town of Elm City, North Carolina. This population was then stratified into two groups: young-old (55-74) and old-old (75 or over). The two

Wilson, Vanessa (Continued)

groups were then divided into four categories: thirty (30) young-old and old-old males; and forty (40) young-old and old-old fe-males. The findings of this study indicate that on the Life Satisfaction (A) scale, religion, health, reminiscence and educa-tion were important in explaining the variance found in life sa-tisfaction. However, the Life Satisfaction (B) scale, social activity, religion, age, health and sex were important for pre-dicting high levels of life satisfaction. Of all the variables chosen for analysis, socioeconomic status was found to have no significant relationship to life satisfaction, concludes Dr. Wilson.

13.   BLACK AGED IN SUBURBIA

295.   Huling, William E. "Aging Blacks in Suburbia: Patterns of Culture Reflected in the Social Organization of a California Community." Unpublished Doctoral Dissertation, University of Southern California, 1978. 191 pp.

The primary objective of this study is to provide qualitative information about the effects of culture on the social organiza-tion of a Southern California suburban Black community, known here as Pierce Park. Key social systems of the mostly self-segregated enclave are examined for cultural patterns shared by a sample of aging, long-time residents who migrated to the com-munity in its formative years. The social organization of Pierce Park is aligned with cultural similarities of its residents, states Prof. Huling. The relationship between cultural patterns and survival skills varies according to the amount of external tension present. In the absence of disturbing tensions, life-style increases and survival skills become dormant or extinct. Inter-generational differences reflect a changing value system between the elder residents and their offspring, and is threaten-ing the survival of the community. Self-segregation is a method of preserving lifestyle, concludes Dr. Huling.

14.   COMPARATIVE BLACK AND WHITE AGED

296.   Curran, Barbara W. "Getting By With a Little Help From My Friends: Informal Networks Among Older Black and White Urban Women Below the Poverty Line." Unpublished Doctoral Disserta-tion, University of Arizona, 1978. 186 pp.

The underlying assumption in this research was that ethnicity affects human behavior with respect to growing old. It was an-ticipated that differences resulting from ethnic factors could be observed in the ways respondents used formal and informal support systems. One hundred women, aged sixty or over, living in a Southwestern city, were interviewed. All had incomes below the poverty level and were living without marital partners. The sample was equally divided between Black and White women. Com-parison between ethnic groups revealed substantially greater use of both formal and informal support systems by older Black women. Black women made greater use of alternative medical systems, had

Curran, Barbara W.   (Continued)

larger networks of family and friends, participated at greater rates in institutional support systems, and rated themselves higher with respect to health and happiness than did White women, states Dr. Curran.   These differences were attributed to the closely cooperative lifestyles of Black women.   These patterns of mutual support were thought to be a highly sophisticated cultural adaptation to historic and economic circumstances.   While individual White women shared these cooperative values at times, as a group, patterns were at significant variance by ethnicity and White women appeared to exhibit independence, not interdependence. Other influential factors in this sample were discriminatory patterns of housing segregation for Black women and a rural southern background common to most Black respondents, but to only a few White women in the sample, asserts the author.

297.   Davis, Dolores Jean.   "Guide for Minority Aging Program at The Institute of Gerontology, University of Michigan: Student Perception Approach."   Unpublished Doctoral Dissertation, University of Michigan, 1974.   142 pp.

The purpose of this study was to develop a guide for a minority aging program at the Institute of Gerontology, University of Michigan (U-M).   A twenty-five item questionnaire was constructed to assess U-M gerontology students' perceived needs, interests and attitudes related to (1) the need for additional minority aged curricula, (2) assessment of the present minority aged content in the U-M gerontology curriculum in meeting their educational and training needs, (3) perception of how these needs can be satisfied.   The questionnaires were distributed in gerontology courses and/or mailed to all (120) gerontology students enrolled during the 1974 spring term.   The total response rate of 79, 15 Black respondents (100%) and 64 White respondents (60%) was considered to be a normal distribution of U-M gerontology students for any given term.   The guide for the minority aging program included the following recommendations: (1) A minimum of 20% of the gerontology curriculum should pertain to the study of minority aging; (2) Minority aged content should be incorporated in all gerontology courses where appropriate and taught as special courses; (3) An Ethnicity and Aging course should be a required course for all gerontology majors; (4) Additional faculty with competencies in this area of specialization should be hired; (5) Recruit additional minority students; (6) The three major components of the minority aging program should consist of research, training and service.

298.   Eaton, Thelma L.   "Social Functions and Personal Autonomy in Black and White OAS Recipients."   Unpublished Doctoral Dissertation, University of Southern California, 1973.   234 pp.

The purpose of this study was to examine the nature of the association between social functioning and personal autonomy in Black and White aged.   It also sought to explore what influence such

Eaton, Thelma L.   (Continued)

variables as race, socioeconomic status, coping and health might
have on this association. The study was designed to investigate
these four independent variables for their relationship; first,
to social functioning; second, to personal autonomy. The stratified random sample consisted of 80 elderly persons (40 Black, 40
White) drawn from the OAS clientele of the Department of Public
Social Services of Los Angeles County. These 80 individuals were
selected from over 354 clients who were English-speaking, noninstitutionalized and ambulatory. Eighteen participants were
determined to have high levels of social functioning and 62 low
levels of social functioning. Scores were based on five vital
areas of life experiences; work and interest, finance, friendship, family and intrapersonal relationships. Apparently, most
of these OAS recipients were experiencing limited amounts of
satisfaction in their efforts to cope, states Prof. Eaton. The
Black subgroup and the White sub-group had similar patterns of
satisfactions. Blacks derived the most satisfaction from contacts with friends and Whites from family relationships. Both
gained the least satisfaction from financial situations. Social
functioning of the White sub-group was more in jeopardy than that
of the Black subgroup, according to the author. Statistical analysis of the data revealed that there was no significant association between the level of social functioning and race, lifetime
socioeconomic status, coping or health. Forty-two participants
had high levels of personal autonomy and 38 low levels. Therefore, these aged persons cannot be characterized as basically dependent individuals. There were more low than high determiners
in the Black subgroup. The reverse was true for the White subgroup. Neither race, socioeconomic status, coping or physical
health was statistically related to levels of personal autonomy,
concludes Dr. Eaton.

299.   Engler, May. "A Comparative Study of the Needs of Black and
        White Functionally-Impaired Elderly." Unpublished Doctoral
        Dissertation, Fordham University, 1982. 235 pp.

        This study sought to determine similarities and differences in
        needs of Black and white functionally impaired, 60 and over, re-
        ceiving federally-funded home care services in an urban center,
        and to determine as well the extent of the interrelatedness of
        characteristics: physical health, mental health, and functional
        ability. It also sought to identify patterns of supports and
        services utilized, requested, and provided for the two study
        groups (N=219 white), and to describe selected demographic
        characteristics. The findings identified a severely functionally
        impaired, but not homogeneous population receiving far fewer
        services than they needed. Moreover, Black and white elderly
        are more alike than different in their needs, condition, and
        services. Although in somewhat better condition than white el-
        derly, Black elderly were less likely to receive needed services,
        declares the researcher. Black elderly were younger and receiv-
        ing medical care from municipal hospitals or clinics. Thus, the
        use of older age (75 and over) as the focus for special services

Engler, May (Continued)

would place an unfair burden on the functionally impaired, particularly Black elderly. Regarding medical care, patterns of utilization should be considered before implementing changes to
avoid unfair burdens on local populations, according to the
author. The study also found a less than perfect relationship
between functional ability and either physical or mental health.
Since it is possible to measure functional ability on an easily-
administered checklist of activities of daily living, this can be
important in training programs and service program organization,
concludes Dr. Engler.

300.   Gold, Joan Beth Klemptner. "A Study of Kinship Ties and the
        Institutionalized Aged: The Relationship Between Sources of
        Referral and Payment for Institutional Care of the Aged in
        Chicago, and Their Geographic Distribution, Their Nearest Rela-
        tives, and Their Last Non-Institutional Address." Unpublished
        Master's Thesis, University of Illinois at Chicago Circle, 1971.
        71 pp.

        The title tells what this work is about. Various references are
        made to the Black aged throughout this work. The author points
        out that the racial composition of the long-term care aged is
        overwhelmingly White (91 percent): non-Whites comprise less than
        7 percent. In 1960, 8 percent of the aged population in metro-
        politan Chicago was non-White. Looking at the Black population
        only, the author found a larger proportion of males (36 percent)
        among this population than in the total institutionalized aged
        group. Sixty-three percent of the Blacks have been referred by
        Public Aid while only 17 percent have been referred by them-
        selves or their families. This is due to a combination of fac-
        tors, including the low socio-economic status of the Black popu-
        lation, contends Gold. The major source of payment for the
        Blacks makes it evident that social class is operating to some
        extent. Although only 63 percent had been initially referred by
        Public Aid, 75 percent are not having their care paid for by
        Public Aid; 10 percent are paid for privately, and 15 percent by
        medical insurance and other sources. Since the Black population
        is different from the larger institutionalized group in several
        ways, special consideration was given to them in the analysis.
        The author states that for the Black population, referral source
        is not related to the distance variables, but major source of
        payment is. Blacks who pay privately live closer to nearest re-
        latives but farther from their last non-institutional community
        than do Black Public Aid clients, concludes the author.

301.   Ruberstein, Daniel I. "The Social Participation of The Black
        Elderly." Unpublished Doctoral Dissertation, Brandeis Univer-
        sity, 1972. 357 pp.

        This study was based on a subsample of 487 Black, 3,419 White
        men and women 65 years of age and older from a national survey
        of elderly persons entitled Residential Physical Environment and

Ruberstein, Daniel I. (Continued)

Health of the Aged. The purpose of this study was to explore
the social participation and well-being of the Black elderly (in
comparison with the White elderly). Through the examination and
analysis of data (obtained from personal interviews) the following objectives were addressed: (1) to describe the household
situations and present an associational analysis of the participation of the respondents with their families and kin, friends
and neighbors, and social organizations, and to measure the effect that this participation had on their morale or well-being:
(2) to gather relevant information on the aged Black person; and
(3) to relate the findings of this study to the provision of more
effective social welfare services for the Black elderly through
recommendations. The findings of this study suggested the following recommendations for programs for the elderly: (1) efforts
should be made to raise income levels, and also Old Age assistance, as it is now practiced, should be replaced structurally
by a less stigmatizing and more equitable and inclusive procedure
of ensuring economic security; (2) the means of communication
(telephone, transportation, etc.) for the Black elderly should
be increased to expand opportunities for social interaction and
social service; (3) group participation by the Black elderly
should be encouraged and discriminatory barriers against participation should be eliminated; and (4) base line demographic data
for program planning and development should be developed and
further study and research on the Black elderly sub-group in
Social Gerontology should be encouraged.

302.   Seelback, Wayne Clement. "Filial Responsibility and Morale
        Among Elderly Black and White Urbanites: A Normative and Beha-
        vional Analysis." Unpublished Doctoral Dissertation, Pennsylva-
        nia State University, 1976. 178 pp.

        This study is concerned with an examination of the normative and
        behavioral dimensions of filial responsibility, and the bearing
        which these two dimensions themselves and the congruence or in-
        congruence between them might have upon the morale of aged
        parents. The sample consisted of 595 low-income, urban elderly,
        seventy-five percent of whom were Blacks; their ages ranged from
        sixty-five to ninety-nine. The data were collected by teams of
        two or three interviewers who were mostly indigenous to the
        neighborhoods in the study. Data were analyzed by the Lazarsfeld
        Partial Table Method, with square and gamma employed as measures
        of significance and strength of association, respectively. Under
        both zero and first-order conditions, there were no significant
        racial differences in (a) type of expectation for filial respon-
        sibility, (b) levels of realized filial responsibility, or (c)
        patterns of normative-behavioral congruence. However, signifi-
        cant zero-order associations were found between type of expecta-
        tions for filial responsibility and age, marital status, income,
        health, and the extent to which a parent engaged in certain soli-
        tary activities. Similarly, significant zero-order associations
        were also discovered between levels of realized filial responsi-
        bility and gender, marital status, income, health and proximity

Seelback, Wayne Clement (Continued)

of offspring. And also at the zero-order level gender, marital status, income, health and solitary activity were significantly associated with types of normative-behavioral congruence. A significant inverse zero-order association was found between morale and types of filial responsibility expectations. This association was further found to be conditioned upon race, gender, age, marital and occupational statuses, solitary activity, religion, and proximity of children. Specifically, the inverse association held only for Blacks, females, unmarried, low occupational status, low solitary activity, Protestants, and persons whose children lived relatively near.

303. Stojanovic, Elisabeth J. "Morale and Its Correlates Among Aged Black and White Rural Women in Mississippi." Unpublished Doctoral Dissertation, Mississippi State University, 1970. 125 pp.

It was the purpose of this study to assess the level of morale of aged (60 and over) Black and White, low-income, rural women and to determine the relationship of their morale with activities and selected demographic, economic, social and attitudinal characteristics. The data were part of a larger nonage-stratified sample of households in six low-income counties in Mississippi, collected in 1961. The author declares that Black women had relatively high morale. They preferred outdoor activities, such as gardening and fishing, as their pastimes. Better housing and recreational facilities were among their expressed needs. Self-reported place on the ladder was an important predictor of the self-image about statics which, in turn, was significantly and positively correlated with morale. The White women did not appear to possess the high morale displayed in the Blacks. Their greatest concern was about their health. The higher the activity score, the lower their morale. They tended to engage in variety pastimes, especially reading and television viewing. The latter was significantly and negatively correlated with morale and was the most important predictor of morale, concludes Dr. Stojanovic.

304. Stone, Virginia. "Personal Adjustment in Aging in Relation to Community Environment: A Study of Persons Sixty Years and Over in Carrboro and Chapel Hill, North Carolina." Unpublished Doctoral Dissertation, University of North Carolina, 1959. 280 pp.

The author discusses the Black people of both Chapel Hill and Carrboro that form a community between the two boundaries of the towns, with the railroad track, as usual, being one of the dividing lines. This makes us have Community A, Chapel Hill White; Community B, the Black population; and Community C, the Carrboro White. A census was conducted to determine the number of persons who were 60 years and over. A total of 910 people 60 years and over were located in this area. The author found 552 in Community A, 206 in Community B, and 152 in Community C. In gathering this information, she selected this on a demographic basis, getting sex, age, and race. The oldsters of Community B were often

Stone, Virginia (Continued)

the sons and daughters of slaves. Most of these oldsters had sub-
stitute parents, and the father figure may have been completely
absent. It is this old Black who had built the family pattern
that we are accustomed to. So, the old Black still maintains
more family control than either of these White communities. In
fact, very few of them live alone--a small percentage of them are
living alone, 8.7 percent. Over one-fourth of them are living
with relatives. One of the fascinating factors about this is
that the young Black moves in with the old Black. The old Black
owns the home, and since the young move in with the old, the old
Black maintains his role as head of the household. Hence, there
is not the same role change in this community as there is in the
other two communities, states Prof. Stone. The old Black had
nothing to turn to outside of work but religion, and religion
offered him the outlet to release those things that were pent up
in him for so long. The older Black of today is dissatisfied
with the Black church of today because "The church has gone fan-
cy," and it doesn't provide him the opportunity for the expression of emotionalism that the old church did, asserts the writer.
One of the interesting things about the church pattern here is
that the author found that the older Black usually maintains his
membership in the rural church but comes under the watchcare of
the town church, so that he still has a tie with the church that
gives him a chance for expression. . . .

305.   Votan, Thomas E. "Death Anxiety in Black and White Elderly Sub-
        jects in Institutionalized and Non-Institutionalized Settings."
        Unpublished Doctoral Dissertation, Auburn University, 1974. 88 pp.

        This study was designed to investigate the effects of three vari-
        ables on the level of death anxiety in an aged population. The
        variables were: (1) Race (Black vs. White), (2) Sex (male vs.
        female), and (3) Institutionalization (institutionalized vs. non-
        institutionalized). A personality inventory was also utilized to
        examine the relationship between personality factors and level of
        death anxiety. Eighty (80) elderly volunteers, equally divided
        with respect to the three variables, served as Ss. An effort
        was made to control for age, mental and physical health, religion,
        intelligence, length of institutionalization, and social class.
        Statistical analysis indicated that institutionalized Ss mani-
        fested significantly higher death anxiety levels than non-insti-
        tutionalized Ss (p .001), but the variables of race and sex had
        no effect. Institutionalized Ss also showed significantly more
        "neurotic" symptomology than non-institutionalized Ss; correla-
        tion analysis revealed a significant positive correlation between
        level of death anxiety and degree of neurotic preoccupation as
        measured by Mini-Mult scales: (1) (Hypochondriasis, r=.28), (2)
        (Depression, r= .31) and (3) Hysteria, r= .29). Personality in-
        ventory differences were found between Black and White Ss, but
        were interpreted with caution due to recent evidence that postu-
        lates these differences may well be due to subcultural differen-
        ces rather than the idea that Blacks are more "pathological"
        than Whites.

306.   Williams, Michael R. "The Effects of Social Security's Title I
        and Title II Programs Amendment Changes Upon the Social/Economic
        Well-Being of Elderly Black Americans (1935-1972)," Unpublished
        Doctoral Dissertation, University of Michigan, 1984. 208 pp.

This historical retrospective policy analysis examined the effects of the Title I and II legislation upon the Black elderly
population. More specifically, the study outlined the effects
of the original legislation and the subsequent amendments of
1939, 1950, 1954 and 1972 upon this population of American citizens. Major findings of the study were: first, the Black elderly, both in an economical and social sense, fared worse than
their white counterparts under the legislation in question. Second, the Black elderly was more likely to remain impoverished
under the original and present old-age legislation. Third, the
Black elderly was more likely to be negatively stigmatized under
these programs. This was due in large part to the fact that the
Black elderly was likely to be more dependent upon the welfare-
oriented Title I program because of low annual earnings. The
overall findings of the study supported the major thesis of the
work--namely that if the needs of all the nation's citizens are
not considered in a major policy decision, then various groups
within the population will be differentially affected, possibly
in a negative fashion, by the decision, concludes Dr. Williams.

15. MINORITY AGED

307.   Adams, James P., Jr. "Social Service Needs By Minority Elderly:
        A Critical Cross-Cultural Analysis." Unpublished Doctoral Dis-
        sertation, University of Minnesota, 1979. 246 pp.

This study was undertaken with two specific objectives in mind:
(1) to determine if a common network pattern emerges relative to
the preference of assistance for certain types of service needs
within and between older members of three ethnic groups--Blacks,
Japanese-Americans and Latinos--in San Diego County; (2) to determine if there is an association between types of service needs
preferred and other factors such as age, education, family member living status and income. It was found that minority elderly
preferred to seek out "intimate" types of arrangements more frequently than they did "informal" and "formal" arrangements. La-
tinos were the most consistent in preferring "intimate" arrangements; Blacks preferred "informal" arrangements more frequently
than any other minority group under investigation while the Japa-
nese-American elderly were more flexible in their preference towards a variety of arrangements depending on the particular service needs, concludes Dr. Adams.

308.   Chen, Pei Ngor. "Continuity/Discontinuity of Life Patterns
        Among Minority Elderly in Nutrition Programs." Unpublished Doc-
        toral Dissertation, Univ. of Southern California, 1978. 304 pp.

The study aimed to determine the extent to which life patterns
represented by food patterns, health status, social interaction,
and program activities, of Black, Mexican-American, and Chinese-

Chen, Pei Ngor (Continued)

American elderly, were reflected by participation in three nutrition programs; particularly to test hypotheses regarding conti-
nuity/discontinuity theory in social gerontology. According to
Dr. Chen, the majority of the participants were not poor, but
sociable and gregarious elderly in fairly good health. Opinions
of staff coincided with the participants' in certain aspects,
such as preferences for food and activities, but differed in
other aspects, such as objectives for participation in the nutrition program. The ethnicity of the participants had influenced
administration of the nutrition programs and the selection of
friends. There were considerable differences and similarities
among ethnic groups regarding life patterns at age 40 and now,
states the author. Using 1970 United States Census poverty
thresholds as comparison, only one-fourth of the total sample
could be considered poor. The Chinese-American elderly had
slightly lower monthly income than the other groups. The Black
elderly were well assimilated into the American way of life. The
Chinese-American elderly were the most isolated and lonely group.
The Mexican-American elderly were the most sociable and healthy
group. However, nutrition programs had helped most participants
to improve their physical health and happiness and prevented
greater loneliness. Opportunities for socialization rather than
food or program activities were the main attraction of nutrition
programs, concludes the researcher.

309.   DeRidder, Joyce A. "Sex Related Roles, Attitudes, and Orienta-
tion of Negro, Anglo, and Mexican-American Women Over the Life
Cycle." Unpublished Doctoral Dissertation, North Texas State
University, 1976. 142 pp.

The focus of this study is the relationship among (1) attitudes
toward sex-based differentiation in adult leisure activities and
socialization of boys and girls, (2) attitudes toward housekeeping, and (3) combinations of marital, maternal, employment, and
head of household statuses among Negro, Anglo, and Mexican-
American women in three categories and from two socio-economic
levels. It is concluded that the lack of association between the
two attitudinal variables and the role structure variable may be
the result of the lack of refinement in the attitudinal and role
combination measures, due to limitations of a secondary analysis
of data. It is recommended that future studies direct attention
to the differences created by ethnicity and various familial sex
role constellations, concludes the author.

310.   Gitelman, Paul. "Morale, Self-Concept and Social Integration:
A Comparative Study of Black and Jewish Aged, Urban Poor." Unpublished Doctoral Dissertation, Rutgers University, 1976. 250 pp.

In this study two distinct groups of aged, urban poor, Blacks and
Jews, form the study population. The respondents reside in de-
teriorating urban areas, characterized by low income. Adjustment
to old age was measured by the major dependent variables, morale,

Gitelman, Paul. (Continued)

self-concept and social integration, each subdivided into four
dimensions. A questionnaire was constructed for the Jews through
selection of items from Faulkner and Heisel's questionnaire with
adjustments made for specific group-related differences. Hypotheses were formulated regarding the relationships of designated
ideal-types with dependent variables. From the findings it is
confirmed that religion, race and ethnicity have an impact on
adjustment to old age. Current objective circumstances seem to
be of secondary importance in regard to one's life satisfaction
while levels of previous attainment provide important perspectives on life satisfaction. The writer states the position of
the aged study group members as societal survivors is highlighted
and the hypothesized strength of the married Jewish female, the
stereotypical "Jewish Mother", is not confirmed. The limited
utility of morale as a measure of actual need is indicated and
the profound actual and potential impact of religion for the respondents is stressed.

311.   Phillips, Gayle Y. "The Quality of Life Among Black and Hispanic
        Elderly in Three Southern Cities." Unpublished Doctoral Disser-
        tation, University of Pennsylvania, 1983. 313 pp.

Social indicators have evolved over time to monitor the quality
of life in American residential environments. Objective indicators are used more frequently in policy and planning activities
than subjective indicators. Subjective assessments should be
considered along with objective indicators in monitoring environmental conditions. Few research studies have examined in a
causal manner the multiple societal forces operating in the residential environment and upon the lives of racial-ethnic elderly.
While residential satisfaction and environmental quality are associated with residential mobility, the elderly tend to be long-
time dwellers in their neighborhood and prefer to remain in fami-
liar settings rather than to move. In lieu of moving, citizen
participation is an alternative to increase levels of residential
satisfaction and quality, asserts Prof. Phillips. By utilizing
an existing data set from the four year national evaluation of
the Community Development Block Grant Program, the descriptive
and multivariate findings reveal that objective and subjective
indicators are influential in determining the quality of life
among racial-ethnic minority elderly in the South. From the
findings, future research endeavors should explore changes in
quality of the experiences among racial-ethnic minorities in
several age groups, concludes Dr. Phillips.

16. BLACK AGED AND HISTORICAL STUDIES

312.   Pollard, Leslie J. "The Stephen Smith Home for the Aged: A
        Gerontological History of a Pioneer Venture in Caring for the
        Black Aged, 1864 to 1953." Unpublished Doctoral Dissertation,
        Syracuse University, 1978. 250 pp.

Pollard, Leslie J. (Continued)

The purpose of this dissertation is to provide historical perspectives of the Black aged. The emphasis on the extended family
has obscured a salient fact of the Afro-American experience:
that the Black community provided a many-sided support of the
elderly. A balanced view of the care of elderly Blacks must include mutual aid societies, benevolent associations and old
folks' homes. The dissertation is also designed to fill a gap in
gerontological literature by providing a study of institutional
care in an historical context. The involvement of Quakers in the
Home sheds greater light on an historic interracial contact.
Over 2,200 residents lived in the Home between 1865 and 1953.
The great majority came from Philadelphia, having migrated there
from such neighboring states as Virginia and Maryland. The Home
was run under a dominant Quaker influence best described as pa-
ternalistic. Viewing the residents as children, the managers defined their needs and provided what they considered best for
them. The writer argues that old age was viewed as a time of
leisure, reflection, and preparation for death. Though some did
not object to this concept of old age, others degenerated mentally in an atmosphere of resignation. Not a few clashed with administration, rebelling against enforced idleness and lack of
stimulation. Since management denied work outside the Home, it
emphasized entertainment, with an undue emphasis on religion.
The author concludes that poverty and family breakdown were important factors that brought residents to live in the Home.
Where relatives existed they were an important asset, providing
personal care to the sick, engaging physicians, inquiring about
proper treatment, and withdrawing the mentally ill, concludes
Dr. Pollard.

313.   Reilly, John T. "The First Shall Be Last: A Study of the Pattern
       of Confrontation Between Old and Young in the Afro-American
       Novel." Unpublished Doctoral Dissertation, Cornell University,
       1977. 203 pp.

       Most often the elder represents the protagonist's past, his heri-
       tage, and the ethos of his people, and the lessons he attempts to
       teach the protagonist are in sum the formidable and ubiquitous
       truths of Black life that he, himself, has learned from his ex-
       periences since slavery times. To survive, to define himself,
       to understand himself in relation to the world around him, to
       prosper, and/or to maintain his humanity, the protagonist is
       required to accept his elder's wisdom, or, in some way, to become
       reconciled with him, states Dr. Reilly. In a sense, his elder is
       the roots to which he, the young tree of Black life must be
       joined if he is to flourish. One of the significant facts dis-
       closed by this dissertation is that while this pattern of con-
       frontation somewhat varies from novel to novel, the concern for
       the Black heritage of struggle for freedom and advancement re-
       mains a constant, concludes the author.

314. Sherman, Eugene G., Jr. "Social Adjustment of Aged Negroes of
      Carbondale, Illinois." Unpublished Master's Thesis, Southern
      Illinois University, 1955. 68 pp.

      The hypotheses, in the present study, were grouped under five
      categories: 1. Living Arrangements, 2. Source of Income, 3.
      Childhood Happiness, 4. Religion, and 5. Health. Forty-five
      males and forty-five females age sixty-five and over were inter-
      viewed using a revised form of the Cavan Schedule to secure data
      to test the hypotheses. These hypotheses, with the conclusions
      based on the data of this study, are summarized as follows:
          1. Among the aged Blacks in general, the majority of persons
      reside in the home of near relatives.   SUPPORTED
          2. Among the aged Blacks, more women than men reside in the
      home of their children.   SUPPORTED
          3. Among the aged Blacks, there are more individuals who re-
      ceive financial assistance from their near relatives than there
      are individuals whose support comes from Old Age Assistance.
                                                       NOT SUPPORTED
          4. Among the aged Blacks, more women than men receive aid from
      their near relatives.   SUPPORTED
          5. The degree of childhood happiness influences the adjustment
      in old age.   SUPPORTED
          6. Attendance at religious services tends to become more
      frequent in old age.   NOT SUPPORTED
          7. Good health is an important factor in adjustment to old
      age.   SUPPORTED
          8. In comparison with the state of health at age fifty, there
      is a marked decline in the state of health for the aged Blacks
      sixty-five and over.   NOT SUPPORTED
          In view of the present study the idea is advanced that the
      aged Blacks of Carbondale, Illinois, reflect a high degree of
      adjustment. The persons reflected the following characteristics:
      (1) Decreased participation in activities with age. (2) Increase
      in economic dependency with age. (3) Increased feeling of secu-
      rity and derivation of satisfaction from religion. (4) Belief in
      life after death. (5) Slight decline in health after passing
      sixty-five.

315. Washington, Harold Thomas. "A Psycho-Historical Analysis of
      Elderly Afro-Americans: An Exploratory Study of Racial Price."
      Unpublished Doctoral Dissertation, University of Massachusetts,
      1976. 151 pp.

      This is a study of racial pride across four historical periods
      based on retrospective interviews with elderly Afro-Americans.
      The four major Afro-American historical periods spanning from the
      1890s to the present include: segregation, integration, Black
      power, and Black nationalism. Three measures of racial identifi-
      cation were developed: racial pride scale, attitudes toward Black
      leadership scale, and the leadership awareness index. The general
      hypothesis reflecting significant differences in leadership aware-
      ness across the four historical periods was made during the inte-
      gration phase and the lowest assessment was made during the Black
      power period. People from the higher SES group were significantly

Washington, Harold Thomas (Continued)

more aware of Black leaders than people from the lower SES group
in both the integration period (t=3.06, p. less than .01) and in
the Black power period (t=3.51, p. less than .01). The Southern
sample was significantly more aware of Black leadership than the
Northern sample (t=4.13, p. less than .001), suggests Prof.
Washington.

5.

GOVERNMENT PUBLICATIONS

1. BLACK AGED FEMALES

316. Jackson, Jacquelyne J. "Improving the Training of Health Para-Professionals." Mental Health: Principles and Training Techniques in Nursing Home Care. Margaret S. Crumbauth, Editor. Rockville, MD.: National Institute of Mental Health, 1972, pp. 56-57.

This brief paper concentrates specifically upon one group: nursing, housekeeping, and food service paraprofessionals employed or likely to be employed in the South, the vast majority of whom are or are likely to be Black females. Many of these Black females are family heads or, if in husband-wife families, significant contributors to their total family income. Most often, they labor diligently for wages at or below the poverty level without even minimally desirable fringe benefits, such as those of an established period of two consecutive days away from and five days at work during each week. Dr. Jackson feels strongly that it is very important to initiate or upgrade training in mental health in these various curricula within high schools, vocational schools, or other technical training programs so that students would be certified to work in the field following the completion of the course or courses. Some attention should be given to developing internship programs in conjunction with the formal training on the high school level, underwritten by such funds as those available from the Neighborhood Youth Corps (NYC). Appropriate rewards--including pay for internship in nursing homes under supervision--should be included. Beyond that, there must be significant upgrading in wages and fringe benefits and fewer deadending jobs for such workers if there is to be a real attempt to reduce heavy personnel turnover, states Dr. Jackson. There may well be a need to consolidate smaller nursing homes, even if it means transferring residents to a larger complex since any home under 200 or so beds would be extremely unlikely to provide an atmosphere especially conducive to training and effective utilization of training as well as opportunity for upgrading personnel. Above all, attention must be given to defining precisely who is to be trained by whom, for what, and when, where, and how, argues Dr. Jackson. Currently, the researcher believes that any training program designed for Black female paraprofessionals should include training personnel who are themselves Black.

2. BLACK AGED AND THE FAMILY

317. Huling, William E. "Evolving Family Roles For The Black Elderly."
      Aging, September-October, 1978, pp. 21-27.

      The researcher argues that historically, older Blacks have pro-
      vided a cohesiveness for the family by offering both material and
      spiritual support to their children and grandchildren. He further
      contends that the practice of treating the aged as assets rather
      than as liabilities to the family has been demonstrated through
      the years by Southern Blacks. The author states that the process
      of acculturation and assimilation into the major social system is
      expected to dilute, if not destroy, both the traditional and cul-
      tural vestiges found in the Black family of past generations. Dr.
      Huling concludes that as more Blacks become urbanized, it appears
      that the persistence of traditional roles for the Black aged is
      highly uncertain.

3. BLACK AGED AND HEALTH CONDITIONS

318. Jackson, Jacquelyne J. "Special Health Problems of Aged Blacks."
      Aging, September-October, 1978, pp. 15-20.

      The writer discusses primarily health perceptions, age changes,
      prevalent diseases, functional health, and the use of health re-
      sources as they relate to aged Blacks. She argues that perhaps
      the most significant issue is the conditions under which health
      resources should be color-blind or color-specific for aged Blacks.
      The sociologist states that health is a crucial problem for most
      aged Blacks. Dr. Jackson concludes that since the few Federal
      attempts to set forth research needs for aged Blacks in the past
      have generally ignored critical participants, including biomedical
      researchers, epidemiologists, health planners, and health providers
      experienced in treating aged Blacks.

319. Ostfeld, Adrian M. "Nutrition and Aging--Discussant's Perspec-
      tive." Epidemiology of Aging. Adrian M. Ostfeld and Don C.
      Gibson, Editors. Washington, DC: United States Government Print-
      ing Office, no date given. DHEW Publication No. (NIH) 75-711, pp.
      215-222.

      The author points out that reliable data regarding diseases among
      aged Blacks are fragmented. Neither is much known about relation-
      ships between various conditions, such as obesity and strokes,
      nor between their morbidity. Recent mortality rates, based upon
      the underlying cause of death, show that diseases of the heart,
      malignant neoplasms, and cerebrovascular diseases account for
      about three-fourth of the deaths of all aged Blacks. The writer
      questions the traditional assumptions about undernutrition and
      overnutrition in older persons. Also some forms of heart or
      cerebrovascular diseases commonly thought to be affected sub-
      stantially by obesity may not be so affected among the aged,
      concludes the writer.

320. Shank, Robert E. "Nutrition and Aging." Epidemiology of Aging.
      Adrian M. Ostfeld and Don C. Gibson, Editors. Washington, DC:
      United States Government Printing Office, No date given, DHEW
      Publication No. (NIH) 75-711, pp. 199-213.

      The limited nutritional data available about aged Blacks suggest
      that their mean caloric intake is below standard, regardless of
      income level, as based upon body weight for age, sex, and height.
      Below standard, however, does not necessarily imply insufficien-
      cies. The researcher concludes that the diets of Blacks, 60 or
      more years of age, were characteristically low in iron, thiamine,
      and calcium, but they showed no serious deficiencies.

4. BLACK AGED AND HOUSING

321. Johnson, Roosevelt. "Barriers to Adequate Housing for Elderly
      Blacks." Aging, September-October, 1978, pp. 33-39.

      Dr. Johnson concludes that if the Federal government is serious,
      prototype models can be developed and implemented to achieve the
      goals of adequate housing for elderly Blacks and to eradicate
      traditional barriers. Moreover, contends the author, the perva-
      siveness of racism and its negative effects will, by necessity,
      be lessened.

5. BLACK AGED AND INCOME

322. Lindsay, Inable B., Editor, Consultant. U.S. Senate. Special
      Committee on Aging. The Multiple Hazards of Age and Race: The
      Situation of Aged Blacks in the United States. Report Number 92-
      450. Washington, DC: U.S. Government Printing Office, September,
      1971.

      The editor states that statistics for 1971 on persons below the
      low income level in 1971 indicate that almost twice as many Blacks
      65 years and over still fall below the low income level (38.4 per-
      cent) as compared to the same age group of Whites (19.9 percent).
      Dr. Lindsay contends that because of higher mortality rates for
      Blacks and less longevity, a substantial number of Black males in
      the age group 55 to 64, die before reaching the age of eligibility
      for such social security benefits as they might be entitled to.
      She states that a proposal for differentials in age eligibility
      met considerable opposition, being called by some plea for "pre-
      ferential treatment." She also relates that housing is another
      problem for the Black aged. According to the 1970 census, about
      30 percent of the housing units occupied by the elderly were
      judged substandard. For the Black elderly, the situation is
      doubly distressing. In 1969, 63 percent of the Black aged relocat-
      ing in public housing were moving from substandard housing compared
      to only 30 percent of the Whites who were relocating, concludes
      the scholar.

323. Orshansky, Mollie. "The Aged Negro and His Income." Social Secu-
      rity Bulletin, Vol. 27, February 1964, pp. 3-13.

      The researcher contends that the income of the average White work-
      er is more sharply reduced in retirement than the income of the
      Black worker, thus drawing the two groups closer together in the
      common bond of stringency. The author asserts that for some time
      to come, many Blacks reaching age 65 will continue to have limited
      resources and to be more dependent than White persons on public
      aid.

324. Rubin, Leonard. "Economic Status of Black Persons: Findings
      From A Survey of Newly Entitled Beneficiaries." Social Security
      Bulletin, Vol. 37, September, 1974, pp. 16-35.

      Information from the Social Security Administration's Survey of
      Newly Entitled Beneficiaries was analyzed for economic status dif-
      ferences between Blacks and Whites to become entitled to payable
      than to postponed benefits and particularly to full rather than
      reduced benefits. At whatever age they become entitled and what-
      ever their payment status was, they were less likely than Whites
      to have high PIA's (over $150) and retirement pensions other than
      social security. Those whose retirement income was limited pri-
      marily to social security benefits and whose PIA's were less than
      $150 subsisted at a level around the poverty line. Included in
      this low economic status were 88 percent of the Black women, 62
      percent of the Black men, 65 percent of the White women, and 32
      percent of the White men. The writer concludes that earned income
      is especially important for those with inadequate retirement in-
      comes, but low economic status was most often associated with being
      constrained to stop work for health or job-related reasons rather
      than with a positive desire to stop work. The relative disadvan-
      tage of Blacks, and of women, was pervasive, holding for every
      characteristic tabulated, states the author.

325. Social Security Administration, Office of Research and Statistics.
      "Current Medicare Report: Supplementary Medical Insurance--Utili-
      zation and Changes, 1972." Health Insurance Statistics, Septem-
      ber 30, 1975.

      This article states that according to the HEW Medicare Survey
      Report for 1972, over half of the Blacks enrolled in Supplementary
      Medical Insurance (SMI) either received no services or were not
      able to meet the deductible. In other words, the majority of
      elderly Blacks do not benefit from Medicare coverage because they
      cannot afford the payments, and over half of all poor elderly
      Blacks, whether living alone or in families, do not receive any
      Supplemental Security Income.

326. Thompson, Gayle B. "Black Social Security Benefits: Trends 1960-
      1975." Social Security Bulletin, Vol. 38, April 1975, pp. 30-40.

      Blacks and Whites are compared with respect to selected provisions
      of the OASDHI program--type of beneficiary, age of beneficiaries,

Thompson, Gayle B.   (Continued)

size of benefits, and size of covered earnings--for the time
period from 1960-1973. There have been substantial increases in
the number of Black beneficiaries since 1960, and in most benefi-
ciary groups Blacks have increased proportionately more than
Whites. The writer argues that Blacks are heavily represented
among young beneficiaries but are underrepresented among aged beneficiaries. The average monthly benefit of Black beneficiaries
was substantially below that of White beneficiaries in 1973, and
the gap in benefit levels has narrowed only slightly since 1960.
Several reasons for this discrepancy--the most important of which
are differentials in the size of covered earnings and years in
covered employment--are discussed. The scholar concludes that
discrepancies in benefit levels will persist for some time, at
least among men, because of continued earnings within the younger
generation.

327. Williams, Blanche Spruiel. Characteristics of the Black Elderly-
      1980. Washington, DC: United States Government Printing Office,
      1980. 41 pp.

This is a statistical report on the Black elderly that was prepared for the United States Department of Health and Human Services. Patricia Roberts Harris was Secretary of HEW when this
report was issued. The writer discussed such topics as "Size of
the (Aged) Population," "Marital Status," "Living Arrangements,"
"Labor Force," "Income and Poverty," "Education," "Mortality,"
"Life Expectancy," "Health," and "Crime." It was concluded that
the number of elderly Blacks is increasing at a substantially
faster rate than the general population and also the elderly
White population. Moreover, a greater percentage of older Blacks
than Whites are without social security benefits or are recipients
of benefits based on lower wages . . . .

6. BLACK AGED AND NURSING HOMES

328. "Home for Aged Colored Persons." Monthly Labor Review, August
      1929, Vol. 29, pp. 284-288.

This is a study of Black Homes for the aged. A survey was made
in 18 states and the District of Columbia. There were 33 homes
that cared for 742 persons at an annual cost of about $135,000.
The largest number of persons, 185, were in Louisiana. This state
only spent $8,573. Pennsylvania, however, spent $42,277 for 178
people. This article points out that generally speaking the
physical conditions at the Black homes did not equal those at the
homes for Whites. All of the Black homes, except one, had a
Black matron or superintendent.

329. Ingram, Donald K. "Profile of Chronic Illness in Nursing Homes,
      United States, August 1973-April, 1974." Vital and Health Statis-
      tics, Series 13, #29, DHEW Publication (PHS) 78-1780. Hyattsville,
      MD: National Center for Health Statistics, 1977.

      The writer points out that based upon a 1973-1974 survey, there
      were 49,300 Black residents of nursing homes in the United States.
      This represents 4.6 percent of the total number of residents.
      Almost one-fourth of them were under 65 years of age, although
      only 11 percent of all residents were under that age. Little more
      than over half of them were in the South. The author believes
      that this figure may suggest that aged Blacks may experience par-
      ticular difficulties in obtaining institutionalization within the
      South, or that other factors, such as past memories of exclusion,
      play a role.

330. U.S., Congress, Senate, Special Committee on Aging, Trends in
      Long Term Care, 92nd Cong., 1st sess., 1972. Testimony by Hobart C.
      Jackson at public hearing on August 10, 1971, pp. 2475, 2476.

      Mr. Jackson points out that because of the universal focus on pro-
      viding alternatives to institutionalization for frail or other-
      wise dependent elderly, which has been overlooked, is actually the
      reverse: "The problem . . . is not one of how to keep the older
      Black person out of a nursing home or similar institution," he
      said, "it is rather, how to get him or her in a good one . . . ."

7. BLACK AGED POPULATION

331. Hill, Robert B. "A Demographic Profile of the Black Elderly."
      Aging, September-October, 1978, pp. 2-9.

      The author discusses population size, urbanization, educational
      attainment, marital status, life expectancy, Family composition,
      housing, amount of income, poverty, sources of income, employment
      status, and standard of living of the Black elderly. The re-
      searcher argues that the social and economic status of elderly
      Blacks today are significantly better than they were a decade ago.
      Between 1970 and 1975, the life expectancy of Blacks increased by
      almost three years and the gap with Whites narrowed by at least
      one year. Thus, there has been a sharp decline in the proportion
      of elderly Blacks who are widowed. Dr. Hill concludes that al-
      though elderly Blacks have made significant strides, they still
      have a long way to go in achieving an equitable and adequare
      quality of life.

332. United States Bureau of the Census. "Estimates of the Population
      of the U.S. by Age, Sex, and Race: 1970 to 1977." Current Popu-
      lation Reports, Series P-25, No. 721, 1978.

      Since 1970, the Black aged population has been increasing more
      than twice as fast as the overall Black population. While the to-
      tal Black population increased by 11 percent, the number of Blacks

United States Bureau of the Census (Continued)

65 and over increased by 25 percent--from 1.6 million to 1.9 mil-
lion--raising the proportion of elderly persons in the total
Black population from 7 to 8 percent.

8. BLACK AGED AND POLITICS

333. Chunn, Jay. "The Black Aged and Social Policy." Aging, September-
October, 1978, pp. 10-14.

The writer declares that the social policy in the United States
designed to serve the aged continues to be fragmented and at times
contradictory. He continues to state that a higher level of political consciousness must be developed for the elderly vote because
politicians tend to respond to those constituencies that vote together. The researcher feels that the presence of an adequate income level for aged Blacks would help to alleviate many problems
suffered by this population. More adequate food could be purchased, services would be more accessible through money for transportation, more adequate housing could be maintained or secured
and so on. He concludes that there is a sense of urgency that
should be recognized within the body politic of public policy as
it determines social policy outcomes. The quality of life of aged
Blacks is, perhaps, declining, instead of improving. The policy,
programs and services needed by the Black aged and all elderly
must ultimately be set forth and must prevail in the public arena,
contends the writer.

9. MINORITY AGED

334. Koch, Hugo K. "National Ambulatory Medical Care Survey."
Vital and Health Statistics, Series 13, #33, DHEW Publication
(PHS) 78-1784. Hyattsville, MD: National Center for Health
Statistics, 1978.

The author points out that in 1975, non-White aged accounted for
only 1.1 percent of all visits to office-based physicians in
patient care. Of those who visited, about 11 percent were new
patients with new problems, and the remaining 71 percent were old
patients with old problems. The physicians felt that about 31 percent of these patients had serious problems, about 36 percent,
slightly serious problems, and the problems of the remaining 33
percent were not serious, according to Koch.

335. U.S., Congress, Senate, Special Committee on Aging. A Pre-White
House Conference on Aging. Summary of Developments and Data.
92nd Cong., 1st sess., 1971, Rpt. 92-505.

This report states that it is becoming increasingly clear that the
problem (of elderly Blacks in need) is really one of multiple
jeopardy, compounded by a shortage of reliable statistical information on key matters. In fact, this information gap has emerged
as a vital issue in all Committee on Aging research related to
minority groups, according to the study.

10. COMPARATIVE BLACK AND WHITE AGED

336. Abbott, Julian. "Socioeconomic Characteristics of the Elderly:
     Some Black-White Differences." Social Security Bulletin, Vol. 40,
     July, 1977, pp. 16-42.

     This article compares several characteristics of the Black and
     White population aged 60 and older in March 1972. To distinguish
     race from economic-status effects the population is divided into
     quintiles of elderly units ranked by size of money income, and com-
     parisons of selected demographic and economic characteristics are
     made within and across quintiles. Differences between social
     security beneficiaries and nonbeneficiaries are also analyzed to
     ascertain the effects of social security benefits. The researcher
     states that the educational and occupational disadvantages of
     Blacks were evident even at the highest income level--a status more
     likely to be achieved by married Black couples with both spouses
     working. The writer concludes that Black elderly units were less
     likely than Whites to have social security benefits, other govern-
     ment or private pensions, or income from assets. They were
     generally more likely to have earned income or to receive public
     assistance payments.

337. Mallan, Lucy B. "Women Born in the Early 1900s: Employment,
     Earnings, and Benefit Levels." Social Security Bulletin, Vol. 37,
     March, 1974, pp. 3-16.

     In general, Black women earn much less than White women, and Black
     men earn much less than White men. Though both earnings and length
     of employment are higher for Black men than for Black women (as is
     true for White men and White women), the relative patterns are not
     the same. When the length of covered employment since 1950 is
     examined, distributions for Black women and White women (and for
     Black men and White men) are the same, states Mallan. The writer
     argues when earnings are examined, however, earnings for Black and
     White women and for Black men are, respectively, 31 percent, 54
     percent, and 63 percent of White men's. The author states earnings
     of Black men are closer to those of White women than to those of
     White men and about twice those of Black women. The author con-
     cludes these differences in earnings would have been even greater
     had the data included postponed as well as payable awards, since
     White men and women (with their higher earnings) postpone their
     awards more often than Black men and women postpone theirs.

338. Manuel, Ron and Marc L. Berk. "A Look at Similarities and
     Differences in Older Minority Populations." Aging, No. 339, May-
     June, 1983, pp. 21-29.

     The authors declare that there are important differences not only
     between older Whites and older Blacks, but also among the elderly
     members of the various minority groups. The minority aged are de-
     finitely not a homogeneous population. While older Blacks were
     not more disadvantaged than their nonBlack counterparts on several
     of the health indicators, evidence of greater disadvantage was

Manuel and Berk (Continued)

generally found on the income measures. Racial and cultural distinctions have produced a population of older citizens with differing health, income and demographic circumstances. "We need
studies designed so that summary data on older nonwhites, and on
whites also, can be disaggregated in order to learn more about the
special circumstances of aging within the many different cultural
groups in the United States," conclude Manuel and Berk.

339.   Roberts, Jean. "Blood Pressure Levels of Persons 65-74 Years,
       United States, 1971-1974." Vital and Health Statistics, Series
       11, No. 203, DHEW Pub. No. (HRA) 78-1648. Washington, DC: United
       States Government Printing Office, 1977.

The author asserts that hypertension is more prevalent among aged
Blacks than Whites. She points out that between 1971-74 the prevalence rates per 100 for definite hypertension for persons 55-64
years of age were 54.5 for Black females, 49.9 for Black males,
31.7 for White females, and 31.1 for White males; for persons 65-
74 years of age, 58.8 for Black females, 50.1 for Black males,
42.3 for White females, and 35.3 for White males.

340.   Thompson, Gayle B. "Black-White Differences in Private Pensions:
       Findings from the Retirement History Study." Social Security
       Bulletin, Vol. 42, No. 2, February, 1979, pp. 15-22.

This article compares older Black workers and older White workers
on coverage under private pension plans, the receipt of pension
benefits upon retirement, and the job characteristics associated
with both coverage and receipt. Data are from the 1969 and 1975
interviews of the Retirement History Study and describe pre-ERISA
(Employee Retirement Income Security Act (ERISA) of 1974) conditions among persons in their late fifties to mid-sixties. Black
workers were much less likely than White workers to have been
covered by a private pension on their longest job. Moreover, among
those who were covered, they were less likely to have received
benefits. The racial differences appear to result in part from
substantial differences on job characteristics, particularly in-
dustry. Nevertheless, some evidence shows that workers of both
races with the same combination of job characteristics are almost
equally likely to have been covered by a private pension, concludes the researcher.

341.   United States Bureau of the Census. "Characteristics of House-
       holds Purchasing Food Stamps." Current Population Reports,
       Series P-23, No. 6, 1976.

This article declares that during the peak of the 1975 recession,
only one-fifth of all elderly Black couples and one-fourth of all
elderly Blacks living alone purchased food stamps, compared to 3
percent of all elderly Whites living alone.

342. United States Public Health Service, National Center for Health
      Statistics. "Final Mortality Statistics, 1976." Monthly Vital
      Statistics Report, Vol. 26, No. 12, 1978, Supplement 2.

      This article states that, since 1970, Blacks have narrowed the
      life expectancy gap with Whites by at least one full year. In
      1970, White men were expected to live to 68.0 years from birth,
      while Black men were expected to live only 61.3 years--a gap of
      6.7 years. But by 1976, White men had a life expectancy of 69.7
      years, compared to a life expectancy at birth of 64.1 years among
      Black men--a gap of 5.6 years.

343. White House Conference on Aging. "The Aging and Aged Blacks."
      Toward A National Policy on Aging, Vol. 2, Washington, DC: U.S.
      Government Printing Office, 1971, pp. 177-196.

      The Black delegates at this conference were especially concerned
      with three major and related issues. One was the insufficient--
      and generally lack of attention given to minority groups, includ-
      ing Blacks, in the formation of issues presented at the conference.
      A second issue was a general feeling of Black underrepresentation
      as Delegates and particularly so as linked with other minority
      groups. Insufficient time to prepare their preliminary report
      constituted the third overriding issue. It was also stated that
      the 1970 United States population contained 608,000 Black males
      65 or more years of age. Located in EVERY state, twice as many
      Black aged as White dwelled in poverty. The delegates argued that
      between 1959 and 1969, dollar income gaps between Black and White
      aged actually widered. Also three of every four Black aged live
      in substandard housing.

                   11.   BLACK AGED AND THE NATIONAL
                          CENTER ON BLACK AGED

344. Paris, June B. (Editor). "Job Bank Lists Blacks in Field of
      Aging." Aging, August, 1977, p. 24.

      The National Center on Black Aged initiated a Job Bank Service as
      a means of introducing Black professionals and paraprofessionals
      in the field of gerontology to employers seeking qualified person-
      nel. The Job Bank is a repository for information about positions
      currently available in the field of aging and for the qualifica-
      tions and backgrounds of persons seeking employment. Applications
      will be screened and those which match specified job descriptions
      will be forwarded to employers. As a special feature, the service
      includes assistance in the placement of older persons seeking part-
      time, paid employment or volunteer positions in the field of aging.
      The Center has as its primary concern the socio-economic needs and
      welfare of aged Blacks. One of its major goals is promoting the
      placement and advancement of Black professionals and paraprofes-
      sionals in the field of gerontology to meet these needs. NCBA is
      encouraging employers and job seekers in aging and related areas
      to utilize the service, which is free to members of the organiza-
      tion. Prospective job candidates who are not members of NCBA are
      charged $2.00 to cover postage fees for one year from the date of
      registration.

6.

ARTICLES

1. BLACK AGED AND ABUSE

345. Cazenave, Noel A. "Elder Abuse and Black Americans: Incidence, Correlates, Treatment and Prevention." Abuse and Maltreatment of the Elderly: Causes and Interventions. Jordan I. Kosberg, Editor. Boston: John Wright and PSG Inc., Publishers, 1983, pp. 187-203.

The author suggests that any effective attempt to eliminate elder abuse among Black Americans must involve attacking racism and economic exploitation, respecting and building on the strengths of family-kin-community networks, helping the Black aged maintain their health and independence for as long as possible, and the building of better, less stressful environments and circumstances. He suggests that the problems faced by the Black aged are complex and varied, and do not occur in a vacuum. The solutions, therefore, must be imaginative, diverse, and mindful of the complexity of every level of the social system, concludes the author.

346. Gordon, Jacob U. "Use of Aging Services By Elderly Blacks in Douglas County, Kansas." Journal of Minority Aging, Vol. 4, No. 3, June, 1979, pp. 88-92.

This descriptive study of 54 elderly Black residents of Douglas County, Kansas, provided some limited data about their use of and attitudes toward the Douglas County Planning Council on Services for Aging, Inc., and the services under its aegis. A majority of the subjects were unaware of the Council, although a few of these unaware persons did use some of its services, observed Prof. Gordon. The use-rate was 33.3 percent, which may or may not be adequate. In the absence of needs-assessment data, the appropriate use level could not be determined, according to the researcher. Any needs-assessment data related to aging services available within the county should also contain some information about the eligibility of elderly Black residents for each of the extant services, suggests the writer. The major implications of this study were the need for an assessment of the needs of elderly Black residents for services related to their overall well-being, an evaluation of the extent to which those needs could be met appropriately through

Gordon, Jacob U. (continued)

existing services, and, if any gaps occur between needs and existing services, the development and implementation of plans more useful in aiding elderly Blacks as they age, concludes the author.

2. BLACK AGED AND ALCOHOLISM

347. Blum, Lawrence and Fred Rosner. "Alcoholism in the Elderly: An
      Analysis of 50 Patients." Journal of the American Medical Associa-
      tion, Vol. 75, No. 5, May, 1983, pp. 489-495.

      It was found in this research that a higher number of elderly alco-
      holics were veterans, widowed, and had a long history of alcoholism
      when compared to younger alcoholics. The authors argue that the
      physician should have a high index of suspicion for alcoholism
      when he is dealing with the elderly patient who presents a combina-
      tion of the following characteristics: depression, bereavement,
      retirement, loneliness, marital stress, economic hardships, and
      physical illness since the psychosocial stresses of aging are
      thought to be the major causal factors of alcoholism among the
      elderly. This study was done in New York City.

3. BLACK AGED AND BLACK ORGANIZATIONS

348. Coiro, Cynthia. "Why the National Caucus on Black Aged?"
      Harvest Year, Vol. 11, November, 1971, pp. 13-18.

      The writer argues that there is a definite need for The National
      Caucus On Black Aged because The Black Aged have special problems
      and concerns that are different than those of the White elderly.
      This organization is the official spokesman for the Black Aged and
      espouses their causes at the local, state, and national levels.
      The author gives an excellent argument for such an organization.

349. Jackson, Hobart C. "National Caucus On The Black Aged: A Progress
      Report." Aging and Human Development, Vol. 2, August, 1971,
      pp. 226-231.

      The Chairman of the National Caucus on The Black Aged (NCBA) dis-
      cusses the "Formation of NCBA," "NCBA Activities," and "The Work
      Ahead." He points out that with the cooperation of the U. S.
      Senate Special Committee on Aging, and Dr. Inable Lindsay, the
      NCBA has been able to update certain information on the Black El-
      derly with respect to their life style, geographical distribution,
      estimated average income and assets, incidence and extent of chro-
      nic illness, longevity expectations, employment patterns, quality
      of housing, effectiveness of Federal programs, and in a few other
      areas. Jackson concludes that one of the great barriers to the
      accomplishment of the NCBA, however, is the absence of current
      definitive usable data.

350. Jackson, Jacquelyne J. "The National Center on Black Ages: A
      Challenge to Gerontologists." Gerontologist, Vol. 14, June, 1974,
      pp. 194, 196.

      The author states that gerontologists can meet the challenge of
      the National Center on Black Aged (NCBA) by:
          Becoming active members of NCBA.
          Sharing all relevant materials and ideas.
          Using individuals knowledgeable about Blacks in the United
              States as key spokesmen about Blacks.
          Encouraging aged Blacks to increase, where necessary, their
              active political involvement on local, state, and national
              levels.
          Involving more Blacks at all governmental and private levels in
              planning stages for the aged.
          Encouraging and aiding Black participation in undergraduate,
              graduate, and other training programs from recruitment through
              successful program completion.
          Electing political officials and legislators who shall reduce
              racism and make certain that old Blacks shall not live in
              poverty and substandard housing.
          Recognizing that Blacks constitute a legitimate and separate
              minority group within the United States.
          Reducing efforts to lump Blacks as a minority group with other
              legitimate minority groups, such as Native Americans, and
              such illegitimate minority groups as the aged, homosexuals,
              and fat people.
          Helping to make real the major recommendations made by the
              Special Concerns Session on Aging and Aged Blacks at the
              1971 White House Conference on Aging, including NCBA's
              "Social Security Proposal" to reduce existing racial inequi-
              ties in the distribution of OASDHI income to primary benefi-
              ciaries.
          Urging the most appropriate and feasible collection, presenta-
              tion, and interpretation of data about aging and aged Blacks
              by the federal government.
          Encouraging others to know and understand realistically various
              patterns and processes of aging among Blacks.
          Helping to increase the life expectancies and longevities of
              Black males and females.

351. Kastenbaum, Robert J. "National Caucus on The Black Aged (Edito-
      rial)." Aging and Human Development, Vol. 2, 1971, pp. 1-2.

      The editor of the above journal points out that to be Black and
      aged is truly to be in double jeopardy. He also declares that
      there is a huge gap in our knowledge and understanding of Black
      aging. Prof. Kastenbaum concludes that the National Caucus on
      the Black Aged is trying to inform the public about the special
      problems of the Black aged. He also states that we cannot claim
      to have developed a comprehensive science of human aging when we
      know next to nothing about those Black Americans who grow old--
      and those who do not.

4. BLACK AGED AND CHILDREN

352. Jackson, Jacquelyne J. "Sex and Social Class Variations in Black
Aged-Parent-Adult Child Relationships." Aging and Human Development, Vol. 2, August, 1971, pp. 96-107.

This article deals with a pilot investigation involving thirty-two
aged Black parents and their eighty-three adult children. It revealed that significant sex and social class differences were apparent with respect to patterns of instrumental aid to and from
these parents and their children, as well as their affectional relationship. Dr. Jackson concludes that most of the Black aged
surveyed did not consider themselves nor their children as mutual
sources of moral support, with the major exceptions of manual
fathers and their daughters and nonmanual fathers and their children; but nonmanual parents were more likely to perceive themselves
in this regard than were manual parents, as was true of fathers
more often than of mothers....

353. _____. "Negro Aged Parents and Adult Children:
Their Affective Relationship." Varia, Spring, 1976, pp. 1-14.

Essentially, the focus of this article was that of sharing certain
findings, and hypotheses derived therefrom, obtained in a pilot
investigation of aged Black parents' perceptions of their affective involvement with their adult children, and of some of the
factors which affect such involvement. Dr. Jackson surmises that
theoretically, the data tended to suggest that common cultural
interests and affection may be sufficiently binding to provide
continuity and substance to those parent and child nuclear families
maintaining economic self-sufficiency, but that, in the absence of
such self-sufficiency, affection and common cultural interests
were not sufficiently binding to provide such continuity and substance. Thus, it appears that economic self-sufficiency is a
variable with significant implications for aged parent-adult relationships, states Dr. Jackson. The author declares that the
data tends to suggest that more attention ought to be placed upon
the social relationships or role interactions, as well as role
structures, and the meanings which such role interactions have for
the participants as indicated by the participants, as well as their
quantity, in studying not only Black aged parents and their children, but also in studying generally the Black family. The writer
concludes that, as might have been expected on the basis of other
literature not cited herein, the pilot investigation indicates
that, in all probability, most aged Black parents prefer to live
independently of, but in close contact with, their children; that,
in those situations defined as "crises," most such parents assist
or are assisted by their children; that most such parents tend to
prefer a daughter, as opposed to a son; and that their affectional
involvement with or their affects toward their children are influenced by a number of variables, not the least of which are the
sex and socioeconomic status of the parent and the child, the
early parent-child relationships, and degree of dominance or
authority by either parent of child within their present relationships, concludes the sociologist.

354. Pihbald, C. T. and Robert W. Habenstein. "Social Factors in Grand-
      parent Orientation of High School Youth." Older People and Their
      Social World, Arnold M. Rose and Warren A. Peterson, Editors.
      Philadelphia: F. A. Davis Co., 1965, pp. 163-180.

      This article is based on the assumption that kinship ties in the
      contemporary family are directly related to the degree of knowledge
      held by grandchildren of their grandparents. The authors compared
      White and Black high school youths. They concluded that more than
      twice as many White as compared with Black students were able to
      report the occupations of both grandfathers. The writers also
      state that only one-fifth of the White students as compared with
      half the Blacks reported the occupation of either grandfather.

                    5. BLACK AGED AND COPING

355. Carter, James H. "Psychosocial Aspects of Aging: The Black
      Elderly." Journal of The National Medical Association, Vol. 76,
      No. 3, March, 1984, pp. 271-275.

      Dr. Carter states that having survived to reach their Senior Years
      is testimony to the individual emotional and physical ruggedness
      of aged Black men and women. The coping styles that led to their
      survival have antecedents in youth. Consequently, suggests the
      author, the measure of strength of aged Blacks can be judged only
      within the framework of their whole lives. He concludes: "As an
      overreaction against racism, Black psychiatrists may have at
      times inappropriately de-emphasized the genetic, metabolic, and
      enzymatic factors that are essential to aging. Longitudinal
      studies are needed to address the totality of important questions
      about the Black aged."

356. Gibson, Rose C. "Blacks at Middle and Late Life: Resources and
      Coping." Annals of the American Academy of Political and Social
      Science, Vol. 464, November, 1982, pp. 79-90.

      An analysis of national data collected in 1957 and 1976 reveals
      that older Black Americans' use of their informal support network
      and prayer in times of distress is distinct from that of older
      white Americans. Black-white disparities in income, education,
      and widowhood were large and appeared to widen from middle to late
      life. Blacks, in coping with distress, drew from a more varied
      pool of informal helpers than whites, both in middle and late
      life, and were more versatile in substituting these helpers one
      for another as they approached old age, states the author.
      Whites, in contrast, were more likely to limit help seeking to
      spouses in middle life and to replace spouses with a single family
      member as they approached old age. Blacks were much more likely
      than whites to respond to worries with prayer, but prayer, as a
      coping reaction among Blacks, declined between 1957 and 1976. The
      role of the special help-seeking model of older Blacks in their
      adaptation to old age is discussed.

357.   _____. "Older Black Americans: Relationships and Coping."
        Generation, Vol. 10, No. 4, Summer, 1986, pp. 35-39.

        Dr. Gibson asserts that the lifetime rehearsal in using combina-
        tions of family members and friends; flexibility in interchanging
        these helpers at critical life points; and being able to manipulate
        the level, quantity, and type of help available by manipulating
        the helpers--coupled with the fact that Blacks may also be more
        socialized to adapt to uncertainty and change within their lives--
        make up a dynamic coping package that is sensitive to life's chang-
        ing circumstances and changing needs. She concludes, in part:
        "This coping package, used at successive transitions may become
        increasingly polished; those Blacks who learn to use the package
        most effectively at previous stages overcome roadblocks more suc-
        cessfully at successive stages. These survivors thus arrive at
        the penultimate transition--old age-- more fortified, more rehear-
        sed, and better able to adapt to its exigencies, despite fewer
        economic and social resources. For Blacks, then, the move into
        old age may be more transition than crisis. The critical issue of
        whether the strategies contained in this coping package are corre-
        lated with psychological survivorship remains open to question.... "

357a.   Stretch, John J. "Are Aged Blacks Who Manifest Differences in
        Community Security Also Different in Coping Reactions?" Aging and
        Human Development, Vol. 7, 1976, pp. 171-184.

        This article was based on seventy-two aged Blacks, equally divided
        between those residing in a high-rise public housing project and
        those living in the community awaiting admission. They were inter-
        viewed to test the theory that differences in community security
        would predict differences in coping reactions. Data on perceived
        community security and reported medical, social and mental coping
        reactions were collected, using a simply and directly worded, pre-
        coded, stimulus-response instrument developed by the author. Re-
        spondents were assigned to either a high or to a low community
        security group by two methods: first, they were assigned a place
        of residence; next they were assigned according to their obtained
        community security score. Dr. Stretch concludes that the results
        in general supported the theory. Of the two empirical indicators
        of community security, however, larger differences in coping reac-
        tion scores were found in the high scoring and low scoring commu-
        nity security groups than in the high-rise and community groups.

358.   Swanson, William C. and Carl L. Harter. "How Do Elderly Blacks
        Cope in New Orleans?" Aging and Human Development, Vol. 2,
        August, 1971, pp. 210-216.

        This article was based on case histories from a representative sam-
        ple of twenty Black men and women age fifty-five or older residing
        in New Orleans. The authors provide several insights into signi-
        ficant life features of elderly Blacks in that city. First, it was
        found that many of these Blacks suffered from financial and health
        problems; yet, by no means did they feel that life was unbearable.
        Secondly, these elderly Blacks do not feel they have ever had any
        serious personal problems. Thirdly, these poor elderly Blacks are
        NOT high suicide risks. The authors conclude that though they may

Swanson, William C. and Carl L. Harter (continued)

be poor, old, sick, and Black, being alive is still good and preci-
ous--to the aged Blacks in New Orleans.

6.   BLACK AGED AND COUNSELING

359. Burgess, Alexena Irving. "Reflections on Counseling Elderly
      Blacks." Journal of Non-White Concerns in Personnel and Guidance,
      Vol. 5, No. 1, October, 1976, pp. 45-48.

      The author believes that specific training for counselors of the
      Black aged is needed. More Black elderly counselors are also
      needed. It was stated that if the counselor is to understand the
      world of the Black counselee, he or she must be knowledgeable about
      the history, sociology, economics, and psychology of Blacks. Knowl-
      edge in these areas can prove to be a very important factor in the
      overall counselor-client relationship. The significance of the en-
      tire relationship is sometimes based on whether the aged Black
      client feels that the counselor is genuinely interested enough in
      his or her prior experiences to be interested in his or her present
      well-being, argues the writer. She concludes, in part: "We must
      not forget that the elderly Black client's past experiences are im-
      portant factors in determining what his or her present situation is.
      There is a definite need for Black counselors to be trained to meet
      the needs of aged Black clients. Counselor education programs
      should begin to devote energies to seeing that Black materials are
      included in their curricula." The researcher continued, "The
      elderly Black client expects no more from the counseling situation
      than any other person. If he or she needs help and seeks it, he or
      she expects to receive it from a person who is knowledgeable, well-
      trained, and alert to his or her needs--a person who genuinely
      cares for him or her as an individual."

360. Mosley, John C. "Problems of the Black Aged." Journal of Non-
      White Concerns in Personnel and Guidance, Vol. 6, No. 1, October,
      1977, pp. 11-16.

      The author contends that some of the problems of the Black elderly
      are that they live at or below a poverty level fixed by the federal
      government at a ridiculously low level. They live in dilapidated
      housing, suffer from malnutrition, and have a variety of special
      health problems. The Black elderly's educational level is generally
      low, so that aged Blacks find it difficult to avail themselves of
      the government services that are available to them, and employment
      to supplement low retirement incomes is hard to find. In addition
      to these distinctive disabilities, elderly Blacks are subject to
      all the problems that the aged in the United States endure. These
      problems include loneliness, a loss of freedom, and psychological
      problems involving awareness of the approach of death, surmises the
      writer. He concludes, in part: "In view of their needs, much more
      must be done in taking care of the Black aged. Not enough money is
      being spent for counseling services at both the federal and state
      levels. The level of expertise of counseling needs desperately to

Mosley, John C. (continued)

be raised. Insufficient attention has been paid to the problems
of elderly Blacks when counseling models and programs for the
aged are developed. Additional research funds at all levels are
needed to develop understanding of the counseling problems of
this group. More time, more attention, more funds, and more
skills are needed in dealing with the problems of the Black aged."

7. BLACK AGED AND CRIME

361.   Japenga, Ann. "Fear of Youth Flaws Blacks' 'Golden Years'."
        Los Angeles Times, May 10, 1985, pp. 1, 22.

The reporter states that elderly Blacks told her that youths take
advantage of them and prey on them. It was also pointed out that
"the elderly have a greater fear of crime and may restrict their
lives in ways that reduce their chances of being victimized."

8. BLACK AGED AND DEPRESSION

362.   Farakhan, Asia, et al. "Life Satisfaction and Depression Among
        Retired Black Persons." Psychological Reports, Vol. 55, No. 2,
        October, 1984, pp. 452-454.

Correlates of life satisfaction of 30 elderly Black persons were
studied by means of a three-session, phase-focused (Pre-retire-
ment, immediate post-retirement, and current) interview that included the Ecosystem Activity Record (EAR) and the Depression
Adjective Check List (DACL) administered to 23 women and 7 men
whose ages ranged from 52 to 97 years. Findings over the three
phases were: (1) an overall decrease in activities but an increase in time spent with family and home and an increase in
participation in church or religiously oriented functions, (2)
an over-all pattern of relatively high life satisfaction, and (3)
relatively low levels of depressive mood. Relationships among
demographic variables also were noted, declare the authors.

363.   Smith-Ruiz, Dorothy. "Depressive Symptomatology in a Nonclinical
        Sample of Elderly Blacks: The Effects of Marital Status."
        Journal of the National Medical Association, Vol. 77, No. 11,
        November, 1985, pp. 879-884.

This article showed that marital status among elderly Blacks is
a significant factor that contributes to depression. A relationship was found between sex and depression, but no significant
distinction was evident, declared the author. She concluded that
marital status among elderly Black individuals is a more significant predictor of depression than the sex variable....

9. BLACK AGED AND ECONOMICS

364. Beattie, Walter M. "The Aging Negro: Some Implications for
      Social Welfare Services." Phylon, Vol. 21, Summer, 1960, pp. 131-
      135.

      This article is an attempt to raise questions as to whether the
      patterns of health, welfare and leisure-time services which are
      emerging for our aging population throughout the United States
      have relevance or meaning for the aging Black and his family. It
      is essential that this question be raised, especially as one con-
      siders the fact that the greater part of our planning for such
      services is taking place in metropolitan centers where the popula-
      tion is comprised of a significant proportion of Blacks, contends
      the author. In addition, those areas of the city known sociologi-
      cally as the "zones of transition" are increasingly becoming the
      place of residence for the aged, both White and Black as well as
      for the Black population of all ages. We must be constantly aware
      of individual differences in carrying out our responsibilities of
      planning for all older persons, states Beattie. The writer sur-
      mises, however, in our concern over the individuality of all older
      persons, we must also give recognition to the racial and socio-
      economic differences between those groups of persons who comprise
      our older population. The author declares if we can do this
      through the development of more basic knowledge as to the composi-
      tion or our aged population, we will begin to go a long way toward
      meeting people where they are and in helping them to achieve the
      utmost for which their capacities allow. He concludes if we do
      not, we will be creating community programs for older persons in
      the image of those groups and interests with which we may have
      the most acquaintance. This, certainly, is a bias which social
      welfare programs must avoid if they are to truly relate to the
      interests and concerns of all older persons in each of our commu-
      nities, continues the researcher.

365. Davis, Donald L. "Growing Old Black." Employment Prospects of
      Aged Blacks, Chicanos, and Indians. Washington, DC: National
      Council on the Aging, 1971, pp. 27-51.

      The author points out that as Blacks grow old they have little to
      look forward to. In many cases Blacks have to continue to work
      after they reach retirement age because they cannot make ends
      meet on their Social Security Benefits.

366. Davis, Frank G. "The Impact of Social Security Taxes Upon the
      Poor: The Cases of the Black Community." Economics of Aging.
      Ann Arbor: Institute of Gerontology, University of Michigan-
      Wayne State University, 1976, pp. 41-53.

      The writer states that the Black community suffers most from
      Social Security Taxes because many Blacks die before they can re-
      ceive Social Security benefits. Moreover, most Blacks cannot
      afford increases in Social Security Tax because they have a lower
      income than Whites; therefore, their take-home pay checks are
      smaller.

367. Gillespie, Bonnie J. "Elderly Blacks and The Economy." Journal of Afro-American Issues. Vol. 3, Summer/Fall, 1975, pp. 324-335.

This paper briefly outlines the general situation of the elderly Black, the present economy, and the interaction effect. The author states that there are approximately 1.7 million elderly Black. They live in all parts of the country, but about 3/5 of them live in the South and most tend to live in urban areas in the South. Dr. Gillespie points out that the disproportionate distribution of income sources by total aggregate incomes, as well as by percent of families receiving incomes of specified types, indicate a considerable need for revising sources of both higher dependable and increased incomes for aged Blacks. He concludes that as long as racism abounds in America the problems of Black elders will continue to be acute. When we attack racism and its institutionalization we assist in bringing about the economic or material and psychological well-being or quality of life of the elderly Black.

368. Henderson, George. "The Negro Recipient of Old-Age Assistance: Results of Discrimination." Social Casework, Vol. 46, 1965, pp. 208-214.

This article is based on an exploratory study of 100 aged Blacks who were recipients of Old-Age Assistance grants in Detroit, Michigan. The main purpose of this article was to examine some of the problems peculiar to aged Blacks. The writer argues that racial discrimination is the cause of many of the problems of today's (1965) aged Blacks, and until it is eliminated, we shall merely be attacking effects, not causes. He surmises that today's aged Black is different from today's aged White because he is "Black" by society's definition, with its socioeconomic consequences. Mr. Henderson suggests that this is his uniqueness, and this alone should be an adequate basis for compensatory treatment. For he has, indeed, been played in double jeopardy; first, by being Black, and second, by being old. The author concludes that it is safe to predict that with a continued racial discrimination, there will be an increasing number of aged Blacks living on public assistance programs.

369. Hudson, Gossie Harold. "Social and Economic Problems Facing the Black Elderly." Share, Vol. 3, No. 2, (Black Educators' Council For Human Sciences, North Carolina A & T State University), January 7, 1975, pp. 1-6.

The writer states that psychological damages help to compound the problems of social and economic insecurity. Dr. Hudson contends that there is a need for more research in the area of Black gerontology by students as well as scholars of history.

370. Oliver, Mamie O. "Elderly Blacks and the Economy." Journal of Afro-American Issues, Vol. 3, Summer/Fall 1975, pp. 316-323.

The writer argues that elderly Black Americans experience a vital balance or survival quotient resulting from a blend of strategy, inner integrity, "style," pride and positive spirit.

Oliver, Mamie O. (continued)

Despite group suppression, rampant racism, racial exploitation, second class citizenship, psychological "trips" focused on despair, physical weakness (hypertension, etc.), old age is a considerable achievement for many elderly Black Americans. The author states it could be said that stress, in this instance, produces with the years, fervor, inner growth, and courage. The elderly Black American, this writer submits, is the possessor of integrity and balance and is capable of defending the dignity of his own life style against all physical and economic threats. Oliver concludes the Black elderly knows solidarity in the midst of racial prejudice, low economic status, and personal suffering, a commitment to justice for ALL mankind. All this should serve to challenge the Black family in America and other youngsters and oldsters to take and pursue life--it is the opportunity and blessing afforded all mundane humans, states Oliver.

371.   Palm, Charles H. "The Future of The Black Aged in America." Proceedings of Black Aged in The Future. Jacquelyne J. Jackson, Editor. Durham, NC: Center for the Study of Aging and Human Development, Duke University, 1973, pp. 86-93.

The author asserts that the future of the Black Aged in America ultimately depends upon the emergence of human values as being the primary focus, a redeployment of our federal, state and county resources, reordering of our priorities and the motivation to seek solutions for our numerous problems by means of a horizontal approach in lieu of a simplistic vertical or linear approach. He concludes that the problem of the Black Aged in America is an extension of the problem of the Aged in America in general and more particularly an extension of the problem of the economically deprived aged in a culture which focuses on youth and which frequently attempts to solve its problems by formulas, slogans and cliches.

372.   Taylor, Robert Joseph and Willie H. Taylor. "The Social and Economic Status of the Black Elderly." Phylon, Vol. 43, No. 4, Winter, 1982, pp. 295-306.

This article presents a demographic profile of the Black elderly, examining their population size, regional distribution, and marital and family status. Their income and poverty levels are examined, and the proportion of income derived from Social Security and private pensions is highlighted. The employment needs and occupational status of the Black elderly are analyzed, with emphasis on unemployment and labor force dropout rates. The level of formal education of the Black elderly is also examined as well as the relationships between education and income and occupation. In addition, the paper assesses the housing adequacy and health status of the Black elderly....

10. BLACK AGED AND EDUCATION

373. "College Coed--At 76." Ebony, December, 1966, pp. 79-83.

This article discusses Mrs. Carolina Cooper who attended Fresno
City College. The learning process, as Mrs. Cooper sees it, is
not only desirable for the older person, it is essential. She
argues "the greatest and most tragic waste of our nation's economy
is the waste of human minds." Mrs. Cooper concludes "that many
older people's minds die long before their bodies do. There's
nothing left for them but their bodily bulk. Then they just sit
around and gossip. Gossip becomes a disease with them. It's a
horrible waste of human life, and I refuse to be among the
waste," declared Mrs. Cooper.

374. Jackson, Jacquelyne J. "A Bicentennial Tribute to Older Blacks:
Black Professionals in North Carolina." Black Aging, Vol. 2,
Nos 2 and 3, December, 1976 and February 1977, pp. 9-21.

This essay, which concentrates upon the relative growth, individual contributions, and opportunities for professional education
for Blacks in North Carolina, showed a numerical increase in
Black professionals between 1930 and 1970, but no real growth or
progress within their professional status. In comparison with all
professionally employed persons within the state, Blacks were
better off in 1930 than in 1970. Non-Black professional employment was much more swift in growth over that time. The unfortu-
nate trend of decreased Black employment within the labor force
was quite alarming. The vignettes about four Black professionals
born between 1763 and 1923 (John Chavis, Joseph Charles Price,
Charlotte Hawkins Brown, and Reginald Armistice Hawkins) provide
contrasting examples of Black professional contributions to the
state's well being. The abbreviated review of state provisions
for Black professional education since the American Revolution
showed better opportunities now than ever before, with those opportunities having been expanded primarily through Black and
federal pressures, and with the state usually restricting itself
to minimal federal or accrediting requirements, concludes the
writer.

375. "Lifelong Dream Realized: High School Diploma at 75." Crisis,
Vol 89, No. 8, October, 1982, p. 22.

This article discusses Mrs. Sadie Patrick of Denmark, South
Carolina, who graduated from Denmark Technical School at age 75.
She states that she went back to school so that she "could do
better work in the Church (Mt. Zion Baptist Church)".

11. BLACK AGED AND FAMILIES

376. Anderson, Peggye Dilworth. "Family Closeness Between Aged Blacks
and Their Adult Children." Journal of Minority Aging, Vol. 6,
Nos. 3 & 4, 1981, pp. 56-66.

Dr. Anderson found, as other researchers have, that the majority
of aged Blacks, like their White counterparts, interact frequently

Anderson, Peggye Dilworth (continued)

with their children as well as express feeling close to them. The
respondents' perceptions and descriptions of closeness to their
children stem primarily from having a reliable exchange of support
system and feeling needed and wanted by them. Therefore, a close
relationship means that the subjects have dependable, concerned
and devoted children who show affection for and sensitivity toward
their parents. She concludes that not only do we know how often
elderly Blacks interact with their children, we also better understand the affective aspects of their interaction. In addition,
the findings made in this study provide us with insight into the
role children play in providing their aged parents with economic,
social and psychological support. These findings can be instrumental to policy makers and social planners when attempting to
provide their parents with other support mechanisms. Further,
because elderly Blacks greatly depend on their children for support, we need to find ways to assist in maintaining and strength-
ening family relationships, concludes the author.

377. Cazenave, Noel A. "Family Violence and Aging Blacks: Theoretical
      Perspectives and Research Possibilities." Journal of Minority
      Aging, Vol. 4, No. 4, September-December, 1979, pp. 99-108.

      This article served as a prolegomenon for the development of re-
      search strategies for the study of aging and family violence. A
      conflict approach to minority aging should offer many insights
      into day-to-day interactions, family development and societal
      transactions affecting their lives. Research on family violence
      and aging Blacks can serve as the prototype for all subsequent
      research on violence and aging, states Prof. Cazenave. The aged
      can be studied as family violence controllers or agitators, vic-
      tims or aggressors. The extended nature of many Black families
      should make research on aging in multi-generational households
      and the effectiveness of potent support systems particularly
      fruitful, according to the author. He concludes, "Finally, because
      of the many social and economic restraints on the full expression
      of masculinity for Black males, Black men can provide key insights
      into the relationship between middle age and aging developmental
      crises and marital violence. In brief, Black aging families pro-
      vide an important arena from which a wide range of ecological and
      developmental variables related to violence and aging can be
      studied. In crossing the currently unexplored frontier of aging
      and family violence, the study of Black aging or of minority
      aging should provide heuristic insights that will prove useful
      in blazing new trails into this heretofore neglected area."

378. Dilworth-Anderson, Peggy. "Family Closeness Between Aged Blacks
      and Their Adult Children." Journal of Minority Aging, Vol. 6,
      Nos. 3 & 4, 1981, pp. 56-66.

      Using a sample of 153 elderly Blacks, this study focused on as-
      sessing the meaning of feelings of closeness between the subjects
      and their children. Through the use of open-ended questions, un-
      structured interviewing and a ten-item Likert scale, the writer
      found that the subjects described closeness as involving an array

Dilworth-Anderson, Peggy (continued)

of factors that augment one another to provide a dynamic process of
sharing goods and services as well as emotional support. The
major components of this process include a reliable exchange of
support system and the elderly feeling needed and wanted by their
children, states the author. It was also pointed out that contact
between aged people and their children continues despite the fact
that many parents live in separate households.

379. Jackson, Jacquelyne J. "Family Organization and Ideology."
Comparative Studies of Blacks and Whites in The United States.
Kent S. Miller and Ralph M. Dreger, Editors. New York: Seminar
Press, 1973, pp. 405-445.

One section is devoted to the "Aged Roles and Statuses." Dr.
Jackson argues that it appears that effective kinship networks
characterize the family lives of both aged Blacks and aged Whites,
that parental and child sex preferences persist into aged parent-
adult-child relationships, and that there are presently no significant differences by sex between the two racial groups as measured by their marital statuses and by the proportions who live
alone and do not live alone.

380. _____ . "Kinship Relations Among Older Negro Americans."
Journal of Social and Behavioral Sciences, Vol. 16, 1970, pp. 5-17.

This article has three major purposes. The first is the proffer-
ing of some cautious and categorical generalizations about older
Blacks. The second is that of providing some findings about specific kinship relations among a specific sample of older Blacks.
The third is that of commenting upon some of the implications of
these generalizations and findings as they may relate to the concept of racial subculture in kinship relations among older Americans. Dr. Jackson argues that essentially, kinship of relations
among older Black Americans displayed no gross structural differences from those of other older Americans. She concludes that
despite the wide communication given to the "increasing polariza-
tion of Black and White," the increasing separation between Black
America and White America, it appears to her that the concept of
racial subculture, when employed in descriptions and analyses of
kinship relations of older persons in the United States, is of
relatively little conceptual value.

381. _____ . "Marital Life Among Aging Blacks." Family Coordinator, Vol. 21, January, 1972, pp. 21-27.

The author states that while this article has focused specifically
upon selected marital patterns among married aging Blacks, much
more attention must also be given to those supportive familial
patterns available for aged Black males and females without spouses. At present, it appears that such individuals still depend,
as they have in the past, upon their own families as the first
line of resource or assistance. When they have children, they
turn toward them, and, most often, their children respond. In
the absence of children, they direct their needs toward other

Jackson, Jacquelyne J. (continued)

relatives, and those relatives respond as well. It thus appears that family functioning among Blacks is still highly supportive, to the extent possible, for aged family members. Dr. Jackson asserts ineffective family functioning which may occur can best be attributed to the lack of strongly societal factors. The author concludes a guaranteed annual income providing at least a moderate living for aging and aged Blacks, and other non-Blacks in need, may be a step in the right direction. It can help strengthen family functioning for aged Blacks, declares the author.

382.   Rao, V. V. Prakasa and V. Nandini Rao. "Gender Differences in The Familial Help Patterns of Older Blacks in Jackson, Mississippi, 1978." Journal of Minority Aging, Vol. 10, No. 1, 1985, pp. 16-24.

A purposive sample of 240 noninstitutionalized Blacks over 60 years of age, who lived in Jackson, Mississippi in 1978, was used to explore gender differences in the help they gave to and received from their children and grandchildren and to determine the various factors that influenced their help patterns. Each respondent included in the analysis had children and grandchildren. In general, a majority of the respondents in the survey reported that both gave help to and received help from their children or grandchildren. The gender differences were insignificant in terms of help received or given, state the writers. The independent variables that best explained the variations in the help patterns differed by gender. According to the professors, this study was most helpful in pointing toward the need for more sophisticated studies of the help patterns of older persons and their children and grandchildren, including, perhaps, the collection of data with respect to the helping patterns between each parent and child and each grandparent and grandchild. The authors argue that more knowledge about the intergenerational patterns of kinship exchange in helping patterns among older and younger Blacks is especially important in that the larger proportion of poor older Blacks than poor older Whites makes the former especially vulnerable to the need for intergenerational exchange of goods and services....

383.   Reiff, Janice L., Michael R. Dahln, and Daniel Scott Smith. "Rural Push and Urban Pull: Work and Family Experiences of Older Black Women in Southern Cities, 1880-1900." Journal of Social History, Vol. 16, No. 4, Summer, 1983, pp. 39-45.

The researchers conclude that the immediate impact of the city was not negative for these older Black women, at least in the first years after emancipation. The city was not a destroyer, instead it provided options that were not available to Black women living in the country. This essay contended that urban effects should be understood by contrasting the conditions in the rural areas of origin to the special features of the urban environment itself. Old women, particularly old widows and most especially those without living children, were partially pushed from their rural homes. Although they found only modest economic opportunity in the city, their chances were superior to what was available in the country. Moving to the city made sense to them, and it should make sense to historians, conclude the researchers.

384.   Smith, Daniel S., Michael R. Dahln and Mark Friedberger. "The
       Family Structure of the Older Black Population in the American
       South in 1880 and 1900." Sociology and Social Research, Vol. 63,
       No. 3, April, 1975, pp. 544-565.

       This article explores the relations between southern Blacks and
       White old people and their adult children. The data derive from
       samples of persons over age 65 taken from the U.S. manuscript
       censuses for 1880 and 1900. The families of older Blacks and
       whites were similar in several important ways. Only half of old
       Blacks, however, lived with children compared to nearly seventy
       percent of whites. Co-residence of adult generations was related
       to family economic activity and to the provision of welfare to
       needy kin, state the writers. Economic factors account for part
       of the Black-white differential and for differentials within the
       Black population. Both Black and white families served welfare
       functions, but welfare in the Black family flowed more from older
       to younger generations, conclude the researchers.

385.   Taylor, Robert Joseph. "The Extended Family As A Source of Sup-
       port to Elderly Blacks." Gerontologist, Vol. 25, No. 5, October,
       1985, pp. 488-495.

       The writer declares that among elderly Blacks, children are more
       a source of support than are relatives. Among childless elderly,
       however, having an available pool of relatives was of singular
       importance in predicting familial assistance. Further, elderly
       Blacks without children or relatives were not significantly less
       likely to receive support, suggests Prof. Taylor. The author's
       study of the Black elderly was unique in that a national sample
       of older Blacks was used and the relationships were examined
       within a multivariate context....

386.   Wolf, Jacquelyn H., et al. "Distance and Contacts: Interactions
       of Black Urban Elderly Adults With Family and Friends." Journal
       of Gerontology, Vol. 38, No. 4, July, 1983, pp. 465-471.

       Distance is the major factor determining the frequency of social
       interaction with family and friends for elderly whites. Age, sex,
       marital status, length of residence, and income also affect the
       number of social contacts. These relationships have not been
       studied for elderly Blacks, according to the authors. Utilizing
       data from a survey of 655 Black urban residents 60 years old and
       older, this study investigated contacts with family and friends.
       The major finding was that the neighborhood is an important place
       for socializing with both family and friends for this population
       as is the case for working-class white elderly adults. A surpris-
       ing finding is that, whereas social contacts increase with higher
       income for working-class elderly whites, for these Black elderly
       adults who are of the working class and poor, social contacts
       decrease with higher income, conclude the researchers.

387. Yelder, Josephine. "The Influence of Culture on Family Relations: The Black American Experience." Aging Parents. Pauline K. Ragan, Editor. Los Angeles: Ethel Percy Andrus Gerontology Center, University of Southern California Press, 1979, pp. 83-93.

This essay considers the experiences of aging Blacks and their families. The topics examined here include demographic background, historical considerations, and patterns of family structure. It was stated that older Black females are more likely to take children into their own households than to move into the households of their adult children or other relatives.

12. BLACK AGED AND HEALTH CONDITIONS

388. Calloway, Nathaniel O. "Medical Aspects of the Aging American Black." Proceedings of Black Aged in the Future, Jacquelyne J. Jackson, Editor. Durham, NC: Center For The Study of Aging and Human Development, Duke University, 1973, pp. 50-56.

The author focused on two themes in this essay. First, he gives a brief description of the overall health of aged Blacks and some needed research. Second, he compared selected non-White with White life expectancies, and mortality rates and causes. Dr. Calloway argues that currently (1973) old Blacks represent a biologically superior population in comparison with younger Blacks and old Whites, primarily because they represent SURVIVORS of a cohort group detrimentally oppressed by various hazards who were able to adjust and adapt in various ways to their environments. The writer concludes that better health status in the younger years will contribute to longer Black life-expectancies and, of course, larger populations of aged Blacks, but will not, at present, contribute to longer life span.

389. Greene, D. Richard. "Health Indicators and Life Expectancy of the Black Aged: Policy Implications." Health and The Black Aged, Wilbur H. Watson, et al. Editors. Washington, DC: National Center on Black Aged, 1978, pp. 32-45.

This article focused on vital statistics, including mortality data, as indicators of the differential health statuses of older persons. As conditional factors, the author included sex and residence according to census tract. A major difference between this study and others was its focus on a local metropolitan community. This approach was intended to reduce some of the data ambiguities inherent in national studies. The author used vital statistics from 1969-70 along with 1970 census data for the City of Seattle, Washington. Ten thousand records of vital statistics were available for analysis. The aim of the study was to develop a framework for policy recommendations and appropriate interventions for the reduction of race-related mortality differentials. Greene contends that policy should reflect obvious and more subtle factors which relate to race-related differences in longevity and their implications. The writer found that the older patients had a larger proportion of conditions that were due to degenerative vascular

Greene, D. Richard (continued)

diseases and the younger ones had more diagnoses related to trauma. The writer was able to demonstrate that with advancing age
there was decreasing functionability as reflected in the statistically significant lower frequency with which older persons left
their homes. This latter finding suggested that the older group
may have had other sub-clinical chronic conditions that were related to the major rehabilitation diagnoses and that were expressed in lower levels of functioning.

390.   Haber, David. "Health Promotion to Reduce Blood Pressure Level
        Among Older Blacks." Gerontologist, Vol. 26, No. 2, April, 1986,
        pp. 119-121.

        Ninety-eight low-income elders, 91% of whom were Black, completed
        a 10-week health promotion program for the purpose of lowering or
        stabilizing blood pressure levels. Comparisons were made between
        classes that met weekly versus 3 times a week, and between yoga
        and aerobics formats. A peer-led class was developed that con-
        tinued for 10 months after the professionally-led class was termi-
        nated. Dr. Haber concludes, peer-led programs have the potential
        to continue health promotion activities without cost, while en-
        hancing the capacity for self-determination among older persons....

391.   Hawkins, Reginald. "Dental Health of Aged Blacks." Proceedings
        of Black Aged in The Future. Jacquelyne J. Jackson, Editor.
        Durham, NC: Center for The Study of Aging and Human Development,
        Duke University, 1973, pp. 57-77.

        The author surmises that there is an alarming number of older
        Blacks needing early dental care. Among those 55-64 years of age,
        78.5 percent of Black males and 79.2 percent of Black females
        needed such care. He concluded that dental health is generally
        poor for most Blacks, and it tends to become increasingly poor
        with age. Dr. Hawkins also points out that those interested in
        curriculum building for the aged must also be interested in in-
        creasing the number of Black dentists available to treat aged
        Blacks....

392.   Henry, Melvin. "Perceived Health Status of the Black Elderly in
        an Urban Area: Findings of a Survey Research Project." Health
        and the Black Aged. Wilbur H. Watson, et al, Editors. Washington,
        D.C.: National Center on Black Aged, 1978, pp. 72-79.

        The author's findings indicated that elderly Blacks in the Los
        Angeles area did not fit the commonly held stereotype of the Black
        elderly as feeble, dependent, decrepit, emaciated, generally in
        poor health and people who are worse off then any other group in
        the society. Further, the elderly in the author's sample seemed
        to have very few problems in gaining access to available health
        care services; they were infrequently represented on the rolls of
        public welfare and lists of persons receiving Supplemental Securi-
        ty Income. The majority of the Blacks in this sample rated their
        health as very good, good, or fair and believed that their health
        was at a level equal to or better than that of other people their

Henry, Melvin (continued)

own age. Functionally, these elderly Blacks were able to take
care of routine activities of daily living and experienced little
or no problems in getting good medical treatment. The costs for
medical care were covered by government programs or private insurance. The majority of the respondents attributed responsibility
for securing health care for the elderly to the federal level of
government. In general, this sample of Black elderly reported
few problems relative to health care. The major areas of concern
were restricted employment and mobility. In particular, there
were difficulties in holding a regular job and walking up three
flights of stairs. Some also reported insurance problems involving difficult instructions and explanation of benefits, long
delays in receiving reimbursement for medical expenses and transportation problems concludes the writer.

393. Jackson, Jacquelyne J. "Action and Non-Action." Action For Aged
      Blacks: When? A Conference of The National Caucus on the Black
      Aged. Washington, DC: National Caucus on The Black Aged, 1973,
      pp. 12-17.

      The author discusses the history of the National Caucus on The
      Black Aged beginning with its origins in 1971. She states that
      some of the programs that affect Black people and specifically
      older Blacks are only receiving "piecemeal" money for their sup-
      port. Since various Black groups are competing for the "same
      monies" to keep their programs going, in terms of action and non-
      action, they get caught in the game of divide and conquer, argues
      Dr. Jackson. The sociologist also points out that the absolute
      gap between old Blacks and old Whites has not only continued to
      increase over the past several decades, but is continuing to in-
      crease.

394. Kovi, J. et al. "Gastric Cancer in American Negroes." Cancer,
      Vol. 34, No. 1, July, 1974, pp. 765-770.

      There were 110 males and 40 females in this study, a male to fe-
      male ratio of 2.75:1. A number of American series of stomach
      cancer have reported male predominance in sex ratios ranging from
      2.6:1 to 2.0:1. The patients' ages ranged from 25 to 87 years.
      The mean age for males was 62.3 years and for females was 64
      years. Corresponding figures for American Caucasians were 65.0
      years for males and 62.1 years for females. This study was done
      at Howard University Hospital.

395. Lewis, Edward A. "High Blood Pressure, Other Risk Factors and
      Longevity: The Insurance Viewpoint." American Journal of Medi-
      cine, Vol. 55, September, 1973, pp. 281-294.

      The writer points out that in the United States, the proportion
      of Black men aged 45 to 65 with distinctly elevated systolic or
      diastolic blood pressures appears to be about double that of White
      men. In Black women aged 45-54, the proportion with such elevated
      blood pressures is about two and a half times that among White
      women; however, among Black women aged 55 to 64 the proportion

Lewis, Edward A. (continued)

with distinctly elevated pressures is only about a third higher
than among White women. This is because the proportion of hypertensive Black women is rather high at ages under 45 and does not
increase with advancing age as sharply as in White women, among
whom the prevalence of elevated blood pressures at ages under 45
is relatively low. The higher blood pressures of Blacks do appear
to be related to their generally lower socioeconomic status. This
was brought out in a study of the race differentials in mortality
attributed to hypertension in which the blood pressures of Whites
and non-Whites in various occupations and at various income levels
were compared; the mortality from hypertensive disease was much
higher in non-Whites regardless of occupation or socio-economic
class. A number of investigations disclose a wide variation in
blood pressure levels among different racial and ethnic groups.
It has been suggested that the higher blood pressures noted among
Blacks in the United States may reflect a genetic factor. This
conclusion is based partly on observations that hypertension is
quite common in West African tribes, whereas average blood pressures in several East African tribes resemble more nearly those
of Whites in the United States, surmises the writer. Average
blood pressures distinctly higher than those among Blacks in the
United States have been recorded in young Polynesians and Melane-
sians, concludes the researcher.

396. McDowell, Arthur. "Health Data On Aging Persons." Proceedings
of The Research Conference on Minority Group Aged in the South.
Jacquelyne J. Jackson, Editor. Durham, NC: Center for the Study
of Aging and Human Development, Duke University Medical Center,
1972, pp. 117-124.

The writer states that the prevalence of heart disease is higher
for Blacks than Whites. About 16 percent of the adult White male
population has heart disease of all types, as compared with about
36 percent of their Black counterparts. A stronger differential
exists comparing the older adult population by race. Hypertension
shows a White male prevalence rate of about 18 percent and a Black
male rate of about 37 percent. Corresponding data are 21 percent
for White and 40 percent for Black females. Over and over again
you see this difference. Really significant is the concealed
classification such as income. There you see much of the apparent
racist difference as an income difference. Much the same is true
of such other measures as limitation of activity. About two-
fifths of those 65+ years of age suffer a limitation in their ability to do their regular work or housework due to some chronic
condition, with a clear racial differentiation unfavorable to
Blacks, states the author. While there is not such a clear differential in the 45-64 year-old group or at least not quite as
big a rate when the age group under consideration is broadened,
you are still looking at limitation of activity related to income.
There is a very clear relationship. More chronic conditions
cause great disability among the poor, concludes the researcher.

397. Newman, Gustave, et al. "Alterations in Neurologic Status With
     Age." Journal of the American Geriatrics Society, Vol. 8, No. 12,
     December, 1960, pp. 915-917.

     The 200 persons studied were volunteers who lived in the community
     in and around Durham, North Carolina. Their ages ranged from 60
     to 93 years (average 70 years). Males and females of both the
     White and Black races were included. The neurologic examination
     was conducted using only the more common standard tools, such as a
     reflex hammer, a tuning fork, a straight pin and some cotton. The
     findings were recorded in the usual clinical manner, that is, as
     indicating normal, moderately impaired function, or severely im-
     paired function. Of 27 items from the neurologic examination, the
     9 which presented the greatest number of deviations from normal
     were selected for closer scrutiny. These variables were gait,
     reflex activity, movements associated with gait, involuntary move-
     ments (tremor), vibratory sensibility (128 tuning fork), two-point
     discrimination, touch, pain and olfaction. The writers argue that
     variables such as palsies of the cranial nerves were of such in-
     frequent occurrence as to be of no value in a statistical study.
     The foregoing 9 neurologic variables were cross-indexed against
     the 4 basic demographic variables of sex, race, age and socio-
     economic status, and tested for significance of variability by the
     chi square test. It was pointed out that alterations of reflex
     activity were much more highly correlated with race, the White
     subjects tending to be hyper-reflexive, whereas the Blacks were
     hypo-reflexive. This racial difference was statistically much
     more significant than the sex difference, and had a P value of
     .001; that is, the probability was 1 in 1,000 that it was due to
     chance, conclude the authors.

398. Nichols, Gloria J. "Drugs and Nutrition." Journal of the Nati-
     onal Medical Association, Vol. 70, No. 10, October, 1978, pp.
     737-738.

     According to the writer, in our society, the elderly are the prin-
     cipal drug users. Patients over 65 make up somewhat less than 11
     percent of the population, but they spend more than 25 percent of
     all monies expended for drugs. They may take prescription medica-
     tions for the treatment of one or more diseases or they may self-
     medicate for symptoms associated with old age. The elderly spend
     a great deal of time watching television, where they are bombarded
     by commercials with claims that a particular pill can relieve an
     aching back, indigestion, swollen legs, or some other distressing
     health problem. They will often go the corner drugstore for medi-
     cations hoping to get instant relief. Excessive use of laxatives
     by older people may be due to the widespread, but erroneous, be-
     lief that one must have daily bowel movements and that simple
     constipation resulting from improper diet must be controlled with
     laxatives, contends the author. The elderly constitute a sub-
     group in which nutritional depletion or malnutrition deficiencies,
     including lack of knowledge about drugs they are taking, foods
     that should be avoided or included in their diet, social isolation,
     physical disability, mental disturbance, and poverty. As second-
     ary factors, dulled taste buds, false teeth, and irregular cooking

Nichols, Gloria J. (continued)

habits contribute to inadequate diets. A drug can be potentiated
by an empty stomach or an undernourished body. Aging is associated with many chronic diseases that can reduce appetite, cause
malabsorption, and decrease nutrient utilization. Such diseases
include congestive heart failure, diabetes, and cancer. Because
of the pathophysiological changes produced by aging, elderly patients tend to absorb drugs at a slower rate, distribute them differently, and eliminate them less efficiently than middle-aged
patients, concluded the author.

399. Nowlin, John B. "Successful Aging: Health and Social Factors In
An Inter-Racial Population." Black Aging, Vol. 2, Nos. 4-6,
April, June and August, 1977, pp. 10-16.

This article proposes a tentative definition of "successful aging"
and examines data collected from an older population in the context of this definition. Any specific definition of "successful
aging" will necessarily be, at least in part, arbitrary, states
the author. Two criteria, both with prima facie validity, would
be chronologic age itself and health status. With respect to
chronologic age, the older person, by virtue of remaining alive
and accruing years, reflects some degree of success in dealing
with vicissitudes of aging. The particular age at which an individual can be considered "successful" in coping with these "vicissitudes" is moot. Yet another gerontologic "talking point" at
present equally informal as that of "successful aging," is consideration of later life in terms of "younger old-age" and "older
old-age"; the age of 75 has been suggested as the dividing point
between these two age groups, according to Nowlin. Attainment of
age 75 then could serve as a reasonable age criterion for definition of "successful aging." Other than chronological age, it is
difficult to conceive of a factor more fundamental to any notion
of "successful aging" than health status. The pervasive role of
health in all aspects of coping for any age group needs little emphasis. Since senescence itself often is associated with loss of
physiologic resources, health status seems an obvious second criterion for "successful aging," concludes the writer.

400. Primm, Beny J. "Poverty, Folk Remedies and Drug Misuse Among the
Black Elderly." Health and the Black Aged. Wilbur H. Watson, et
al., Editors. Washington, DC: National Center on Black Aged, 1978,
pp. 63-70.

The author points out that pharmacists must be alerted to the
problems of possible over-medication resulting from prescribed
and over-the-counter drugs. Physicians must learn to care for
the elderly, not just cure them: (1) They must take time to talk
to their patients; (2) They must explain the condition for which
a drug is prescribed; and (3) They must look for inexpensive, gene-
ric (not brand name) drugs to prescribe. In sum, they must teach
prevention. State and national legislators must rectify some
basic problems in this area by law. For example, every drug sold
in America for senior citizens should be required to state, in
large type, exactly what the consumer should know: How many to

Primm, Beny J. (continued)

take, what not to take it with, et cetera. A comprehensive national health plan would also help. Health care must be a right,
not a privilege, concludes the writer.

401. Ruiz, Dorothy S. and Theresa A. Herbert. "The Economic of Health
Care for Elderly Blacks." Journal of The National Medical Association, Vol. 76, No. 9, September, 1984, pp. 849-853.

It was pointed out that inflation, medical expenses, and the ineffective buffering of public assistance programs have made
health care for older Blacks a scarce commodity. They conclude:
"Low income is merely another barrier to adequate medical care in
American society. However, with the rising number of older Blacks
with diminishing incomes, it is becoming an increasingly effective barrier."

402. "Sam Johnson Is Still Horsing Around at 99." Jet, November 22,
1973, pp. 62-63.

Article concerns a 99-year-old ex-slave who worked very hard as
a stablehand, exercise boy, a one-race (in 1973) jockey, trainer
and groomer for 81 years. He credits "soul food" for much of his
good health. "Soul food ain't nothing new. It's older than me,"
reminded Johnson. At 99 years old he still walked at least one
mile a day--in morning and evening installments--from his home in
Elmont, Long Island, NY to Belmont Park race track and back.

403. Shafer, Stephen O. "Brain Infarction Risk Factors in Black New
York City Stroke Patients." Journal of Chronic Diseases, Vol. 27,
1974, pp. 127-133.

The author points out that of 527 consecutive stroke patients at
Harlem Hospital, 22 percent had had a previous stroke: 57 percent
had hypertension: 28 percent had diabetes mellitus: 24 percent
had advanced heart disease: 19 percent had none of these conditions identified. These proportions match those from White
series, except for the low prevalence of heart disease, which was
recorded only in clinically symptomatic stages. When the series
was divided in half by age, diabetes, heart disease and previous
stroke were each more common in patients 65 and older. Hypertension was significantly (p is less than 0.02) less frequent. The
Health Examination Survey estimated that 52 percent of Blacks age
65-74 and 60 percent of those aged 75-79 are hypertensive. In
Harlem stroke patients, by contrast, the prevalence of hypertension at ages 65-74 was 48 percent. It fell to 37 percent for
ages 75 and over. In more aged patients, hypertension seemed to
be less common than estimates, concludes the writer.

404. _____. et al. "The Contribution of Nonaneurysmal Intracranial Hemorrhage to Stroke Mortality in New York City Blacks."
Strokes, Vol. 4, November/December, 1973, pp. 928-932.

The authors surmise that of 527 unselected stroke patients (98%
Black) in a New York City hospital, 80 (17%) had nonaneurysmal

Shafer, Stephen O. (continued)

intracranial hemorrhages, with a fatality rate of 85%. Of 216
inhospital deaths 37% were due to such hemorrhages. In patients
aged 65 and less, 52% of 90 fatal events were hemorrhagic. Only
in patients below age 46, however, did cerebral hemorrhage account for more deaths than infarction. The incidence of hemorrhage and the proportion of inhospital deaths from it were higher
than in three White American and lower than in one Black African
series. The differences were not major, and could be explained
by varying definitions and hospital use. The mean age of patients was 61 years. When the inhospital mortality is extrapolated
into annual mortality estimates, the following conclusions according to the authors may be drawn about spontaneous aneurysmal
intracranial hemorrhage in New York City Blacks: (1) above age
45, it does not account for more deaths than infarction, (2) it
is not much more common or lethal in Blacks than in Whites, and
(3) it does not occur at earlier ages in Blacks than in Whites.

405.   Staggers, Frank. "Carcinoma of the Prostate Gland in California:
       A Candid Look at Survival Trends in Regards to Stage, Race and
       Social Class." Health and The Black Aged. Wilbur H. Watson et
       al., Editors. Washington, DC: National Center on Black Aged, 1978,
       pp. 18-30.

Cancer of the prostate is the most frequent category of all cancers occurring in Black males after the age of 65, states the
author. The presence of the disease can be detected by rectal
examination. As indicated by the California Tumor Registry for
Alameda County between 1942 and 1969, White males with cancer of
the prostate seemed to have had a higher survival rate than Black
males, according to Staggers. However, when type of treatment
setting was controlled, White males treated in county hospitals
had a lower survival rate than all other groups, including Black
males. The author concludes that while it was clear that there
were race-related differences between Black and White males in
the rate of cancer of the prostate, there were also differential
treatment effects that may have reflected class and technological
differences between intervention systems when patients were admitted to private versus county (public) hospitals.

406.   Thompson, Larry W. et al. "Relation of Serum Cholesterol to Age,
       Sex, and Race in an Elderly Community Group." Journal of Geron-
       tology, Vol. 20, 1965, pp. 160-164.

Total serum cholesterol determinations were made on 198 elderly
persons (60-93 years) living in or around Durham, N.C., as part
of a comprehensive study of human aging. Repeat determinations
were obtained on 74 of these people after a three-year interval.
White and Black community volunteers of both sexes and a wide
range of socio-economic levels were included. No over-all age
effect was observed. Females in their seventh and eighth decades
had significantly higher serum cholesterols than males; but sex
differences were less pronounced in the oldest group (80-93 years).
The data suggest that females reach a peak value in their 60s followed by a gradual decline, while males above 60 undergo little

Thompson, Larry W. et al. (continued)

change with time, state the authors. A sex by race interaction was also apparent, with the Black males having significantly higher levels than the White males; the difference between White and Black female groups was minimal according to the writers. A comparison of Ss with and without clinical evidence of cardiovascular disease revealed no differences, which suggests that cholesterol level may play a less significant role in the development of pathological processes in senescence than in middle age.

407.   Weaver, Jerry L. "Personal Health Care: A Major Concern For Minority Aged." Comprehensive Service Delivery System For The Minority Aged. E. Percil Stanford, Editor. San Diego, CA: Center on Aging, School of Social Work, San Diego State University, 1977, pp. 41-62.

Poverty, Discrimination, segregation and little or no access to scientific health care providers seem to have produced a selected body of elderly--perhaps only the strong survive--because the mortality picture of very old Blacks (over 75 years) is generally better than that of their Anglo peers, argues the author. Nevertheless, for all Black elderly, there is a persistent pattern of higher incidence of most chronic diseases, days of forced inactivity and visits to physicians. There is very little detailed information about the relative well-being and health care needs of Black aged. Studies which lump non-elderly with elderly are misleading, while studies of Black elderly alone document conditions without offering a yardstick for determining the relative severity or frequency of problems for Blacks, states the author. The author concludes that while sickle-cell anemia has captured the attention of many Americans, the most severe health problem of Black elderly, and for the overall community, is hypertension. As early as 1966 it was reported that "in any age group the likelihood of heart disease with hypertension is greater for Blacks than for White persons." Especially threatened are Black women: fully 71 percent of Black women over 50 years of age in a study of New Orleans residents were found to be hypertensive, concludes the author.

408.   Wilson, James L. "Geriatric Experiences With the Negro Aged." Geriatrics, Vol. 8, February 1953, pp. 88-92.

The author states that while there are no sharp differences in the majority of diseases affecting the Black aged and those affecting the White race in the same age bracket, there are certain differences in etiologic factors and incidence of ailments which merit consideration and correction. On the basis of a study of an active Negro population between the ages of 55 and 91, the diseases encountered may be listed in the order of their occurrence as: (1) cardiovascular disease, with or without hypertension; (2) arteriosclerosis, generalized; (3) hypertrophic and infectious arthritis and osteoarthritis; (4) calcified fibroma uteri; (5) hypertrophied prostate; (6) carcinoma of breast, uterus and stomach; (7) pneumonia and influenza; (8) diabetes mellitus with complicating infections and gas gangrene; (9) pulmonary tuberculosis; (10)

Wilson, James L. (continued)

aneurysm; (11) leg ulcers, due to varicose veins, arteriosclerosis, trauma or sickle-cell anemia; (12) cirrhosis of the liver; (13) senile dementia, cerebral arteriosclerosis and cataracts; (14) vitiligo; (15) arterio-venous fistula due to trauma; and (16) ainhum. The author points out that the FACTORS determining the incidence of certain ailments in aged Blacks are primarily economic. Where they exist, a low wage scale and long working hours tend to undermine body resistance. Poor housing and overcrowding with attendant unsanitary conditions predispose to infectious diseases. The existence of crowded districts and alleys in cities promotes disease and crime. Trauma encountered in hazardous occupations is responsible for production of certain surgical ailments. Inadequate diet promotes low serum proteins which retard tissue repair. In certain areas some hospitals refuse to admit Blacks who, in many instances, are not hospitalized when necessary. Of nearly equal significance is the refusal of several medical schools to give postgraduate and refresher courses to Black physicians. Not withstanding these economic and educational barriers, the span of life and the total Black population have continued to increase. Scientific investigation serves to stress the need for greater opportunities for the Negro population, especially in economic, educational, health and hospitalization areas. The writer declares that there are essentially no major differences between the diseases of the Black aged and those of the White race in the same age bracket. Certain diseases, however, have a higher incidence in the Black: hypertensive heart disease, advanced generalized arteriosclerosis and pulmonary tuberculosis. The author concludes that the latter is on the decline. Incidence of carcinoma, as a whole, is lower than in the White race, but fibromyoma uteri is more commonly found. Vitiligo is seen more frequently than in the White race, and the rare finding of ainhum has not been reported in the White man. Only the latent cases of sickle-cell anemia live to reach an old age.

409. Wolf, Jacquelyn H., et al. "Access to Medical Care of the Black Urban Elderly." Journal of the National Medical Association, Vol. 75, No. 1, January, 1983, pp. 41-46.

This article was based on access to medical care of 492 Black urban respondents 60 years of age and older that was measured in a house-to-house study. 93% indicated that they had a regular source of medical care and 88% reported a visit to a physician or clinic within the past year. The researchers conclude that the respondents who reported poorer physical and mental health were more likely to have a regular source of care and to have seen a physician in the past year.

410. Wright, Roosevelt, et al. "The Black Elderly and Their Use of Health Care Services: A Causal Analysis." Journal of Gerontological Social Work, Vol. 2, No. 1, Fall, 1979, pp. 11-27.

In this essay, the authors attempt to develop a conceptual framework which provides a theoretical linkage between predisposing, enabling, and need for care factors and the utilization of

Wright, Roosevelt, et al. (continued)

physicians' services within an elderly Black population. The study uses a path analytic approach in order to determine the relative importance of different explanatory variables in determining the use of such services. Apart from its substantive findings, it also suggests that it is possible and desirable to use sophisticated multivariate analytical techniques in order to enhance our understanding of the causal relationship between the variables used to explain utilization. More importantly, however, the current study recognizes the need to pay more attention to the unique characteristics and needs of the Black elderly, argue the researchers.

411.   Young, John L., et al. "Incidence of Cancer in United States Blacks." Cancer Research, Vol. 35, November, 1975, pp. 3523-3536.

Incidence rates for the Black population of six Standard Metropolitan Statistical Areas in the United States are examined using data collected in the Third National Cancer Survey, 1969 to 1971. For all sites combined, Black males had the highest rates among the four major race-sex groups; Black females had the lowest rates. For fourteen common sites accounting for 80% of the cancers among Blacks, Black/White ratios, survival data, trends between 1935 and 1969, and geographic variation are presented. United States Black data, adjusted to an African Standard, are compared with similar data from Nigeria, Rhodesia, and South Africa. It has been suggested that the high rates among Black males can be explained by census underenumeration. However, it has shown that, while there was considerable underenumeration of Black males, aged 20 to 54, there was an overenumeration of Black males aged 65 and over, state the writers. None of the patterns previously discussed were significantly altered. Thus, high rates among Black males cannot be explained on the basis of denominators that were too low, declare the authors. An analysis of survey data by socioeconomic status is currently being undertaken by the National Cancer Institute utilizing census tract data. It is hoped that such an analysis will enable the Black/White differences noted in this report to be further understood, conclude the researchers.

13.   BLACK AGED AND HOUSING

412.   Brown, Diane Robinson, et al. "Home Equity Conversion: Income Generation for Black Elderly Homeowners." Urban Research Review (Howard University), Vol. 11, No. 3, 1987, pp. 5-8.

Overall, findings from this pilot study suggest that receptivity to home equity conversion as a mechanism for generating additional income is not shared by the majority of urban Black elderly homeowners. Most were not interested and did not view home equity conversion as offering possible benefits to meet their needs, state the researchers. Nonetheless, a substantial number did

Brown, Diane Robinson, et al. (continued)

express an interest in home equity conversion as reflected in slightly more than 40 percent of participants in the survey, conclude the authors. This article was based on a study done on elderly Black homeowners in the District of Columbia.

413. Isserman, Abraham.   "Housing For The Aged Blacks." Proceedings of Black Aged in the Future. Jacquelyne J. Jackson, Editor. Durham, NC: Center for the Study of Aging and Human Development, Duke University, 1973, pp. 34-39.

The writer points out that housing for Blacks and for the elderly Blacks has been blocked by The Department of Housing and Urban Development's rules and regulations. He gives fourteen housing needs of the Black elderly. These needs are applicable in most part to all elderly persons. Mr. Isserman concludes that to fulfill these needs will require strong dedication and intensive work in building coalitions of all people and organizations of goodwill determined to put America back on a course where its resources will be devoted to the well-being of the people of this country.

414. Jackson, Hobart C. "Housing and Geriatric Centers for Aging and Aged Blacks." Proceedings of Black Aged in The Future. Jacquelyne J. Jackson, Editor. Durham, NC: Center for The Study of Aging and Human Development, Duke University, 1973, pp. 23-33.

The author feels that there are general inadequacies in our social institutions and specific housing inadequacies for Aged Blacks. Because of this, he recommended very strongly that a movement be undertaken for the development of geriatric centers in Black communities. He concludes that a redistribution of income is vital if the Black elderly are to be removed from the kind of grinding poverty that no one was meant to endure. Jackson continued to surmise that the implementation of a goal of power for the powerless would give the minority elderly the priority position they deserve.

415. Jackson, Jacquelyne J. "Social Impact of Housing Relocation Upon Urban, Low-Income Black Aged." Gerontologist, Vol. 12, Spring, 1972, pp. 32-37.

The author did a comparison of successful and non-successful Black aged applicants for a public, age-segregated housing complex in Durham, North Carolina to determine characteristics favoring acceptability. Those whose objective characteristics (e.g. being male and married) more nearly approximated dominant social patterns and whose subjective characteristics (e.g. dependency) tended to conform to traditional stereotypes of Blacks gained admission more often than those rejected. One significant social impact, in the microcosm, is that of the social consequences of such discriminatory selectivity among Blacks only. One major implication of the study is an apparent tendency for the selection processes to favor those among the Blacks who, in some sense, may be the least deprived. In other words, here as in other areas involving

Jackson, Jacquelyne J. (continued)

younger and older Blacks, those "who get in" are those who tend,
on the one hand, to approximate more nearly those objective characteristics (such as being male, younger, or married) favored by the
larger society, and, on the other hand, who display subjective
characteristics not favored by the larger society, except as they
may be found within minority groups (such as dependence), argues
Dr. Jackson. Hence, this study suggests, anew, serious considerations of the consequences of selectivity outward of the "best,"
and rejection of the "rest" of the Blacks, whether it be in housing for the aged, education for the youth or employment for the
adults, concludes the sociologist.

14. BLACK AGED AND HYPERTENSION

416. Flamenbaum, Walter. "Management of Unique Hypertensive Situations:
A Focus on Difficult, Problematic, Elderly Black Patients."
Journal of the National Medical Association, Vol. 19, Supplement,
March, 1987, pp. 31-34.

According to this researcher, the pharmacokinetics of labetalol
have been studied in the elderly patient and are predictable and
appropriate for the treatment of this age group. Its bioavaila-
bility has been shown to be the same in both young and old patients, while its elimination when administered either orally or
intravenously is prolonged in the elderly as compared to younger
patients. This knowledge allows therapeutic application of labetalol in the elderly hypertensive patient, which can be easily
managed for optimal benefits, concludes Dr. Flamenbaum.

417. Lewis, Irene. "The Study of Hypertension Compliance in a Group
of Elderly Third World Patients." Health and The Black Aged.
Wilbur H. Watson, et al., Editors. Washington, DC: National
Center on Black Aged, 1978, pp. 4-17.

The article focuses on identifying factors that could be relied
upon to indicate a patient's potential for high compliance with a
treatment plan for hypertension. The author attempted to determine whether any such factors could be manipulated by the provider
to increase the likelihood of compliance. Each patient's compliance with a treatment plan was assessed informally. The degrees
of compliance were loosely put as "low," "medium," and "high."
Out of nine cases, one person was judged low, three as medium,
and five (5) as high compliers. Recent audits of patient records
at the clinic where the author conducted this study showed that
her findings were generally representative of compliance behavior,
maintains the author.

15. BLACK AGED AND LIFE SATISFACTION

418. Bild, Bernice R. and Robert J. Havighurst. "Senior Citizens in
Great Cities: The Case of Chicago." Gerontologist, Vol. 16, No.
1, February, 1976, pp. 1-8.

The researchers discussed the Black elderly in Chicago in the following areas: "Economic Welfare," "Housing," "Problems of Elderly
Chicagoans," "Health," "Family and Social Support," "Life Satisfaction," and "Knowledge and Use of Services." It was pointed
out that the Black elderly were probably the worst off economically of any other aged groups in Chicago. On the whole, income,
education, and employment have greater effect than age. Blacks
register lower levels of (life) satisfaction than whites, mainly
but not entirely attributable to income differences, conclude
the authors.

419. Donnenwerth, Gregory V., et al. "Life Satisfaction Among Older
Persons: Rural-Urban and Racial Comparisons." Social Science
Quarterly, Vol. 59, No. 3, December, 1978, pp. 578-583.

In the present study the analysis of covariance indicates that the
variance produced in life satisfaction by race is not due primarily to race per se but to income. Although the significance of
residence and race are explained primarily through income and
frequency of social contacts, the interaction of residence and
race remains largely unexplained, state the researchers. A partial explanation can be offered by examining the cross-classifica-
tion of residence and race with income and frequency of contacts
than rural whites. Third, rural Blacks have a higher mean income
and higher levels of social contacts than rural whites. The difference in social contacts and income provide a reasonable explanation for the higher life satisfaction among urban versus rural
whites and rural versus urban Blacks, conclude the authors.

420. Jackson, James S. et al. "Life Satisfaction Among Black Urban
Elderly." Aging and Human Development, Vol. 8, 1977-78, pp. 169-
179.

This article was based on a sample of 102 Black retired adults
residing in noninstitutionalized settings. The sample was purpose-
ly selected from predominantly Black older adult centers located
in the Detroit metropolitan area. Individuals in the sample
ranged from fifty-four to eighty-three years of age with a mean
of 69.5 years. Females comprised 71.6 of the persons interviewed
and were over-represented based upon the 1973 census estimates
for this population. In addition to the racial homogeneity of the
respondents, 80.9 percent reported a high school education or less.
Reported annual income for the majority of the sample (87%) was
less than three thousand dollars. A large proportion (62.6%) of
the respondents were born and raised in the South. The authors
conclude that their findings, when viewed in the context of the
societal barriers which perpetually confront Blacks across the
life span, suggest that adjustment to aging, particularly psycho-
logically, might be a different and perhaps relatively easier task
in comparison to the adjustment of White majority individuals.

421. Kivett, Vira R. "The Importance of Race To The Life Situation of the Rural Elderly." Black Scholar, Vol. 13, No. 1, January/February, 1982, pp. 13-20.

This study examined the frequency with which race was of relative importance to several variables important to the quality of later life. Results from multivariate procedures showed race to be of relative importance in three of sixteen analyses: adequacy of income, decision to live with a daughter rather than a son, and life satisfaction. Race was of no relative importance to the extent of social interaction; morale, retirement satisfaction, and loneliness; decisions to live alone or with others; health; transportation; and service utilization, states Prof. Kivett. The results suggest that in a rural area race is of less frequent relative importance to the life situation of older adults than health and other social and economic factors, concludes the researcher. In summary, data from 418 rural adults aged 65 to 99 years show older Blacks to differ from older white adults in four areas important to quality of life-health, educational background, housing, and marital status. Race, per se, however, is an infrequent predictor or discriminator of life situations of the rural elderly. Despite more negative life situation indicators, older Blacks report higher levels of life satisfaction than their white counterparts, suggests the author.

422. Osgood, Nancy J. "The Impact of Creative Dramatics on Black Elderly." Journal of Minority Aging, Vol. 9, No. 1, 1984, pp. 60-72.

This study was designed to explore the impact of participation in a program of creative dramatics of Black elderly. A sample of 103 elderly, 95% of whom were Black, was chosen from seven nutrition sites in Virginia. A matched control group of 27 was chosen from two of the study sites. The members of the experimental group participated in a 10-month program of creative dramatics (including pantomime, improvisation, dance, motion, and intergenerational theatre). Members of the experimental and control groups were pretested and posttested on life satisfaction, self-perceived loneliness, and subjective age identification. Analysis of change scores revealed significant change on all dependent variables for members of the experimental group, as compared to members of the control group, who did not participate in drama sessions, states the researcher. Qualitative analyses of leaders' diaries, systematically-recorded observations of group leaders, and interviews with elderly participants supported the quantitative analyses. Elderly Blacks who participated in the creative drama program for 10 months were indeed significantly happier, less lonely, and saw themselves as younger after participation than did those in the control group who had not participated in the drama program, concludes the author.

423.   Rao, V. Nandini and V. V. Prakasa Rao. "Life Satisfaction in the
        Black Elderly: An Exploratory Study." Aging and Human Development,
        Vol. 14, No. 1, 1981-1982, pp. 55-66.

        The major purpose of the study was to determine whether the Life
        Satisfaction Index (LSIA) was unidimensional or multidimensional
        and to examine the different dimensions of the scale to either
        validate or reject the factors on elderly Blacks. The data for
        the study were collected from a sample of 240 Black elderly in
        Jackson, Mississippi in Spring 1978. The LSIA was tested for re-
        validation and reliability by the use of item analysis, biserial
        correlation, discrimination values, and factor analysis. The
        study failed to support the existence of five dimensions that were
        supposed to form the life satisfaction scale as high intercorrela-
        tions were found among "mood tone," "zest," "self-concept," "reso-
        lution," and "congruence." The cluster of items derived from
        factor analysis was not similar to clusters obtained by other
        writers. The data, however, revealed that the scale was highly
        reliable in measuring life satisfaction among Black elderly, con-
        clude the researchers.

424.   _____. "Determinants of Life Satisfaction Among Black
        Elderly." Activities, Adaptation, and Aging, Vol. 3, No. 2,
        Winter, 1982, pp. 35-48.

        The researchers suggest that the adjustment to aging with respect
        to life satisfaction may be different for Black elderly males com-
        pared to females. Demographic, social, and familial variables
        have different impacts on the well-being of the sample across sex
        groups. The results of the study suggest that the adjustment-to-
        age models are quite different for Black elderly males and females.
        The needs of Black females are quite different from those of Black
        males, declare the writers. The findings support earlier argu-
        ments that the Black elderly should be treated as a heterogeneous
        group in formulating and designing social services programs. Be-
        fore drawing broad generalizations about the patterns of adjust-
        ment of aging among Blacks with no regard for sex differences,
        systematic research on familial, social, economic and psychologi-
        cal factors must be conducted in samples in the future with larger
        population that are more representative of the Black elderly, con-
        clude the authors.

                    16. BLACK AGED AND LEGAL SERVICES

425.   Grilfix, Michael. "Minority Elders: Legal Problems and the Need
        for Legal Services." Comprehensive Services Delivery System for
        the Minority Aged. E. Percil Stanford, Editor. San Diego, CA:
        Center of Aging, School of Social Work, San Diego State University,
        1977, pp. 131-141.

        The researcher states that particular legal problems of elder
        minority persons include the following: (1) They suffer from an
        extraordinarily high incidence of poverty. (2) They are more de-
        pendent on public benefits and encounter more difficulties in

Grilfix, Michael (continued)

obtaining them. (3) They may be more susceptible to consumer
fraud and consumer abuses than Anglo elders. (4) They are beset
by problems that may be unique to their race. (5) They suffer
from the residual effects of discrimination--both individual and
institutional--experiences at younger ages. Although some steps
have been taken to address these problems, our legal institutions
have not satisfied them. Nor, for that matter, have legal service
programs for elders been sufficiently sensitive to minority persons, argues the author. By identifying a number of the most
salient issues and suggesting remedial measures, it is the hope of
the author that more attention will be given minority elders by
legal service providers....

17. BLACK AGED AND LEISURE TIME

426. Anderson, Monroe. "The Pains and Pleasure of Black Folks."
      Ebony, March, 1973, pp. 123-130.

      The writer points out that in 1973 about 60 percent of the Black
      aged still lives in the South and the greatest single concentra-
      tion of them can be found in New York City. It is also mentioned
      that 20 percent of the Black aged have no living children and that
      the majority of those with children do not live with them. Many
      Black aged feel that besides poverty, the major psychological
      problems of being old are that many times you are lonely, you do
      not have many friends left and you do not have anything to do.
      Several Black aged women are interviewed in this article, and they
      tell what it is like to be old, female, poor, and Black.

427. Lambing, Mary L. "Social Class Living Patterns of Retired
      Negroes." Gerontologist, Vol. 12, Autumn, Part 1, 1972, pp. 285-
      289.

      This study investigates the life-style of American Blacks retiring
      from the minor professions, from stable blue-collar work, and from
      the service occupations, domestic work, and common labor. Data
      were collected through interviews with 33 men and 68 women ranging
      in age from 48 to 105. Income differentials and leisure-time
      activities were found to have implications for planners in recre-
      ation and social welfare. Dr. Lambing believes future studies of
      the Black aged might focus on two groups not included here, those
      retiring from the major professions, such as law and medicine,
      and those who need the help of Public Assistance payments but are
      not willing to have a lien on their property in order to qualify.
      She concludes that many older Blacks in the lower classes have
      inadequate income even though they may have pensions or Old Age
      Assistance; those without the additional help of Social Security
      benefits must live a spartan life indeed. Social planners need to
      recognize these shortcomings in the present system. Gerontolo-
      gists planning recreational facilities for Blacks can benefit by
      recognizing social class differences in leisure-time activities,
      argues Prof. Lambing.

428. Marshall, Marion. "Differential Use of Time." <u>Workshop on</u>
      <u>Community Services and The Black Elderly</u>. Richard H. Davis,
      Editor. Los Angeles: Andrus Gerontology Center, University of
      Southern California, 1972, pp. 12-16.

      The author feels that it is much more difficult to get the older
      Black person to use his leisure time in involvement activities,
      for they have not had this encouragement from society. Marshall
      concludes that we must help the Black elderly to move away from
      being told what to do. They must plan together what to do and
      then take the responsibility of getting it done.

                   18. BLACK AGED AND LONELINESS

429. Creecy, Robert F., et al. "Correlates of Loneliness Among the
      Black Elderly." <u>Activities, Adaptation, and Aging</u>, Vol. 3, No. 2,
      Winter, 1982, pp. 9-16.

      The findings of this study indicate that perceived poor health and
      perceived financial inadequacy are directly linked to feelings of
      loneliness. Negative assessments of health and personal income
      tend to reduce mobility and prevent the Black elderly from ventur-
      ing beyond their residential contexts to participate in activities
      and social groups that may thwart feelings of loneliness. Health
      care services, both preventive and rehabilitative, should be im-
      plemented to address the health needs and requirements of Black
      older people, suggest the authors. Special provisions such as re-
      duced fares for public transportation would be very helpful to
      those individuals who have limited incomes. The implementation
      of these measures may increase the mobility of older Black adults
      and influence their predisposition to seek out and capitalize on
      social opportunities in the broader community arena, declare the
      researchers. Fear of crime, as do poor health and inadequate
      finances, leads to involuntary social isolation which, in turn,
      gives rise to feelings of loneliness. The implementation of
      security escort services and the installation of crime prevention
      devices such as mercury vapor lights may help minimize this fear
      and provide the elderly with increased opportunities for social
      interaction, observe the writers. They conclude, in part: "....
      In addition to focusing on Black elderly residents of the conven-
      tional community, these investigators should draw their sample
      from among Black elderly who reside in the various institutional
      settings. The results of these efforts would enhance our under-
      standing of loneliness and assist in developing a broad based
      strategy for loneliness intervention within the Black Elderly
      population."

430. Kivett, Vira R. "Loneliness and The Rural Black Elderly: Perspec-
      tives on Intervention." <u>Black Aging</u>, Vol. 3, Nos. 4 and 5,
      April and June, 1978, pp. 160-166.

      Results from this article show that three out of five older rural
      Blacks surveyed experienced varying bouts of loneliness which
      could be partially explained by intra-group differences on several

Kivett, Vira R. (continued)

population characteristics. Social rather than physical factors generally contributed to loneliness by creating the social as well as emotional isolation of older adults. Inadequate transportation and the loss of a spouse through death, separation or divorce were significant influences on both occasional and frequent loneliness. The flexibility to travel from one place to another, whether it be for the purpose of shopping, visiting with family, or for other reasons seemed to be crucial to feelings of loneliness, states the author. The frequency with which older rural Blacks telephoned friends, relatives, or others appeared to be an index to the extent of loneliness being incurred. The frequently lonely showed considerable effort to circumvent their feelings of loneliness through a "reaching out" to others via the telephone. Despite the observation of the similarity between the occasionally and the frequently lonely, important distinctions could be made between the two groups based on adequacy of eyesight, marital status, and educational level. The observation that older Blacks who were frequently rather than sometimes lonely were more likely to have poor eyesight, to have a higher education, to be married rather than divorced, and to report that they had no one in whom they could trust or confide suggested the relatively weak role that marriage may play as an emotional support among certain groups of older married Black adults, specifically, the higher educated, visually impaired, argues the writer. Several variables failed to separate older Blacks according to frequency of loneliness. Some appeared to be suppressed because of the relative homogeneity of the rural sample, i.e., socioeconomic characteristics based on previous work type and education, concludes the author.

19. BLACK AGED AND MENTAL HEALTH

431. Bengtson, Vern L. and Linda M. Burton. "Mental Health and the Black Elderly: Competence, Susceptibility, and Quality of Life." Journal of Minority Aging, Vol. 7, Nos. 3 & 4, 1981-1982, pp. 25-31.

This article speculates about the possible vulnerability of aged Blacks to mental illnesses and suggests that coping mechanisms they may have acquired through their lifetimes, and particularly in response to racism, may, in fact, make them less susceptible. The researchers' concerns about competence, vulnerability, and susceptibility all point toward the need for increased research in these important areas. A critical research need is in the areas of cross-ethnic and cross-cultural research, so as to determine the commonalities and distinctions between minority and majority aged with respect to their socially-imposed vulnerability in old age to mental health disorders, state the authors. Because of their distinctive life experiences, it has been suggested that America's Black elderly face special challenges as they negotiate the changes of aging. Many of those challenges are directly related to issues of competence, susceptibility, and quality of life in old age, conclude the professors.

432. Carter, James H. "Differential Treatment of The Elderly Black:
      Victims of Stereotyping." Postgraduate Medicine, Vol. 52,
      November, 1972, pp. 211-214.

      Dr. Carter discusses two case studies involving elderly Blacks.
      He points out that aged Black persons, far from being homogeneous,
      make up heterogeneous groupings. The writer argues that many
      Blacks do not seek early Social Security or public assistance but
      instead want gainful employment. He observes that the generaliza-
      tion that the elderly Black will find gratification outside the
      world of work seems to be a gross misunderstanding. The author
      concludes that with a view toward correcting past and present
      mistakes, he would suggest that a starting point could be an inde-
      pendent cultural education including community involvement, study
      of pertinent social data, and a hard, honest look on the part of
      physicians at cultural issues as they relate to the elderly Black.

433. _____. "A Psychiatric Strategy For Aged Blacks in the Future."
      Proceedings of Black Aged in the Future. Jacquelyne J. Jackson,
      Editor. Durham, NC: Center for the Study of Aging and Human De-
      velopment, Duke University, 1973, pp. 94-100.

      The author observes that witnin the past decades psychiatry has
      made only token efforts to combat racism and to improve psychia-
      tric care for Black patients, especially elderly Blacks. He also
      points out that in spite of preventive measures, he anticipates
      that aged Blacks in the future will be suffering some mental ill-
      ness. The writer declares that the White therapist can be effec-
      tive with Black patients if he learns to understand the cultural
      and social values of Blacks.

434. _____. "Psychiatry's Insensitivity to Racism and Aging."
      Psychiatric Opinion, Vol. 10, No. 6, December 1973, pp. 21-25.

      According to Dr. Carter, racism, clearly a mental health problem,
      places every Black American in the position of being "psycholo-
      gically tyrannized, socially minimized and economically ignored."
      Because of racism, mental health professionals have been guilty
      of making too many invalid generalizations about the Black elderly,
      with too little selective research regarding the relevance of
      race to aging. Few psychiatrists will deny that they should carry
      a special responsibility to combating racism. Yet most seem
      hesitant to become personally involved in solving those problems
      stemming from racism. Obviously, the "good-will" of psychiatry
      is encouraging, but it does very little to combat racism, states
      Dr. Carter. What is actually needed is a personal involvement in
      attacking racism, which gives rise to most of the mental health
      problems of the Black patient. The Black, elderly psychiatric
      patient, whose problems would be expected to be compounded by age,
      constitutes a special group of patients who generally defy all of
      our current "accepted criteria for treatment." This clearly, ac-
      cording to the author, indicates that we need to begin to evaluate
      our traditional methods of treating Black patients. The Black,
      elderly patients may be seen as being special in that they are not
      only discriminated against because of age, but because of race.
      Seemingly, most psychiatrists have found little satisfaction in

Carter, James H.   (continued)

treating Black patients, and it would be expected that they will
find still less gratification in taking care of aged Black patients. Further, the private practice of psychiatry, which typically treats the middle-class neurotic patient, is obviously more re-
warding financially than service in public clinics or mental hospitals that treat the aged and the severely mentally disturbed
patient, concludes the author.

435.   _____. "Psychiatry, Racism and Aging." Journal of the
American Geriatrics Society, Vol. 20, No. 7, July 1972, pp. 343-
346.

The basis for present inadequacies in the treatment of aged Black
psychiatric patients is discussed. Training programs in psychiatry should include working with people of a different race. The
philosophical and social aspects of Black culture should receive
more attention. There is often a direct relationship between
social status and type of mental illness. Many of the Black patient's problems are related to race, and he is confronted with
more obstacles in obtaining appropriate help, argues the author.
For elderly Black people, there is a pressing need for better integration of mental health services with other health and social
services, concludes the author. Dr. Carter states that the nation
must eventually develop programs to make it possible for all
Americans to cope, regardless of their race or age. Without a
reasonable amount of research and evaluation, it is possible to
go down the wrong road to the point of no return. It is time that
psychiatrists, in addition to looking at Black pathology, review
the possibilities for relieving system deficiencies, including the
impact of racism, concludes the author.

436.   _____. "Psychiatry, Racism, and Aging." Proceedings of The
Research Conference on Minority Group Aged in the South.
Jacquelyne J. Jackson, Editor, Durham. NC: Center for the Study
of Aging and Human Development, Duke University Medical Center,
1972, pp. 125-130.

Up to the present time, approximately nine out of every ten psy-
chotic Black patients have been institutionalized and given protective or custodial care instead of active treatment, contends
the author. As for the less severely disturbed, most clinics,
finding traditional therapy ineffective, have been content to let
the Black patient drop away, rather than break with custom and
tradition to develop alternative treatment methods. Effective
treatment of Black and lower income groups seems to require multiple forms of intervention. The author argues that historically
there have been three lines of approach to the treatment of mental illness--the physical, the psychological and the social.
While all three forms of intervention are utilized to some extent,
at the present time it is characteristic for Black patients to receive the physical approach (chemical-somatic). Conditions of
life of the Black patient, particularly from low income families,
are such that a simultaneous attack on all levels is frequently
required. The writer points out, for example, combining active

Carter, James H. (continued)

environmental manipulation, such as job modification, with physical therapies, to effect the speediest amelioration of symptoms,
with appropriate forms of psychological intervention. There is a
pressing need to achieve fuller integration of mental health services with other social, health and welfare services in the community, and this especially applies to the aged. Families on the
lower socio-economic ladder have a multiplicity of unmet health,
economic, and social needs. The author states that it is difficult
to see how effective mental health services can be rendered by a
community mental health facility which pays no attention to the
totality of needs, and which endeavors to dispense physiological
prescriptions without regard to the whole life situation of the
patient, concludes Dr. Carter.

437.   _____. "The Black Aged: A Strategy For Future Mental Health
Services." Journal of the American Geriatrics Society, Vol. 26,
No. 12, December, 1978, pp. 553-556.

According to Dr. Carter, during the past decade psychiatry has
made only token efforts to combat racism and to improve psychiatric care for Black patients, especially elderly Blacks. The
United States Senate Special Committee on Aging, with limited con-
sultation from Black psychiatrists, is to be commended for legislation passed to date which is aimed at improving the health of
the elderly, states Prof. Carter. Much remains to be done in the
areas of prevention and treatment. To meet the mental health
needs of elderly Blacks successfully, consideration must be given
to their culture and value systems and most importantly, to the
realities of racism, concludes the author.

438.   Elam, Lloyd C. "Critical Factors For Mental Health in Aging Black
Populations." Ethnicity, Mental Health and Aging. Los Angeles:
Gerontology Center, University of Southern California, April,
1970, p. 2.

The author surmises that one of the critical factors for mental
health in the Black aged populations is the proper understanding
of more and better mental technique needs to be employed in dealing with this group. Unlike the White aged, the Black elderly
have special problems: they are poorer, have had a harder life,
are in poor health, and racism is ever-present.

439.   Faulkner, Audrey Olsen, et al. "Life Strengths and Life Stress:
Exploration in the Measurement of Mental Health of the Black
Aged." American Journal of Orthopsychiatry. Vol. 45, January,
1975, pp. 102-110.

This paper describes an attempt to understand the self-concept,
social characteristics, personal strengths, and frailties of a
group of older Black men and women in order to tailor mental health
and social work services to their needs. Difficulties inherent in
obtaining such information were minimized by a methodology that
integrated the research and service aspects of the project. Results of the pilot study, and service implications, are discussed.

Faulkner, Audrey Olsen <u>et al</u>. (continued)

The results show that in spite of a life full of stress and difficulties, the majority of the Black men and women in this group
have a highly positive self-concept, compare themselves favorably
with other people their age, and express relatively high satisfaction with life and themselves, all indices which show their
strength, and which we consider highly relevant to mental health.
They do, however, tend to feel victims of their environment
(which, in view of the very high crime rate in the area they live
in, is a realistic appraisal) and some seem socially isolated in
spite of their eagerness for contact, conclude the authors.

440. Hawkins, Brin D. "Mental Health and the Black Aged." <u>Mental Health:</u>
      <u>A Challenge to the Black Community</u>. Lawrence E. Gary, Editor.
      Philadelphia: Dorrance & Co., 1978, pp. 166-178.

The author discusses the stress factors that affect the mental
health of the Black Aged. These factors include the lack of sufficient income, housing and health care. He also states that isolation and lack of social contact and communication can be as
physically debilitating as health dysfunctions and may lead directly to emotional stress. The older person who has lost family,
friends, and satisfying social roles may lose the will to eat, to
participate, and eventually the will to live. Dr. Hawkins concludes that these stresses are compounded for a large number of
Black elderly who are left without the necessary economic and
personal resources to maintain an active and meaningful social
life.

441. Jackson, Jacquelyne J. "Epidemiological Aspects of Mental Illness
      Among Aged Black Women and Men." <u>Journal of Minority Aging</u>, Vol.
      4, No. 3, 1979, pp. 76-87.

Urging an epidemiology of mental illness of aged Blacks, and improved preventive and treatment resources in mental health for
them, this article describes demographically aged Blacks, assesses
epidemiological literature about their mental illnesses, speculates about major predictors of their social involvement, psychological well-being, and life satisfaction, and the implications
thereof, especially for research and manpower needs. Emphasized
is Black determination of the qualifications of white institutions
to include them, and affirmative action, where necessary, to upgrade those institutions. Also discussed are recent mortality
trends by sex showing heightened rates among some age-specific
groups from all causes, mental disorders, suicide, and homicide.
Prof. Jackson argues that much of the mental illnessess exhibited
by aged Blacks...could be reversed or modified, as is occurring
to a small degree through improved governmental programs for the
aged....

442. _____. "Negro Aged in North Carolina." <u>North Carolina Jour-</u>
      <u>nal of Mental Health</u>, Vol. 4, No. 1, 1970, pp. 43-52.

The author points out that, in North Carolina, more active intervention by community mental health and other agencies in areas of

Jackson, Jacquelyne J. (continued)

critical social concerns must take place. Apparently, too many
day centers within the state are yet too much concerned about the
racial identity of the clients whom they will and will not service,
or yield only to token desegregation. According to the author,
too few psychiatrists and others speak up "loud and clear" about
such problems, as did too few North Carolinians generally about
the recent events which indicated that some state workers were receiving wages below the minimum wage scale--a fact which some persons may interpret as unrelated, e.g., to Black aged, but which
is quite related inasmuch as, again, we are back to income. Income affects, in various ways, adjustment in old age, states Dr.
Jackson. Community mental health centers, it seems to the author,
might assist further in helping to deal with such problems as
those of poverty--including employment and sufficient income, racism, youth problems and suicides. A resolution of these types of
problems would help to improve considerably the conditions and
mental health statuses of Blacks and of other aged within North
Carolina, contends Dr. Jackson. This paper about Black aged in
North Carolina was concerned chiefly with providing some limited
demographic data about such persons; with pointing out the need
for further studies about them, with :special emphasis upon factors affecting their mental health statuses; and with suggesting
that community mental health centers throughout the state might--
in fact, should--play significant roles in helping to reduce the
types of social conditions which tend to affect adversely the mental health statuses of Blacks, and of others who are aged, concludes the scholar.

443. Jackson, James S., Linda M. Chatters, and Harold W. Neighbors.
      "The Mental Health Status of Older Black Americans: A National
      Study." Black Scholar, Vol. 13, No. 1, January/February, 1982,
      pp. 21-35.

This study examined mental health status in a large national sample of the Black elderly. Previous studies of mental health and
illness in this population have been either geographically limited
or based upon small national samples that have not permitted reasonable investigation of important demographic differences, according to the authors. In addition to using traditional measures
of self-reported mental health functioning, the present study also
included measures of well-being in an attempt to explore the multi-
dimensional nature of the mental health concept in the Black elderly. The findings of the present analyses indicate a great deal
of heterogeneity among the Black elderly as well as significant
relationships between global measures of well-being and measures
of psychological distress, conclude the writers. The implications
of these findings for a multi-dimensional conception of mental
health in Black Americans are discussed.

444. Markides, Kyriakos S. "Minority Status, Aging and Mental Health."
      Aging and Human Development, Vol. 23, No. 4, 1986, pp. 285-300.

      Available data show that Blacks of both sexes and of all age
      groups are overrepresented in mental institutions. For example,
      for all ages, the rate of admissions per 100,000 population was
      over twice as high among Blacks than among Whites in 1975. The
      same held true for those aged sixty-five and over.... Class dif-
      ferences and discrimination mostly serve to explain the under-
      representation of Blacks in nursing homes, but do not constitute
      satisfactory answers to overrepresentation in mental hospitals.
      Blacks and poor people can be expected to be overrepresented in
      "deprived institutions" such as state mental hospitals. Thus,
      "mental hospitalization of the aged is a consequence not only of
      mental disorder but of social characteristics as well....When a
      Black older person requires institutional care, state hospitals
      are the only facilities routinely available....", according to the
      author. The little evidence available does not suggest that the
      greater representation of older Blacks in mental institutions is
      necessarily the result of greater psychiatric impairment. Consi-
      derable evidence suggests that for older Blacks and other ethnic
      elderly, the state mental hospital functions as a nursing home.
      It is a way of assuring long-term care for people who cannot af-
      ford nursing home care, concludes the author.

445. Polansky, Grace. "Planning for the Specially Disadvantaged
      Minority Groups: Clinical Experience." National Conference on
      Alternatives To Institutional Care For Older Americans: Practice
      and Planning. Eric Pfeiffer, Editor. Durham: Center for the
      Study of Aging and Human Development, Duke University Medical
      Center, 1973, pp. 116-121.

The researcher contends that the older Black comes to the clini-
cian because he is feeling pain and has grossly unmet common human
needs. Remember that this is relative, that Blacks have the same
range as Whites, have achieved just as satisfying and effective
and useful a level of functioning in many cases; could in all,
given equal opportunity in every sphere for development of individual potential. He may come with hostility, distrust, open or
masked, may not want to come at all, may need more encouragement,
a glimmer of hope that, here, he is going to be treated with
dignity unthreatened, with respect, with his rights of self determination seen as strong as anyones, states Dr. Pfeiffer. He may
put you on, may continue any of a variety of responses he'd had to
learn to survive in an essentially hostile world. Dependence may
have worked, throttled back expression of true feelings may have
been or seemed necessary. His "security" may have seemed to him
to be within the White, benevolent world, he tells us. His sense
of status is a mirror image in some cases, reflected. He sees himself as others see him. Or he may come proudly. The Black who
has lived in the North for decades and returned seems often to
feel more hope, more power, not to be so often caught in the help-
less, hopeless, powerless syndrome, argues the author. The activities of the largely younger Blacks may have liberated something
in them too dangerous for many to express openly before; "more
often with the people in our clinical setting it seems to have

Polansky, Grace (continued)

been frightening, I think, as suppressed rage stirs, threatens to get out of control, feels dangerous," declares the writer. "There is rage, understandably, on some level, and this is where our job comes in, to help this be a force for constructive change," concludes the writer.

446. Reynold, David K. and Richard A. Kalish. "Anticipation of Futurity as a Function of Ethnicity and Age." Journal of Gerontology, Vol. 29, No. 2, March, 1974, pp. 224-231.

This article is based on a larger study of attitudes and expectations: 434 residents of Greater Los Angeles, approximately equally divided by four ethnic and three age groups, stated how long they wished to live and how long they expected to live. The authors anticipated that the older persons expected to and wanted to live longer than the younger age cohorts. The writers were surprised that the Black respondents were significantly more likely to expect to live and want to live longer than Japanese Americans, Mexican Americans, and White Americans. The aged Blacks did not fear death. They concluded that other differences, such as their sex, between ethnic groups were minimal.

447. Scott, Judith and Charles M. Gaitz. "Ethnic and Age Differences in Mental Health Measurements." Diseases of the Nervous Systems, Vol. 36, No. 7, July, 1975, pp. 389-393.

The sample included 1441 respondents stratified by sex, the three major ethnic groups of Houston--Anglo (an ethnic designation used commonly in the southwest, meaning White, non-Mexican-American), Black, and Mexican-American, two family socioeconomic levels (working class and lower-middle class), and six age groups ranging from a 20-29 age group to a 75-94 age group. To increase the validity of responses, the interviewers were matched ethnically to the respondents. One hypotheses of the relationships of social stress and mental illness states that, because of the effects of racial prejudice, minority groups would suffer more psychological stress than the dominant ethnic group; and that the added stress should be reflected in more psychological-symptom expression. To support such an hypothesis the authors would predict, for example, higher mean symptom reports from, first, the Blacks, secondly, from the Mexican-Americans, and then the lowest score from the Anglos. The data, however, show the opposite. The writers found the highest level of symptom expression by Anglos, then by Mexican-Americans, and finally the lowest level of symptom expression by Blacks.

448. Shader, Richard I., and Martha Tracy. "On Being Black, Old, and Emotionally Troubled: How Little is Known." Psychiatric Opinion, Vol. 10, No. 6, December, 1973, pp. 26-32.

This article reviewed multiple factors in pursuing answers to the questions regarding the identification and management of elderly Blacks in one well-circumscribed, well-covered catchment area. Evaluating all of the statistics which the authors have gathered,

Shader, Richard I., and Martha Tracy (continued)

there are few hard conclusions to be drawn. They service a Black
elderly population which is, at the minimum, one percent of our
total population. Black elderly patients comprise only 3.7 percent of our geriatric inpatient experience. A significant age
difference exists between the writers' elderly White and Black patients. Although many explanations have been considered in evaluation of low number of Black geriatric patients, no single explanation appears to account for the very small numbers of elderly
Blacks. The writers declare it is probably that several causes
contribute in varying degree in various communities. Superimposed
on a background of early mortality, these factors could begin to
explain the relatively low frequency of Black geriatric patients
seen in our urban psychiatric facilities, conclude the authors.
It seems very important to them, however, to acknowledge how
little we know, declare the authors.

449. Solomon, Barbara. "Ethnicity, Mental Health and the Older Black
      Aged." Ethnicity, Mental Health and Aging. Gerontology Center,
      University of Southern California, Los Angeles, 1970, pp. 10-13.

The writer points out that the Black aged have special mental
problems than those of other ethnic groups. Therefore, they need
special attention.

450. Whanger, Alan D. and H. Shan Wang. "Clinical Correlates of the
      Vibratory Sense in Elderly Psychiatric Patients." Journal of
      Gerontology, Vol. 29, No. 1, January, 1974, pp. 39-45.

The authors state that the vibratory threshold (VT) was measured
quantitatively at the wrist and knees of acutely admitted and
chronically hospitalized elderly psychiatric patients and compared
with a cohort of elderly persons living in the community. The VT
was markedly elevated in all groups as compared with a young controlled group. The VT of the psychiatric patients was significantly higher (hence implying neurologic impairment) than that of the
community volunteers. The measurement at the wrists was the more
useful one clinically. The VT of Black subjects was significantly
lower than that of White subjects. Those on inadequate diets had
a significantly elevated VT, as did those using tobacco, when compared to non-users. Subjects with diabetes, syphilis, and severe
organic brain syndromes also had significantly elevated VT, conclude the writers.

                20. BLACK AGED AND NURSING HOMES

451. Gibbs, Eddie. "Nursing Home Action." Action for Aged Blacks:
      When?: A Conference of the National Caucus on The Black Aged.
      Jacquelyne J. Jackson, Editor. Washington, DC: National Caucus
      on The Black Aged, 1973, pp. 55-57.

The writer declares that the majority of the people in nursing
homes today (1973) are aged people--the aged Blacks, or what we

Gibbs, Eddie (continued)

believe to be the poorest of works against aged Blacks. Blacks
also need to own and operate their own nursing homes, argues
Gibbs. He concludes that Black people should become more and
more involved, in every way, in trying to improve the nursing
home for the Black aged.

452. Jackson, Hobart C. "Overcoming Racial Barriers in Senior Centers."
       National Conference on Senior Centers, Vol. 2, 1965, pp. 20-28.

       The writer points out that for the most part, the Black aged are
       treated very poorly in senior centers. This is due to some de-
       gree on the part of the staff and their racial attitudes and lack
       of proper training. The aged Black in these centers usually is
       alone and without family and friends and has little personal con-
       tact with others in the centers.

453. Solomon, Barbara. "Social and Protective Services." Workshop on
       Community Services and The Black Elderly. Richard H. Davis,
       Editor. Los Angeles: Andrus Gerontology Center, University of
       Southern California, 1972, pp. 1-11.

       The author contends that many Black older people are in institu-
       tional settings in nursing homes, state mental hospitals or what
       have you because of the lack of services in the community to sup-
       port them and allow them to remain independent in the community.
       She argues that Black professionals should start to work hand in
       hand with the Black residents in the community.

454. Sullivan, Ronald. "Study Charges Bias in Admissions to Nursing
       Homes." New York Times, January 28, 1984, p. 27.

       The "Friends and Relatives of the Institutionalized Aged," of New
       York City, issued a report that suggested that nursing homes in
       New York City systematically excluded Blacks and Hispanic patients
       in defiance of Federal and State laws barring racial discrimina-
       tion. "Out of 153 public, voluntary and proprietary nursing homes
       in the city, 54 have all-white or virtually all-white resident
       population," concluded the study. The article also gave a break-
       down by region (Queens, Bronx, Brooklyn, Staten Island, and Man-
       hattan) and race of the patients in New York's 153 Nursing Homes.

21. BLACK AGED AND PLANNING

455. Arling, Greg. "Race and Subjective Economic Well-Being in Old
       Age." Journal of Minority Aging, Vol. 9, No. 1, 1984, pp. 49-59.

       This study shows the importance of close ties with family and
       friends, face-to-face visiting and telephone talk, religiosity,
       and going to church with friends as factors that help to induce
       a sense of subjective well-being among older Blacks. While the
       findings about the importance of family, friends and church parti-
       cipation are well documented elsewhere in the literature, the

Arling, Greg. (continued)

importance of visiting behavior and telephone conversation have
received much less research attention, asserts the author. Given
the importance of our understanding of the determinants of objective and subjective well-being, especially the policy relevance of
this understanding for planning programs of long term care, future
research should pay closer attention to the significance of visiting behavior and telephone talk as well as other sources of social
support among older Blacks, concludes the writer.

456. Jackson, Hobart C. "Planning For The Specially Disadvantaged."
      Alternatives To Institutional Care for Older Americans: Practice
      and Planning. Eric Pfeiffer, Editor. Durham, NC: Duke Univer-
      sity, 1972, pp. 94-101.

      The late Mr. Jackson declared "We've got to learn how to plan
      with people instead of for them." He asserts we must recognize
      the strength of elderly minorities in developing and helping to
      carry plans that are going to be in their best interests. Mr.
      Jackson believed that there are a few Black elderly who may want
      to enter existing nursing homes in predominantly white situations.
      They should have that opportunity. But there are also those who,
      for whatever reasons, want to remain in their own communities.
      Such a choice should not be penalized by inadequate services, dis-
      criminatory practices, and open hostility. It should be simply
      one choice that they should be free to make, suggested the author.
      He concluded, in part: "It is certainly time that the Federal
      Government and other interests began to work with the development
      of viable systems of health and social care and services in Black
      and minority communities with and through Black and minority in-
      stitutions and people; rather than continue to pursue a punitive
      approach of establishing standards criteria for them, without pro-
      viding the accompanying resources with which to meet the criteria.
      This process usually results in closing those institutions that
      do exist and keeps others from even getting underway and thereby
      results in the systematic erosion and deterioration of services
      to Blacks and other minorities." The writer continued, "We call
      for positive approaches rather than regressive measures in Black
      communities--ones that, instead of being abhorent and repugnant
      to Black people, as most of the current approaches are, would per-
      mit them to use their talents and skills in the injection of some
      much-needed humanity in our work with older people."

457. Jackson, Jacquelyne. "Really There Are Existing Alternatives to
      Institutionalization for Aged Blacks." Alternatives to Institu-
      tional Care for Older Americans: Practice and Planning. Eric
      Pfeiffer, Editor. Durham, NC: Duke University, 1972, pp. 102-107.

      The writer believes that perhaps the most important alternative to
      institutionalized care for old Blacks is that practice and planning
      must not concentrate so much on those who are already old. "We
      must begin now to concentrate more upon those who are being born
      today and tomorrow and tomorrow and tomorrow. We must make cer-
      tain that we reverse this creeping tide of racism. We must ensure
      that young Blacks will be able to grow and develop in environments

Jackson, Jacquelyne. (continued)

permitting them to mature and to become both independent and interdependent beings," states Dr. Jackson. She believes that many of
those who are Black and institutionalized in this country today
are those who have never really been allowed a chance to grow up.
That is, they have never really become adults. There may be some
critical distinctions between noninstitutionalized and institutionalized old Blacks today, with the latter remaining children
and the former, despite all the odds, somehow having become adults.
Hence, the vital alternative for us is that of maximizing conditions for adult growth and development for Blacks, argues the
author. These responsible Blacks will then make their own decisions about their need for institutionalization or alternatives
to institutionalization. When health conditions do not permit
them to make such decisions directly, then their spouses, children,
or other responsible family members or friends will make the decisions for them, concludes the writer.

458. Lightfoot, Orlando B. "Preventive Issues and the Black Elderly:
      A Biopsychosocial Perspective." Journal of The National Medical
      Association, Vol. 75, No. 10, October, 1983, pp. 957-963.

      Dr. Lightfoot suggests that preventive services in an elderly
      population must focus on maintaining physical health, supporting
      psychological well-being, and sustaining an adequate economic base
      and a dependable social-service network. High-risk factors in
      the elderly include being Black, being poor, living alone, experi-
      encing major life changes, being recently bereaved, or being re-
      cently discharged from a hospital. Important issues involved in
      maintaining good psychological and mental health include previous
      psychological health, previous intellectual capability, and the
      response to diminished physical health and to other major life
      changes. The physician concludes than an adequate social network
      must include maintaining or developing friendships, capitalizing
      on the strengths of subcultural identifications, and having ready
      access to social, legal, health, and political-action groups....

459. Watson, Wilbur H. "Crystal Ball Gazing: Notes on Today's Middle
      Aged Blacks with Implications for Their Aging in the 21st Century."
      Gerontologist, Vol. 26, No. 2, April, 1986, pp. 136-139.

      Based upon current data and trend analysis, patterns of occupa-
      tional segregation seem likely to continue with only minor shifts
      of Blacks from the periphery to core positions. Where shifts oc-
      cur, improvements in income and reductions in other disparities
      can be expected. So far as today's middle aged Blacks continue to
      suffer occupational discrimination and the associated risks of
      underemployment and low income, they will most likely rank among
      the poorest of the poor among the elderly as the United States en-
      ters the 21st century, suggests Dr. Watson. In addition to the
      associated risks of poor housing, little or no health insurance
      or Social Security benefits, poor middle aged Blacks who reach 60
      or 70 in the 21st century can be expected to delay seeing a doctor
      when needed and be severely impaired when they finally receive the
      attention of a health care professional, concludes the author.

22. BLACK AGED AND POLITICS

460. Jackson, Jacquelyne J. "NCBA, Black Aged and Politics." Annals of The American Academy of Political and Social Science. Vol. 415, 1974, pp. 138-159.

The author discusses the National Caucus on Black Aged and the needs for such an organization. Dr. Jackson argues that it will only be an effective agency for dealing with the problems of the Black Aged if it has the necessary support from both Blacks and Whites. Dr. Jackson surmises that this organization, like others, should be free from politics. Unfortunately, it is not, she concludes.

461. Robinson, Henry. "Political Action and the Black Aged." Action For Aged Blacks: When? A Conference of the National Caucus on The Black Aged. Jacquelyne J. Jackson, Editor. Washington, DC: National Caucus on The Black Aged, 1973, pp. 32-34.

The author states that in 1970 there were nearly 1,500,000 Blacks 65 years or older making up about 8% of the Black population. He argues that if this large proportion of people were brought together as a cohesive force they could play a significant role in the political area. Robinson argues that the Black aged have all the problems of the aged plus the handicaps of discrimination, poverty, poor housing, inferior health facilities, and faulty nutrition, to name just a few. The writer asserts that the Black aged must not only register to vote, he must exercise that vote on election day.

23. BLACK AGED AND POPULATION

462. Dowd, James J. et al. "Aging in Minority Population: An Examination of the Double Jeopardy Hypothesis." Journal of Gerontology, Vol. 33, 1978, pp. 427-435.

Utilizing data from a large (N=1269) multistage probability sample of middle-aged and aged Blacks, Mexican-Americans and Anglos living in Los Angeles County, indicators of relative status and primary group interaction were analyzed to determine the degree and nature of any ethnic variation. It was found that differences among the three ethnic groups do exist in some cases, particularly on income and self-assessed health, constitute a case of double jeopardy for the minority aged. But while double jeopardy was found to be an accurate characterization of the Black and Mexican-American aged on several variables, the data also suggest that age exerts a leveling influence on some ethnic variation over time. Variables such as frequency of interaction with relatives as well as, for Black respondents, the life satisfaction factors of Tranquillity and Optimism all evidence a certain decline in the extent of ethnic variation across age strata.

463. Ehrlich, Ira F. "Toward a Social Profile of The Aged Black Popula-
      tion in The United States: An Exploratory Study." Aging and
      Human Development, Vol. 4, Nov. 3, 1973, pp. 271-276.

      This article was based on a stratified random sample of Black men
      and women aged 70 and over. This study was developed in two high
      rise, age segregated urban housing units in St. Louis. Normative
      activity was classified in terms of three life styles: alone,
      reciprocal and non reciprocal. An internal comparison was made
      with a Black sample and an external comparison with a White sample
      differing on several major demographic characteristics. Although
      the modal activity pattern was to do things alone, the findings
      were equivocal with respect to the disengagement framework. In-
      volvement with others tended to increase with age, and was usually
      of a religious or leisure time nature. Findings of this study
      suggest the desirability for encouraging flexible life style op-
      tions. The author concludes that his study suggested a non-homo-
      geneous sample--particularly in relation to such variables as age,
      income, health and education. Marital status was suggested as a
      variable that may account for significant racial differences.

464. Smith, T. Lynn. "The Changing Number and Distribution of the
      Aged Negro Population of the U.S." Phylon, Vol. 18, 4th Quarter,
      1957, pp. 339-354.

      The writer asserts that the first half of the Twentieth Century
      the number of Blacks aged sixty-five and over increased by 229
      percent whereas Blacks of all ages gained only 70 percent. Even
      so, however, the aging of the Black population was less rapid than
      that of the total population, for comparable figures for the lat-
      ter are almost 300 percent for the aged contingent and just under
      100 percent for those of all ages, declares Smith. In 1900 only
      one Black out of every thirty-four had passed the sixty-fifth
      birthday, whereas by 1950 the comparable ratio was one out of
      every eighteen. He argues that there will probably be about
      1,150,000 Blacks aged sixty-five and over in 1960, and the number
      will probably continue to rise until 1990. A slight decrease in
      absolute numbers is likely to take place before the census of the
      year 2,000. Unless one can forecast the numbers of future births,
      the proportions of the aged in future years cannot be forecast with
      any degree of accuracy, argues Smith. The author concludes that
      it seems unlikely that the proportions of the aged among Blacks
      will equal that among Whites prior to the year 2,000.

                  24. BLACK AGED AND POVERTY

465. Lacklen, Cary. "Aged, Black, and Poor: Three Case Studies."
      Aging Human Development, Vol. 2, No. 3, August, 1971, pp. 202-207.

      The author discusses three elderly Blacks who lived in an urban
      high-rise apartment complex. The aged Blacks were: Walter Galton,
      Sam Smith, and Bess Casper. The researcher drew no conclusions
      about their lives.

25.   BLACK AGED AND PROFESSIONAL TRAINING

466.   Jackson, Jacquelyne J.   "Education and Training Priorities For
Ethnic Groups." Conferences on the Role of Institutions of Higher
Learning in the Study of Aging, 1972. Richard H. Davis, et al.,
Editors. Los Angeles: Ethel Percy Andrus Gerontology Center,
University of Southern California, 1973, pp. 131-132.

The author points out that at this conference recommendations were
made in four areas: The structure of problem-solving groups; al-
location of federal funds; priorities for training Blacks; and the
content of training programs. (a) Problem-Solving Groups, it was
suggested, should organize themselves separately according to type
of minority. Then they may join to solve their common problems.
(b) It was felt that substantial money should be allocated each
minority group at least in proportion to its representation in the
population. The attitude of the National Caucus on the Black Aged
is that 12% of federal funding for aging and the aged should be
allocated to the Black Aged. Each minority group should decide
how the money will be used. (c) Initial priorities for training
Blacks were articulated. Professionals and paraprofessionals will
be prepared to be decision-makers in various categories such as
medicine, economics, law and the clergy. Once these persons are
trained as professionals with input into the decision-making
structure, they in turn will train the less educated, who may then
support the interests of the group. (d) One component to the
content of training programs, it was felt, should be political education for participation in the system. One member of the workshop felt that content should include teaching ways to solve the
problems of all older persons, regardless of race or ethnicity.

467.   _____. "Social Stratification of Aged Blacks and Implications for Training Professionals." Proceedings of Black Aged in
the Future. Durham, NC: Center for the Study of Aging and Human
Development, Duke University, 1973, pp. 114-132.

The author is primarily concerned with specifying some aspects of
social similarities and differences among aged Blacks, and relating those data to existing or desired training and curricular
needs. The most important conclusions, contends Dr. Jackson, are
the diversification of aging and aged Blacks, and the need to increase substantially adequate knowledge and understanding of aged
Blacks, Black aging professionals, and the future.

468.   Reed, John. "Prospects for Developing Gerontological Training
Programs at Black Institutions." Proceedings of The Research Conference on Minority Group Aged in the South. Jacquelyne J. Jackson, Editor. Durham, NC: Center for the Study of Aging and Human
Development, Duke University Medical Center, 1972, pp. 145-147.

The writer contends that many Southern legislatures have not yet
recognized as a problem those who are Black and aged and needy.
Most Blacks, in fact, never live long enough to become aged problems in the South--or elsewhere for that matter, argues Reed. The
1970 census data show us that the proportion of persons 65 or more
years of age in the Black population is higher than it was in 1960,

Reed, John. (continued)

states the author. Yet, the Black population in 1970 is younger
than it was in 1960. The recognition that Blacks have a sizeable
population 65 or more years of age has not yet come in many quarters. In fact, we have a sizeable healthy, aged population, suggests the writer. When the Whites recognize that a crucial area
of research and training may fall within the realm of ascertaining
significant information about the relatively good health of most
aged Blacks, only then may we get such programs--and only after
they have been instituted in White institutions, concludes the
author.

469. Smith, Stanley H. "The Developing Gerontological Training Program
at Fisk University." Proceedings of the Research Conference on
Minority Group Aged in the South. Jacquelyne J. Jackson, Editor.
Durham, NC: Center for the Study of Aging and Human Development,
Duke University Medical Center, 1972, pp. 139-142.

The author believes that in its total configurational thrust, a
graduate program in social gerontology at a school such as Fisk
University should not be similar in its totality to a graduate
program in gerontology at the University of North Carolina or the
University of Michigan. It should be reflective of Fisk. He believes that there is a uniqueness to an institution and that its
program should reflect this. A student desirous of enrolling at
Fisk on the undergraduate level should go there knowing what Fisk
emphasizes. These are the kinds of expectations that we would
like students to have, argues Smith. The same principle is applicable at the graduate level. This particular stance is reflected
adequately in this seminar. There is a whole gap of concern, omissions and commissions about the Black aged. This seminar has
sought to address itself to these issues and problems. In the same
way, the curriculum in "Social Gerontology" at Fisk should cer-
tainly reflect that particular concern, concludes the scholar.

26. BLACK AGED AND SENIOR CITIZENS DAY CARE CENTERS

470. "Day Care: A Novel Way of Keeping Oldsters 'Young'." Ebony,
Vol. 35, No. 11, September, 1979, pp. 74, 76-77.

This article discusses a Senior Citizens Day Care Center in Chicago. The center is fully staffed and has a four-part curriculum:
arts and crafts, body dynamics, nutrition and humanities. The
average age of the Blacks who attended this center was 77.

471. Ralston, Penny A. "Senior Center Utilization By Black Elderly
Adults: Social Attitudinal and Knowledge Correlates." Journal of
Gerontology, Vol. 39, No. 2, March, 1984, pp. 224-229.

This study examined factors that affect utilization of senior centers by three groups of Black elderly adults: Attenders (n=46)
and non-attenders (n=33) of a neighborhood senior citizen center
in one community and non-attenders (n=27) in a comparable community

Ralston, Penny A.   (continued)

without a neighborhood senior center. Variables investigated included social contact (with family and friends), attitudes (disengagement potential, acceptability to others, commitment to become involved in senior centers) and knowledge (perception of senior centers). Results of the multivariated analysis of variance showed
that sex, age, marital status, health, and transportation did not
have a significant effect on the six variables studied, concludes
Prof. Ralston. The three groups differed in commitment to become
involved in senior centers, perception of senior centers, contact
with family, and contact with friends. Similarities between the
attenders and non-attenders in the comparable community suggest
that the latter group are potential senior center participants,
suggests the author.

472.   Woolf, Leon M. "Serving Minority Persons in a Senior Center."
       Challenges Facing Senior Centers in the Nineteen Seventies. Alice
       G. Wolfson, Editor. New York: National Council on the Aging,
       1969, pp. 146-152.

The writer discusses the Metropolitan Senior Citizens Center of
Baltimore, Maryland. He declares that when we talk about serving
minority persons in senior centers, we almost always think in
terms of racial and religious minorities, particularly Blacks.
The author submits that there are growing numbers of aged persons
belonging to other minorities, unrelated to race or religion, whom
we must learn to attract and serve. He cites a few examples.
There are retired professional people, physically handicapped
people, people with advanced educational backgrounds, poverty-
stricken individuals, retired business executives, and men in
general. He asks the question, Is the concept of the multipurpose
senior center broad enough and secure enough to encompass and
serve an increasingly multifaceted clientele?

27. BLACK AGED AND SEX

473.   West, Malcolm R. "Who Says You Get Too Old To Enjoy Sex? Not
       These Youngsters!" Jet, August 11, 1977, pp. 22-24.

This article discusses the sex lives of several of Chicago's
senior citizens who have been experiencing the joys of sex for
more than sixty years. These aged Blacks discuss how frequently
they have sex. Some stated they had sex every week. Others declared they had sex every other week and still others said once a
month.

28. BLACK AGED AND SUICIDE

474.   Hill,Robert B. "A Profile of Black Aged." Proceedings of the Re-
       search Conference on Minority Group Aged in the South. Jacquelyne
       J. Jackson, Editor. Durham, NC: Center for the Study of Aging
       and Human Development, Duke University Medical Center, 1972, pp.
       92-96.

Hill, Robert B. (continued)

Dr. Hill states that because of the historic oppression of Blacks
one would ordinarily predict that suicide rates would be greater
for Blacks than Whites. It is also interesting to note that the
gap is even greater among the elderly. For example, Black males,
65-69, have a suicide rate of 12.8, but 65-69 year-old White males
have a suicide rate of 35.6. And when we look at those between
75 and 79, the suicide rate for Black men is 15.0, but it is 42.5
among elderly White men, contends Dr. Hill. One of the most interesting aspects of the suicide rates is that they are lowest
among Black women, who are probably the most oppressed group in
America, according to Dr. Hill. Thus, the story of the Black elderly is really an inspiring saga of courage and determination
against adversity. In many ways, the elderly Blacks, perhaps more
than any other age group, best exemplify the historic fortitude
and resilience of Black people in America, concludes the researcher.

475. McIntosh, John L. and John F. Santos. "Methods of Suicide By Age:
Sex and Race Differences Among the Young and Old." Aging and
Human Development, Vol. 22, No. 2, 1985-1986, pp. 123-139.

The author points out that Blacks in general and Black females in
particular, have overall low suicide rates. Dr. McIntosh did men-
tion that older Black males employed firearms in noticeably higher
proportions than younger Black males, when they did commit suicide.
He concludes, in part: "...the use of firearms was proportionately higher among elderly Black males than for any other group or
any other method...."

29. BLACK AGED AND SUPPORT SERVICES

476. Anderson, Peggye. "Support Services and Aged Blacks." Black
Aging, Vol. 3, No. 3, February, 1978, pp. 53-59.

Although aged Blacks and other groups of elderly people seek and
expect support from their families, the findings in this article
reveal that older Blacks frequently underutilize resources in the
community. However, in many instances the elderly and their families need the support of community resources to reduce the potential and actual strain families experience as a result of caring
for and/or supporting aged family members, suggests the author.
The writer asks a crucial question at this point: "How do we max-
imize on the resources available to older people?" If we consider
family members as resources for the aged, we can better design programs to help them assist the elderly, argues the writer. Such
programs can take the form of intergenerational workshops so that
elderly parents and their adult children can better understand one
another through sharing experiences with other families in similar
situations. Day care facilities for older people, which are slow-
ly appearing in our society, could also eliminate or delay institutionalization and could give adult children free time to pursue
their interests or goals. Another resource that could be further
utilized in the Black community to support the elderly and their

Anderson, Peggye (continued)

families is the church. Traditionally, the Black church has been,
and is, to a less extent today, the focal point of social interaction in the Black community, states the author. The Black
church has also been the major vehicle through which the needs of
the elderly are addressed. Therefore, we need to place more emphasis on the use of the Black church in providing services and
dissemination of information about services that are available to
the elderly in our communities, concludes the author. The author
surmises that in pursuing this research further, we need to tap
more services and support mechanisms of the elderly. Therefore,
we can better understand the major roles or functions that the
family plays in providing support to aged Blacks.

477. Jackson, Hobart C. "Easing the Plights of the Black Elderly."
      Perspectives on Aging, Vol. 4, 1975, pp. 21-22.

      The writer contends that the only way to ease the plights of the
      Black aged is for local, state, and federal governments to have
      effective programs to meet their needs. These needs include
      better housing, more income and better social services and health
      facilities.

478. Jackson, Jacquelyne J. "Compensatory Care for the Black Aged."
      Minority Aged in America. Occasional papers in Gerontology, Uni-
      versity of Michigan-Wayne State University, 1973.

      The writer states that more compensatory care needs to be devoted
      to the Black aged because they suffer more economically than most
      other elderly. She also contends that more attention should be
      devoted to the particular problems of the Black elderly.

479. Kent, Donald P. et al. "Indigenous Workers as a Crucial Link in
      the Total Support System for Low-Income, Minority Group Aged: A
      Report of an Innovative Field Technique in Survey Research."
      Aging and Human Development, Vol. 2, August 1971, pp. 189-196.

      This article traces the development of a concept of involvement of
      indigenous workers of all age grades in work with the low income,
      minority group aged from its inception in a survey research con-
      text. Employment of indigenous workers as research interviewers
      contributed to the lessening of distance between respondents and
      interviewers that was, in turn, necessary if appropriate data was
      to be secured. Problem referral work in the research context led
      the authors to investigate broader areas in which the communica-
      tion skills and community commitment of the indigenous worker
      could be brought to bear in fostering social change to alleviate
      the deprivation of low income, minority aged as a group. Recog-
      nition is given to problems of maintaining the unique contribution
      of the indigenous worker when his role becomes institutionalized
      in establishment agencies.

480.   Rao, V. V. Prakasa and V. Nandini Rao. "Factors Related to the
        Knowledge and Use of Social Services Among the Black Elderly."
        Journal of Minority Aging, Vol. 8, Nos. 1-2, 1983, pp. 26-35.

        This study was undertaken to examine factors related to the two
        dependent variables of knowledge and use of social services by
        Black elderly. Stepwise multiple regression analysis yielded
        models for the total sample, the female subsample and the male
        subsample. It is interesting to observe that for each of the two
        dependent variables most of the strongest variables found in the
        male models do not appear in the female models, assert the profes-
        sors. For example, life satisfaction, intergenerational help
        given to children/grandchildren, and income were the only common
        variables found in both subsample models. This means that the
        predictor variables explaining the knowledge of social services
        for males and females were different, according to the authors.
        The findings support the argument that the Black aged are hetero-
        geneous by sex in terms of socioeconomic and family related vari-
        ables. Public officials, policy makers, program designers, and
        public and private agencies should be cognizant of the different
        factors affecting the knowledge and use of social services by
        males and females, concluded the writers. Social and cultural
        factors affecting the attitudes and beliefs of the aged popula-
        tion should be recognized before any programs are developed to
        meet their needs, argue the researchers.

481.   Waring, Mary L. and Jordan I. Kosberg. "Life Conditions and the
        Use of Social Welfare Services Among Aged Blacks in Northern
        Florida." Journal of Minority Aging, Vol. 5, No. 2, March, 1980,
        pp. 233-240.

        The purpose of this study was to describe the life conditions
        (housing, health, finances, and social activities), level of pro-
        gram participation, and use of social welfare services of all 55
        aged Blacks utilizing a Congregate Meals Program in a non-urban
        community in Northern Florida. Data were collected through the
        use of an interviewer-administered questionnaire. Conclusions
        reached from the study include: attachment to a neighborhood
        might be more important than the condition of one's dwelling;
        there is a fear of insufficient income to meet health care costs;
        social activities are extensive; and though the Congregate Meals
        Program met several needs of the participants, all the services
        available were not being utilized. The professors believe that
        their findings are important for service provision and program
        planning activities....

                    30. BLACK AGED AND RELIGION

482.   Jericho, Bonnie J. "Longitudinal Changes in Religious Activity
        Subscores of Aged Blacks." Black Aging, Vol. 2, Nos. 4-6, April,
        June and August, 1977, pp. 17-24.

        This article is primarily concerned with the temporal stability of
        religious activity subscores among aged Blacks, as well as with

Jericho, Bonnie J. (continued)

factors, including religious attitude subscores, which may affect that stability. Using secondary data from the Duke University Longitudinal Study, it has three specific purposes. The first is an examination by sex of the longitudinal stability of the religious activity subscores of the Blacks in both Rounds 1 and 3 of the Duke study. The second is the isolation of some of the variables affecting the stability of those subscores over time. The third is a discussion of certain gerontological and religious implications of the findings. The study of change in the stability of the religious activity subscores of aged Blacks between roughly the years 1955 and 1965 showed no consistent decrease with increasing age among them. The stability of their religious activities was affected by socioeconomic status. In general, the lower the socioeconomic status the greater the decrease in religious activities. This phenomenon probably occurred because aged Blacks of lower socioeconomic status compensate for their reduced church attendance with increased reading of religious literature and other types of compensatory activities measured by the religious activity scale, argues the author. This would also suggest that the study is historically bound, states Jericho. The percentage of lower socioeconomic aged Blacks who would have access to a television and available means of transportation in 1955 to 1965 would have increased by 1977 and such factors would not affect the religious activity subscore in the same way. The author concludes that perhaps the most important gerontological implications of this study are (1) the need for the development of a more sophisticated instrument to measure longitudinal changes in religious patterns among older persons; and (2) the need for a carefully designed and self-executed study of religious patterns among older Blacks. Such a study contains a sufficiently large number of Blacks, so as to permit cross-variable comparisons of a meaningful nature. According to the writer, one of the current problems in the gerontological literature concerning Blacks is the insufficient sampling of Blacks makes it almost impossible to obtain valid findings about them. Particularly worthy of investigation are the effects of socioeconomic status (including sex) and widowhood upon religious activities and attitudes in the later years. Theorists in the area of religion and aging should devote more attention to the effects of socioeconomic status upon religious activities and attitudes of elderly people as they continue to age, as well as to the prior effects of socioeconomic status upon the religious activities and attitudes which accompany them into old age, argues the writer.

483. Heisel, Marsel A. and Audrey O. Faulkner. "Religiosity in an Older Black Population." Gerontologist, Vol. 22, No. 4, August, 1982, pp. 354-358.

The researchers interviewed 122 urban Blacks, ages 51-90, about their religious practices and beliefs. The results were analyzed using a multi-dimensional scale based on Glock's conceptual framework. Religiosity did not appear to vary with age but church membership did. Women had higher scores than men, and religiosity was positively related to life satisfaction and to frequency of church attendance regardless of age and sex, conclude the authors.

484. Taylor, Robert Joseph. "Religious Participation Among Elderly
      Blacks." Gerontologist, Vol. 26, No. 6, December, 1986, pp. 630-
      636.

      Religious participation among elderly Blacks was examined using
      data from a national sample of Black Americans. Three indicators
      of religious participation were utilized: frequency of religious
      service attendance, church membership, and the degree of subjec-
      tive religiosity. The findings of this study suggest that reli-
      gion and the church are important and salient aspects of the lives
      of elderly Blacks. The practical implications of these results
      suggest that churches can encourage participation (including regu-
      lar attendance as well as more intense organizational involvement)
      by removing any transportation and other (i.e., physical access)
      attendance barriers. Social service providers can incorporate the
      strong religious beliefs system of elderly Blacks when delivering
      services to this population. Given the attachment of older Blacks
      to church and religion, social service agencies might employ the
      organizational structure of the church in their efforts to provide
      assistance to this population, declares the author. These results
      also demonstrate that elderly Blacks vary in their level of reli-
      gious involvement. Those who are male, unmarried, and urban tend
      to display lower levels of religious involvement. From a minis-
      terial viewpoint, it would be important to ensure continued parti-
      cipation following the loss of a spouse....Similarly, since di-
      vorced older Black couples may not want to maintain membership in
      the same church, ministers should help facilitate involvement of
      one of the spouses in another church, concludes the writer.

485. _____ and Linda M. Chatters. "Church-based Informal Support
      Among Elderly Blacks." Gerontologist, Vol 26, No. 6, December,
      1986, pp. 637-643.

      Sociodemographic and religiosity factors were examined as predic-
      tors of the receipt of church-based support among a national sam-
      ple (n = 581) of older Black Americans. Frequency of church at-
      tendance was the most important predictor of both frequency and
      amount of support. The relationship between age and support was
      modified by the presence of children and church membership. So-
      cioemotional support during illness was the most prevalent form
      of reported aid, assert the researchers.

486. Walker, Bishop John. "How Organized Religion Can and Should Meet
      the Needs of Aged Blacks." Action for Aged Blacks: When? A Con-
      ference of the National Caucus on The Black Aged. Jacquelyne J.
      Jackson, Editor. Washington, DC: National Caucus on The Black
      Aged, 1973, pp. 52-54.

      The writer surmises that the whole question of a ministry to the
      aging is one which has traditionally been within the Church's
      realm and sphere of activity. He asserts that the organized
      churches of America, be they Christian or non-Christian, will com-
      bine their resources and work together to develop communities that
      are rich and fulfilling for the young and old alike. The Bishop
      concludes that the young need the aging, as the aging need the
      young. Together they can develop creative programs and creative
      life styles for all our people.

487. Watson, Wilbur H. "Sitting Location as an Indicator of Status of
      Older Blacks in the Church: A Comparative Analysis of Protestants
      and Catholics in the Rural South." Phylon, Vol. 48, No. 4,
      December, 1986, pp. 264-275.

      This article is based upon a comparative analysis of 1639 older
      Blacks, 1354 Protestants and 285 Catholics living in the rural
      southeastern United States between 1978-1980. According to the
      researcher, the results of his study clearly show that older per-
      sons among congregations of Protestants and Catholics are not ran-
      domly distributed by sitting location during religious services.
      Instead, sitting location in the church is organized by age, eco-
      nomic class, church status, and sociosexual identity, states the
      writer. Basically, the elderly, 60 years and older, as a group,
      tend to sit from the middle to the front of the church during or-
      ganized religious services. By contrast, youth, as reported by
      the elderly in this study, sit nearer the middle to the back of
      the church, except when held close by their parents, or when a
      special status, such as membership in the youth choir, requires
      close proximity to the front, points out the author. While the
      elderly as a group tend to sit up front, there are differences
      among them. Older women, for example, are far more likely than
      older men to sit up front during religious services. However, it
      was not the oldest, 82 to 92 years among the old, but the young-
      old (60-70 years) who accounted for most of the variance in the
      sex differences in up front sitting. There was no clear explana-
      tion for this finding, maintains Dr. Watson. He concludes, in
      part: "The results of this study also show an association between
      sitting location, home worth, measured in terms of the elderly
      owner's report of the market value of his or her home, number of
      years of education, and contributions made by the older person to
      the church and community. The finding of a close association be-
      tween "up front sitting" and indicators of high socioeconomic
      class among the elderly in their community suggests two conclu-
      sions: Sitting location can be interpreted as an indicator of
      status in the church, and as behavior which symbolizes the class
      of the older person in the context of the broader community. How-
      ever, the present research also revealed differences between
      Protestants and Catholics in the organization of sitting location
      in the church, as well as differences among the elderly related
      to personality, health, and other factors...."

                31. BLACK AGED AND THE FEDERAL GOVERNMENT

488. Flemming, Arthur C. "Action and Aged Blacks: The Post-White
      House Conference on Aging." Action for the Aged Blacks: When?
      A Conference on the National Caucus on the Black Aged. Jacquelyne
      J. Jackson, Editor. Washington, DC: National Caucus on The Aged,
      1973, pp. 43-51.

      The writer discusses his nomination as Commissioner on Aging and
      what he would do that would affect Black people in that position.
      He stated that he wanted Blacks in policy-making positions in his
      organization and on all policy-making levels of government,

Flemming, Arthur C. (continued)

expecially those that affect the aged, including the Social and
Rehabilitation Service, Social Security Administration, U. S. Department of Agriculture, Department of Health, Education and Welfare and the Office of Economic Opportunity.

489. Dubrousky, Gertrude. "Growing Old Black is Double Difficult."
New York Times, March 21, 1982, (NJ Section), p. 4.

The writer points out that growing old and being Black is doubly
difficult, especially if you're old and sick. Health problems are
closely linked to poverty. Consequently, poor Blacks and minorities must rely more heavily on the Medicaid program than do other
segments of the population....

490. Eaglin, J. P. "The Nation's Black Elders: This Is Not Progress."
Generation, Vol. 6, No. 3, Spring, 1982, pp. 29-30, 54.

The essence of this short article is that although the Black aged
are somewhat better off today (1982) than they were several years
ago, they still have not progressed. Even though social security
has increased, so has inflation. The majority of the Black elderly
are in poor health and need assistance. Although the Black elders
have paid their dues, they are given little respect by the larger
community....

491. Jackson, Jacquelyne J. "Aged Blacks: A Potpourri in the Direction of the Reduction of Inequities." Phylon, Vol. 32, No. 3,
September, 1971, pp. 260-280.

The triple focus of this article is upon (a) a description and
analysis of Southern urban Black grandparental roles, emphasizing
certain implications for current policies surrounding Black aged;
(b) the National Caucus on the Black Aged, stressing its urgent
missions of dramatizing the plight of the Black aged and having
a significant impact upon the forthcoming 1971 White House Conference on Aging, where policy recommendations for the aged in the
decade ahead will be formulated, as well as its general concern
for increasing substantially services to training for and research
about Black aged; and (c) a specific proposal to reduce the minimum age-eligibility requirements for recipients of Old-Age, Survivors, Disability and Health Insurance (OASDHI, a form of Social
Security) so as to reduce the racial inequities not extant, where-
in Blacks are far less likely to receive proportionate benefits as
Whites, even though they may be very likely to have invested proportionately more of their life-time earnings into Social Security,
inasmuch as they tend to die earlier than do Whites. Prof. Jack-
con argues that the interfacing of these foci occurred largely in
that the grandparental data point toward the need for improved economic and housing conditions for grandparents, for their children
and for their children's children. The National Caucus on the
Black Aged is significantly concerned about improving these adverse
conditions and, in this connection, seeks assistance from all relevant resources (including those Blacks who are not yet aged). The
scholar concludes that the specific proposal to realize greater

Jackson, Jacquelyne J. (continued)

racial equity between aged Whites and Blacks is one response to
the need to improve the deplorable income plight of many Black
aged: in this case, a specific improvement in obtaining benefits
which Black aged themselves have earned.

492.   _____. "Aging Black Families and Federal Policies: Some
Critical Issues." Journal of Minority Aging, Vol. 5, No. 1,
September-December, 1979, pp. 162-169.

Concerned about the unwarranted consequences of federal policies
which are not colorblind upon aging Blacks, this article deals
with the issues of the need for differential age-eligibility requirements by race for primary beneficiaries of Social Security
retirement pensions and issues arising from the 1978 report of the
Human Resources Corporation to the Federal Council on Aging. It
also stresses the insufficiency of current data for making definitive and comprehensive recommendations about federal policies and
programs for aging Blacks as they relate to familial support, as
well as the likely probability that the U.S. Civil Rights Commis-
sion would not be able to produce a valid and reliable study of
racial and ethnic discrimination in aging programs, as mandated
by 1978 federal legislation. Finally, some recommendations related to the federal government and aged Blacks are offered, with
the most important ones being that no ethnic-specific legislation
nor set-asides in the areas of research, training and services be
set up, that at least in the South area agencies on aging should
not ignore feasible cooperation with existing anti-poverty agencies, and that the Federal Council on Aging should take appropriate caution, so that strategies they propose for minority aged
will not, in fact, slow up the movement of them into the main-
stream, concludes Dr. Jackson.

493. Mitchell, Parren J. "Mutual National Caucus on The Black Aged
(NCBA) and The Congressional Black Caucus (CBC) Concerns About
Aged Blacks and Recommended Legislation for Action." Action for
Aged Blacks: When? A Conference of The National Caucus on the
Black Aged. Jacquelyne J. Jackson, Editor. Washington, DC:
National Caucus on The Black Aged, 1973, pp. 76-87.

This Black ex-Congressman from Maryland states what the CBC was
doing to help the Black aged. He declares that the astronomically
high unemployment among Black people has significant implications
for senior Black citizens; because if Blacks are unemployed at a
high rate, then they cannot possibly help support Black senior
citizens. The Congressman also pointed out that the CBC was working with the NCBA in the development of a legislative program that
would implement some of the recommendations made at the 1971 White
House Conference on Aging.

494. Sheppard, N. Alan. "A Federal Perspective on The Black Aged:
From Concern to Action." Aging. September-October, 1978. pp. 28-
32.

This article highlights the need for Federal efforts in the aging
field by presenting a profile of the elderly population and their

Sheppard, N. Alan. (continued)

concerns/needs. He contends that the Federal Government needs to provide a perspective on the minority aged, in general, and aged Blacks in particular; to show by example how a Federal agency such as the Federal Council on the Aging can move from concern to action for the minority aged. The researcher concludes that the commitment of the Federal Government must be firm, steadfast, and built upon a sound and effective strategy for dealing with the Black Aged.

495.   Weaver, Eyvette Marie. "Attitudinal Perceptions of the Old Age Survivors Insurance Programs (OAS) Among Residents of Washington, DC, 1983." Journal of Minority Aging, Vol. 10, No. 1, 1985, pp. 62-91.

This essay addressed the applicability of describing aged Blacks as being doubly jeopardized by their race and age, described and compared some recent demographic trends of aged Blacks and whites, analyzed in a very limited way the adequacy of major federal programs for aged Blacks and related racial issues, and offered some recommendations that could, if implemented, improve the quality of life for aged Blacks and their families. The most important of the major conclusions were that the concept of double jeopardy is extremely limited as a theoretical or empirical concept, but highly useful as an advocatory concept; that far more data are needed to determine the adequacy of existing federal programs for aged Blacks; that Social Security should become a true means-tested program, without any current modifications in the health entitlements of World War II veterans; that the effects of the relatively new prospective payment method of Medicare needs to be monitored carefully to determine its effects on the health well-being of the aged; that the delivery of federal services to the aged are most rational and efficient when they are delivered directly (as in the case, e.g., of OASI); and that additional research and training are yet needed to improve the nature and modes of the delivery of federal goods and services to the extremely heterogeneous population of aged Blacks, concludes Prof. Weaver. The author states that available data do not show that the overall or economic status of aged Blacks declined between 1981 and 1984. Thus, it is highly doubtful that the various federal budget cuts had a significantly negative impact on the well-being of aged Blacks during those years.

32. AGED BLACKS AND VOLUNTEER SERVICES

496.   Faulkner, Audrey Olsen. "The Black Aged As Good Neighbors: An Experiment in Volunteer Service." Gerontologist, Vol. 15, December, 1975, pp. 554-559.

Prof. Faulkner suggests that there should be more testing of the central hypothesis that self-image can be enhanced in the Black elderly by voluntary service to others. If proof is forthcoming that the volunteer program does indeed enrich the life of the

Faulkner, Audrey Olsen (continued)

Black senior, we will need to reach out for volunteers as we now attempt to reach out to the potential recipients of direct social services. Social workers can then be less concerned about what the volunteer produces for others and accept as most valuable the positive results of volunteering. The writer concludes that careful attention must be given to the tasks projected for the volunteers. These should clearly provide special enrichment to the elderly Black population but should not be the basic services that are provided to other populations by paid personnel, such as homemakers, home health aides, information and referral service, nutrition services, etc.

33. BLACK AGED FEMALES

497. Cantor, Marjorie H., Karen Rosenthal, and Louis Wilker. "Social and Family Relationships of Black Aged Women in New York City." Journal of Minority Aging, Vol. 4, No. 1, June, 1979, pp. 50-61.

Using data obtained from 376 aged Black women in New York City in 1970, this article discusses their background characteristics, prevailing kinship patterns, and the relationship between the type of family structure and the extent and nature of the interaction between them and their kin. Among the most important findings is the fact that the nature of the family structure was the single most important predictor of help given by children to these women. Those most likely to receive help lived in an extended or augmented family household, state the researchers. The continued involvement of older Black women in the day-to-day family life may be a crucial factor in their mental health and their relatively high level of morale in old age. In this respect, it is significant to note that among the 376 Black elderly women studied, those living in extended/augmented households scored higher on several measures of life satisfaction than did women living alone or even those with husbands, conclude the writers....

498. Clarke, John Henrik. "A Search For Identity." Social Casework, Vol. 51, No. 5, May, 1970, pp. 259-264.

In a moving personal account, Mr. Clarke tells of the forces and influences in his life that led him to develop creative and well-documented Black Studies. One of the forces that influenced him was his great grandmother, "Mom Mary," who had been a slave in Georgia and later in Alabama. Mom Mary was the historian of the author's family and told him stories about his family and how it had resisted slavery. Prof. Clarke concludes, "I think that my search for identity, my relationship to the world began when I listened to the stories of that old (Mom Mary) woman." He also recalls that she was a deeply religious woman and her concept of God was so pure and practical that she could see that resistance to slavery was a form of obedience to God. She thought that anyone who had enslaved any one of God's children had violated the very will of God, states the writer.

499. Daly, Frederica Y. "To Be Black, Poor, Female and Old."
      Freedomways, Vol. 16, No. 4, Fourth Quarter, 1976, pp. 222-229.

      The author argues that as Black women age, they who have experi-
      enced racism and sexism encounter in these most vulnerable, older
      years, the additional demeaning prejudice of ageism. For elderly
      Black women in this country, contends Day, too often men oversee
      their passage from "nigger" through "broad" to "old bag," a des-
      picable history of deepening and widening unacceptability in di-
      rect ratio to the diminution of their strength as they grow old.
      The writer surmises that as if inadequate housing, poor health
      care and societal rejection were not enough, the elderly also suf-
      fer from those who seemingly care yet refuse to allow the elderly
      to share themselves and their accumulated life learning experien-
      ces with others. She continues to assert that we need to bring
      pressure on government to reorder our national spending priorities
      to include as major priorities programs that will enhance the
      human quality of life for the elderly poor. The author suggests
      that these programs should include health reforms, expanded Medi-
      care coverage, manpower programs for older workers, health and
      nutrition education programs and for older workers, a watchdog
      mechanism to prevent and punish swindling and exploitation by
      those in the professions. She concludes that individuals as advo-
      cates have the power to do personal things that can help the el-
      derly poor such as asserting constant disapproval of ageism in the
      neighborhood, on our jobs, in the media, wherever. Further, advo-
      cates can help educate the elderly about anti-discrimination laws
      and teach them how to identify illegalities and the agencies
      available to them when they believe they are victims of ageism,
      sexism and racism. Above all, the advocates must act as publi-
      cists and facilitators, supporting the elderly's rights to do for
      themselves, surmises the writer.

500. Gibson, Rose C. "Work Patterns of Older Black Female Heads of
      Households." Journal of Minority Aging, Vol. 8, Nos. 1 & 2, 1983,
      pp. 1-16.

      This study used The Panel Study of Income Dynamics to examine work
      patterns, and factors related to those patterns, among older Black
      female heads of households over a six-year period. The older
      Black women were compared with their Black male and white male
      and female counterparts. The Black females were found to be the
      most likely to exhibit disadvantaged work patterns--they had been
      with their employers the shortest time, and had worked the fewest
      years, weeks, and hours per week. They lost their positions in
      the continuity of work hierarchy, as they aged, to older white
      women. Black women who were better educated, received transfer
      income, were older, and lived in areas of high unemployment experi-
      enced the most discontinuous patterns. Surprisingly, asserts
      Prof. Gibson, poor health was not related to interrupted work.
      These "working poor" appeared unable financially to leave the
      labor force....

501. Gillespie, Bonnie J. "Black Grandparents: Childhood Socialization."
      Journal of Afro-American Issues, Vol. 4, Nos. 3 & 4, Summer/Fall,
      1976, pp. 432-444.

      According to Dr. Gillespie, as a result of this overall study of
      Black grandparent and childhood socialization, the following con-
      clusions have validity. 1. Black grandparents traditionally and
      presently have played a significant role in the socialization of
      Black children and adolescents. 2. Telling stories, family visits
      are several of the mechanisms through which childhood socializa-
      tion occurs via Black grandparents. 3. The Black extended family
      or multigenerational family exists today--although not in large
      numbers, and grandparents play significant and important roles in
      such families. 4. The Black maternal grandmother was indicated
      in this study as being the main factor in Black childhood and
      adolescent socialization outside of the immediate nuclear family.
      5. The Black maternal grandmother in almost all instances was
      viewed as a "second mother" and she treated her grandchildren like
      they "were her own." 6. The male respondents tended to have signi-
      ficantly greater affection and interaction with grandparents than
      the female respondents. 7. The profile of selected grandparents
      by student respondents indicated a diversity of education and oc-
      cupation. Most tended to be male, Baptist, and Democrat. 8. The
      predominant relationship between Black children and grandparents
      was one of "love," "affection," "compatibility," and "dependabili-
      ty." 9. The Black church is an important link and socializing
      agent for Black grandparents and grandchildren. 10. Today's modern
      American industrial society tends to have a detrimental effect on
      Black grandparental relationships with grandchildren--mainly due
      to mobility. 11. As a subset of the Black elderly, on occasion,
      Black grandparents suffer many of the inequities of this subpopu-
      lation via inadequate income: housing, and social/material envi-
      ronment. 12. Constructive work and programs for the elderly have
      had a significant positive effect on the elderly and their grand-
      parent subset therein. 13. The research of Black grandparental
      relationships, effects on grandchildren, and the Black elderly is
      rewarding and intellectually stimulating to the Black researcher,
      because it has great significance and implications for him/her,
      concludes Dr. Gillespie.

502. Himes, Joseph S. and Margaret L. Hamlett. "The Assessment of Ad-
      justment of Aged Negro Women in a Southern City." Phylon, Vol.
      23, Summer, 1962, pp. 139-147.

      The article showed that although the 100 aged Black women who were
      studied in Durham, North Carolina were markedly similar in level
      of adjustment, they were concentrated at the upper end of the ad-
      justment range. This fact agrees with findings reported in other
      studies of the aged, both Black and White, in both Southern and
      Northern communities. Adjustment appeared to be less adequate in
      the economic rather than in the social and psychological areas,
      contend the authors. Differences in level of adjustment were
      shown to be related significantly to variations of employment ex-
      perience, home ownership, education and health conditions. The
      evidence from this and other studies suggests that these variables
      comprise clusters of factors that are significant in the experiences

Himes, Joseph S. and Margaret L. Hamlett (continued)

of aged persons. The authors conclude that the women exhibited the greatest social adequacy in managing the household, social participation, and personal decisions, and the least in respect to exclusion from leadership roles. Psychological adjustment was best with respect to self expression, reality definitions and self images, and poorest with respect to role satisfaction. In the economic sphere greatest adequacy of adjustment issued from sufficiency of income and control of economic activities, while most dissatisfaction came from inadequate income and lack of opportunity for training and gainful employment, conclude the writers.

503. Jackson, Jacquelyne J. "'But What I Really Said Was...' or Categorical Differences of Older Black Women." Journal of Minority Aging, Vol. 5, No. 3, March-October, 1980, pp. 279-285.

The primary purpose of this article was to provide an interpretative exercise for gerontological studies interested in the implications of editorial changes which may be made in manuscripts concerning older Black women. Although this practice is not widespread when the changes are substantive, it does occur on occasion. Some consideration should also be given to factors or motives underlying the changes. Specifically, the case study used in this article concerns modifications made in print by Generations, a publication of the Western Gerontological Society, in an invited manuscript, in which the author wrote, entitled, "Categorical Differences of Older Black Women." An exercise of this type should be especially useful on the advanced undergraduate level, where professors may help their students increase their critical or analytical skills, as well as to learn more about factors affecting given viewpoints, particularly since assumptions held by writers, researchers, and others often affect outcomes, states Dr. Jackson. Some notable gaps remain in the general area of furthering social understanding of the kinds of social problems confronting older women in the United States. Two such gaps concern the stereotypes of older Black women held by many aging or aging-related specialists of all races, and the impact of those stereotypes on issues concerning older Black women. These types of problems, of course, are not restricted to aging; they permeate many aspects of contemporary society, including much of the academic world, in the United States. These issues, however, have often been suppressed in many gerontological or aging courses when the subject is minority aging, and particulatly when it is Black aging, according to the author. Thus, most undergraduates and graduate students of aging probably have little or no exposure to them. One of the problems concerns the reinterpretation of positions taken by others; it may be entitled "but what you really meant was..." and viewed as an honest attempt to improve an oral or written presentation. However, much subjectivity underlies this game, concludes the professor.

504. _____. "Categorical Differences of Older Black Women."
Generation, Vol. 4, No. 3, Spring, 1980, p. 17.

The sociologist points out that elderly Black women have different
needs than other aged women. Besides being Black, they are poorer, less educated, receive less Medicaid attention and are given
little attention by the larger society....

505. _____. "Comparative Life Styles and Family and Friend Relationships Among Old Black Women." Family Coordinator, Vol. 21,
January, 1972, pp. 477-485.

The total sample upon which this article was based contained 74
women living with their spouses (hereafter married women) and 159
women without their spouses (hereafter spouseless women), all of
whom were 50 or more years of age. Data were collected in personal interviews in 1968-1969 from predominantly low-income women
representative of a Black, urban renewal target area in Durham,
North Carolina, and from a nonrandom sample of middle-income women
scattered through or peripheral to that target area. The author
declares that while the most important conclusion may be the great
similarity between these married and spouseless women, the presence or absence of spouse may be significantly related to such
variables as number of close friends, sharing commercial recrea-
tion with friends, dependence upon or participation with children
in emergencies of any sort and in shopping, mutual assistance pat-
terms between mothers and youngest children, choices between spending more time with friends or relatives, and specific preferences
for greater affinal or consanguinal contact.

506. _____. "Introduction-The Black Elderly: Reassessing the
Plight of Older Black Women." Black Scholar, Vol. 13, No. 1,
January/February, 1982, pp. 2-4.

According to this scholar, the economic plight of older Black
women (and particularly so for Black women over sixty-five years
of age, or the aged) was dire. Today, despite some improvements
in their economic conditions, many aged Black women remain poor.
Much of the economic improvement of aged Black women over time
occurred through federal programs providing income, medical, food,
and housing subsidies. Whatever terminology is employed to dis-
guise the nature of these subsidies, the undisputed fact remains
that they are welfare subsidies, suggests Dr. Jackson. She believes that the problem of racial inequities in the receipt of
Social Security benefits, due in part to differential patterns of
longevity by race, could be overcome if Social Security were a
true insurance program. Because Social Security for the aged has
become a "hot potato" politically now, however, Blacks and other
Americans require considerable education about the real status of
the currently bankrupt and illogical system of Social Security,
declares the sociologist. Prof. Jackson argues that advocates for
aged Blacks should act sagaciously by reviewing those recommendations which must, by law, be presented for consideration to the
Congress of the United States. In subsequent congressional hear-
ings which may occur, these advocates should promote the legislative enactment of Social Security as only a social insurance

Jackson, Jacquelyne J. (continued)

program. The benefits to Blacks and their heirs could be enormous.
Steps must be taken to make certain Blacks investing in Social Security, or at least their heirs or assignees, will receive all of
their benefits, with appropriate interests, asserts the writer.
Other methods must also be developed to increase the socioeconomic
well-being of older Black women, said Prof. Jackson. Many of
these efforts, as well must be directed to their earlier years,
including the reduction of the high proportion of Black women now
bearing illegitimate children. The author emphasizes the fact
that the qualitative (and not merely the quantitative) education
level of Black women merits categorical improvement. To this end,
more attention must be concentrated on realistic assessments of
what it means to be "Black and female" in the world of today and
tomorrow. The earlier assessment of the plights of older Black
women was also hampered by the inadequate availability of gerontologic data about them. This problem still exists, but the gaps
have narrowed somewhat since then, concludes Dr. Jackson.

507. _____. "Menopausal Attitudes and Behaviors Among SENESCENT
Black Women and Predictors of Changing Attitudes and Activities
Among Aged Blacks." Black Aging, Vol. 1, August/October, 1976,
pp. 8-29.

The authors major purpose in this article was to share some hypotheses from an exploratory study of a nonrandom sample of 51 post-
menopausal Black women about psychological and sociocultural
events related to the menopause. Emphasized most are relationships between demographic variables and menopausal symptoms, expected and occurred symptoms, and variables related to attitudes
about reproductive loss. Also considered are symptomatic cluster-
ing and the women's use and evaluation of medical treatment. Dr.
Jackson points out that a key explanatory concept for good social
and psychological adjustment in growing older for both Black women
and Black men, and for successful adjustment to menopause among
Black women, may well be that of social integration. The greater
the integration into social units meaningful to the individual and
the greater the individual's satisfaction with that integration,
the greater is her or his successful adjustment to aging. Growing
older is generally more successful when individuals share that
continued aging with intimate others, and especially with satisfactory spouses.

508. _____. "Plights of Older Black Women in the United States."
Black Aging, Vol. 1, Nos. 2 & 3, December, 1975 and February 1976,
pp. 12-22.

In this essay Dr. Jackson gives her assessment of the plights of
economics, loneliness, mortality and isolationism confronting the
category of older Black women as they age within the United States.
Insufficient data prevented any definitive assessment at this
time, but minimal assessments relying largely upon relevant demographic data were made. Generally, the types of adverse conditions confronting Black women as a categorical group in their
younger years merely become more exacerbated in their older years.

Jackson, Jacquelyne J. (continued)

Some other changes, such as that of diminishing size of their family and friendship circles, occur at later points in their life
cycles, and interact with the variables leading to plights of economics, loneliness, mortality, and isolationism. Overall, it does
appear that it may be unprofitable for older Black women to focus
considerable energies upon the resolution of problems which confront them because they are old and Black and female, as opposed
to more gross attacks from many angles and with many different
kinds of individuals of varying ages upon the problems which they
share in common with other groups, according to the author. Dr.
Jackson states, the proliferation of an increasing number of highly specialized protest groups is unprofitable in resolving the
critical socioeconomic and other problems confronting those who
are old and Black and female. Finally, it is important that individuals who are aging and Black become more cognizant of recent
trend reversals in generalizations which were previously valid and
reliable, so as to avoid "chasing dead issues," concludes the
sociologist.

509.   _____. "The Plight of Older Black Women in the United States."
       Black Scholar, Vol. 7, April, 1976, pp. 47-55.

This essay provided a cautious assessment of the plights of economics, loneliness, mortality and isolationism confronting aggregated older Black women as they age in the United States. Although
insufficient data prevented any definitive assessment at this
time, minimal assessments relying both upon relevant demographic
data and the writer's own value system were possible and were so
provided. Generally, the aggregated conditions of older Black
women which were prevalent when they were younger continue into
old age, merely becoming more exacerbated. Perhaps the most exacerbated plights related to those of insufficient monies and insufficient men, states the writer. Dr. Jackson surmises that
there is a need to improve significantly not only the use of health
care and delivery of preventive health care, but also to reexamine
seriously the extent to which the needs of older persons are met
more effectively through organizations, services, and other resources being based upon race, sex, and age, et cetera, or upon
more salient and combinable characteristics. She concludes that
this is especially important for older Black women who have for
too long already been isolated from the central core of longevity.

510.   Johnson, Elizabeth F. "Look At It This Way: Some Aspects of the
       Drug Mix-up Problem Among Blacks, Poor, Aged, and Female Patients."
       Journal of the National Medical Association, Vol. 70, No. 11,
       October, 1978. pp. 745-747.

The writer declares that elderly Blacks seldom have sufficient
funds to seek proper medical advice. They frequently diagnose
their own physical problems and decide that they are minor. They
are vulnerable to slick Madison Avenue advertising that a pill or
a drug which can be purchased without a doctor's prescription will
give relief in a short time. This is especially true of drugs ad-
vertised to give relief to the pains of arthritis. And if one

Johnson, Elizabeth F. (continued)

receives even the minimal relief, the taking of the drug soon becomes habit-forming, according to the author. The inability to
read labels with understanding continues to create problems for
persons with limited education, especially the elderly, concludes
the author.

511.   Jones, Faustine C. "The Lofty Role of the Black Grandmother."
        Crisis, Vol. 80, January, 1973, pp. 19-21.

        The writer contends that the role of the grandmother is one of
        love, strength, and stability for the Black family. She argues
        that no matter what social and economic conditions the Black fami-
        ly has faced, the Black grandmother has been a steady, supporting
        influence, as well as a connecting link between branches of the
        extended family. Dr. Jones points out that even during slavery
        the Black grandmother, during the first five or six years of her
        grandchildrens' lives, sought to make them happy, comfortable,
        secure in her love for them, and conscious of their worth in her
        eyes. The writer surmises that there was no "generation gap" be-
        tween the Black grandmother and her descendants after the era of
        slavery had ended. She concludes, it is clear that although the
        role of the Black grandmother has changed and has been diminished,
        she remains a source of love and strength as well as a stabilizing
        factor for the Black family. The author continues to state that
        Black people, seeking to know and appreciate their heritage, must
        understand the role of the Black grandmother in the survival,
        growth, and development of the Black family in America.

512.   Penn, Nolan E. "Ethnicity and Aging in Elderly Black Women:
        Some Mental Characteristics." Health and The Black Aged. Wilbur
        H. Watson, et al., Editors, Washington, DC: National Center on
        Black Aged, 1978, pp. 80-96.

        According to the writer, aged Black and Indian women held more
        positive attitudes toward Children, "past" and "present," than
        did Caucasian women. In this sense, Black and Indian women did
        not seem to disengage; Black women held more positive attitudes
        toward parents in the "present" and "past" than did Caucasian and
        Indian women; and Caucasian women held more positive attitudes to-
        ward work "past" and "present" than did Black and Indian women.
        In fact, Black women's attitudes toward work were significantly
        more negative than those attitudes observed in the other two eth-
        nic groups, concludes the researcher.

513.   Smith, Alicia D. "Life Satisfaction and Activity Preferences of
        Black Female Participants in Senior Citizens' Centers: An Investi-
        gative Inquiry." Black Aging, Vol. 3, Nos. 1 and 2, October and
        December, 1977, pp. 8-13.

        This study was conceived of as an investigative inquiry into the
        life satisfaction and learning preferences of Black older adults.
        The purpose was to observe and report on behavioral issues which
        affect aging adjustment. Measurements were made of individual
        life satisfaction and additional data was collected on personal

Smith, Alicia D. (continued)

motivation for utilizing the center, responses to a list of activities, and on the perceptions of both participants and administrators with regard to the needs of the elderly. Fifty participants
and four administrators, at four centers, were identified. The results of this inquiry indicate that three variables: age, health
and length of residency are significant correlates of life satisfaction and that length of residency is the single best predictor
of satisfaction. The indications are also that members prefer
health and personal oriented activities. It is concluded that cultural experiences and values play a significant role in defining
individual needs, and that for this population, aging adjustment
means engaging in and enlarging upon social interactions and experiences rather than disengaging, concludes the writer.

34. BLACK CENTENARIANS

514. "Charlie Smith, 137, Nation's Oldest." Newsday, (Garden City, NY)
      October 7, 1979, p. 20.

      Charlie Smith, brought to the United States as a slave in 1854 and
      considered by Social Security officials to be the nation's oldest
      person at 137, died in Bartow, Florida, October 6, 1979. Mr.
      Smith was originally stolen from Liberia (West Africa) in 1854 and
      brought to New Orleans, where he was sold on the auction block to
      a Texas rancher named Charles Smith who gave him his name.

515. Clifford, Terry. "The Oldest Man in New York." New York Magazine,
      May 28, 1979, p. 120.

      This article is about Mr. Henry Jones, who was 106 years old in
      1979 and believed to be the oldest man in New York City. "First
      thing I do every morning, I get me a cup of black coffee, eat two
      raw eggs, and have a drink of whiskey. Then I'm gone with the
      wind," said Mr. Jones. When asked what others can do to live as
      long as he, Mr. Jones argues: "God Almighty made me. His will
      brought me to what I am. Ain't nothing but God Almighty's will.
      If it's not in His will, you're a dead duck."

516. Drane, Francesca. "At 104, She Has Sage Advice on How to Live."
      New York News World, March 12, 1978, pp. 1A, 12.

      Mrs. Clementine Ryan Sheppard was born in Aiken, South Carolina in
      1874 and was living in Harlem, NY in 1978. She attributed her
      success as a mother and as a person to her faith in God. She said
      the secret of a long and happy life is to "Let nothing bear on
      your heart and let nothing worry your mind."

517. Drummond, Steven. "Brotherhood of Sleeping Car Porters." Alexan-
      dria Gazette (Virginia), March 28, 1985, p. 3.

      This article is about Mrs. Rosina C. Tucker, who was 104 years old
      in 1985. She was the wife of a Pullman porter and was the union's

Drummond, Steven (continued)

first international secretary-treasurer. She was a member of the first Black labor union, the Brotherhood of Sleeping Car Porters, in the United States which was founded in 1925. Mrs. Tucker recalls that she missed being elected president of the Brotherhood by only two votes. She also discusses the part that A. Philip Randolph played in forming the Brotherhood of Sleeping Car Porters.

518. Harvey, James. "At 106, He's Going Home: Harlem (NY) Man Returning to His Roots in Africa." New York Daily News, September 4, 1983, p. 10.

Mr. Charlie Lee, West Harlem's oldest resident, left the United States to spend his remaining years in Dakar, Senegal, a West African nation. Asked how he managed to live so long, Mr. Lee said: "I owe it all to God; nothing happens to you unless God lets it happen."

519. "I Have to Work." Christian Science Monitor, December 4, 1979, p. 10.

This article is about Willie Brew, thought to be 104 years old and was, perhaps, in 1979, the oldest working American. For $58.00 a week, he cut weeds and picked up trash in the Osceola National Forest in Northern Florida. He lived in Olustee, Florida, a small town 50 miles west of Jacksonville, Florida.

520. Meyer, Eugene L. "District Woman Celebrates Time of Her 105-Year Life." Washington Post, November 3, 1986, pp. D1, D3.

Mrs. Rosina C. Tucker was born November 4, 1881 in the District of Columbia. Even at her age she was alert, articulate and amazing in her recall of a century of history. She had visited schools throughout the metropolitan area to impart oral history to the younger generation....

521. Nadeau, Dot. "She Has a Story to Tell." Brattleboro Reformer (Vermont), July 2, 1983, pp. 3-9.

This article is about Miss Daisy Turner who was 100 years old and lived in Grafton, Vermont. Miss Turner discusses her family's roots from Africa to the present (1983). "On the whole, I've found young people have no prejudice of feeling like a certain age of people have. You have to be big enough not to let these things make you bitter or prejudiced. You got to be big enough to learn something from these things and still go on," declares Miss Turner.

522. Schaap, Dick. "Meet the Oldest Man." Parade Magazine, November 20, 1983, pp. 5, 6.

Mr. Arthur Reed was 123 (in 1983) and was born June 28, 1860 in Buffalo, NY. In 1983 he was living in Oakland, CA. He lived under 25 presidents and said FDR was the best. Mr. Reed's advice to the world is: "Be good to one another because God is good to us. Wasn't for God, we wouldn't be here today. God is good to every one."

523. Smith, Earl. "Two Brothers: 100 Years of Caring." <u>Jet</u>, October 10, 1974, pp. 22-23.

This article discusses Albert Peters, who was 102 years old and his brother Paul Peters, who was 94 years old and blind. Albert took care of his brother and has been doing so for nearly most of his adult life. Both are deeply religious men and are regular churchgoers.

524. Thompson, Vernon C. "William 'Mac' Pinckney: 116-Year-Old Recalls His Early Days as a Sharecropper." <u>Washington Post</u>, February 8, 1979, p. 20.

Mr. Pinckney, who was once declared the oldest man in Prince George's County (Maryland) discusses his youth, parents and friends. He said his secret of old age is simple. "As long as I walk upright and keep His (God's) command, He will lengthen my days."

525. Toner, Mike. "116-Year-Old Recalls His Night of Terror." <u>Atlanta (GA) Journal and Constitution</u>, August 31, 1986, p. 12.

Mr. Willie Dewberry, who at 116 years old in 1986, remembers the 1886 earthquake. He was 16 at the time. Mr. Dewberry said he would never forget the great Charleston earthquake. He discussed the events that occurred during the earthquake near his father's farm in Summerville, South Carolina.

526. "The 130 Year Old Man." <u>Newsweek</u>, October 2, 1972, p. 74.

This article discusses Charlie Smith, an ex-slave, who was thought to be (in 1972) the "oldest" man in the United States. He lived in Bartow, Florida and ran (in 1972) a candy and soft-drink store. Smith outlived three wives. He had a quick sense of humor, a desire to keep active and a firm belief in God. "I ain't so perfect," says Charlie Smith, "but I do try to live nearer to the Commandments."

35. BLACK OCTOGENERIANS

527. "For These 'Youngsters,' Life Begins at 80." <u>Ebony</u>, Vol. 36, No. 4, February, 1981, pp. 58-60, 62.

This article discussed some octogenerians who had productive lives long past retirement age. They included: Dr. Charles H. Wesley, Historian; A. G. Gaston, Businessman; William O. Walker, Publisher of the <u>Cleveland (Ohio) Call and Post</u>; Dr. Howard Nash, Physician; Alberta Hunter, Vocalist; Reverend Martin Luther King, Sr., Minister; Elizabeth Cotten, Folk-blues guitarist; Dr. Benjamin E. Mays, Educator; James Van Der Zee, Photographer; and Estelle (Mama) Yancey, Blues Singer.

36. MYTHS ABOUT THE BLACK AGED

528.   Jackson, Jacquelyne J. "Black Aged in Quest of the Phoenix."
        Triple Jeopardy--Myth or Reality. Washington, DC: National Coun-
        cil on the Aged, 1972.

        The author, while not denying the heterogeneity among the Black
        elderly, forcefully argues that "race is a reality and we should
        not deny it. . . . Insofar as Black old people are concerned, I
        think that we should not now begin to treat them as if they were
        the same as white old people. They are not." Racism has adverse-
        ly affected their preparation for old age, concludes Dr. Jackson.

529.   _____ and Bertram E. Walls. "Myths and Realities About Aged
        Blacks." Readings in Gerontology. Mollie Brown, Editor. St.
        Louis, MO: C. V. Mosby Co., 1978, pp. 95-113.

        The development of gerontological knowledge about Blacks has been
        hampered severely by racial biases and vested interests. The sig-
        nificant differences between aged Blacks and Whites typically
        stressed by advocates for aged Blacks are largely myths. Geronto-
        logists have generally abetted the perpetuation of these myths
        through ineffectual controls of the variables of race in their
        contrasts of aged Blacks and Whites. This study, which was prima-
        rily concerned with the resolution of prevalent myths about aged
        Blacks and Whites, was based on an analysis of the 1974 Harris
        data about aging attitudes and behaviors in the United States.
        The finding of a general absence of any significant racial differ-
        ences between paired groups of low- and high-income aged and young
        Blacks and Whites in the Harris survey suggested strongly the vast
        similarity of aging process and patterns among American Blacks and
        Whites, argue the writers. An examination of variables related to
        sociodemographic characteristics, aging images and attitudes, ag-
        ing activities, aging problems, and patterns of familial assistance
        showed striking similarities between low-income, as well as high-
        income, aged Blacks and Whites. For example, comparisons of ap-
        propriately controlled groups of aged Blacks and Whites by income
        levels indicated insignificant differences by such variables as
        activities, instrumental assistance from and to families, religion,
        and health. The few significant differences reported herein would
        undoubtedly wash out with more stringent controls for socioemic-
        mic status. In other words, current myths about significant dif-
        ferences between aged Blacks and Whites have little, if any, va-
        lidity, state the writers. The authors conclude that the most im-
        portant implication of their study for aging programs involving
        Blacks is the need to structure such programs on adequate knowl-
        edge about the conditions under which race is and is not a factor.
        Furthermore, advocates for racially separated programs should avoid
        hiding behind aged Blacks when they are clearly more concerned
        about building Black power bases for themselves. Finally, aging
        training programs should place greater emphasis on training indi-
        viduals of various races to provide services to individuals of va-
        rious races. They should also aid their students in distinguish-
        ing clearly between significant differences between populations,
        such as aged Blacks and Whites, and significant differences between
        individuals who happen to be aged Blacks or Whites, surmise the
        researchers.

37.   RURAL BLACK AGED

530. Blake, J. Herman. "'Doctor Can't Do Me No Good': Social Concomitants of Health Care Attitudes and Practices Among Elderly Blacks in Isolated Rural Populations." Health and the Black Aged. Wilbur H. Watson, et al., Editors. Washington, DC: National Center on Black Aged, 1978, pp. 55-62.

The author surmises that practitioners must recognize that, frequently, there are major gaps between their expectations and the ability of the elderly to appropriately respond. He found repeated instances of people being given prescriptions or other instructions when they were unable to read. Many of the people have not spent a day in school. Many were functionally illiterate even if they had attended and, as a consequence, the patients would often end up either following instructions improperly or not at all. In either case, medication often produced no improvement and thus confirmed the belief that "The doctor can't do me no good." As we attempt to extend the benefits of health care to the Black elderly we must always bear in mind that rural residents born 1910 came to their adulthood in a society very different from the one we now take for granted, argues the author. To the extent that their lives still reflect the conditions and experiences of a much earlier generation, their beliefs and practices will also reflect those conditions. If we would truly do them any good, we must "listen eloquently" to their experiences, and respond with sensitivity and understanding, concludes the researcher.

531. Bourg, Carroll J. "A Social Profile of Black Aged in a Southern Metropolitan Area." Proceedings of the Research Conference on Minority Group Aged in the South. Jacquelyne J. Jackson, Editor. Durham, NC: Center for the Study of Aging and Human Development, Duke University Medical Center, 1972, pp. 97-106.

The writer argues that in household or family composition he found that the extended family remains an unexplored notion. He contends we are without adequate terms to identify the various arrangements which have been arrived at among Black elderly. In addition, it is characteristic of Black elderly, in contrast to White elderly, that the presence of adult children or other relatives in the household usually means that they have been brought into the homes of the elderly person(s). If we limit ourselves and government programs to the now accepted identifications of households, heads of household and so on, we exclude large numbers of Black elderly who can made do and can make do well in households that combine various persons all cooperating to the maintenance of the home, argues Bourg. If the supplementary assistance of governmental agencies can be directed to the actual situations, much can be done to fortify the manifest strengths of the Black elderly, even though they have been persons living in a southern metropolitan area, concludes the author.

532. Ford, Johnny. "Black Aged in The Future in a Predominantly Black
      Southern Town." Proceedings of Black Aged in The Future. Jacque-
      lyne J. Jackson, Editor. Durham, NC: Center for the Study of Ag-
      ing and Human Development, Duke University, 1973, pp. 1-10.

      The researcher discusses Tuskegee, Alabama as a site for a compre-
      hensive housing complex for the elderly. Such a complex would pro-
      vide social services, as well as housing, recreation, health ser-
      vices, economic opportunities, and social activities. He declares
      that those who are concerned about the aged in this country should
      look South, and to create strategies which will develop and mold
      the resources for the aged ending up in the South. Ford concludes
      that Black and poor people, and older people especially, need mo-
      ney and resources, not words.

533. Jackson, Jacquelyne J. "Aged Negroes: Their Cultural Departures
      From Statistical Stereotypes and Rural-Urban Differences." Re-
      search Planning and Action for the Elderly: The Power and Poten-
      tial of Social Sciences. Donald P. Kent, et al., Editors. New
      York: Behavioral Publications, Inc., 1972, pp. 501-513.

      The major purposes of this article were those of suggesting some
      areas where aged Blacks tend to become "cultural departurers" from
      statistical stereotypes, and of also suggesting certain variables
      which may be useful in distinguishing between rural and urban aged
      Blacks. Essentially, both tasks were only partially successful,
      due to the scarcity of available data about aged Blacks, and, no
      doubt, to the value judgments which the author has imposed upon
      those data. Given those limitations, however, Black aged tend to
      depart from such statistical stereotypes as those which hold that
      their marital statuses are significantly different from those of
      White aged: that their life expectancies are typically less than
      those of Whites (they may be longer at the later age periods);
      that they differ significantly from Whites by importance placed
      upon their families, or that they are more religious, in poorer
      health, or less active in formal organizations than Whites. Some
      variables which may be useful in distinguishing between rural and
      urban Blacks in southern areas, at least, include those of income
      sources, material possessions, health, family, and household fac-
      tors, friendship and social contact, church attendance and parti-
      cipation in church-related organizations, and attitudes toward the
      desirability of homes for the aged and toward death, declares the
      author. According to the writer, age-eligibility requirements for
      Blacks to receive retirement and other old age benefits must be re-
      duced. It is also necessary for various local, county, and state
      governments to become more concerned about, and more actively in-
      volved in programs, planning, and evaluation for Black aged, states
      the writer. Dr. Jackson concludes that social gerontologists and
      practitioners utilizing their findings have such responsibilities
      as those of enhancing the validity and reliability of statistical
      stereotypes about Black aged, and of working among and for Black
      aged to eliminate those valid stereotypes which are undesirable,
      and of augmenting those which are desirable.

534. _____ and A. Davis. "Characteristic Patterns of Aged, Rural Negroes in Macon County." A Survey of Selected Socioeconomic Characteristics of Macon County. B. C. Johnson, Editor. Tuskegee, AL: Macon County Community Action Office, 1966.

The title tells what this work is about. The authors point out that the Black aged in Macon County, Alabama were at the bottom of the social and economic ladder. They surmise that the various social agencies in the county showed no real interest in meeting the pressing needs of Black senior citizens.

535. Pearson, Jean and Vira R. Kivett. "The Widowed, Black, Older Adult in the Rural South." Family Relations, Vol. 29, No. 1, January, 1980, pp. 83-90.

In this study, 72 widowed Black aged from a rural area were studied with regard to various characteristics and service needs. Observed needs were then compared to recent national policy recommendations for the general population of the elderly. The data showed that the rural Black elderly who are widowed are disadvantaged more than corresponding rural elderly with regard to health status, income, education, home ownership, transportation, and organizational activity. Older widowed Blacks were less economically autonomous than the rural elderly in general as observed through their heavier reliance upon Medicaid, Medicare, and family resources. The rural church and relatives figured prominently in their support systems, conclude the authors....

536. Ruberstein, Daniel I. "Social Participation of Aged Blacks: A National Sample." Proceedings of the Research Conference on Minority Groups Aged in the South. Jacquelyne J. Jackson, Editor. Durham, NC: Center for the Study of Aging and Human Development, Duke University Medical Center, 1972, pp. 48-62.

This study found that more of the White elderly lived alone than did the Black elderly. Moreover, twice as many White and Black elderly lived in households consisting solely of respondent and spouse (presumably husband and wife), states the author. In addition, more Whites than Blacks were found living with a spouse in households containing others. However, examination of larger households showed that the Black elderly lived with more people in their households than did the Whites. Contrary to the stereotype of separated, broken, discontinued families among the Blacks, it was found that only four out of ten Black elderly did so. This family belonging was further evidenced by the finding that more than twice as many Blacks as Whites would be found in companionship households. Intergenerational continuity in households was also found more prevalent for Blacks than for Whites: the Black elderly were more than three times as likely to live in households with grandchildren than were White elderly, according to the author.

537. Scott, Jean Pearson and Vira R. Kivett. "The Widowed, Black, Older Adult in the Rural South: Implication for Policy." Family Relations, Vol. 30, No. 1, January, 1981, pp. 83-90.

Scott, Jean Pearson and Vira R. Kivett (continued)

The researchers examined the characteristics and needs of the widowed, Black, older adult. Special attention was given to the implications for policy. The sample was composed of 72 widowed
Blacks who were drawn from a larger random sample of 418 rural
elderly adults (65-99 years). The general economic plight of widowed Blacks suggested the need for a basic floor of defined vital
services that would speak to income, health, housing, and transportation needs, stated the authors. The vital role of the family
and of the church in the support systems of widowed Blacks is discussed. A strategy for bringing services to disadvantaged communities where constituent action is unlikely, was recommended by
the writers.

538.   Smith, Stanley H. "The Older Rural Negro." Older Rural Americans:
A Sociological Perspective. E. Grant Youmans, Editor. Lexington:
University of Kentucky Press, 1967, pp. 262-280.

This article discusses some selected demographic characteristics
of aged rural Blacks; data on educational level, employment, and
income. In all cases, aged rural Blacks are far behind in all
these categories. The writer also gives some data on the involvement of aged rural Blacks in American life; and a small amount of
data which are designed to give an assessment of some of the subjective reactions of aged rural Blacks to their social and economic conditions. The author concludes that aged rural Blacks have
three things against them: old age, rural residence, and minority-
group status.

539.   Tucker, Charles J. "Changes in Age Composition of the Rural Black
Population of the South from 1950-1970." Phylon, Vol. 33, Fall,
1974, pp. 268-275.

The author states that of a decline of 1.5 million persons in the
South's rural Black population between 1950 and 1970, a net minimum of 1.9 million Blacks moved to cities within the region or
moved outside the region altogether; therefore, accounting for all
the decrease. Had it not been for relatively high fertility among
those who remained, declines would have been greater still. The
estimates of migration presented in this paper are based on the application of 1950-1970 cohort ratios for the total U.S. Black population during the period and do not include estimates of migration among those persons born after 1950. These ratios were applied to the age structure of the Black rural population of the
South in 1950. He said for total losses, the heaviest were obviously found among the farm segment of the rural population. The
farm population declined by no less than 86 percent over the twenty years. Within this population, losses were heaviest among farm
youth who were younger than 20 years of age in 1950, most of whom
must have migrated to urban places. For older persons who had already become established in farm occupations by 1950, migration
was not as heavy and when it occurred, was probably directed to
nonfarm areas or entailed a shift in occupation from farm to other
activities without a movement to urban places and jobs. The writer concludes that shifts in occupation or residence on the part

Tucker, Charles J. (continued)

of many farm Blacks of older ages had the effect of increasing the
number of nonfarm Blacks by more than 50 percent over the twenty
year period. Young adult age groups barely increased in number at
all. There is little wonder, then, that the dependency ratio of
nonfarm Blacks increased drastically due to the shortage of young
adults, contends the researcher.

540. Watson, Wilbur H. "Indicators of Subjective Well-Being Among
      Older Blacks in the Rural Southeastern United States: Some Find-
      ings and Interpretations." Journal of Minority Aging, Vol. 9,
      No. 1, 1984, pp. 39-48.

This study focused primarily upon six indicators of subjective
well-being among older Blacks between 60 and 92 years of age.
These factors include an absence of feelings of loneliness; feelings of being useful, for example, in performing valued social
roles within the family; feeling that things were not getting worse
as one grew older; not taking things hard as an older person, a
sense of satisfaction with one's life situation, and not having a
lot to be sad about.... The significant factors that help to account for the unexpected high level of subjective well-being among
Blacks are their religiosity, supportive networks of church-going
acquaintances and close ties with family and friends, argues Dr.
Watson.

38. URBAN BLACK AGED

541. Bailey, L. B. et al. "Folacin and Iron Status and Hematological
      Findings In Predominantly Black Elderly Persons from Urban Low-
      Income Households." American Journal of Clinical Nutrition, Vol.
      32, No. 11, November, 1979, pp. 2346-2353.

The researchers found that the iron status of the Blacks whom they
studied appeared to be normal and the dietary histories of those
individuals indicated that only 20% were taking supplemental iron.
Therefore, it appeared likely that dietary iron was adequate, concluded the authors.

542. Barg, Sylvia K. and Carl Hirsch. "A Successor Model for Community
      Support of Low-Income Minority Group Aged." Aging and Human De-
      velopment, Vol. 3, 1972, pp. 243-252.

The authors argue that experience in research and community outreach work with low-income urban aged led to the development of a
multifocal program approach. The program approach includes case
referral and advocacy work with the target population as well as
the organization of neighborhood-based groups of elderly residents.
The two approaches are intended to achieve both treatment of extant social symptons of age discrimination and social and political power by the aged to eliminate discrimination on the basis of
age. The two approaches provide mutual reinforcement for the success of each, and are based on tenets of social interaction theory

Barg, Sylvia K. and Carl Hirsch (continued)

as well as an analysis of the social and political powerlessness
of the aged in the Model Cities Neighborhood of Philadelphia. The
researchers conclude that experience in the Model Cities Senior
Wheels East has led to considerations involving cross-generational
ties between worker and client to achieve senior power, the role
of indigenous community workers in social welfare agencies working
with the aged as well as the successful application of the approach
to the Black, Puerto Rican, and foreign-born White aged residing
in the area.

543. Clemente, Frank, et al. "Race and Morale of the Urban Aged."
Gerontologist, Vol. 14, August, 1974, pp. 342-344.

Racial differences in morale were analyzed in this article for
comparable samples of 721 Black and 211 White residents of Philadelphia age 65 and over. The authors argue that a hypothesis suggesting Blacks have lower morale than Whites was derived from the
literature and tested by regression analysis. The standardized
partial regression coefficient was of negligible magnitude, and
the hypothesis was rejected.   They conclude that possible reasons for the failure of race to emerge as even a moderate predictor of morale include Messer's (1968) argument that elderly Blacks
view old age as a reward in itself and McCarthy and Yancey's (1971)
contention that presumed racial differences in morale have received
little actual empirical support.

544. _____. "The Participation of Black Aged in Voluntary Associations." Journal of Gerontology, Vol. 30, July, 1975, pp. 469-
478.

Racial differences in membership in and attendance of voluntary
associations were analyzed for comparable samples of 753 Black and
260 White residents of Philadelphia age 65 and over. A hypotheses
suggesting aged Blacks have higher rates of participation than
aged Whites was derived from the literature and tested by regression analysis. The authors declare potentially confounding variables, e.g., health and socioeconomic status, were entered into
the regression equation as controls. They state the results of
the regression analysis indicated the Black aged belonged to more
associations than the White aged and had higher rates of attendance.
The writers ocnclude examination of findings previously reported
indicate part of the difference is due to the greater participation of aged Blacks in church-related activities. Implications
of the findings are briefly discussed.

545. Craig, Dorothy. "Aged Blacks: The Story of Cleveland, Ohio."
Action for Aged Blacks: When? A Conference of The National
Caucus on The Black Aged. Jacquelyne J. Jackson, Editor. Wash-
ington, DC: National Caucus on The Aged, 1973, pp. 27-31.

The author discusses senior citizen programs in Cleveland, Ohio,
beginning with the organization Outreach. She also points out
that there are 20,000,000 Americans over age 65 (for the year
1973) and a quarter of them live in poverty. Craig acknowledges

Craig, Dorothy (continued)

that almost half of all older Americans did not complete elemen-
tary school while little more than 1,000,000 are college graduates;
and 3,000,000 older people are considered functionally illiterate.
She believes that while the picture may be grim for older people,
it does not have to be. With some understanding, effort, and
friendliness from the rest of society, the elderly can be made to
feel useful and wanted, concludes the writer.

546. Hearn, H. L. "Career and Leisure Patterns of Middle Aged Urban
      Black." Gerontologist, Vol. 11, Winter, 1971, pp. 21-26.

The lack of formal education and opportunities generally have been
a tremendous handicap to the aged Black in America. From the author's research on the aging artist it was found that second ca-
reers which impart meaning, prestige, and supplement income in the
later years are a source of satisfaction and positive self feelings
to those so engaged. The author concludes that if the aging Black
American views his work as a necessary evil which entails little
self-involvement, perhaps a second career, which could start at
almost any time, will lend more satisfaction to his retirement
years, combining, as it can, "leisure activity" with income sup-
plementation.

39. COMPARATIVE BLACK AND WHITE AGED

547. Conway, Katherine. "Coping with the Stress of Medical Problems
      Among Black and White Elderly." Aging and Human Development, Vol.
      21, No. 1, 1985, pp. 39-48.

This is a preliminary study looking at the coping responses of a
group of Black and White urban elderly women to the stressful
event of a medical problem. Cognitive and active coping responses,
as well as social support, were explored. Findings revealed these
women were similar in many of the ways in which they responded to
the stress of medical problems. However, there were some definite
racial differences. These included level of social support, use
of prayer in coping, and use of nonprescription drugs; the Black
elderly engaged in these latter behaviors more frequently, according to the author....

548. Creecy, Robert F. and Roosevelt Wright. "Morale and Informal Ac-
      tivity with Friends Among Black and White Elderly." Gerontologist,
      Vol. 19, No. 6, December, 1979, pp. 544-547.

This article examines the nature of the relationship between informal activity with friends and morale among a sample of White
and Black elderly. The data indicate a statistically significant
relationship between these variables within the White sub-sample,
but within the Black sub-sample this relationship was substantially insignificant. The major implication of this research re-
volves around the finding that informal activity with friends was
not associated with morale among Black elderly. While it was

Creecy, Robert F. and Roosevelt Wright (continued)

suggested that the lack of intimacy in the friendships of Blacks may account for this finding, this was not tested since a measure of intimacy was not included in the data, according to the writers. The writers conclude that the future efforts of policy-makers and planners and the activities of practitioners should focus on the development and implementation of improved social service programs that enhance the opportunity for social interactions and friendship formation among the Black elderly, thereby minimizing the risk of social isolation among this population subgroup.

549. Davidson, William B. and Patrick R. Cotter. "Sense of Community Identity, Social Networks, and Psychological Well-Being Among Black and White Elderly: A First Look." Journal of Minority Aging, Vol. 9, No. 2, 1984, pp. 85-90.

The sense of community identity was studied in 200 Black and White older people in two Southern cities. This social identity was correlated significantly with psychological well-being among whites but not among Blacks. It was also significantly related to membership in multiple organized groups and having family nearby for whites and frequent contact with neighbors for Blacks.

550. Davis, Katherine C. "The Position and Status of Black and White Aged in Rural Baptist Churches in Kansas." Journal of Minority Aging, Vol. 5, No. 3, March-October, 1980, pp. 242-248.

This descriptive study explores the position and status of the aged in three Baptist churches (two Black, one white) in the rural area of Pike County, Missouri. It concentrates on the major roles of the aged in the churches, as well as their participation and seating arrangements. Also explored was the degree of respect obtained by the aged in their churches. Findings from the data, collected through interviews and observation, indicated that racial differences existed. The position and status of the aged in the Black churches were more clearly defined and respected than was true in the white church, states the author. It could be argued that the church is important to many rural dwellers, but that it holds special significance for rural Blacks. The rural Black church is able to unify activity for its members. Historically, the Black church has been the longest-living institution....

551. Deimling, Gary, et al. "Racial Differences in Social Integration and Life Satisfaction Among Aged Public Housing Residents." Aging and Human Development, Vol. 17, No. 3, 1983, pp. 203-212.

The effects of social activity, social resources, health, and functional status on the life satisfaction of Black and white aged were examined, based on interviews with 330 residents of age-integrated and age-segregated public housing estates in Cleveland, Ohio. The results of multivariated analysis call into question previous conclusions that age-segregated is conducive to greater life satisfaction. However, the findings do lend support to previous research indications that social integration has a greater degree of importance in determining the life satisfaction of Black than of white aged, conclude the researchers.

552. Durant, Thomas J., Jr. "Residencé, Race and Sex Differences Among
the Aged." Journal of Social and Behavioral Sciences, Vol. 24, No.
2, Spring, 1978, pp. 85-101.

The author tested six hypotheses with data collected by the personal interview technique on 458 persons of 65 years of age and over
from two Louisiana parishes. The study found that all four dimensions of alienation, group isolation, powerlessness, normlessness,
and personal isolation, existed to a substantial degree among the
aged studied, but powerlessness was particularly more prevalent.
Level of alienation did not vary by rural and urban residence and
in only one instance by sex. More powerlessness was found among
males than among females, and Blacks were more alienated than
Whites, especially in terms of group isolation. The status resource variables, especially education, were found to be greater
sources of variance in alienation than were the social interaction
variables. Status resource variables also served as greater sources of variance in alienation for Whites than for Blacks and for
urban residents over rural residents. No difference was found by
sex, in this regard, according to the writer.

553. Gatz, Margaret, Elissa I. Gease, Forrest B. Tyler, and John A.
Moran. "Psychosocial Competence Characteristics of Black and
White Women: The Constraining Effects of 'Triple Jeopardy'."
Black Scholar, Vol. 13, No. 1, January/February, 1982, pp. 5-12.

In this study patterns of competence of 114 Black and white older
and adolescent women were examined using a model based on M.
Brewster Smith, Jacquelyne J. Jackson, and Forrest B. Tyler. Sense
of personal control proved to be an important component of competence, as it was correlated with active, planful coping skills,
and it distinguished more effective from less effective criterion
groups, state the authors. Patterns of competence were different
within the age and race sub-groups, supporting the notion that
social conditions which restrict opportunity will constrain the
development of competence. The writers conclude that their study
offers support for a picture of competence in which the central
attributes are active coping skills and perception of personal control. The patterns of attributes appear to be systematically in-
flüenced by restrictions of opportunity, such as "triple jeopardy."
However, the effect of "triple jeopardy" is to constrain the pattern of competence rather than to reduce competence. In fact, the
older Black women in this study exhibited real strengths, capabi-
lities, and resilience as people, suggest the researchers.

554. German, Pearl S., et al. "Health Care of the Elderly in a Changing Inner City Community." Black Aging, Vol. 3, Nos. 4 & 5, April-
June, 1978, pp. 122-131.

The city discussed in this article was Baltimore, Maryland. The
researchers found that in this city, greater length of time at an
address, and living alone were associated with greater use of services. They conclude that if older people, particularly those who
may be cut off from more traditional support systems, look to hospitals, doctors, nurses, and other services closely connected to
maintaining independence in later life can be initiated and coordinated.

555. Golden, Herbert   "Black Ageism." Social Policy, Vol. 7, No. 3,
      November/December, 1976, pp. 40-42.

      The author argues that what is clear is that attempts to apply re-
      search findings based on undifferentiated comparisons between
      Black and White elderly toward the solution of problems faced by
      Black elderly are doomed to ineffectiveness. Social scientists by
      and large agree that race is an American social reality and as such
      must be regarded as an independent variable in any study attempting
      to offer policy and/or planning objectives. It is then only when
      Blacks are studied as a group without necessarily making compari-
      sons to the larger White elderly population that we will have a
      good base for attacking the unique problems that this minority
      group membership imposes on peoples' adaptation to aging, concludes
      the writer.

556. _____ and Comeilda Weinstock. "The Myth of Homogeneity
      Among Black Elderly." Black Aging, Vol. 1, Nos. 2 & 3, December,
      1975 and February 1976, pp. 1-11.

      The writers state that because empirical evidence is sparse, the
      heterogeneity of Black elderly is frequently denied. The research-
      ers attempted to show that the mythology surrounding such charac-
      teristics as marital status, living arrangements, education, and
      family style ignore the possibility of any variability in this
      large population. They suggest that when Blacks are studied as a
      group without implying comparison to the white elderly population,
      we have a better understanding of the particular and unique prob-
      lems that minority group membership imposes on adaptation to
      aging....

557. Goldstein, Sidney. "Negro-White Differentials in Consumer Pat-
      terns of the Aged, 1960-1961." Gerontologist, Vol. 11, Autumn,
      1971, pp. 242-249.

      The writer asserts that since 1960-1961, the income of both White
      and Black aged units has improved, but even in 1968, older Black
      income levels were only about two-thirds as high as those of White
      units, and the percentage of Black units classified as below the
      poverty level remained substantial, especially for unrelated in-
      dividuals. This being so, it seems likely that important differ-
      ences also continue to characterize the expenditure dimensions of
      the consumer behavior of White and Black aged units. The scholar
      concludes the compounding influences of age and race make the eco-
      nomic situation of older Black units particularly bleak and war-
      rants special attention to this segment of the aged population.

558. Haber, David. "Yoga As a Preventive Health Care Program for
      White and Black Elders: An Exploratory Study." Aging and Human
      Development, Vol. 17, No. 3, 1983, pp. 169-176.

      A ten-week yoga program was implemented with sixty-one and forty-
      five low-income Black elders at two community sites, along with a
      pretest-posttest control group research design with random assign-
      ment at each site. White elders attended class regularly, prac-
      ticed yoga on their own on a daily basis, improved psychological

Haber, David   (continued)

well-being, and lowered their systolic blood pressure level, in
comparison to a control group.   Black elders, on the other hand,
attended the once-a-week class regularly but did not practice on
their own on a daily basis.   Thus, they did not improve psychological well-being nor reduce blood pressure level in comparison to
a control group.   Social analysts suggest that low-income minority
elders need more frequent contact with structured leadership in
order to adhere to a daily routine that may lead to psychological
and physical change, suggests the researcher.

559.   Hanson, Sandra L., et al.   "Racial and Cohort Variations in Filial
Responsibility Norms."   Gerontologist, Vol. 23, No. 6, December,
1983, pp. 626-631.

This study examined whether racial differences exist in the endorsement of five filial responsibility norms and the extent to
which age and cohort effects influence these patterns.   Tabular
analysis of responses from 339 Black and 1,611 white respondents
demonstrated stronger support for filial norms among the white respondents than for the Black, with the racial difference being
sharply attenuated among the oldest respondents.   An inverse association was found between age and endorsement of the norms, according to the researchers.   The research findings suggest considerable
differences between Blacks and whites under age 60 in their support for filial responsibility.   The largest difference was in support of married couples wanting a home with room for their parents
to feel free to move in.   Some of these differences may stem from
differing physical and financial resources.   Children in general
may be anxious about their competence in taking care of elderly
persons.   This anxiety is well-founded in that the American family
does not have the structure, organization, or economic resources
necessary to care for older persons over long periods of time,
state the authors.   Because Blacks in general have fewer resources
and opportunities than Whites, some of the differences in children's support of filial responsibility norms may stem from the
greater worries and fears Blacks have with regard to being able
to provide support for their parents, assert the writers.

560.   Hays, William C. and Charles H. Mindel.   "Extended Kinship Relations in Black and White Families."   Journal of Marriage and the
Family, Vol. 35, No. 1, February, 1973, pp. 51-57.

This study is an attempt to compare and explain the differences in
extended family cohesion of Black and white families.   The Black
family is not approached as deviant or pathological, but from the
view of a separate subculture within a pluralistic society.   Comparisons were made in terms of both intensity and extensity of
interaction of Black and White families with their extended kin.
Specific comparisons were made of contact and help patterns, number of kin living in the household, and salience of kin.   It is
shown that the extended kin network is a more salient structure
for Black families than it is for white families.

561. Heyman, Dorothy K. and Frances C. Jeffers. "Study of the Relative
     Influences of Race and Socio-Economic Status upon the Activities
     and Attitudes of a Southern Aged Population." Journal of Geronto-
     logy, Vol. 19, No. 2, April, 1964, pp. 225-229.

     Analysis of the data, by the authors, indicated that: (1) differ-
     ences in activity patterns were found to be socio-economic rather
     than racial, (2) for attitudes, racial differences were again not
     dominant and socio-economic differences were found only within the
     Negro group, (3) both activity and attitude sub-items showed con-
     siderable variation in association with socio-economic race factors:
     religion and economic security revealed the most differentiation,
     state the authors.

562. Hicks, Nancy. "Life After 65." Black Enterprise, May, 1977, pp.
     18-22.

     The writer points out that less than five percent of all people
     over 65 live in nursing homes. About 60 percent of the Black aged
     and 55 percent of the White live in and around cities, although
     more than half of the Blacks are still in the South. According to
     Miss Hicks about one-quarter live on farms. It is stated that
     there are many reasons why a larger percentage of Black elderly
     live with their children: the importance of the role of grand-
     mother, because mother works or is away; the need for sharing of
     income within a family, including the older person's Social Secu-
     rity and public assistance payments; and the respect and sense of
     responsibility said to exist more strongly in Black households, in
     caring for and protecting one's parents, particularly the aged
     mother.

563. Hirsch, Carl. "A Review of Findings on Social and Economic Condi-
     tions of Low-Income Black and White Aged of Philadelphia." Pro-
     ceedings of The Research Conference on Minority Group Aged in the
     South. Jacquelyne J. Jackson, Editor. Durham, NC: Center for
     the Study of Aging and Human Development, Duke University Medical
     Center, 1972, pp. 63-81.

     This is a report on an inquiry into the conditions of urban low-
     income elderly persons. The study population of this research was
     selected to yield information about both low-income aged Blacks
     and Whites. Virtually all of the more than 1,000 persons inter-
     viewed may be classified as low-income. About 3/4 or those inter-
     viewed were Black. The consideration prompting the study was a
     need to explore the role of the resources and agencies available
     to the aged and the conditions and adjustments of the aged. The
     decision to focus upon the low-income elderly was prompted by a
     number of considerations. Among them was the finding that most
     earlier studies of the aged had utilized samples from either of
     two groups: Institutionalized aged or middle-class aged. The need
     is great for comparable data on the aged living within the commu-
     nity, but in poor economic circumstances, concludes the author.

564. _____. "Serving Aged Residents of Central City Neighborhoods." Challenges Facing Senior Centers in the Nineteen Seventies. Alice G. Wolfson, Editor. New York: National Council on the Aging, 1968, pp. 134-145.

This article discusses aged Blacks in Philadelphia. The author found evidence of a higher rate of affiliation with voluntary associations among low-income Blacks than among low-income Whites. The difference in the writer's sample is perhaps explained by the greater rate of religious activity among Black respondents and their greater potential for memberships in church or religious groups. The essential conclusions, drawn from Dr. Hirsch's study, relate to serving that particular minority of aged persons who reside in the low socio-economic neighborhoods of central cities. The concerns are: the lack of effective communication between agencies and the aged; the demonstrated potential of an outreach mechanism that attempts to deliver coordinated services to the aged individual at his door; and the importance of the aged person's concept of life space and the functional relevance of services to him which, if ignored by those delivering and developing services, can hinder and retard utilization, concludes the author.

565. _____, et al. "Homogeneity and Heterogeneity Among Low-Income Negro and White Aged." Research Planning and Action for the Elderly: The Power and Potential of Social Science. Donald P. Kent, et al., Editors. New York: Behavioral Publications, Inc., 1972, pp. 484-500.

The availability of medical care to low-income aged in a metropolitan setting is well documented by the data from this study. More than one-third of the study group (again, no racial differences) had had an eye examination during the previous year. More than 80% wore glasses. While only a fifth had visited a dentist during the preceeding year, 60% had dentures. Again, difference between the races was slight. These data give too favorable a picture. A contextual analysis and the case material collected bring to light less favorable aspects. Clinics and hospitals often are located too far from the neighborhoods of the low-income aged. Public transportation is frequently non-existent, often inconvenient, and almost always too expensive. Health personnel at times fail to communicate with the old. At times the health professional assumes a greater medical sophistication on the part of the aged patient than exists; and at other times the health workers are amazingly blind to the social needs of the elderly patient, declare the authors. His medical needs will be well diagnosed and the appropriate prophylactic prescribed; but at the same time his social needs will be completely disregarded with the result that the latter quite negate the hoped-for medical therapy. Since, in many respects, the Black church follows a traditional pattern, it may more nearly meet the cultural expectations of the present group of elderly. Conceivably, the greater interest of the Black aged in religion reflects not a greater inner need but rather a greater adaptability of the Black church to the desires of the aged. The writers argue that perhaps the White church in its open efforts to reach the young has developed a service and message less congenial to the White aged, conclude the researchers.

566. Hudson, Gossie Harold. "The Black Aged: Some Reflections By a
      Layman." Proceedings of the Workshop Series on the Black Aging
      and Aged and the Conference on the Black Aged and Aging. Jean
      Dorsett-Robinson, et al., Editors. Carbondale, IL: College of
      Human Resources, Southern Illinois University, 1974, pp. 113-119.

      Dr. Hudson contends that the social and economic problems of older
      Blacks, compounded by race and age, are particularly bleak and war-
      rant special attention in the literature. Contemporary scholars
      in the field of gerontology generally agree that the difficulties
      of unemployment are more severe among non-white workers who are
      doubly disadvantaged because they are often discriminated against
      on the basis of both age and minority group status. In fact, un-
      employment among elderly Blacks is almost triple the rate of that
      experienced by elderly Whites. However, the socio-economic prob-
      lems confronting the Black aged are undoubtedly a continuation of
      earlier disadvantages rather than solely a reflection of currently
      inadequate income. Therefore, to reduce poverty in old age, de-
      privation must be attacked in the early years, argues Dr. Hudson.
      To be sure, adequate income cannot be abruptly established at age
      65 or age 62. Dr. Hudson declares that a mere perusal of the
      sources will show that despite the general upgrading of the labor
      force in this generation, Blacks are still far too well represen-
      ted among those who are employed at jobs at which even White work-
      ers average low earnings throughout a lifetime. Moreover, current
      efforts have not resulted in better employment opportunities for
      Blacks, states the writer. This suggests, of course, that when
      younger Blacks reach old age, they will probably share in the po-
      verty that earlier stalked them and their children just because
      of the color of their skin, concludes the historian.

567. _____. "Some Special Problems of Older Black Americans."
      Crisis, Vol. 83, No. 3, March, 1976, pp. 88-90.

      The writer points out that about 16 percent of all Black house-
      holds are headed by elderly persons. Among the Black elderly, one-
      third of the women and one-fourth of the men live alone. About
      one-fourth of all the old men never had any children. About one-
      half live in poverty, and well over one-half reside in substandard
      housing. While the life expectancy of Black males continues to be
      approximately seven years less that that of either Black females
      or White males, those Blacks who have survived to very old age
      have a higher remaining life expectancy than do Whites. When
      younger Blacks reach old age, they will probably share in the po-
      verty that earlier stalked them and their children because of the
      color of their skins and the rampant racism in the society. There-
      fore, to reduce poverty in old age, relative deprivation must be
      attacked in the early years because adequate income cannot be
      abruptly established at age 65, contends Dr. Hudson. The total
      mean income for all aged Black females is only 59.7 percent as much
      as that of their male counterparts; those with high school and col-
      lege education measure 54.7 and 69.2 percent, respectively. Actu-
      ally the same type of ever-widening gaps in income patterns when
      Blacks and Whites in the United States are compared over the past
      few decades are also present when comparing Black females and
      males. As the absolute income earnings of Whites are becoming

Hudson, Gossie Harold (continued)

continuously larger than those of Blacks, the absolute income earnings of Black males are also becoming continuously larger than
those of Black females. In general, older Black people have had
less education than Whites and therefore have had less choice in
work opportunities. The Black woman's median years of schooling
is about 6th grade, while for men it is 4th grade. Today, about
16 percent of older Black people are illiterate while the rate for
Whites is only 2 percent. Housing, too, is poorer for aged Blacks
than for aged Whites. Less than 3 percent of the people in nursing homes or homes for the aged are Black. Older Blacks do not
have the financial ability to enter homes for the aged, and are
often discriminated against by the homes. In addition, few of the
homes are located in the Black community, states the writer. An
even greater problem is recognized when one knows that most of the
agencies trying to serve the Black community are short of funds.
Psychological damages help to compound the problems of economic
and social insecurity. The development of negative self-attitudes
often causing self-hatred and rejection of others like one's self,
obsessive sensitivity, dependence, and alienation are some of the
observed consequences of minority status. The corrosive effects
of prejudice and discrimination reach their zenith when the minority group internalizes cultural definitions of inferiority.
"Ageism," like its cousins, "racism" and "sexism," festers in the
older person the haunting fear that all the stereotypes held about
him are accurate. The resulting passivity, anxiety, and withdraw-
al can be viewed as accommodative actions by the aged as they attempt to adjust to prevailing cultural definitions. Also, the high
rates of suicide, behavioral disturbances, and mental aberrations
are qualifiable measures of the consequences of older people's en-
counter with institutional and personal discrimination. Dr. Hudson concludes that these personal pathologies reflect a deep and
pervasive malaise in the American social structure.

568. Jackson, Jacquelyne Johnson. "Death Rates of Aged Blacks and
      Whites, United States, 1964-1978." Black Scholar, Vol. 13, No. 1,
      January/February, 1982, pp. 36-48.

      According to Prof. Jackson, comparison of comprehensive mortality
      and morbidity rates for aged Blacks and Whites in the United States
      could resolve an ethnogerontologic issue of the relative ill-
      health position of these two groups, provided that socioeconomic
      controls were appropriately applied in the comparisons. The cur-
      rent absence of such data continues to fuel the contradictory con-
      clusions surrounding this issue, argues the sociologist. She be-
      lieves that much more comprehensive data are needed to describe
      and explain the similarities and differences in mortality patterns
      of aged Blacks and Whites. Overall, however, the fact that aged
      Blacks, a younger population than aged Whites, continue to die, on
      the average, earlier than aged Whites means, inter alia, that aged
      Blacks do not receive old-age pensions under Social Security for
      as long a period of time as do aged Whites, asserts Dr. Jackson.
      The solution to this inequitable problem, however, is not to modi-
      fy the minimum age/eligibility requirements so that Blacks may be-
      come primary beneficiaries at an earlier age, concludes the

Jackson, Jacquelyne Johnson (continued)

scholar. The more appropriate solution is more in line with Peter
J. Ferrara's well-reasoned argument to separate entirely the social insurance and welfare functions of the current Social Security
system, a separation which could benefit greatly older Blacks and
their heirs, states the author.

569. Jenkins, Mercilee M. "Age and Migration Factors in the Socioeconomic Conditions of Urban Blacks and Urban White Women." Industrial Gerontology, Vol. 9, Spring, 1971, pp. 13-17.

The author concludes that part-time and seasonal employment or non-
participation in the labor market are more characteristic of Black
than of White women in all three urban-size types. Among Black
workers, young women in large cities enjoy the greatest occupational success, whereas older Black women in small cities usually
have low-status jobs and earn the least. Extreme poverty is more
frequently experienced by White families, both young and old, who
have always lived in the city. For Black families, the situation
is reversed; particularly in the middle-class and large urban areas
it appears that migrants are not a burden to the cities as is commonly believed. As a group they are not poorly educated and prone
to unemployment or welfare roles; indeed, it seems that some have
actual advantages over native urbanites, concludes the author.

570. Kalish, Richard A. "Death and Dying: A Cross-Cultural View."
Proceedings of Black Aged in The Future. Jacquelyne J. Jackson,
Editor. Durham, NC: Duke University, Center for the Study of
Aging and Human Development, 1973, pp. 11-22.

Dr. Kalish compares Blacks with Asians, Mexicans, and Whites in
Los Angeles and concludes that Blacks displayed the greatest wish
for and expectation of longer life. He argues that to understand
the general processes of aging, both social and biological, we
need to recognize his particular culture, its history and its present circumstances; and we need to seek a person's strengths,
while enabling him to deal more effectively with his weaknesses.
Dr. Kalish points out that some of the strengths include durabi-
lity, wisdom, knowledge, faith and loyalty.

571. Kandel, Randy F. and Marion Heider. "Friendship and Factionalism
in a TRI-ETHNIC Housing Complex for the Elderly in North Miami."
Anthropological Quarterly, Vol. 52, January, 1979, pp. 49-59.

The writer used conflict and environmental docility models to ana-
lyze the impact of ethnicity, architectural design and internal
politics on community formation in a U.S. Department of Housing
and Urban Development subsidized development for Black, Cuban and
White English-speaking elderly. Four interlinked levels of community participation (dyadic friendships, ethnic subcommunities,
Tenant's Council political factionalism, and the "community-of-
the-whole") are discussed with particular reference to the roles
of culture brokers, the Tenant's Council's relationship to the
external political structure, and the unique psychological and
social conditions of the elderly. The authors conclude that

Kandel, Randy F. and Marion Heider (continued)

because most residents of communities for the elderly have nowhere else to turn, it is a moral imperative to provide them with the largest possible range of options for achieving life satisfaction. The researchers suggest this can best be done by designing highly flexible residential arrangements and political and social organizations in future retirement communities.

572.   Kasschau, Patricia L. "Age and Race Discrimination Reported by Middle-Aged and Older Persons." Social Forces, Vol. 55, March, 1977, pp. 728-742.

This article was based on a sample of 398 Black, 373 Mexican-American, and 373 White residents of Los Angeles County, aged 45-74, who were asked about their experiences with race and age. Each ethnic subsample identified both race and age discrimination as common in the country today. Smaller percentages of each ethnic subsample (20%-45%) reported that their own friends and acquaintances had experienced race or age discrimination. Finally, respectively smaller percentages of each group (8%-34%) directly identified personal experiences with race or age discrimination. The author concludes that Blacks were considerably more likely to assert the existence of race discrimination at each of these three levels of observation than were Mexican Americans, who, in turn, were moderately more likely to report race discrimination at each level than were Whites. Differences among the ethnic subsamples were less dramatic and less consistent for reported experiences with age discrimination at the three levels of observation, although Black respondents still tended to report greater exposure to age discrimination than the other ethnic groups, concludes the author.

573.   Kernodle, Ruth L. "Sharing the Past: Themes and Values from Early Life." Journal of Minority Aging, Vol. 8, Nos. 1-2, 1983, pp. 56-67.

This article has attempted to summarize the general themes and values expressed through stories of early life by some 500 elderly persons. Most of these older people came from a relatively similar background, spending their childhood and adolescence in the upper rural South where they experienced poverty and hard work. The experiences described as important in shaping their adult lives were quite similar for both Blacks and whites, such things as the influence of a strong family, the church as an important religious and social institution, the sense of community expressed in many ways. The writer observed that there were some important differences between whites and Blacks, since hard work had resulted in upward mobility for most whites, but not for this Black population. Whites yearned for the "good old days," but Blacks felt that, except for their early childhood, and in spite of their present relative poverty, this may be the best time of their lives-- a chance to "rest and enjoy," concludes the author.

574. Koening, Ronald, et al. "Ideas About Illness of Elderly Black and White in an Urban Hospital." Aging and Human Development, Vol. 2, August, 1971, pp. 217-225.

The authors contend that the Blacks evidenced great regard for the hospital where they were lodged and were satisfied with the doctors. Particularly they tended, more than Whites, to prefer the young doctors who can be expected to have been more positively influenced by changing racial attitudes than other physicians. The writers found that in many respects both Black and White aged patients shared common views about illness. They were equally inclined to be realistic about the seriousness of the illness and did not often attribute illness causes to fate or "God's will." They conclude that both groups seemed to regard illness as a problem to be solved and not necessary and predictable concomitant of age.

575. Kosberg, Jordan I. "Differences in Proprietary Institutions Caring for Affluent and Nonaffluent Elderly." Gerontologist, Vol. 13, No. 3, Autumn, 1973, Part I, pp. 299-304.

Prof. Kosberg asserts that being old, poor, and Black compounds the probability of placement into an inferior institution, or preclusion of placement into an Extended Care Facility (ECF) or expensive facility which can meet higher standards. This group of elderly are often on welfare and would be placed in institutions caring for welfare aid recipients. It was pointed out that one-third of Blacks over 75 years of age were receiving Old Age Assistance, while only 1 out of 20 of the Whites were. A Cook County (IL) Department of Public Aid reported that in 1966 of all Blacks in nursing homes, 82% were on Old Age Assistance. The researcher concludes that the elderly poor, who are mainly Blacks, are often institutionalized in small, old, and substandard nursing homes; most converted from private dwellings. The elderly Blacks are further inconvenienced by being placed in facilities which are located further from their families and previous dwellings than is true for the affluent elderly who are usually White. The poor Black elderly also are treated differently by professional and non-professional staff members, states the author.

576. Krause, Neal. "Stress in Racial Differences in Self-Reported Health Among the Elderly." Gerontologist, Vol. 27, No. 1, February, 1987, pp. 72-76.

This article was based on a study done on 351 older adults in Galveston, Texas. Of the above number, 64% were white, 27% were Black, 7% Hispanic, and 1% "others." Analysis of the data, however, was based on the white and Black elderly only. The first goal of this study was to determine if the self-rated health of older Blacks was worse than the self-rated health of older Whites. Preliminary data analysis confirmed this hypothesis and suggested that these differences could not be attributed to the effects of age, sex, marital status, education, response bias, and psychological well-being. Next, the life stress perspective was examined to determine whether it could be useful for explaining the relative health disadvantage of Blacks. Although older Blacks were

Krause, Neal (continued)

found to be more vulnerable to the effects of network crisis events, the data also revealed that older whites were more vulnerable to the deleterious effects of chronic financial strain, according to the author. A number of explanations for these findings were discussed and the most plausible explanation seems one that involves the benefits and costs of social support. This social support explanation, however, was not empirically evaluated here.

577. Manton, Kenneth G. "Sex and Race Specific Mortality Differentials in Multiple Cause of Death Data." Gerontologist, Vol. 20, No. 4, August, 1980, pp. 480-493.

The Black/white mortality crossover is studied by comparing its presence in underlying cause of death data, where one cause is assigned to each death, to its presence in data where deaths may have multiple causes. A number of observations are made which suggest that the basic biomedical aspects of aging and chronic disease are better represented in the multiple cause of death data. The constraint of assigning only one cause to a death distorts the picture of age variation in chronic disease mortality and limits the use of underlying cause of death data in the study of certain aspects of population aging processes, concludes Prof. Manton.

578. _____. "Temporal and Age Variation of United States Black/White Cause-Specific Mortality Differentials: A Study of Recent Changes in the Relative Health Status of the United States Black Population." Gerontologist, Vol. 22, No. 2, April, 1982, pp. 170-179.

The relative age-specific medical progress of United States Blacks and whites is examined by studying detailed age variation in their cause-specific relative mortality risks for the period 1962 through 1975. The results show considerable variation in both the change and absolute level of sex-and age-specific relative mortality risks for major causes of death during the period. Interesting observations about the relative mortality risks are the tendency for Black females to have decreasing relative risks at early ages, the relative increases in cancer risks for Black males, and the decreases in the relative risks of stroke for both sexes, states the author.

579. _____ and Sharon Poss. "The Black/White Mortality Crossover: Possible Racial Differences in the Intrinsic Rate of Aging." Black Aging, Vol. 3, No. 3, February 1978, pp. 43-53.

The authors state that the ages at which mortality crossovers were consistent with the observations of other studies. The crossover was observed, to some degree, both within sex and for Black males and White females for all diseases studied. Furthermore, substantial total and disease-specific crossover of hazards was observed, albeit at somewhat different ages, no matter whether unsmoothed or three or five-year smoothing was applied, or whether hazards were formed with synthetic mortality cohort data or unadjusted census data. The basic determinant of the crossover seemed to be the

Manton, Kenneth G. and Sharon Poss (continued)

different functional form manifested by Blacks and whites for most diseases, especially atherosclerotic diseases, suggest the research- ers. They also believe that the markedly different forms of the disease-specific hazard plots suggest that it is useful to propose and investigate models of the biologic processes that determine the progression of chronic disease and their manifest effects on health. At this point, it is still an open question as to the relative con- tributions of measurement artifact, biological selection, exposure determination of intrinsic rates of aging and genetic differenti- als to the Black/White mortality crossover, assert the authors. However, the evidence strongly suggests that some biological fac- tors contribute to the crossover. Furthermore, the characteris- tic forms observed for the hazard plots of various disease groups strongly suggest a variety of biologic mechanisms, related to phy- siological aging or wear, that serve to determine mortality out- comes. Thus, though it will be necessary to develop more intensive and detailed studies of individuals to isolate and verify the va- rious components of the crossover, the use of mortality models can serve as a useful starting point in the development of working hypotheses about the basic aging and disease mechanisms implicated, conclude the writers.

580.   _____, Sharon Poss and Steven Wing. "The Black/White Morta- lity Crossover: Investigation from the Perspective of the Compo- nents of Aging." Gerontologist, Vol. 19, No. 3, April, 1979, pp. 291-300.

Several possible explanations for the lower mortality rates of Blacks relative to whites at advanced ages in the United States population are discussed and evaluated. The plausibility of the "crossover" is investigated via an analysis of the cause and age- specific mortality rates for the United States population in 1969. An evaluation of two proposed models accounting for processes lead- ing to the crossover effect is made by determining their consis- tency with both the observed mortality data and independent biolo- gical, clinical and epidemiological evidence on racial differences in the etiology of the causes of death.

581.   McCaslin, Rosemary, et al. "Social Indicators in Black and White: Some Ethnic Considerations in Delivery of Service to the Elderly." Journal of Gerontology, Vol. 31, January, 1975, pp. 60-66.

A random sample of elderly clients utilizing the Information and Referral Service of the Houston Areawide Model Project were inter- viewed, using DHEW's Social Indicators for the Aged. An analysis of that data by ethnic group revealed that Anglos scored lower than Blacks in all areas measured and that scores of Blacks in this client group were essentially the same as those of Blacks in the general population, while scores of Anglos in the client group were consistently lower than those of Anglos in the general popu- lation. The findings of this study have led the authors to two conclusions: (1) services to the aged, such as those of the Hous- ton Areawide Project, will be utilized by a larger proportion of Black elderly than Anglo elderly due to more widespread need among

McCaslin, Rosemary, <u>et al</u> (continued)

the Black population; (2) at the same time, services will be under-utilized relative to the needs of the Anglo population due to a greater reluctance to admit need for services.

582. McPherson, Judith E., <u>et al</u>. "Stature Change with Aging in Black Americans." <u>Journal of Gerontology</u>, Vol. 33, January, 1978, pp. 20-23.

Five hundred Black Americans were measured to determine if there was a statistically significant decline in height with increasing age. The following conclusions were found: (1) The Black population has a greater decrease in height with aging than does the White population; (2) Black males decrease approximately 4.2 cm in height every 20 years compared to 1.2 cm in the White population; (3) Black males below age 60 have a longer arm-span than Black males over 60; (4) Black females decrease in height approximately 3.4 cm per 20 years; (5) Incidence of skeletal disease is more noticeable in Black females than in Black males and also increases with aging; (6) Black females weigh more than Black males except in the "older" age group.

583. Messer, Mark. "Race Differences in Selected Attitudinal Dimensions of the Elderly." <u>Gerontologist</u>, Vol. 8, Winter, 1968, pp. 245-249.

This article indicates that race differences among the elderly account for considerably more of the variation on three important attitudinal dimensions than differences in age, sex, marital status, education, or health. The importance that may be attached to this finding is primarily due to the fact that, while the other traits have been examined repeatedly in studies of aging, race has been largely ignored. Prof. Messer concludes: (1) elderly Blacks have higher morale than elderly Whites; (2) elderly Blacks have less of a feeling of integration with overall society than elderly Whites; (3) elderly Blacks are less likely to deny their actual age status than elderly Whites.

584. Mindel, Charles H., Roosevelt Wright, Jr. and Richard S. Starrett. "Informal and Formal Health and Social Support Systems of Black and White Elderly: A Comparative Cost Approach." <u>Gerontologist</u>, Vol. 26, No. 3, June, 1986, pp.

This study, based on a probability sample of noninstitutionalized elderly from Cleveland, Ohio, focuses on the types and amount of support given by the social subsystems of elderly Blacks and Whites. Multiple classification analysis indicated racial differences in types and amount of support provided by the informal and formal social support systems but not to the degree suggested by previous research. More interesting to the thrust of this study was the fact that racial differences were small. Black elderly generally received more supportive services from both the formal and informal support systems than did white elderly. But it was only in the area of Basic Maintenance provided by the formal system that race was a significant factor. Very small differences by

Mindel, Charles H., Roosevelt Wright, Jr. and Richard S. Starrett
(continued)

race existed in amount of aid provided by the informal system after
income was controlled, maintain the writers. Consistent with previous research, the elderly in this study were abandoned by their
family and friends. Their aid was offered and received in amounts
comparable to the public formal support system, though it was concentrated in somewhat different areas. While some racial differences were found, they were concentrated in the use of the formal
system rather than in the informal system, state the authors. This
finding challenges some of the literature on the greater viability
and saliency of the Black kin support system over the white, conclude the writers.

585.   _____. "The Use of Social Services by Black and White Elderly: The Role of Social Support Systems." Journal of Gerontological Social Work, Vol. 4, Nos. 3/4, Spring/Summer, 1982, pp. 107-
125.

The major racial difference in patterns of utilization was found
in the more important role of the informal family support system
for the Black elderly than for the White group. The findings in
this study put the aid system in a somewhat clearer perspective,
declare the authors. They suggest that aid to the elderly is not
an alternative to aid from institutional sources but rather it is
a supplement to seeking help from outside sources. The important
difference to be noted however, is that for the White group the extended family support system appears to be absent or at the very
least minimal. For the Black group formal and informal sources of
aid combine to provide important resources for a particularly
needy group, suggest the researchers. Other significant racial
differences found were the more important effect of age on need
and use for the Black elderly, and the greater vulnerability of
the female and small town, rural Black elderly who tended more often to be poorer, and older than their White counterparts. The
writers conclude, in part: "Utilization behaviors among Black and
White elderly, are, without a doubt, affected by different factors...."

586. Mutran, Elizabeth. "Intergenerational Family Support Among Blacks
and Whites: Response to Culture or to Socioeconomic Differences."
Journal of Gerontology, Vol. 40, No. 3, May, 1985, pp. 382-389.

Factors that influence family helping behavior are examined and
comparisons are made between Black and white families. The question of whether family differences are due to culture or socioeconomic reasons is asked. In the analysis, tests are made for the
main and interactive effects of race. Black elderly parents give
and receive more help than white elderly parents after controlling
for age and sex; however, the greater amount of help received by
older Blacks is, to a large extent, the result of socioeconomic
factors. The increased amount of help that they give to the middle and younger generations appears to be a combination of cultural
and socioeconomic factors. Among Black families, attitudes of respect for each generation play a part in determining family support behavior, concludes Prof. Mutran.

587.   Ortega, Suzanne T., et al. "Race Differences in Elderly Personal Well-Being." Research on Aging, Vol. 5, No. 1, March, 1983, pp. 101-118.

The major thesis of this article is that degree of social integration is an important variable in the life satisfaction of older people. Furthermore, since some evidence indicates that elderly Blacks manifest a greater degree of primary group integration than whites. The authors believe that Blacks experience greater satisfaction with life, after other variables are controlled. If this proves to be the case, it would suggest that the failure of other studies of race and life satisfaction among the elderly to produce consistent results may indeed be due to the fact that in previous studies the effect of social integration has not been taken into account, conclude the researchers. This, in itself, however, would not indicate the precise nature of the integration effect. Social integration is multidimensional and may include ties to a variety of other persons, such as relatives, church members, and friends, suggest the writers....

588.   Pieper, Hanns G. "Regression Analysis of Selected Demographic and Social Factors Related to the Life Satisfaction of the Black and White Aged." Journal of Minority Aging, Vol. 6, Nos. 3-4, 1981, pp. 67-78.

In addition to a brief discussion about the preferable use of life satisfaction, as opposed to happiness or morale, because it is the most stable of these three conceptions, this study tested hypotheses about relationships between life satisfaction and predictor variables defined as demographic, health, financial, living arrangement, family, community activity, associational, and religious. The sample of 210 subjects (27% Black) from a midwestern city permitted racial comparisons as well. The major findings showed that age and life satisfaction were not negatively correlated, that higher satisfaction occurred among females than males in the Black, but not the White group; that health and status and health limits activity were significant variables affecting life satisfaction; that financial variables were significantly related to life satisfaction for whites, but not for Blacks; that living arrangements and life satisfaction were significantly related to life satisfaction for both racial groups, while only contact with grandchildren was significant for Whites, and number of close friends for both groups; and that a greater number of religious variables were significantly associated with life satisfaction for Whites than for Blacks. These findings suggest that there is a variation in the major factors influencing life satisfaction for Black and White aged, concludes the author.

589.   Pitcher, Brian L., et al. "Patterns of Migration Propensity for Black and White American Men: Evidence from a Cohort Analysis." Research on Aging, Vol. 7, No. 1, March, 1985, pp. 94-102.

The estimated age effects for the older white men indicate that even when period and cohort effects are controlled, there was a significant gradual increase with age in propensity to migrate. This peaked at about age 65-66 (at or shortly after the institutionalized age of retirement) and declined thereafter, state the

Pitcher, Brian L., et al. (continued)

authors. For the older Black sample there was a general long-term
decline with age in the propensity to migrate. Regarding cohort
effects, there appear to be opposite patterns for Blacks and whites.
The pattern for whites shows an increased propensity to migrate
for the more recent of the cohorts born 1907-1920. The evidence
for Blacks is that the recent cohorts might be slightly less likely to migrate, according to the authors. The time interval patterns indicate that, overall, migration was more likely in 1967-
1969 than in 1969-1971, constant between 1969-1971 and 1971-1973,
and somewhat less likely during the time interval 1973-1975.
There also appears to have been a convergence in race differences
over time, conclude the researchers.

590.   Quadagno, Jill S., et al. "Maintaining Social Distance in a Raci-
        ally Integrated Retirement Community." Black Aging, Vol. 3, Nos.
        4 and 5, April and June, 1978, pp. 97-112.

        The writers declare that it is clear from the survey data that few
        differences exist between Black and White residents in this retire-
        ment community. While Blacks tend to be somewhat more diversified
        in terms of income and education, these differences are not sta-
        tistically significant. Blacks and whites tend to participate
        equally in activities, both in the retirement community and out-
        side it in the wider community. They tend to feel the same about
        their living situation. In spite of this similarity of background,
        behavior and feelings, racial tension does yet exist. This ten-
        sion appeared slightly in the survey data, but was really only ob-
        vious after extensive field work, argue the authors. They point
        out that the expressed satisfaction of the residents seems to con-
        tradict the concern about racial issues. However, these findings
        are not really contradictory. Residents maintain tranquility by
        artificially creating a means of maintaining social distance. By
        defining formal structured activities as work, they are able to
        interact comfortably in these situations. It is only in leisure-
        type activities where the potential for intimate friendships exists
        that tensions interfere with daily interaction. The implications
        of these findings suggest that an increase in formal activities in
        integrated housing may reduce racial tension and segregated pat-
        terns of interaction, conclude the authors.

591.   Register, Jasper C. "Aging and Race: A Black-White Comparative
        Analysis." Gerontologist, Vol. 21, No. 4, August, 1981, pp. 438-
        443.

        The writer points out that Blacks under 65 have more favorable
        attitudes toward the aged than Whites under 65. Dr. Register sur-
        mises that Blacks are more likely than Whites to look forward to
        old age and regard it as a reward; they are, however, disappointed
        with the reality of being old. Blacks over 65 have lower levels
        of morale than Whites over 65. Being Black adds an additional di-
        mension to the handicaps associated with old age. The researcher
        concludes that there are Black-White differences in levels of life
        satisfaction.

592. Rosen, Catherine E. "A Comparison of Black and White Rural Elder-
      ly." Black Aging, Vol. 3, No. 3, February, 1978, pp. 60-65.

      Interviews were conducted on 694 ambulatory rural elderly residing
      in a high poverty region. They were designated as probable members
      of an extremely high risk population. Interviewer-respondent's
      race was matched in order to reduce respondents' inhibitions. Of
      the respondents, 48 percent were Black and 52 percent were white.
      Comparing the life situations of the Black and white high risk
      rural elderly finds that the Blacks had significantly poorer
      health on every index. However, 94 percent of both groups repor-
      ted having a regular doctor and there were no differences between
      ethnic groups on when they last saw a doctor, observes the author.
      The writer reported that there was a significant relationship be-
      tween the race and/or the sex of the elderly person and their pri-
      mary needs. Females reported greater loneliness and transportation
      needs. Males reported more medical problems. Blacks reported
      greater financial and housing problems. Whites reported more emo-
      tional or family problems and concerns about entering nursing homes.
      More whites (40%) than Blacks (26%) were not receiving any kind of
      social or health services. Whites were more critical of the lack
      of community services for the elderly. Morale was related to race.
      Blacks were either more optimistic or more pessimistic than whites,
      concludes the researcher.

593. Ruberstein, Daniel I. "An Examination of Social Participation
      Found Among a National Sample of Black and White Elderly." Aging
      and Human Development, Vol. 2, August, 1971, pp. 172-188.

      Dr. Rubenstein asserts that contrary to prevailing assumptions,
      the Black elderly are no more alone and isolated than are the
      general elderly population, and their emotional state of well-
      being is no different from that of the White elderly. The author
      concludes that the Black elderly as well as the White elderly are
      grown and matured adults who are at that stage of life where, in
      the socialization process, they socialize others, rather than be-
      ing socialized themselves. It is therefore incumbent upon us to
      recognize that the Black elderly must not be viewed as children
      and adolescents, concludes the author.

594. Sauer, William J. "Morale of the Urban Aged: A Regression Analysis
      By Race." Journal of Gerontology, Vol. 32, September, 1977, pp.
      600-608.

      The writer argues that his research, though supporting only a limi-
      ted number of the hypothesized relationships, while at the same
      time explaining what is to the consensus a fair amount of the va-
      riance, did offer some support for activity theory. Prof. Sauer
      concludes for both aged Blacks and aged Whites: (1) There is a
      direct relationship between the health of elderly people and mo-
      rale. There is a direct relationship between the number of soli-
      tary activities an individual engages in and morale. In addition,
      for aged Whites: (1) There is a direct relationship between the
      frequency of interaction with family and morale. (2) Males are
      more likely to manifest high morale than females.

595.   Simpson, Janice C. "Prisoners of Our Silver Ghettos." Black Enterprise, Vol. 12, No. 2, September, 1981, pp. 44-46, 48.

This author points out that the cost of old age can be a grim future of poverty and isolation if we don't act. Older Blacks are three times as likely to be poor as elderly whites. Older Black women who have no living relatives are the poorest, states Ms. Simpson. Dr. Jacquelyne J. Jackson, the leading authority on the Black aged, declares that Blacks should pool their money to fund programs for the aged.

596.   Thune, Jeanne M. "Racial Attitude of Older Adults." Gerontologist, Vol. 7, September, 1967, pp. 179-182.

The writer surmises the results obtained in her early analyses of differences between older Whites and older Blacks indicate that older Blacks are less prejudiced than older Whites; older Blacks believe thay are different from both other Blacks and Whites in that they value personal qualities rather than material objects or pleasure-oriented behavior; and older Blacks feel they have less personal control over their environment and are more controlled by forces outside themselves than do older Whites. The author also found for both older Blacks and Whites a relationship between the amount of prejudice expressed on a social distance measure and the personal feeling of internal vs. external source of control. She concludes those older adults who feel more inner control are those who indicate they would behave in a less prejudiced manner when participating in an inter-racial social situation.

597.   _____, et al. "Interracial Attitudes of Younger and Older Adults in a Biracial Population." Gerontologist, Vol. 11, Winter, 1971, pp. 305-309.

The authors declare that the interracial prejudice as it occurs within young, middle-aged, and older Blacks and Whites and the degree to which prejudice is affected both by episodes of civil violence and by the passage of time have been the focus of a continuing program of research in the Southern city of Nashville, Tennessee. Data indicate that while age affects racial attitudes, particularly of White Southerners, race is an even stronger determiner of prejudice. There were significant differences in the degree of prejudice expressed by Blacks and Whites of all age groups, the magnitude of these differences increasing systematically across age groups due primarily to the higher prejudice of older Whites. The authors conclude that Blacks of all ages stated that they were willing to interact with Whites to a greater extent than Whites of any age stated they were willing to interact with Blacks.

598.   Thurmond, Gerald T. and John C. Belcher. "Dimensions of Disengagement Among Black and White Rural Elderly." Aging and Human Development, Vol. 12, No. 4, 1980-1981, pp. 245-266.

The findings of the present study support some of the revisions of role theory. More white males than Black males in the Southern rural population are likely to have jobs with role relations similar to those in an urban area. The overall pattern of findings

Thurmond, Gerald T. and John C. Belcher (continued)

for role loss should conform more closely to traditional role theory hypotheses among white males than Black males, declare the
writers.... The fact that most white males are still embedded in
rural relationships not primarily determined by the occupational
role would prevent occupational loss from having statistically significant impact in the findings. Similarly, role loss in the form
of widowhood or divorce should have more importance for white women than Black women due to the differential significance of the
husband's occupational role, according to the authors. The findings that morale significantly decreases with role loss more often
with white than Black women gives limited support to this proposi-
tion, state the writers. The failure to account for patterns of
aging in the rural Black population is due to role theory's incor-
rect assumption that marital and occupational roles are the only
important roles and to its subsequent inability to identify other
roles, assert the authors. They conclude, in part: "Morale, perceived life space, formal and informal social participation, and
role loss all appear to be influenced by aging independently of
one another and differently in the race and sex groups sampled.
It makes no theoretical sense to assume that these different dimensions reflect a single process of disengagement. And our findings
do not support such an assumption. Grouping all of these factors
under one dependent variable obscures the findings and necessarily
frustrates theoretical advances."

599. Usui, Wayne M., et al. "Determinants of Life Satisfaction: A
Note on a Race-Interaction Hypothesis." Journal of Gerontology,
Vol. 38, No. 1, January, 1983, pp. 107-110.

A "race interaction" hypothesis would suggest that factors important to the life satisfaction of whites may not be important to
the life satisfaction of Blacks. In this paper the authors suggest that dummy variable regression with interaction terms allows
an assessment of differential effects by race. Using data from
438 white and 219 Black elderly respondents, it was shown that
most factors influencing life satisfaction of elderly people have
similar effects among Blacks and whites. Although greater numbers
of impairments lead to lower life satisfaction for both races, the
negative effect is considerably stronger among Black than among
white respondents, conclude the writers.

600. _____. "Homogeneity of Friendship Networks of Elderly Blacks
and Whites." Journal of Gerontology, Vol. 39, No. 3, May, 1984,
pp. 350-356.

Race and sex were found to be the most salient parameters of friendship. Multivariate analysis revealed that Blacks tend to have
less homogeneous friendship networks than their white counterparts
only in regard to marital status. How close respondents felt to
their friends, on the average, was positively related to the level
of age and sex homogeneity of the network. Respondents' education
was positively related to all five types of homogeneity. It was
found that the size theorem from Blau's primitive theory of social
structure accounted for some of the findings. Exceptions were in

Usui, Wayne M. (continued)

race and education homogeneity, where discrimination and social distance figured into possible explanations, states Dr. Usui.

601. Ward, Russell A. and Harold Kilburn. "Community Access and Satisfaction: Racial Differences in Later Life." Aging and Human Development, Vol. 16, No. 3, 1983, pp. 209-219.

The results of this research suggest that community involvement plays an important role in the processes shaping life satisfaction in later life. This role appears to vary for Blacks and whites. Involvement in the surrounding community does not appear to directly affect the life satisfaction of older Blacks. Community access and mobility are important only indirectly to the extent that they affect or reflect patterns of general social interaction, state the authors. Lifelong patterns of residential segregation, and the social and psychological consequences of this ghettoization may account for these lesser and more localized implications of community involvement. Having become acclimated to a more delimited social territory, restricted access is less consequential for Black elders. The more general implication of this racial difference is that life styles and experiences over the life course shape the nature and consequences of aging, serving as sources of differentiation in the aging experience, conclude the researchers.

602. _____. "The Stability of Racial Differences Across Age Stratus." Sociology and Social Research, Vol. 67, No. 3, April, 1983, pp. 312-323.

The author argues that in his study of Black and White elderly, he found no evidence that Black elders received greater social support than white elders. Racial differences in income, subjective health, and subjective well-being were found to be quite stable across age groups, declares the writer. He concludes that the above assertion suggests that aging and age stratification do little to alter the size or nature of racial differences.

603. Weinstock, Comeilda and Ruth Bennett. "Problems in Communication to Nurses among Residents of a Racially Heterogeneous Nursing Home." Gerontologist, Vol. 8, Summer, 1968, pp. 72-75.

The authors state that all of the Black patients reacted favorably to their roommates, and 75% were satisfied with their neighbors. In marked contrast, only a third of the white patients were satisfied with their roommates and one-quarter with their neighbors. In general, the response of Blacks indicated enthusiasm while the White patients showed marked disaffection. The author states that differences in reactions and types of communication to nurses were found among White and Black patients in a proprietary nursing home. Strained interaction between patients and staff members appeared to result from negative reactions of White patients to the Black staff. They conclude strained interaction did not seem to be a function of staff members' negative attitudes toward the aged since it was reflected mainly in the attitudes of the White group.

604. Wellin, Edward and Eunice Boyer. "Adjustments of Blacks and White
Elderly to the Same Adaptive Niche." Anthropological Quarterly,
Vol. 52, January, 1979, pp. 39-48.

This article discusses three public housing projects for the elderly. The writers argue that in these projects, Black and White
residents make different adjustments in terms of church membership
and other formal social participation, patterns of friendship and
help, leadership, and leisure activities. They conclude that both
daily neighborly contact and desirable organized activities seem
to promote more frequent and harmonious interracial contact than
is common outside the project. These studies were conducted in
Milwaukee, Wisconsin.

605. Wershow, Harold J. "Inadequate Census Data on Black Nursing Home
Patients." Gerontologist, Vol. 16, February 1976, pp. 86-87.

In the course of the investigation on Black and White Nursing Home
Patients (NHP), the author's findings led him to the conclusion
that census data on Black patients in nursing homes (NH) are grossly in error. The 1960 census states that there were, at the time,
no more than 6 Black NHP in NH in Alabama that are "known to have
nursing care" (KHNC), all in state and federal institutions, all
males over 80 years of age. The author later learned, in question-
ing the 1970 data to be presented herein that, even in 1960, there
were already several Black proprietary NH in existence, all of
whom were KHNC. Yet the census somehow missed all of them. The
author asserts the situation has not improved with the publication
of the 1970 census. The author concludes his study discovered at
least 197 Black NHP, 76 males and 121 females, residing in four
black-owned NH KHNC in Jefferson County, Alabama. All are certified and licensed as "skilled nursing homes" and "extended care
facilities" by Medicare and Medicaid, and licensed by the State
Health Department.

606. Whittington, Frank. "Aging and the Relative Income Status of
Blacks." Black Aging, Vol. 1, No. 1, October, 1975, pp. 6-13.

The author asserts that only through a vigorous determination of
the independent effects of age, period and cohort can valid conclusions be reached concerning the nature of change in the relative income of Blacks. It is, after all, an understanding of the
nature of change across the life span which will lead to an explanation of characteristic differences between Blacks and Whites
in the late life, states Prof. Whittington.

607. Wright, Roosevelt, et al. "Medical Care and the Elderly: An Ex-
ploratory Analysis of Factors Involved in the Use of Physicians'
Services by Black and White Elderly." Journal of Minority Aging,
Vol. 5, No. 1, December, 1979, pp. 123-129.

Using a sample of 414 aged residents of elderly public housing in
Milwaukee County, Wisconsin, in 1973, this article reports upon
factors affecting their use of physicians' services, as measured
by self-reports of physician contacts during the preceding year.
Although some similarity by race is present in terms of factors

Wright, Roosevelt, et al. (continued)

influencing the use of physicians' services, racial differences
are also apparent, state the authors. These differences and some
of their implications for social policies are discussed.

40. MINORITY AGED

608. Dickerson, Morgan W. F. "Problems of Black High-Risk Elderly."
Journal of Black Studies, Vol. 14, No. 2, December, 1983, pp. 251-
260.

It was stated that the Black Elderly are ten times more likely to
be on welfare than any other ethnic population. The Black elderly
are faced with many problems which are often unique. They are
discriminated against because of age, income, service delivery
patterns, housing patterns as well as race. As a group they are
best described as, too old to work, too young for Social Security,
and too poor for skilled care. Their life span is shorter than
their nonminority contemporaries and, as a result, they often do
not collect Social Security (if they are eligible), states Prof.
Dickerson. Current trends are toward raising the age of eligibility for Social Security; such a move further threatens the survival of the high risk Black elderly. Legislation at the federal
level to allow for the life span disparity should be considered.
According to the writer, in the case of the Black elderly, there
are some solutions:
(1) Legislation to allow Blacks to receive Social Security at age
     55, which partially offsets the seven-year difference in life-
     span.
(2) Extension or replacement of funds to support or develop aging
     programs in Black neighborhoods under Model Cities type
     grants or other resources--that is, the Administration on
     Aging or HEW.
(3) A national health insurance which will provide high-quality
     care for all aged.
(4) Provision of moneys to provide more alternative care programs
     for the elderly and money to provide training for homemakers
     and other home care specialists.
(5) Requests to Congress for provisions regulating distribution
     of revenue sharing funds which state a given percentage of
     all revenue sharing moneys be designated for aging services.
(6) Train and employ more Black youth and aged in aging services.

609. Hoover, Sally L. "Black and Spanish Elderly: Their Housing Characteristic and Housing Quality." Journal of Minority Aging,
Vol. 5, No. 3, March-October, 1980, pp. 249-272.

Available 1970 and 1975 housing data were used to compare the characteristics and quality of housing of Black, white, and Spanish
households where the heads were over 65 years of age. Based upon
an examination of such indicators as value of the housing unit,
gross rent, condition of plumbing and heating equipment, older
white owners lived in relatively better structures than Blacks or

Hoover, Sally L. (continued)

Spanish, and the Spanish tended to have better housing than the
Blacks. The most problematic housing occurred among older Black
renters. Problems associated with the neighborhood tended to cut
across racial and ethnic lines, suggesting that federal programs
for home improvement cannot be divorced feasibly from neighborhood
rejuvenation. The housing situation of older Americans needs
greater attention than it has presently received, and overhousing
is not an historical accident, concludes the author....

610. Lipman, Aaron. "Ethnic and Minority Group Content for Courses in
      Aging." Gerontology in Higher Education: Perspectives and Issues,
      Papers from the 1977 Meeting of the Association for Gerontology in
      Higher Education. Mildred M. Seltzer, et al., Editors. Belmont,
      CA: Wadsworth Publishing Co., Inc., 1978, pp. 223-227.

The writer points out that while we have become aware that within
that numerical minority there is a subgroup of racial and ethnic
minority aged population clusters that must be clearly delineated,
effectively researched, and the results disseminated in texts and
lectures that teach social gerontology. The four major minority
groups that have been distinguished in the United States and which
should be included in the initial thrust, are the American Indian
or native Americans, Black Americans, Asian Americans and Spanish-
speaking Americans. In studying the minority aged, contends the
author, we need to collect a body of knowledge which will indicate
uniformities in the minority experience of aging, as contrasted
with the dominant group, as well as showing the effects of subcultural differences between various minorities. The author continues to argue that the fund of knowledge we already possess concerning the minority elderly indicates that as a group, they are
more economically disadvantaged than those elderly that belong to
the dominant group. Yet while attention has been given to social
class differences, research has neglected to account for variations
within or across class lines due to the interplay of racial or ethnic factors. Part of the problem with data concerning the poor is
the confounding of the concepts "poor" and "minority." For the
total population at all ages the likelihood of being poor if one
is a member of a minority is four times as great as for that of
the dominant group, states the author. By the time a person reach-
es old age, that proportion is down to twice as great. This is
not necessarily due to an improvement in the fortunes of the poor
elderly minority member as he gets old, but more probably to the
fact that so small a number survive to old age. In 1975, the median income for White families was $14,268, compared with $9,551
for Hispanics and $8,779 for Black families. "Nearly 27 percent
of Hispanics were below the federally defined poverty level of
$5,500 for an urban family of four, compared with 9.7 percent of
Whites and 31.3 percent of Blacks," concludes the writer. In 1975
for those 65 years and over, 13.4 percent of the Whites were below
the poverty level compared with 32.7 percent of the Hispanics and
36.3 percent of the Blacks. The writer also concludes that it is
important to include material about minority groups in our curricula on aging for a number of reasons: There is the purely epis-
temological aim of scientifically expanding our theoretical

Lipman, Aaron (continued)

generalizable base of knowledge concerning the total gerontic population. Secondly, comparative studies on the adjustment of different groups to aging could identify the dynamics that contribute
to that adjustment and by identifying those coping structures and
mechanisms which work for variant subcultural groups in our society, we might also refine our knowledge of the dominant group
adaptation process. Finally, knowledge about minority groups
would help generate action programs and policies targeted for those
individuals who, as a consequence of their membership in an ethnic
or racial minority subgroup, have not been reached by programs
which were designed by and for the dominant white, contends the
researcher.

611. Mindel, Charles H. "The Elderly in Minority Families." Family
      Relationships in Later Life. Timothy Brubaker, Editor. Beverly
      Hills, CA: Sage Publications, 1983, pp. 193-208.

It was pointed out that the Black informal support system supplied
somewhat more home and personal care services, but the white informal support system provided somewhat more basic maintenance
services. The Black elderly received more services from the formal support system than did the white elderly, but only in the
basic maintenance area, argues Dr. Mindel. The researcher concludes, in part: "Care and support of the elderly in time of need
still is a major responsibility of children of all races and ethnic groups."

612. Moss, Frank E. and Val J. Halamandaris. "No Vacancy for Minority
      Groups: Aged Blacks." Too Old, Too Sick, Too Bad: Nursing Homes
      in America. Germantown, MD: Aspen Systems Corp., 1977, pp. 117-
      121.

The researchers state that older Blacks are twice as likely to be
poor; 50 percent live in poverty as compared with 23 percent for
Whites. While over half of them continue to live in the South,
the migration of this minority group into urban areas has created
overcrowded conditions, poor health, drug addiction, and social
and personal violence. To the Black American this means a higher
mortality rate at every stage of life. From 45 to 64, Black women
have twice the mortality rate of White women; from 55 to 64, the
mortality for Black men is ten percent higher than for White men.
Despite higher incidences of acute and chronic disease, an elderly
Black sees a physician at an average annual rate of 4.9 visits as
compared with a White's 6.1 visits. Aged Blacks are experiencing
no temporary aberration, but rather the continuing effect of poverty and racism. "Now in their golden years, they have relin-
quished whatever hopes they had--resigned to an ignominious death
in a subtle form of euthanasia," argue the authors. They declare
that since half of the 1.7 million elderly Blacks are poor, it appears safe to assume that cost would not be an important factor,
the assumption being that the poor are eligible for Medicaid,
which now pays more than 50 percent of the nation's home bill, according to the writers.

613. Stanford, E. Percil. "Theoretical and Practical Relationships
      Among Aged Blacks and Other Minorities." Black Scholar, Vol. 13,
      No. 1, January/February, 1982, pp. 49-57.

      According to Prof. Stanford, theoretically, it is extremely diffi-
      cult to conclude that the elderly represent a subculture; but, for
      the purposes of this article, the premise is that the aged of vary-
      ing backgrounds make changes and adjustments in their lives based
      on their cultural experiences, backgrounds, and environmental li-
      mitations. Obviously, considerable theoretical and practical at-
      tention must be given now and in the future to the advantages and
      disadvantages of governmental policies and programs which fail to
      distinguish between majority and minority aged, or which tend to
      regard minority aged of various racial and ethnic backgrounds as
      merely a homogeneous grouping, according to the writer... Most
      studies tend to compare Blacks with whites, or Protestants with
      Catholics and Jews, without adequate controls for sex, socioecono-
      mic statuses, or generational length in the United States. Such
      studies obscure the between-group and within-group differences,
      states the author. We have only just begun to recognize the need
      for a theoretical framework to describe and explain relationships
      between aging and ethnicity, concludes the author.

              41. RESEARCH ON THE BLACK AGED

614. Chatters, Linda M., et al. "Size and Composition of the Informal
      Helper Networks of Elderly Blacks." Journal of Gerontology, Vol.
      40, No. 5, September, 1985, pp. 605-614.

      Research on the informal support networks of older persons recog-
      nizes that network size and composition (i.e., family vs. non-kin)
      may have important consequences for care. The present study exa-
      mined the relationship of a group of sociodemographic, health,
      family, and availability factors to the size and composition of
      the informal support network. The data were taken from the Na-
      tional Survey of Black Americans and constitute a nationally re-
      presentative sample (N=581) of older Blacks (55 years and older).
      The results for several of the sociodemographic factors (i.e., sex
      and marital status) are consistent with previous work. Regional
      differences in network dimensions, however, suggest new areas of
      inquiry. The findings underscore the importance of availability
      and family factors in support relationships and the relative in-
      effectiveness of health factors as predictors of network size and
      composition, conclude the researchers.

615. Dowell, Daniel D. "Aging Research, Black Americans, and the
      National Institution on Aging." Journal of the National Medical
      Association, Vol. 75, No. 1, January, 1983, pp. 99, 102-104.

      The author discusses Black-oriented research currently (in 1983)
      supported by the National Institute on Aging and the priorities
      which the Institute has established in attempting to meet the op-
      portunities and challenges posed by the "graying" of America. It
      was also stated that elderly Blacks now comprise about 8 percent

Dowell, Daniel D. (continued)

of the 24 million Americans over 65. Elderly people who are also minority-group members have special needs and concerns because of the double handicap posed by ageism and racism, declares the writer.

616.   Ehrlich, Ira F. "The Aged Black in America--The Forgotten Person." Journal of Negro Education, Vol. 44, No. 1, Winter, 1975, pp. 12-23.

The author (1) critically reviewed the literature with particular emphasis on the education component; (2) related his empirical re- search and methodology for the training of gerontologists; and (3) recommended roles in the gerontological education and training which university and community can perform to enhance the quality of life for Black Aged. The writer concludes that educational in- stitutions can and should meet their responsibilities to the Black aged population by (1) creatively developing a network of informal educational communities in which he can participate, and (2) by training professional gerontologists with emphasis on recruitment of more Black students into the field. Dr. Ehrlich declares broad- ening the living horizons of the Black aged person through these augmented resources can provide him with the opportunity of no longer being labeled the forgotten person.

617.   Gibson, Rose C. "Blacks in an Aging Society." Daedalus, Vol. 115, No. 1, Winter, 1986, pp. 349-371.

The author points out that a recurring theme in her research is that not all aspects of old age have negative connotations for Blacks. Elderly whites have somewhat higher morale than elderly Blacks in most of the major national studies, but if we consider the great disparities between the races in functional health, in- come, education, and marital harmony, the gap in morale is not commensurate with the gap in resources, maintains, Dr. Gibson. She asserts that some of the effective mechanisms of Blacks may lie. not only in the role religion plays in their lives, but in their use of special patterns of help-seeking as they adapt to old age. In terms of using informal support networks in times of distress, older Black Americans drew from a more varied pool of informal helpers than did their white counterparts, both in middle and late life, and were more versatile in interchanging these helpers one for another as they approached old age. Whites, in contrast, were more likely to limit help-seeking to their spouses in middle life, and when their spouses were no longer available for this support, to confine their attempts to replace it by calling on single fam- ily members as they approached old age, states the researcher. She concludes, in part: "In spite of their economic and physical handicaps, the Black elderly--the psychological survivors--may turn out to be part of the salvation of the Black family of the future. The unusual strengths of very old Black women (who are perhaps, not so coincidentally, experiencing the most rapid growth of all 80+ groups, considered by sex and race) are well-known. Elderly Black women have been a wellspring of support and nurtur- ance over time...."

618. _____, and A. Regula Herzog. "Rare Element Telephone Screening (RETS): A Procedure for Augmenting the Number of Black Elderly in National Samples." Gerontologist, Vol. 24, No. 5, October, 1984, pp. 477-482.

The writers describe a cost-effective method (RETS) of sampling older Blacks by telephone, taking advantage of information available from an existing telephone survey. It was shown that asking Black respondents between 18 and 54 years of age from a national survey (shortly after they had been interviewed for the second time), as well as others in their households who were Black and within the same age range, for referrals to parents or grandparents yielded a ratio of approximately one (.8) older Black per Black household in the original survey. The writers argue as a rule of thumb, then, the number of telephone numbers of Blacks 55 years old and over in a supplemental sample generated by RETS from an existing survey will come close to the number of Black households in the original survey. It was also demonstrated that refusal by younger Blacks to provide information on parents or grandparents was rare, that most of the telephone numbers obtained by RETS were valid, and that an overwhelming majority of older Blacks thus identified were willing to complete an interview when contacted by telephone, conclude the authors.

619. Hill, Robert B. "A Profile of Black Aged." Minority Aged in America. Ann Arbor: Institute of Gerontology, University of Michigan-Wayne State University, 1972, pp. 35-50.

The title tells what this work is about. The author discusses various aspects of the Black aged such as population, education, marital status, life expectancy, family size, housing, poverty, health, and employment. The writer points out that since 1970, the Black aged population has been increasing more than twice as fast as the overall Black population.

620. Jackson, Jacquelyne Johnson. "Aged Black Americans: Double Jeopardy Re-examined." Journal of Minority Aging, Vol. 10, No. 1, 1985, pp. 25-61.

This essay, written in December, 1984, is the unabridged version of Dr. Jackson's final draft of a manuscript that was commissioned by the National Urban League for its report on The State of Black America 1985. The essay focuses mostly on the current applicability of the concept of double jeopardy to aged Blacks, some very recent demographic trends about aged Blacks (often in comparison with aged whites), and a limited analysis of the adequacy of major federal programs for aged Blacks, some racial issues about those programs, and some related recommendations. The available data suggest the theoretical or empirical limitations of the concept of double jeopardy when it is used to study aging or age changes, as opposed to its use as an advocatory concept, suggests the author. Also, the available data since 1980 or 1981 do not show that aged Blacks have fared badly under the Reagan administration, but they do suggest the need for more race-sex-age specific data for consumers of federal programs and the need for more subsidized housing for eligible aged Blacks. The major recommendations suggested by

Jackson, Jacquelyne Johnson (continued)

the writer, were that Social Security should be transformed into a
true social insurance program, that Medicare and Medicaid should
be combined into a means-tested program, that the health benefits
for World War II veterans should not be modified now, that the delivery of federal services to aged Blacks are more efficient when
they are rendered in terms of direct payments, and that additional
research and training are needed to improve the nature and modes
of delivery of federal services to aged Blacks.

621.   _____. "The Blacklands of Gerontology." Aging and Human
Development, Vol. 2, 1971, pp. 156-171.

Dr. Jackson discusses "The State of the Literature," "Health, Life
Expectancy, and Race," "Social Patterns, Policies, and Resources,"
"Psychology and Race," and "Related Literature." She points out
that two of the most critical research needs are mental illness
among the Black aged, and trends in the use or non-use of nursing
homes by the Black aged. The writer concludes that while it is no
longer true that almost nothing is known about Black aged, it is
still true that we have a long way to go! She further states that
it would be helpful if some of the research, training, and service
needs already identified in her article and elsewhere were executed with greater speed.

622.   _____. "Negro Aged: Toward Needed Research in Social Gerontology." Gerontologist, Vol. 11, Spring, 1971, pp. 52-57.

This article has three major purposes: 1. That of providing both
a brief survey of social gerontological literature concerned with
Blacks and a selected bibliography of the most useful researches
presently available; 2. That of evaluating critically these
available researches on or about Black aged; and 3. That of con-
ceptualizing several of the most important research problems on
areas about aging and aged Blacks in need of further study now
and during the forthcoming decade of the 1970s.

623.   _____. "Really, There Are Existing Alternatives to Institu-
tionalization for Aged Blacks." National Conference on Alterna-
tives to Institutional Care for Older Americans: Practice and
Planning. Eric Pfeiffer, Editor. Durham, NC: Center for the
Study of Aging and Human Development, Duke University Medical
School, 1973, pp. 102-107.

Dr. Jackson argues that perhaps the most important alternative to
institutionalized care for old Blacks is that practice and planning
must not concentrate so much on those who are already old. We
must begin now to concentrate more upon those who are being born
today and tomorrow and tomorrow and tomorrow. We must make certain that we reverse this creeping tide of racism. According to
Dr. Jackson we must ensure that young Blacks will be able to grow
and develop in environments permitting them to mature and to become both independent and interdependent beings. The author believes that many of those who are Black and institutionalized in
this country today are those who have never really been allowed a

Jackson, Jacquelyne Johnson   (continued)

chance to grow up. That is, they have never really become adults.
There may be some critical distinctions between non-institutiona-
lized and institutionalized old Blacks today, with the latter remaining children and the former, despite all the odds, somehow
having become adults. Hence, the vital alternative for us is that
of maximizing conditions for adult growth and development for
Blacks. These responsible Blacks will then make their own decisions about their need for institutionalization or alternatives to
institutionalization. When health conditions do not permit them
to make such decisions directly, then their spouses, children, or
other responsible family members or friends will make the decisions for them. Dr. Jackson concludes that we do not need to
focus attention upon developing services for aged Blacks where
aged Blacks will not be able to exercise any choice in utilizing
those services and where Blacks will have had no meaningful role
in developing and implementing such services. According to the
writer, we must give attention to developing aged and aging Blacks
themselves so that they can be effective producers and consumers
in the market. The types of problems to which she alludes cannot
be resolved merely by changing the race of the caretaker of the
aged. Dr. Jackson also concludes that the problem can only be resolved by individuals themselves being allowed to make viable
choices as long as they can with the hope being that one of the
alternatives to institutionalization will not be poorer care. The
author argues that those aged Blacks experiencing institutionalization will find themselves in environments relatively free from
stress and highly warm and receptive to them, for many institutions
now containing aged Blacks are, intended or not, merely designed
to hasten their deaths.

624. _____. "Selected Statistical Data on Aging and Aged Blacks."
Proceedings of the Research Conference on Minority Group Aged in
the South. Durham, NC: Center for the Study of Aging and Human
Development, Duke University Medical Center, 1972, pp. 173-184.

Dr. Jackson states that one of the chief objectives of this "Research Conference on Minority Group Aged in the South" is assessing the current status of research on Black aged, an invaluable
objective in determining short and long-range research priorities.
Another objective is emphasizing the need for an enlarging cadre
of persons trained in gerontology or geriatrics and sincerely interested in aging and aged Blacks. Good research can provide a
strong base for planning and action, states Dr. Jackson. These
statistical data, culled from advance and subsequent reports of
the 1970 census, provide some background data on older Blacks. At
least two caveats are in order: Some modifications of advance
1970 census data have occurred since these tables were prepared
including a reduction in the enumeration of aged Blacks; and a
statistical picture of Black aged fails often to portray any single aged Black. Statistical profiles often mask the vast heterogeneity of aged Blacks. Despite these cautions, statistical profiles have some uses, concludes the author.

625. _____. "Social Gerontology and the Negro: A Review."
Gerontology, Vol. 7, September, 1967, pp. 168-178.

The purpose of this article was to provide a collection of sociocultural and psychological references on the Black aged and to
share impressions about such references, focusing predominantly on
certain emergent issues. The author asserts that one of the present gaps in social gerontology is empirical research on the Black
aged; and, therefore, few data are available. Although such existing data do show some convergence, more often their findings di-
verge. Dr. Jackson concludes that few valid generalizations beyond the objective socioeconomic statuses of aged Blacks are possible at the present time.

626. Jenkins, Adelbert H. "The Aged Black: Some Reflections on the
Literature." Afro-American Studies, Vol. 3, December, 1972, pp.
217-221.

This article gives a review of the literature on the Black aged.
Studies have shown that some samples of aged Blacks depart from
stereotypic expectations regarding their adjustment to old age,
concludes the author.

627. Johnson, Christopher Jay. "Toward an Empirical and Theoretical
Framework for Understanding and Developing Positive Images of
Southern Black 'Frail' Elderly: An Africanity and Life History
Approach." Journal of Minority Aging, Vol. 9, No. 2, 1984, pp.
91-103.

This essay advocates the use of an "Africanity" empirical and
theoretical orientation, in combination with a life history
method, to research the quality of life of Southern Black "frail"
elderly. Past theoretical and empirical frameworks have employed
a historical, positivistic, comparative research strategy to study
Black elderly. Moreover, white gerontologists have a limited capacity to understand the social life ("data") of Black elderly,
declares the writer. White gerontologists have often examined the
world of Black elderly through conceptual glasses ground to focus
reality for white people, argues the author. This paper suggests
the need for more qualitative depth in order to understand key
variables or generate new theory in researching the quality of
life of Southern Black elderly. This paper asks social gerontologists to direct their attention to both the strengths and the
problems of Southern Black "frail" elderly in their future research.
This study focuses on both the past and present for an understanding of the quality of life for Southern Black-American "frail"
elderly, and outlines a suggested orientation and research method
to develop new and positive images of Southern Black elderly.
This study also deals with the problems of the intersection of the
biography and history of Black "frail" elderly within the present
social structure of the South.

628. Kastenbaum, Robert J. "Psychological Research Concerns Relative
      to Aging and Aged Blacks." Proceedings of the Research Conference
      on Minority Group Aged in the South. Jacquelyne J. Jackson, Edi-
      tor. Durham, NC: Center for the Study of Aging and Human Develop-
      ment, Duke University Medical Center, 1972, pp. 25-47.

      The writer contends that psychologists should be concerned about
      the same things that psychologically affect the White Aged as the
      Black Aged. Dr. Kastenbaum points out that older Blacks do not
      feel sorry for themselves. He concludes that it is a pity that a
      part of the population among us calling for more Black Studies,
      Black History, et al., often fails to utilize the historical ta-
      lents of its best Black historians. Among those best Black histo-
      rians are many old people who have lived through significant events
      which are often not known to the young--White or Black. They also
      have often had experiences which are not known to a larger propor-
      tion of the American population--White or Black.

629. Lindsay, Inable B. and Brin D. Hawkins. "Research Issues Relating
      to the Black Aged." Social Research and the Black Community:
      Selected Issues and Priorities. Lawrence E. Gary, Editor. Wash-
      ington, DC: Institute for Urban Affairs and Research, Howard Uni-
      versity, 1974, pp. 53-65.

      The researchers highlighted some of the major problems from which
      aged Blacks suffer. They also focused on major strengths which
      may be brought to bear for corrective purposes. It is pointed out
      that it has only been in recent years that aging has commanded the
      prominent attention of researchers in a variety of fields, and the
      Black aged are still very much ignored as a unique minority of the
      elderly population. It is the very uniqueness of the experience
      of the Black elderly in America that makes research such a criti-
      cal issue. They only touched upon a few of the problems and con-
      cerns that confront the Black elderly and undermine their chances
      to grow old in dignity and comfort. The most basic problems rela-
      ted to income maintenance and housing are further reflected in poor
      nutrition, poor physical and mental health, increased vulnerability
      and high mortality. Even in the area of social relationships,
      which has provided a haven of hope for the many Black aged, we
      still find pockets of old Black people in "geriatric ghettos" who
      live out their lives in loneliness and isolation. It is evident
      from the limited data and research that is available that much ac-
      tion is needed to remove the disparities that exist in this soci-
      ety for aged Blacks, contend the authors. It is further evident
      that such action must be preceded by relevant research, because
      action in the face of ignorance has invariably done more harm than
      good, conclude the writers.

630. Morse, Dean W. "Aging in the Ghetto: Themes Expressed by Older
      Black Men and Women Living in a Northern Industrial City."
      Industrial Gerontology, Vol. 3, No. 1, Winter, 1976, pp. 1-10.

      Approximately 100 older Black Americans participated in an "oral
      history" project to record recollections of experiences, thoughts
      and feelings from their early days up to the recent past. A
      sense of worth was closely related to the meaning of work activity

Morse, Dean W. (continued)

in the minds of older Blacks. But work was not pleasurable; it
was a necessary cross to bear. Retirement meant being confined
to the urban environment. For those covered by Social Security,
the monthly check is the difference between a life of dependence
and independence....

631.   Petty, Douglas and George A. Robinson. "Common Philosophical
        Themes in the Oral History and TCB Content of Four Black Octoge-
        narians." Journal of Non-White Concerns in Personnel and Guid-
        ance, Vol. 10, No. 2, January, 1982, pp. 57-63.

        The instrument used in this study was the Themes Concerning
        Blacks (TCB). Four Black octogenarians were interviewed individu-
        ally via an oral history procedure. The authors give a summary of
        their philosophies:
        1.   Trust in the Lord; treat everyone fair and just; help those
             who cannot help themselves; help those who need help; work
             hard and don't give up. Don't forget to show concern.
        2.   Trust in the Lord; think before acting; treat everyone
             nice all the time even when they do you wrong. Whatever you
             have, be willing to share it with others. Work hard, don't
             give up; always strive to do better, and love everyone.
        3.   Trust in the Lord; remember the Golden Rule; work hard; share;
             don't avoid responsibility; keep your word; respect yourself
             and everyone else, and love one another.
        4.   Trust in the Lord; love everybody, treat everyone right even
             when they do you wrong; take care of yourself; don't be afraid
             of responsibility; work hard, and share whatever you have.
        The authors maintain that obtaining the philosophy or world view
        of an individual adds another dimension to the psychological as-
        sessment process in understanding personality functioning. The
        philosophy of an individual contains at least as much and some-
        times more information than a projective test is able to obtain
        alone; as was evidenced by this study, state the researchers.
        They conclude, in part: "It is quite revealing that none of the
        subjects' philosophies contained any negative (pathological) con-
        tent. One wonders what might have been the case if the TAT had
        been used as the projective test...."

632.   Smith, Stanley H. "Major Concerns: A Summing Up of Gerontological
        Research and Training." Proceedings of the Research Conference on
        Minority Group Aged in the South. Jacquelyne J. Jackson, Editor.
        Durham, NC: Center for the Study of Aging and Human Development,
        Duke University Medical Center, 1972, pp. 152-154.

        The writer states that there is an increasing urgency for the col-
        lection of hard data on the Black Aged. Complete reliance cannot
        be placed on longitudinal studies. The time could be reduced con-
        siderably by combining the longitudinal and the cross-sectioned
        approaches. Increasing reliance could also be placed on smaller
        samples without negatively affecting reliability and validity. It
        may not be inconceivable to deal with sample sizes of twenty-five
        by sample selection devices based on rapidly defined social cate-
        gories, states the author. This will permit more in-depth

Smith, Stanley H. (continued)

interviews and more precise recordings of behavioral observations,
argues the writer. Research must be careful not to superimpose
definitions of social phenomena on their subjects. This has been
done much too frequently on Black people. On the contrary, greater emphasis should be placed on how these persons define or concep-
tualize the social phenomena in question. For example, instead of
assuming that persons are not married because they have not been
"churched," one should be more concerned with how these persons
define their relationship with each other and if they have accepted responsibility for the functions of child bearing and child
rearing. Prof. Smith concludes that in research and particularly
on Black people, it is safe to make the assumption that there is a
certain order and, therefore, concentrate on recognizing, and as a
consequence, analyzing the nature of that order. This might conceivably make more relevant and appropriate the methodological approach followed. Different definitions and assumptions will determine a different methodological approach. This, in turn, will
affect conclusions and hopefully, policy, continues the writer.

633. Solomon, Barbara. "Better Planning Through Research." Comprehen-
sive Service Delivery Systems for the Minority Aged. E. Percil
Stanford, Editor. San Diego: Center on Aging, School of Social
Work, San Diego State University, 1977, pp. 19-29.

The researcher argues that research should be an integral part of
planning services including services to minority elderly. Since
research is eventually a set of tools, the important issue is the
nature of the questions which research is asked to answer. There
are questions in regard to minority elderly which need answers,
states the writer: Should there be culturally specific programs?
If so, how should they differ in regard to structure, content and
process? To what extent do minority-specific variables enter into
program evaluation? Systematic, programmatic research would appear
to be one of the most effective ways to arrive at answers. At the
same time, the suggestion that there is possibly not enough uniqueness about the Black elderly to warrant special attention in research institutes is reflective on the negative valuation placed
on minorities in our racist society, states Solomon. According to
the writer, there are thousands of research institutes in this
country with some very esoteric as well as mundane interests, e.g.,
there is an Institute for Research in Acting; an Institute for
Research in Practical Partisan Politics; an Institute for the Study of the Future; and an Institute for the Study of Earth and Man.
To suggest that minority elderly are not sufficiently unique to
study separately in a special institute is strangely contrary to
the values and practices in the research establishment, but entirely consistent with the low valuation placed on our minority populations, concludes the author.

APPENDICES

Black Old Folks' Homes, 1860–1988

Home for Aged Colored Women
Boston, MA
Founded ca. 1860

Home for Aged and Infirm Colored Persons
Philadelphia, PA
Founded by Stephen Smith in 1864 and is still in existence 1988

Home for Aged Men
Springfield, MA
Founded by Primus Mason for all races ca. 1868

The Colored Old Folks' and Orphans' Home
Mobile, AL
Established in 1871

Old Folks' and Orphans' Home
Memphis, TN
Founded ca. 1880

The Liner's Harvest Home
New Orleans, LA
Established by Edward Liner in 1886

Widows' and Orphans' Home
Jackson, MS
Started date unknown; probably between 1880-1900

Carter's Old Folks' Home
Atlanta, GA
Establishment date unknown; probably between 1880-1900

St. James Old Folks' Home
Louisville, KY
Organized in 1887

Bethel Old Folks' Home
Baltimore, MD
Founded ca. 1890

Crawford's Old Folks' Home
Cincinnati, OH
Founded ca. 1890

The Centenary Church Home
Charleston, SC
Organized ca. 1890

Old Folks' and Orphans' Home
Birmingham, AL
Started ca. 1890

Lincoln Old Folks' and Orphans' Home
Springfield, IL
Founding date unknown; probably between 1890-1903

Old Folks' Home
St. Louis, MO
Establishment date unknown; probably between 1890-1905

Old Folks' Home
Augusta, GA
Establishment date unknown; probably between 1890-1905

Masonic Home
Columbus, GA
Establishment date unknown; probably between 1890-1905

Cleveland Home for Aged Colored People
Cleveland, OH
Started by Mrs. Eliza Bryant in 1893

Old Folks' and Orphans' Home
Kansas City, MO
Founded by Samuel Eason, a Black man, in 1894

Old Folks' Homes
Norfolk, VA
Started in 1894 and was still in operation in the late 1930s.

Colored Aged Home Association
Newark, NJ
Started in 1895. (Moved to Irvington, NJ in 1905.)

Aged Men's and Women's Home
Baltimore, MD
Started ca. 1895

Old Folks' Home
St. Louis, MO
Establishment date unknown; probably between 1895-1904

Home for Aged and Infirm Colored People
Chicago, IL
Started by Mrs. Gabriella Smith ca. 1896 and was still operating in
1920 on West Garfield Boulevard

Ashley River Asylum
Charleston, SC
Started ca. 1896

Old Ladies' and Orphans' Home
Memphis, TN
Started ca. 1896

The Sarah Ann White Home for Aged and Infirm Colored Persons
Wilmington, DE
Founded in 1896

The Widow's Faith Home for Colored Destitutes
New Orleans, LA
Organized ca. 1896

New Bedford Home for the Aged
New Bedford, MA
Established in 1897 by Miss Elizabeth C. Carter

Tents' Old Folks' Home
Hampton, VA
Organized in 1897 by a Society of Women called "Tents." This home was
still operating in the early 1940's.

The Stoddard Baptist Home
Washington, DC
Established ca. 1897 by Mrs. Maria Stoddard

Home for Aged Colored Men and Women
Philadelphia, PA
Started ca. 1898

Old Folks' Home
Columbus, OH
Establishment date unknown; probably ca. 1898

Woman's Home Mission Society Home
Baton Rouge, LA
Started ca. 1898

The Negro Baptist Old Folks' Home
Richmond, VA
Established ca. 1899 and still in existence in the early 1940's

Green Memorial Home for the Aged and Infirm
Evansville, IL
Establishment date unknown; probably ca. 1899

City Home
Petersburg, VA
Started before 1900 and was still in existence in the early 1940's

Alpha Home Association
Indianapolis, IN
Founded ca. 1900

Home for Aged Colored Women
Cincinnati, OH
Established ca. 1900

Home for Aged and Infirm Colored Women
Pittsburgh, PA
Founded ca. 1900

Home for Negro Aged Men
New York, NY
Founded before 1900 and was still in existence in 1943

Home for Negro Aged Women
New York, NY
Established before 1900 and was still operating in 1943

Home for Destitute Children and Aged Persons
San Antonio, TX
Founding date unknown; probably ca. 1900

Iowa Home for Aged and Orphans
Des Moines, IA
Founded ca. 1900

Old Folks' Home
Birmingham, AL
Started ca. 1900

Old Folks' Home
Chicago, IL
Founded by John Johnson and his family ca. 1900

Old Folks' Home
Providence, RI
Starting date unknown; probably ca. 1900

Rescue Home for Orphans and Old Folks
Jacksonville, FL
Started ca. 1900

The Lafon's Old Folks' Home
New Orleans, LA
Established by Thomy Lafon ca. 1900

Old Folks' Home
Westham, VA
Organized by the True Reformers ca. 1900

The Lincoln Hospital and Home
New York, NY
Founded ca. 1900

The Women's Twentieth Century Club
New Haven, CT
Organized in 1900 by Mrs. J. W. Stewart

Old Folks' Home
Richmond, VA
Founded ca. 1900 and still operating in the late 1930's

M. W. Gibbs Colored Old Ladies' Home
Little Rock, AK
Established ca. 1900

Taborian Home for Aged and Indigent Members
Topeka, KS
Establishment date unknown; probably between 1900-1905

Home for the Aged
Brooklyn, NY
Organized ca. 1901

Home for Aged and Incurable
Atlantic City, NJ
Started ca. 1901 by Dr. C. Fayerman

Old Folks' Home for Colored
Portsmouth, VA
Started ca. 1901 and still in operation in the late 1930's

The Priscilla Brown Mercy Home
Selma, AL
Organized in 1902 by the City of Selma

Tent Sisters' Old Folks' Home
Raleigh, NC
Established ca. 1904

Colored Masonic Home and Orphanage
Linglestown, PA
Organized ca. 1905 by the Grand Lodge of Colored Free and Accepted
Masons of Pennsylvania

Colored Aged Home Association
Irvington, NJ
Established in 1905

Phillis Wheatley Home
Detroit, MI
Started in 1907 by the Labor of Love Circle

Old Folks' Home
Gloucester, VT
Started in 1907

Old Folks' Home
Alexandria, VA
Started ca. 1907

Evergreen Old Folks' Home
Savannah, GA
Organized in 1908

Home for Colored Aged Women
Anniston, AL
Started ca. 1908

Old Folks' Home
Natchez, MS
Founded ca. 1910 by the Faithful Few Circle of the King's Daughters

Old Folks' Home
Pensacola, FL
Started ca. 1911

Selected Periodicals
with Articles Pertaining
to the Black Aged

Activities, Adaptation, and Aging

Afro-American Studies

Aging

American Historical Review

American Journal of Medicine

American Journal of Orthopsychiatry

Annals of the American Academy of Political and Social Science

Anthropological Quarterly

Black Aging

Black Enterprise

Black Scholar

Cancer

Cancer Research

Crisis

Daedalus

Diseases of the Nervous System

Ebony

Encore

Family Coordinator

Family Relations

Freedomways

Generation

Geriatrics

Gerontologist

Harvest Years

Industrial Gerontology

International Journal of Aging and Human Development

Journal of Afro-American Issues

Journal of Black Studies

Journal of Chronic Diseases

Journal of Clinical Nutrition

Journal of Gerontological Social Work

Journal of Gerontology

Journal of Minority Aging

Journal of Negro Education

Journal of Negro History

Journal of Non-White Concerns in Personnel and Guidance

Journal of Social and Behavioral Sciences

Journal of the American Geriatrics Society

Journal of the National Medical Association

Monthly Labor Review

Negro Digest

North Carolina Journal of Mental Health

Phylon

Postgraduate Medicine

Psychological Reports

Research on Aging

Share

Social Casework

Social Forces

Social Policy

Social Science Quarterly

Social Security Bulletin

Sociology and Social Research

Strokes

Index

Including authors, joint authors, and editors. Numbers refer to individual entry numbers.

About the Compiler

LENWOOD G. DAVIS is Professor of History at Winston-Salem State University, North Carolina.